P9-CAE-311

Family Communication

THIRD EDITION

Family Communication

COHESION AND CHANGE

Kathleen M. Galvin
NORTHWESTERN UNIVERSITY

Bernard J. Brommel
NORTHEASTERN ILLINOIS UNIVERSITY

HarperCollins*Publishers*

Sponsoring Editor: Melissa A. Rosati
Project Coordination, Text and Cover Design: P. M. Gordon Associates
Cover Photo: Alan Oddie
Photo Research: Carol Parden
Production: Michael Weinstein
Compositor: Omegatype Typography Inc.
Printer and Binder: R. R. Donnelly & Sons, Company
Cover Printer: New England Book Components

Text and photo credits appear on pages 336–337.

Family Communication: Cohesion and Change, Third Edition

Copyright © 1991 by HarperCollins Publishers Inc.

All rights reserved. Printed in the United States of America. No part of this book may be used or reproduced in any manner whatsoever without written permission, except in the case of brief quotations embodied in critical articles and reviews. For information address HarperCollins Publishers Inc., 10 East 53d Street, New York, NY 10022.

Library of Congress Cataloging-in-Publication Data

Galvin, Kathleen M.
    Family communication : cohesion and change / Kathleen M. Galvin,
Bernard J. Brommel. — 3rd ed.
        p.   cm.
    Includes bibliographical references and index.
    ISBN 0–673–46120–3
    1. Communication in the family—United States.   2. Interpersonal
communication—United States.   I. Brommel, Bernard J., 1930–   .
II. Title.
HQ734.C2515   1991   90–46205
306.87—dc20   CIP

90 91 92 93 9 8 7 6 5 4 3 2 1

To my family: The Galvins, Wilkinsons, Nicholsens, and Sullivans, plus the special friends I consider as my family.

KMG

To my children: Michaela Ann, Brian, Debra, Brent, Brad, and Blair; with thanks to Randy Treff, Grace Laird, Vic Silvestri, and Perry Rudman. I dedicate my part of this edition to the memory of my sister Florence Cairo. Her dying gave new meanings to my sense of the importance of family.

BJB

Contents

Preface

It is a pleasure to introduce the third edition of *Family Communication: Cohesion and Change,* the first textbook to have addressed the family from a communication perspective. The first and second editions have been used by students and teachers of family-related courses in communication, psychology, sociology, counseling, home economics, theology, and health.

Historically, family interaction received attention solely within medical and therapeutic perspectives. Only recently have scholars turned their attention to interaction within functional families. The past decade has witnessed growing interest in ordinary family interaction processes within all of the social sciences. Increasing numbers of communication scholars are devoting research efforts to specific aspects of family communication.

The basic premise of this book is that communication aids family functioning. Using a systematic approach, we consider, in depth, the communication processes within the family as well as the extent to which they affect and are affected by larger social systems.

The focus of the text remains descriptive rather than prescriptive, because we believe that description provides the understanding necessary to the eventual development of valid approaches and strategies. We examine how family members typically perform primary family functions—regulating cohesion and adaptability—and secondary family functions—developing appropriate family images, themes, boundaries, and biosocial beliefs.

The first four chapters establish the foundation for what follows by presenting basic communication concepts, an overview of family demographics, a framework for analyzing family communication, and an explanation of how family meanings develop and illustrations of the role of one's family-of-origin in establishing communication patterns. Later chapters explore communication issues related to basic family interaction: relationship development, intimacy, roles, power, conflict, developmental stages, and adjustment to unpredictable crises. The final chapters focus on the physical and temporal context for communication patterns and on approaches toward the improvement of family communication.

With each edition we have attempted to reflect the rapidly changing family experience. In this edition we focus extensively on diverse family forms, and gender and ethnicity, all critical issues in current family research. We believe this edition synthesizes the best of current related research on communication and in the social sciences.

Throughout the book we present honest first-person examples (names and identifying data have been changed) and quotations that complement and expand on the content. We hope these demonstrate the direct application of the concepts.

Many persons contributed to the completion of the Third Edition. We received valuable feedback on manuscript drafts from Arthur Bochner, University of South Florida; Mary Ann Fitzpatrick, University of Wisconsin at Madison; Christina Gonzalez, Rutgers University; Judith K. Jones, University of Oregon; Jeffry H. Larson, Brigham Young University; Joan D. Lynch, Villanova University; Sheila McNamee, University of New Hampshire; John W. Monsma, Northern Arizona University; Helen Newman, Hunter College of the City University of New York; Don Orban, Emporia State University; Karen M. Roloff, Northwestern University; Timothy Stephen, Rensselaer Polytechnic Institute; Colleen Thomas, George Brown College; Leanne O. Wolff, Heidelberg College; and Barbara Wood, University of Illinois at Chicago. We remain indebted also to the people who provided feedback on the first two editions.

We are grateful to the Harper Collins editorial staff: Barbara Muller, Melissa Rosati, Vikki Barrett, and Louise Howe for their supportive encouragement and guidance. Our students and clients provided insightful commentaries and examples. Rebecca Holloway and Bernadette Burke typed the manuscript. Charles Wilkinson supplied numerous examples from his family practice.

Our own families have grown and changed over the past decade, a process that has taught us a great deal more about family life and family communication. To our family members we express our gratitude for their exceptional patience and moral support.

Finally, this book comes from our own commitment to, and enthusiasm for, teaching family communication. Unlike most other academic courses, students bring their personal experiences to the course content and, thus, start with considerable insight and knowledge of the subject. From them and through our practice and in our research we continue to learn about how families function and what it means to be a member of a family.

Kathleen M. Galvin
Bernard J. Brommel

Family Communication

CHAPTER 1

Introduction to the Family

Families: We are born into a family, mature in a family, form new families, and leave them at our deaths. Family life is a universal human experience. Yet no two people share the exact same experience. Our lives are shaped by family experiences, particularly family communication patterns.

> *"At family gatherings I found myself watching the little things that go on among members—the ways people share affection, the ways secrets travel, how the people use sarcasm other than direct confrontation. These events were part of my School for Living. Many of these patterns have been carried into my current family. When I'm a grandmother I may witness my children acting in similar ways."*

Because the family is such a powerful influence in our lives, we need to examine families and their interaction patterns to understand ourselves better as members of one of the most complex and important parts of society. Therefore, as you read this book, you will examine a subject you already know something about, since you have spent your life in some type or types of family arrangement. Yet, because you have lived in only one or a small number of families, your experience is limited compared with the range of possible family experiences. Your reading should expand your understanding of many types of families.

This book will present a framework for examining communication within families; by the end of the text, you should be able to apply this model to a particular family and understand it as a communication system. We also hope that you will apply what you learn to your own family or to the family you will eventually form, in order to improve communication among its members.

Throughout this book you will find some material written in the first person and set off from the text. These examples, provided by friends, students, and clients, illustrate many of the concepts in the chapters. These statements should enable you to understand the concepts more completely. Some material may remind you specifically of your own family experiences, whereas other material may seem quite different from your background. This is because people relate to each other very differently within what is called a "family."

Because teachers are family therapists, we hold certain basic beliefs that undergird the words on the following pages. We want to share these with you to establish a context for understanding.

1. There is no "right" way to be a family. Family life is as diverse as the types of persons who create families. There are many types of families and numerous ways to relate within each family type. Families are systems created by human beings; the perfect family does not exist. Each family must struggle to create its own identity as it experiences good times and stressful times.

2. Communication is the process by which family members work out and share their meanings with each other. Through this interaction, the members define their own identities and their relationships to each other and the rest of the world. Thus, each family serves as a communication system.

3. Families are part of multigenerational communication patterns. Family members are influenced by the patterns of previous generations as they create their own patterns that will influence generations to come. The family serves as each person's first classroom in communication.

4. Healthy families work at developing functional communication patterns. Developing and maintaining relationships takes work. Healthy families develop the capacity to adapt to and create change, to share intimacy and manage conflict. Healthy families are self-aware; they value the goal of effective communication, understanding that this may be achieved in various ways depending on the people involved. Yet family members consciously work at improving their relationships through their communication.

This text attempts to introduce you to the diverse world of families and their complex communication patterns, and to develop your observational and analytical skills. It will not present prescriptive solutions for family problems. We hope your increased understanding of family communication will be accompanied by an increased appreciation for the complexities and the changes inherent in this area of study.

As an introduction to the family, this chapter will discuss definitional issues and family status. This discussion will establish an understanding of the concept of the family that will be used throughout the rest of the book.

FAMILIES: DEFINITIONAL ISSUES

What images come to your mind when you hear the word *family?* How would you define the term? Although *family* is a word used frequently, reaching agreement on its meaning is much more difficult than you might expect. In the following section you will see the variations implied in the term *family.*

There is no single, widely agreed-upon definition of the term *family*. Traditionally, families have been viewed according to consanguine, or blood, ties and conjugal, or marital, ties. Families have been described as networks of persons who live together over periods of time and have ties of marriage and kinship to one another (Laing 1972). In their attempt to find the essence of family, Fitzpatrick and Badzinski (1985) suggest that the only universal family type is a small kinship-structured group whose primary function is the nurturing and socialization of newborn children. Beutler and colleagues (1989) extend this position, describing a "family realm" that is created by the birth process and the establishment of ties across generations. The core aspect of this "family realm" is the "biological, emotional, social and developmental processes that are inherent in procreation and the nurturing of dependent children," (806), yet their definition includes both intergenerational issues and alternative family forms.

In contrast, a family may be viewed more broadly as a group of people with a past history, a present reality and a future expectation of interconnected mutually influencing relationships. Members often (but not necessarily) are bound together by heredity, by legal marital ties, by adoption, or by a common living arrangement at some point in their lifetime (Kramer 1980, 43). Clearly, this definition emphasizes the personal, connected relationships among family members, instead of relying solely on blood ties or legal contracts as the basis for a family.

As we talk about families in this book, we will take a broad, inclusive view; therefore, if the members consider themselves to be a family, we accept their self-definition. Generally, we will refer to family as networks of people who share their lives over long periods of time; who are bound by ties of marriage, blood, or commitment, legal or otherwise; who consider themselves as family; and who share future expectations of connected relationship. Such a definition encompasses countless variations and numerous interaction patterns.

In contemporary society, family diversity abounds. One indication of the complexities of today's families may be found in a review of current literature, which includes such categories as large, extended blood-related families, formal communal groups, stepfamilies, single-parent families, gay-parent families, and families of various races and socioeconomic situations. This book's authors represent two very different family orientations. One grew up on an Iowa farm in a family of nine children, married, fathered six children, divorced, and is now a grandfather. The other grew up in New York City as an only child. After her parents died, she acquired an adopted family with three siblings. Currently, she is married and raising three children, one of whom is adopted. Although blood relatives are important, each also has friends who are considered to be family members.

You may have grown up in a small family, large family, or three- or four-generation household. Your brothers and sisters may be blood related, step, or adopted. Some of you may be single parents, stepparents, or foster parents. Whereas some of you may have experienced one long, committed marriage, others may have experienced divorce, death, and remarriage. No simple pattern exists.

There are many categories of families. We will use a simple category system encompassing the following styles of family formation: two-parent biological family,

A two-parent biological family is no longer the most common family form.

single-parent family, blended family, extended family, and partners without children. These are not discrete categories; some families may belong to more than one.

A two-parent biological family consists of two parents and the children who are from the union of these parents. Thus, blood ties and the original marriage bond characterize this type. Although frequently thought of as "typical," this type of family no longer represents the most common family form.

A single-parent family consists of one parent and one or more children. This formation may include an unmarried man or woman and his or her offspring; men and women without partners through death, divorce, or desertion, and the children who remain; single parents and their adopted or foster children.

The blended family consists of two adults and their children, all of whom may not be from the union of those two parents. Families may be blended through the remarriage of adults whose spouses have left, a situation that brings the children into new family ties. Families may also be blended through the addition of adopted or foster children. You may have witnessed the common pattern in which a natural family becomes a single-parent family for a period of time, after which certain members become part of a stepfamily.

Although an extended family usually refers to that group of relatives living within the surrounding city or nearby area, it may be more narrowly understood as the addition of blood relatives, other than the parents, to the everyday life of a child. For example, this may take a cross-generational form, including grandparents who live with a parent-child system or who take on exclusive parenting roles for grandchildren.

A single-parent family is one of many forms.

> "*I grew up in an extended family. My great-grandparents were the dominant figures. Most of us lived with our grandparents at one time or another. There were six different households in the neighborhood I grew up in. My great-grandmother, referred to as 'Mother,' babysat for all the kids while our parents were at work.*
>
> "*There are also people who were informally adopted into my family. My mother and one of my cousins were raised by their grandmother, even though their parents did not live there. In my family no one is considered half or step. You are a member of the family, and that is that.*"

Another variation of the extended family is the communal family—a couple or a group of people, some of whom are unrelated by blood, who share a commitment to each other, live together, and consider themselves to be a family. Formal examples of these family types are found in a kibbutz or in religious organizations, whereas other communal families are informally formed around friendship or common interests or commitments. Two families may share so many experiences that over time both sets of children and parents begin to think of each other as "part of the family."

Although we usually think of families as having children, partners without children may form their own familial unit as an outgrowth of their original families. Although their numbers are small, some married couples are choosing to remain child-free, whereas others remain childless due to infertility. Homosexual partners may also be included in this category, as long as the partners consider each other as family members. Partners without children continue to serve as children to the previous generation and as siblings and extended family members to other generations, while at the same time providing loyalty and affection to one another.

It is important to distinguish between two types of family experience: current families and families-of-origin. Families in combination beget families through the evolutionary cycles of coming together and separating. Thus, each person may experience life in different families starting with his or her family-of-origin. Family-of-origin refers to the family or families in which a person is raised. The family in which you grew up is your family-of-origin. Noted family therapist Virginia Satir (1972) stresses the importance of the family-of-origin as "the main base against and around which most family blueprints are designed." She suggests: "It is easy to duplicate in your family the same things that happened in your growing up. This is true whether your family was a nurturing or a troubled one" (200). Recently, multigenerational patterns, those of more than two generations, are being considered as part of the blueprint (Hoopes 1987). As you will discover, family-of-origin and multigenerational experiences are crucial in the development of communication patterns in current families.

Family Systems

The systems perspective provides one way to gain insight into family functioning and family communication. Although Chapter 3 will explore in detail the family as a system, let us examine this concept briefly. Each individual is part of an overall family system, affecting and being affected by that system. Therefore, you cannot fully understand a person without knowing something about his or her family. For example, an individual's behavior may appear strange, but if you understand the whole family context, your perceptions may change. An individual's behavior becomes more comprehensible when viewed within the context of the human system within which he or she functions. What may be viewed as problematic behavior in one setting may be functional in another context.

Within a system, the parts and the relationship between them form the whole; changes in one part will result in changes in the others. This is so, too, in families. Satir (1988) describes a family as a mobile. Picture a mobile that hangs over a child's crib as having people instead of elephants or sailboats on it. As events touch one member of the family, other members reverberate in relationship to the change in the affected member. Thus, if a member of your family gets a raise, flunks out of school, marries, or becomes ill, such an event affects the surrounding family system, depending on each person's current relationship with that individual. In addition, because family members are human beings, not elephants or sailboats, they can "pull their own strings." At some point, a family member may choose to withdraw from the family and, by pulling away, force other members into closer relationships. Thus, as members move toward or away from each other, all members are affected. If you hold a systems perspective, you will always observe and analyze families by paying attention to the relationships among members as opposed to paying attention only to an individual's activity.

Families: Current Status

The contemporary family exists in a world of change and diversity. In order to understand family interaction more completely, you need to examine the current status of family life in America. No matter how old you are, you have lived long enough to witness major changes in your family or in the families around you. These changes reflect pieces of a national picture. In 1955, for example, 60 percent of all households in the United States consisted of an intact marriage, a working father, a housewife mother, and two or more school-age children. Today, only 7 percent of all households fit the traditional family image (Otto 1988). Although research figures shift constantly and various sources provide slightly different numerical data, the overall point is clear: the American family has undergone dramatic changes in the twentieth century. Reports of census data attest to the scope of such change (Current Population Reports, March 1988; Abstract of the United States, 1984).

In 1988 the United States had more than 91 million households, but each contained fewer members than ever. Families accounted for 72 percent of these households, compared with 74 percent in 1980 and 81 percent in 1970. Over half the U.S. families do not have a child under age 18 living at home. Two-parent families are declining, slipping from 40 percent of all households in 1970 to 27 percent in 1988. The impact of recent decades of family change can be demonstrated by the current reality for children. The normal childhood experience of today's youth is for a child to live with only one parent sometime before reaching age 18. Based on 1985 statistics, Otto (1988) estimates the following:

Of every one hundred children born today:

- Twelve are born out of wedlock.
- Forty-one are born to parents who divorce before the child is age 18.
- Five are born to parents who separate.
- Two will experience the death of a parent before they reach age 18.
- Forty-one will reach age 18 without such incidents.

Current trends indicate that first marriages are taking place later; for example, the average marriage age for women was 21 in 1975 and 23 in 1985. For men it was 25.9, the highest since 1900. The average length of a first marriage that ends in divorce ranged from 7.3 years in 1975 to 6.9 years in 1980 and went back up to 7.5 years in 1985.

Until now, incidence of divorce has risen rapidly throughout this century, up 700 percent since 1900. This figure also reflects the longevity of persons in today's society. In earlier times, when more people died at a young age, many unsatisfactory marriages were ended by death rather than divorce. Recently, the divorce rate has remained relatively constant after the significant rise during the 1970s. In 1988, 6.6 percent of men and 8.9 percent of women listed themselves as currently divorced.

Clearly, this population shifts as almost three-quarters of divorced persons, although first divorce percentage has leveled out, remarry. The incidence of redivorce continues to rise (Norton and Moorman 1987).

The majority of women, approximately three-fourths, who divorce eventually remarry, although the proportion who remarry seems to be declining. Childless divorced women under age 30 are most like to remarry, followed by divorced women with children under age 30. At this time remarriage rates are high, and most divorced individuals will form a new partnership. About five out of six men and three out of four women remarry after a divorce. About half of these remarriages occur within three years of the divorce.

As shown by the earlier figures on childhood expectations, we are witnessing the continuing rise of single-parent systems. In 1970, 11 percent of children under age 18 lived with their mothers, 1 percent with their fathers, and 85 percent with two parents. In 1982, 20 percent of children under age 18 lived with their mothers, 2 percent with their fathers, and 75 percent with two parents. The remainder were cared for in an institutional setting. These rates are rising in part because more children are entering life as part of a single-parent system. Whereas in 1960 approximately 5 percent of births occurred to unmarried women, by 1988 that figure had risen to 22 percent.

Recent census data indicate that the number of unmarried-couple households is growing rapidly. Such households are defined as "two unrelated adults of the opposite sex sharing living quarters with or without children present." In 1988 there were 2.6 million unmarried-couple households, nearly a third with children. This figure, more than four times the number in 1970, represents 5 percent of the couples in U.S. households. There were 1,891,000 unmarried-couple households in 1983—more than three times the number in 1970. Although during the 1970s this type grew rapidly, the amount of growth in the 1980s has been comparatively small.

Although census figures on gay-male and lesbian couples are not available, Blumstein and Schwartz (1983) included such couples as a significant part of their study. They suggest that, until the 1970s, gay men and lesbians were a fairly invisible part of the American population. In the late 1960s, the Kinsey Institute found that 71 percent of its sample of gay men between ages 36 and 45 were living with a partner. Other studies in the 1970s and 1980s point toward the desire for couple relationships within the gay-male or lesbian community (McWhirter and Mattison 1984; Johnson 1984).

All these changes are occurring against a backdrop of longer life expectancy. Persons born in 1960 have a life expectancy of 69.7 years, whereas those born in 1986 have an expectancy of 74.9 years. The male expectancy is 71.3 years, whereas the female is 78.3 years. When you consider that most people marry before age 30, a continuous marriage might well be expected to last forty to fifty years. Widowhood has become an expected life event for most women. Over age 65, the ratio of widows to widowers is approximately 6:1.

All these changes are intertwined. These figures are accompanied by major economic changes. Today only 7 percent of households in the United States fit the traditional description of a family with a working father and a mother at home. Working mothers are commonplace (Philip Morris 1989). Approximately 73 percent of women of childbearing age, 18–44, are in the work force. At least 51 percent of married women with babies less than a year old are working. Over 68 percent of female single mothers are working. These figures will increase in the coming decades, because young two-career couples are becoming a larger segment of the 20–30-year-old age group and unmarried single parenthood continues to rise. Because of these changes, the United States is witnessing a phenomenon of "latch key children" who return from school hours before a parent returns from work, and who are expected to contribute to the successful running of the household. Young children may spend many of their waking hours with babysitters or in day-care centers, encountering their parents only a few hours a day.

Another economic factor that impacts directly on family life is poverty. One-third of the homeless are families with children, a figure that is rising rapidly. Although a large number of poor families contain two parents, the female single-parent family is five times more likely to live in poverty. The economic pressures add significant stress to the lives of these family members.

No examination of family status is complete without a discussion of the effect of ethnicity on family functioning. Within the past decades, two forces have combined to bring ethnic issues to the attention of family scholars. First, the overall ethnic composition of U.S. families is changing as the number of black, Hispanic, and Asian families increases. Second, scholars are recognizing the long-term effect of ethnic heritage on family functioning.

American society represents a wide diversity of ethnic and cultural groups. The 1986 census figures indicate that of approximately 237 million persons, 201 million are white, 28.5 million are black, and 18 million are Hispanic. These census figures also indicate that of the 63.5 million U.S. families, approximately 55 million are white, 7 million are black, and 4 million are Hispanic. Whereas the general population averages 2.67 members per household, black families average 2.90 members and Hispanic families average 3.43 members per household.

Hispanic families are growing at the highest rate. Whereas 21 percent of white families had children under 15, 28 percent of black and 30 percent of Hispanic families reported young children.

The life expectancy for white males born in 1985 is 71.9 years and for white females is 78.7 years; for black males born in 1985 the life expectancy is 65.3 years and for black females is 73.5 years.

Although generalizations about cultural groups must always be accompanied by an indication of their many exceptions, a consideration of family ethnicity provides one more perspective from which to examine communication patterns. This perspective will receive increased attention. By the middle of the twenty-first century, Americans of European ancestry will be in the minority. This shift will influence underlying assumptions about how families work.

It is important to consider ethnicity in families because, contrary to popular myth, Americans have not become homogenized in a "melting pot"; instead, various cultural/ethnic heritages are maintained across generations. In her overview of studies in family ethnicity, McGoldrick (1982) points to the increasing evidence that "ethnic values and identification are retained for many generations after immigration and play a significant role in family life and personal development throughout the life cycle." She maintains that second-, third-, and even fourth-generation Americans reflect their original cultural heritage in lifestyle and behavior.

"My parents' marriage reflected an uneasy blend of Italian and Norwegian cultures. My mother included her Italian relatives in on many issues my father considered private. He was overwhelmed by her family's style of arguing and making up, and would retreat to the porch during big celebrations. I came to realize that cultural tension was reflected in many of their differences, including their child-rearing patterns. I carry pieces of those conflicting patterns within me today."

Ethnicity may affect family life through its traditions, celebrations, occupations, values, and problem solving. There are strong variations across cultures and familial issues such as age at first marriage, single parenthood, older marriages, changing marital partners and male/female roles (Dilworth-Anderson and McAdoo 1988; McGoldrick, Anderson, and Walsh 1989). The definition of "family" may differ across ethnic groups. For example, whereas the dominant "White Anglo-Saxon" definition focuses on the intact nuclear unit, black families focus on a wide kinship network, and Italians function with a large, intergenerational, tightly knit family that includes godparents and old friends. The Chinese are likely to include all ancestors and descendants in the concept of "family" (McGoldrick 1982, 10). Each of these definitions has an impact on communication within the family.

Changes in family form and ethnicity hold many implications for the ways in which family members communicate with each other. For example, the rise of two career families alters the amount of time parents and children are in direct contact. Economic stress frequently results in escalating family conflict. The high divorce rate increases the chances that family members of all ages will undergo major stressful transitions, including changes in their communication patterns. The growth in single parent systems and dual-career couples increases a child's interpersonal contact with a network of extended family or professional caregivers. Children in stepfamilies need to function within two different family systems, each with its own communication patterns. As American families reflect greater ethnic diversity, family life will be characterized by a wider range of communication patterns.

Throughout this book, examples and information that reflect changing family forms and ethnic variation will be included.

At this point, it is important to forecast the types of families to be discussed in the upcoming chapters. Historically, most literature on family interaction has focused on dysfunctional or pathological families. Early studies examined families with a severely troubled or handicapped member. In recent years, attention has shifted to understanding the workings of the well-functioning, or "normal," family. As you may imagine from the previous description of the definitions and the status of families, there is little agreement on what is "normal."

Early writers (Offer and Sabshin 1966) provided four concepts from which to view normality: health, utopia, average, and process. Walsh (1982, 5–6) reworked these concepts into four perspectives:

1. Asymptomatic family functioning. This approach implies that there are no major symptoms of psychopathology among family members.
2. Optimal family functioning. This approach stresses positive or ideal characteristics often based on members' accomplishments.
3. Average family functioning. This approach identifies families that appear typical or seem to fit common patterns.
4. Transactional family processes. This approach stresses a systems perspective focusing on adaptation over the life cycle and adaptation to contexts.

Studies of well-functioning families highlight the tremendous diversity of families that appear to be functioning adequately at a particular point in time (Kantor and Lehr 1976; Lewis et al., 1976; Reiss 1981; Walsh 1982; Olson and McCubbin 1983; Fitzpatrick 1988).

In this text, we will focus on communication within the functional family, because this constitutes the primary experience for most of you. This book will attempt to dispel two myths: (1) there is one right way to be a family and (2) there is one right way to *communicate* within a family. Throughout the following pages, you will encounter a wide variety of descriptions of family life and communication behavior. Our purpose is to help you gain a better understanding of the dynamics of family communication, not to try to solve specific problems. Hence, we will take a descriptive, rather than a prescriptive, approach.

We hope there is some personal, rather than just academic, gain from reading these pages. Most of you come from families that have their share of pain and trouble as well as joy and intimacy. It is our hope that you will gain a new insight into the people with whom you share your lives. As you go through this text, read with your own family or other families with whom you have some passing acquaintance. We hope you choose to apply what you learn to your own family, although it may be difficult at times. The words of one of our students describe this process better than we can.

"Analyzing my own family has not been an easy process. As I began, my entire soul cried out, 'How do I begin to unravel the web of rules, roles, and strategies that make up our system?' I do not claim to have all possible answers; certainly my opinions and attitudes are different from those of the others in my family. I also do not claim to have the answers to all our problems. But I have tried to provide answers to my own confusion and to provide some synthesis to the changes and crises that I have experienced. And I have grown from the process."

CONCLUSION

This chapter introduces the world of the family. We shared our basic beliefs about families and communication, and moved on to an examination of family definitions and a consideration of the family as a system. We examined the current status of the American family, touching on issues of trends in marriage, divorce, and remarriage, the rise of dual career couples and single-parent systems, increased life expectancy, economic pressures, and ethnic diversity. Finally, we examined issues related to normal family functioning, indicating that this text would be descriptive rather than prescriptive in its approach.

IN REVIEW

1. At this point in your personal and academic life, how do you define the family?
2. To what extent do you agree with the family categories described earlier? Describe how you would alter these categories, giving reasons for your choices.
3. Demonstrate the basic-systems concept by describing how a change in one member of a family affects the other members. You may use a real or literary example.
4. Identify the family systems of four close friends, and describe them in terms of category types and socioeconomic and ethnic status.
5. At this point in your personal and academic life, how would you describe family normality?

CHAPTER 2

Framework for Family Communication

Families repeat themselves within and across generations. Members become caught up in predictable and often unexamined life patterns that are created, in part, through their interactions with others. This text explores the family as an interaction system, concentrating on the mutual influence between communication and family development, or how communication patterns affect family relationships and how those relationships affect communication. Within the framework of common cultural communication patterns, each family has the capacity to develop its own communication code based on the experiences of individual members and the collective family experience. Most individuals develop their communication skills within the family context, learning both the general cultural language and the specific familial communication code. Because most people take their own backgrounds for granted, you may not be aware of the context your family has provided for learning communication. For example, on a simple level, you may have learned "funny" words for familiar things; on a deeper level, you have learned particular ways to express feelings of affection or conflict. People in other families may have learned these things differently. In order to understand the family as an interaction system, you need to explore the communication concepts and how they can be applied to the family.

THE COMMUNICATION PROCESS

Communication may be viewed as a symbolic, transactional process, or to put it more simply, the process of creating and sharing meanings. In saying that communication is symbolic, we mean that symbols are used to transmit messages. Words, or verbal behavior are the most commonly used symbols; but the whole range of nonverbal behavior, including facial expressions, eye contact, gestures, movement, posture, appearance, and spatial distance, are also used symbolically. Objects and ideas can also be symbols, or referents. Families may use kisses, special food, toys, or poems as symbols of love. Although symbols allow you to share your thoughts on the widest range of possible subjects, the symbols must be mutually understood for the meanings to be shared. For example, if family members do not agree on what activities are "fun," how much is "a lot" of money, or which behaviors imply anger, there will be confusion. If meanings are not mutually shared, messages may not be understood.

> *"In my first marriage, my wife and I often discovered that we had very different meanings for the same words. For example, we agreed we wanted a 'large' family, but I meant three children and she meant seven or eight. I thought 'regular' sex meant once a day, and she thought it meant once a week. I thought spending a 'lot of money' meant spending over three hundred dollars; she thought it meant spending over fifty dollars. In my second marriage we talk very frequently about what we 'mean,' so we don't have so many disagreements."*

To say that communication is transactional means that when people communicate, they have a mutual impact on each other. In short, you do not originate communication, you participate in it (Watzlawick, Beavin, and Jackson 1967). Thus, in communicative relationships, all participants are both affecting and being affected by the others. It does not matter how much more talking one person appears to do; the mutual impact remains the same. The focus is placed on the relationship, not on the individual participants. Participation in an intimate relationship transforms fundamental reality definitions for both partners and in so doing transforms the partners themselves (Stephen and Enholm 1987, 331).

A transactional view of communication and a systems perspective of the family complement each other, because both focus on relationships, and relationships take precedence over individuals. A communication perspective focuses on the interaction of two or more persons. Accordingly, from a systems perspective it is nonproductive to analyze each individual separately. Each individual communicates within an interpersonal context, and each communication act reflects the nature of those relationships. As two people interact, each creates a context for the other and relates to the other within that context. For example, you may perceive a brother-in-law as distant and relate to him in a very polite but restrained manner. In turn, he may perceive your politeness as formal and relate to you in an even more reserved manner.

> *"My father and brother had a very difficult relationship with each other for many years, although each of them had an excellent relationship with everyone else in the family. Dan saw Dad as repressive and demanding, although I would characterize him as serious and concerned. Dad saw Dan as careless and uncommitted, although no one else saw him that way. Whenever they tried to talk to each other, each responded to the person he created, and it was a continual battle."*

In the previous example, knowing Dan or his father separately does not account for their conflictual behavior when they are together. Each influences the other's interaction. Each creates a context for the other and relates within the context. It is as if you say to another: "You are sensitive," or "You are repressive," or "You are

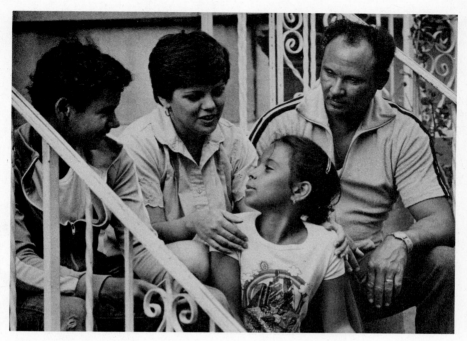

Family members renegotiate their relationships with each passing day.

shiftless," "and that's how I will relate to you." The content and style of the messages vary according to how each sees himself or herself and how each predicts the other will react. In addition to taking the environment or context into account, the transactional view stresses the importance of the communicator's perceptions and actions in determining the outcome of interactions.

Thus, the relationship pattern, not one or another specific act, becomes the focal point. One's perception of another and one's subsequent behavior can actually change the behavior of the other person. A mother who constantly praises her son for his thoughtfulness and sensitivity, who notices the good things in his efforts, may change her son's perception of himself and his subsequent behavior with her and other people. On the other hand, a husband who constantly complains about his wife's parenting behavior may lower her self-esteem and change her subsequent behavior toward him and the children. Thus, in communication relationships, each person (1) creates a context for the other, (2) simultaneously creates and interprets messages, and (3) affects and is affected by the other.

To say that communication is a process implies that it is continuous and changing. Communication is not static; it does not switch on and off but, rather, develops over time. Process implies change. Relationships, no matter how committed, change constantly, and communication both affects and reflects these changes. The passage of time brings with it predictable and unpredictable crises that take their toll on family regularity and stability. Yet everyday moods, minor pleasures, or irritation can shift the communication behaviors on a day-to-day basis.

As each day passes, family members subtly renegotiate their relationships. Today you may be in a bad mood, and people adjust to that with you; tomorrow adaptations may be made around your brother's great report card. Next week a major job change may affect all your relationships. Over time, families change as they pass through stages of growth; members are born, age, leave, and die. As you will see in the chapters on family development and change, communication patterns reflect these developments in family life.

As indicated earlier, communication may be viewed as a symbolic, transactional process, one of creating and sharing meanings. Successful communication depends on the partners' shared reality, or sets of meanings (Bochner and Eisenberg 1987). Now it is necessary to examine meanings and the way in which meanings develop.

Meanings and Messages

How often do people in close and committed relationships find themselves saying, "That's not what I mean" or "What do you mean by that?" According to Stephen (1986), even in the most mundane interchanges, participants' messages reflect their visions of the nature of social and physical reality as well as their values, beliefs, and attitudes. These are referred to as their meanings. Communication involves the negotiation of shared meanings; if meanings are not held in common, confusion and misunderstanding are likely to occur.

How does a person gain a set of meanings? Basically, your perceptions of the world, which affect your meanings and messages, result from your filter systems, which reflect your past experiences and the current situation. You might say that each person has lenses, or filters, through which to view the world. Each individual sees the world through a different filter. You view the world within the context of age, race, gender, religion, culture. In addition, your view of reality will be affected by sibling position and family history, with its myths, party lines, and traditions across generations (Lerner 1989, 71). These factors combine uniquely for each individual and determine how each person perceives and interacts with the world in general and, more specifically, to the surrounding family system. Although this sounds like a very individualistic process, remember the transactional perspective. Each communicator constantly affects and is affected by the other; thus, perceptions occur within the context of a relational system and are constantly influenced by that system.

Development of Meanings. Meanings emerge as information passes through your filter systems. Your physical state, based on human sensory systems (sight, hearing, touch, taste, smell), constitutes the first set of filters. Your perceptions are also filtered through the social system, or the way you use language, your accepted ways of seeing things, and all the socially agreed-upon conventions that standardize parts of your world. Eventually you share some common meanings for verbal and nonverbal symbols with those around you. You may share some very general experiences with many people and much more specific experiences with a smaller group of people. For example, with some persons, you share only global experiences, such as cultural background, including language, geographic area, customs, beliefs, and attitudes. With others, you may also share the specific and narrow experiences of living together in the house at 6945 Osceola Street and learning to understand each other's idiosyncrasies.

Social experiences frame your world. The language you speak limits and shapes the meanings you can ascertain. For example, the current pressure to use nonsexist language reflects a belief that women have formed less-powerful images of themselves because of the emphasis on the masculine in pronouns and other words. Proponents of change believe that perceptions of women will be altered by the new use of language. Current terminology limits easy discussion of certain new family relationships, such as "my stepmother's sister" or "my half-brother's grandfather on his mother's side." Yet, although language may limit meanings, we are capable of broadening such perspectives by learning new terminology, opening ourselves to new experiences.

Thus, the overall culture affects perceptions and meaning, but the immediate groups to which one belongs exert a strong influence on an individual's perceptual set. The family, school, office, and friendship group all provide contextual meaning and influence the way meaning is given to sense data. If giving a handmade gift is considered a special sign of caring, a knitted Christmas stocking may be valued, but an expensive necklace will not. Being a member of the Thurman family, a farmer, a square dance caller, a volunteer fire fighter, or a church elder provides context for giving meaning to the world for the individual and for a small segment of people who surround that person.

Although physical and social systems provide the basic general filters, specific constraints and experiences influence an individual's meanings. Individual constraints refer to the interpretations you create for your meanings based on your own personal histories. Although some of you may have similar histories, each person develops a unique way of dealing with sensory information and, thus, an individual way of seeing the world and relating to others in it. Two members of the Thurman family may share being farmers, square dance callers, fire fighters, and church elders, yet they will respond differently to many situations. For example, many brothers and sisters disagree on the kind of family life they experienced together. One declares, "I had a very happy childhood," which contrasts with a sibling's statement, "I would never want to go through those years again." For each of you, specific events and people affect your meanings. One person may say that his creative third-grade teacher and his summers at Aunt Mary's influenced his view of the world. Hoopes and Harper (1987) suggest that no sibling grows up in the exact same family.

"My sister Diane was considered the 'problem child' in our house. As far as experts can determine, her emotional difficulties stem from an unknown trauma when she was three, when they suggest she was rejected by my parents at a time when she needed love. The reality was that Diane functioned as a scapegoat for all of us. Although Diane and I are very close in age, we had different experiences in our family because of the way she perceived the family and was perceived by its members."

All persons' perceptions are not different. As family members, you also share many similar perceptions with the other family members who have learned to see the world in similar ways.

Over time, communication, or the symbolic transactional process, permits persons to negotiate shared meanings. After each encounter with a person or object, you become better able to deal with similar situations, and your behavior takes on certain patterns. The greater the repetition, the greater the probability of the assigned meaning.

Long-term, enduring relationships are characterized by agreements between members as to the meaning of things. These persons develop a relationship worldview reflecting the members' symbolic interdependence (Stephen 1986). Often people in families develop this worldview.

After you have functioned within a family system, you become comfortable with your ability to handle the symbols, mainly because you are able to interpret them on all levels and feel that you really understand them. As a child, when you heard your mother yell "Johnny" or "Elizabeth-Marie," you were able to tell from her tone of voice just what to expect. Today, you can sit at dinner and hear your younger sister say, "I just hate that Ernie Johnson" and know that she is really falling in love.

Levels of Meaning and Metacommunication. Communication of meaning occurs on two levels: the content level and the relationship level. The content level contains the information, whereas the relationship level indicates how the information should be interpreted or understood. The relationship level is more likely to involve nonverbal messages. When your mother says, "When are you going to pick up those clothes?" she is asking an informational question, but there is another level of meaning. It is up to you to determine if, by her nonverbal tone, she is really questioning at what time of day you will remove the articles, or if she is telling you to get them out of there in the next thirty seconds.

Metacommunication occurs when people communicate about their communication, when they give verbal and nonverbal instructions about how their messages should be understood. Such remarks as "I was only kidding," "This is important," or "Talking about this makes me uncomfortable" are signals to another on how to interpret certain comments, as are facial expressions, gestures, or vocal tones. On a deeper level, many couples or family members have spent countless hours talking about the way they fight or the way they express affection. Metacommunication serves an important function within families, because it allows members to state their needs, clarify confusion, and plan new and more constructive ways of relating to one another.

The ways in which people exchange messages influence the form and content of their relationships. Communication among family members shapes the structure of the family system and provides a family with its own set of meanings. Although we have used many family examples in describing the communication process, we have not explored the role of communication within the family. The following section examines the role communication plays in forming, maintaining, and changing family systems as families perform core functions.

COMMUNICATION PATTERNS AND FAMILY FUNCTIONS

When you come into contact with other families, you may notice how their communication differs from that of the families in which you have lived. Ways of relating, making decisions, sharing feelings, and handling conflict may vary slightly or greatly from your own personal experiences. Each family's unique message system provides the means of dealing with the major functions that give shape to family life. In other words, communication provides form and content to a family's life as members engage in family-related functions. We may define a function simply as something a system must do if it is not to break down (Cushman and Craig 1976). We will examine two primary family functions and four supporting functions that affect and are affected by communication.

Primary Functions

In their attempt to integrate the numerous concepts related to marital and family interaction, researchers Olson, Sprenkle, and Russell (1979) have developed what is known as the circumplex model of marital and family systems. Over the past decade, the model has evolved to include three dimensions: (1) cohesion, (2) adaptability, and (3) communication. The two central dimensions are family cohesion and family adaptability, which are perceived as the intersecting lines of an axis. The third dimension is family communication, a facilitating dimension that enables couples and families to move along the cohesion and adaptability dimension (Olson and McCubbin 1983). In their model, Olson and McCubbin do not develop the communication beyond a discussion of "positive skills," such as empathy and reflective listening, which encourage interpersonal sharing; and "negative skills," such as double messages or criticism, which keep members from sharing feelings. The authors imply the importance of communication but do not elaborate on this dimension.

In this text, the concepts of cohesion and change form a backdrop against which to view communication within various types of families. From this perspective, two primary family functions involve the following:

1. Establishing a pattern of cohesion, or separateness and connectedness.
2. Establishing a pattern of adaptability, or change.

Cohesion.   From the moment you were born, you have been learning how to handle distance or closeness within your family system. You were taught directly or subtly how to be connected to or separated from other family members. Cohesion implies "the emotional bonding members have with one another and the degree of individual autonomy a person experiences in the family system" (Olson et al. 1979, 5). In other words, a family attempts to deal with the extent to which physical or psychological closeness is encouraged or discouraged.

The issue of cohesion has been identified by many scholars from various fields as central to the understanding of family life (Bochner and Eisenberg 1987). Family researchers Kantor and Lehr (1976) view "distance regulation" as a major family function; family therapist Minuchin (1967) talks about "enmeshed and disengaged" families; sociologists Hess and Handel (1959) describe the family's need to "establish a pattern of separateness and connectedness."

Cohesion in a family affects and is affected by the communication among members. It is through communication that family members are able to develop and maintain or change their patterns of cohesion. A father may decide that it is inappropriate to continue the physical closeness he has experienced with his daughter now that she has become a teenager, and he may limit his touching or playful roughhousing. These nonverbal messages may be confusing or hurtful to his daughter. She may become angry, find new ways of being close, develop more outside friendships, or attempt to force her father back into the old patterns. A husband may demand more intimacy from his wife as he ages. He may ask for more serious conversation, make more sexual advances, share more of his feelings. His wife may ignore this new behavior or engage in more intimate behaviors herself.

Families with extremely high cohesion are often referred to as "enmeshed"; members are so closely bonded and overinvolved that individuals experience little autonomy or fulfillment of personal needs and goals. Family members appear fused or joined so tightly that personal identities do not develop appropriately. Enmeshed persons do not experience life as individuals.

"As my sister and I grew up, we were very parental and protective toward each other. When Sara and I were young, and even into our adolescent years, we used to imagine what would happen if one or the other of us were to die. There was clear agreement that the one who remained alive also would have to die soon afterward. Neither of us really believed we could survive without the other. Growing up in an alcoholic home, we relied on one another for physical and emotional survival. Now we both are learning to trust other people also."

"Disengaged" refers to families at the other end of the continuum in which members experience very little closeness or family solidarity, yet each member has high autonomy and individuality. There is a strong sense of emotional separation or divorce. Members experience little or no sense of connectedness to each other (see Figure 2-1).

As you examine cohesion in families you may wish to look at indicators such as "emotional bonding, independence, boundaries, time, space, friends, decision making, and interests and recreation" (Olson et al. 1979, 6). Throughout this book, we will look at ways families deal with issues of coming together or staying apart and how they use communication in an attempt to reach their desired cohesion level.

Figure 2–1 ————————————————————————

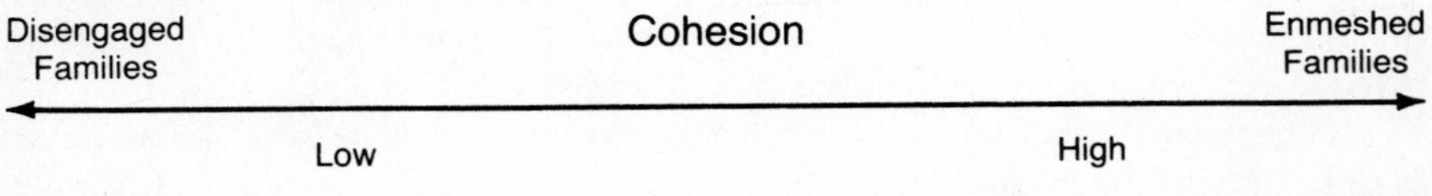

Disengaged Families	Cohesion	Enmeshed Families

←————————————————————————————————————→

Low   High

Families do not remain permanently at one point on the cohesion continuum. Members do not come together and stay the same, as is evident from the previous examples. Hence, change within a family's life must be addressed.

Adaptability. When you think of the changes in your own family over the past five or ten years, you may be amazed at how different the systems and its members are at this point. A family experiences changes as it goes through its own developmental stages and deals with crises that arise in everyday life, such as adapting to the marriage or job transfer of one of its members.

Adaptability may be viewed as "the ability of a marital/family system to change its power structure, role relationships, and relationship rules in response to situational and developmental stress" (Olson and McCubbin 1983, 62). The researchers see family power structure, negotiation styles, role relationships, relationship rules, and feedback as central to the concept of adaptability.

Each human system has both stability-promoting processes (morphostasis) and change-promoting processes (morphogenesis) to maintain itself. Family systems need periods of stability and periods of change in order to function. Families that regularly experience extensive change may be considered chaotic. Because of total unpredictability and stress, they have little opportunity to develop relationships and establish common meanings. At the other extreme, rigidity characterizes families that repress change and growth (see Figure 2-2).

Recently, questions have been raised about the view of extreme flexibility as chaos, seeing it in a negative light as opposed to seeing it as desirable (Lee 1988a). Although most scholars consider an excess or a paucity of change to be dysfunctional, they see the ability of a system to change its structure as generally desirable.

As you think about adaptability, you may think about it as related to internal system change (first order change). This means that a system that is flexible, but not extreme, is most functional as everyday issues are dealt with. On the other hand, when a system undergoes second order change, or change in the entire system's structure, this is so unusual and infrequent that it should not be considered on this model.

Family systems constantly restructure themselves as they pass through predictable developmental stages—marriage, pregnancy, birth, parenting, and the "empty nest." All represent major familial changes. Likewise, when positive or negative stresses arise involving such issues as money, illness, or divorce, families must adapt. Finally, family systems must adapt both structurally and functionally to the demands of other social institutions as well as to the needs of their own members.

Figure 2—2 _____

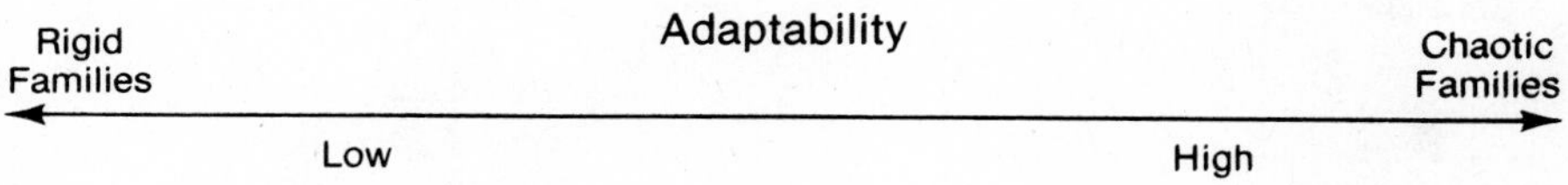

Adaptability

Rigid
Families ←————————————————————————————————→ Chaotic
Families

Low   High

"My son and daughter-in-law adopted an older child and had to adapt their communication patterns to accommodate her. Although lying was forbidden in their family when they adopted Shirley, they had to reassess this position because she had learned to lie for most of her life. My son and daughter-in-law had to learn to be more tolerant of this behavior, particularly when she first joined the family, or they would have had to send her back to the agency."

Communication is central to the adaptive function of a family. Any effective adaptation relies on shared meanings gained through the family message system. Through communication, families make it clear to their members how much adaptation is allowed within the system, while regulating the adaptive behaviors of their members and the system as a whole. Variables that affect this family function include family power structure (assertiveness and control), negotiation styles, role relationships, and relationship rules and feedback (positive and negative). Olson and McCubbin (1983, 13) hypothesize that, where there is a balance between change and stability within families, there will be more mutually assertive communication styles, shared leadership, successful negotiation, role sharing, and open rule making and sharing.

Adapting the work of Olson and colleagues, you can visualize the mutual interaction of adaptability and cohesion within families by placing them on an axis (see Figure 2-3a). By adding the extremes of cohesion (disengagement and enmeshment) and adaptability (rigidity and chaos), you can picture where more or less functional families would appear on the axis (see Figure 2-3b).

The central area represents balanced or moderate levels of adaptability and cohesion, seen as a highly workable communication pattern for individual and family development, although there may be instances when a different pattern could aid a family through a particular developmental point or through a crisis. The outside areas represent the extremes of cohesion and adaptability, less workable for consistent long-term communication patterns.

Figure 2–3
Family Cohesion/Adaptability Axes

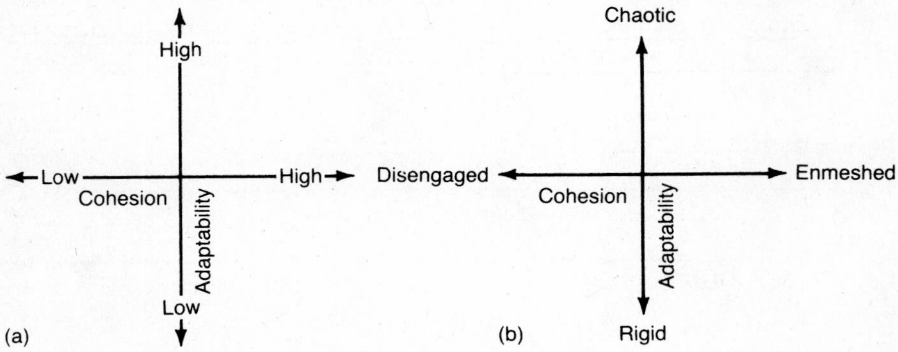

Figure 2-4 —————————————————————————————————
Application of Family Cohesion/Adaptability

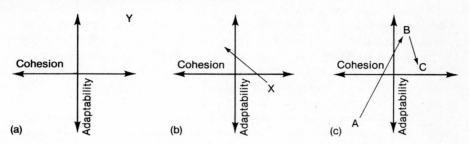

Most well-functioning families are found short of the extremes, except when they are under high levels of stress. In those situations, placement at the extreme may serve a purpose. If a family is faced with the loss of a member through death, a highly cohesive communication pattern may be critical for mourning purposes. In Figure 2-4a, at the time of a family death, members may find themselves at point Y. Such a family may be experiencing extreme closeness among remaining members but chaos in terms of dealing with the changes in roles or in everyday activities.

As another example, a family with an acting-out teenager may find itself shifting from point X to point Z on the axis, as the adolescent demands greater freedom and less connectedness from the family and forces changes upon the system (see Figure 2-4b).

The situation in the following quotation may be graphed as three moves (see Figure 2-4c).

———

"As a small child I lived in an active alcoholic family in which people kept pretty much to themselves. We did not talk about the problems caused by our parents' drinking, and we acted as if things were fine. Yet we were very rigid, because we never could bring anyone into the house and we never let outsiders know about the drinking. My older sister always took care of me if there was a problem, whereas my older brother locked himself in his room. Thus we were at point A. When my parents finally went into treatment the house was crazy in a different way for a while because no one knew exactly how to act, but we did get closer and we were all forced to discuss what was going on. I guess we got closer and almost too flexible or unpredictable (point B). Now, five years later, I'm the only child left home, and my sober parents and I have a relatively close and flexible relationship (point C)."

———

If you think about periods in your family life, you should be able to envision how the family shifted from one point to another on the cohesion-adaptability axis.

Olson and McCubbin (1983) have indicated that families at different stages of development seem to function better in different areas of the model. For example, young couples without babies function best in either the upper right- or lower left-hand quadrants. Adolescents function best in the central, or balanced, area;

older couples relate best in the lower right-hand quadrant. Adolescents function best when they have average cohesion, being neither enmeshed with parents nor disengaged, and when their adaptability is midway between rigidity and chaos. Obviously, these results indicate adolescents' needs for a family system without threats or rigid rules. Older couples function best when cohesion is high but adaptability is low. Possible explanations for these findings will become clearer in the chapters on developmental changes. Although results may differ for families from particular backgrounds or ethnic origins, these findings support maintaining a flexible attitude toward well-family functioning.

When viewing a whole system, you may find certain members who would be graphed in a different place if they were to be pictured individually. These models attempt to represent the group on the axis. Throughout the text, the cohesion/change framework will be used as a backdrop for understanding family communication.

Although the issues related to cohesion and adaptability/change are viewed as the primary functions, these functions do not provide a complete picture. There are additional family functions—supporting functions—that contribute to the understanding of family interaction.

Supporting Functions

There are four supporting functions that, in conjunction with cohesion and adaptability, give shape to family life. Hess and Handel (1959, 4) identify five processes, or family functions, that interact with the development of a family's message system. Because one of these processes relates to cohesion, we will list only the remaining four. The supporting family functions include the following:

1. Establishing a satisfactory congruence of images.
2. Evolving modes of interaction into central family themes.
3. Establishing the boundaries of the family's world of experience.
4. Dealing with significant biosocial issues of family life, such as gender, age, power, and roles.

Each of these processes interacts with a family's point on the cohesion/adaptability axis and influences a family's communication pattern.

Family Images. Relationship patterns can be seen as metaphors. If you had to create a mental image or a metaphor for your family, what would it be? Do you see your family as a nest, a broken wagon wheel, a corporation, a spaceship, or a schoolroom? Every family operates as an image-making mechanism. Each member develops images of what the family unit and other family members are like; these images determine his or her patterns of interaction with the others. Patterns of the marital relationship, which often cannot be communicated through literal language, are explained metaphorically (Norton 1989). A person's image of his or her family embodies what is expected from it, what is given to it, and how important it is (Hess and Handel 1959). Thus, the image has both realistic and idealized components that reflect both the imaged and the imaginer.

"The best family image for my parents and the six kids is fighter planes in formation. My parents are the two fighter planes in front, and the six children are in formation behind. We all go off in slightly different directions, yet always remain behind the parent planes, always remain at full speed ahead, and always remain in some sort of formation. Occasionally, one fighter plane may lose his place in the formation and become lost. Although no one slows down, help is extended over the radio, or in desperate situations, one parent plane goes after the lost plane, bringing it back into formation."

A family's conception of itself affects its orientation to areas such as cooperation versus competition, reaching out versus withdrawal, and it affects communication. According to Jones (1982), the verbal and nonverbal behaviors of the family members are, in part, determined by this imagistic view of their relationship with each other and with the external environment. One dual-career couple described their family as a "seesaw," saying: "We are able to balance each other well and be flexible in allowing the kids to move between us. But if a crisis hits and we have to move in new patterns, such as sideways, we run into problems."

If you think about metaphors within interactive systems of interaction, individual behaviors and relationships may be seen as metaphors. One set of siblings may be seen as "two peas in a pod"; another set may be "oil and water." If the persons involved hold very different images of their relationship to each other, this difference will be reflected in communication patterns. If two people's images of each other are congruent and consistent for a period of time, a predictable pattern of communication may emerge in which both are comfortable. For example, if a mother sees her son as a helpless and dependent creature, she may exhibit many protective behaviors, such as keeping bad news from him. If the son's image of his mother is as a protector, the congruence of the images will allow harmonious communication, but if the child sees his mother as a jailer, conflict may emerge. If one child sees the mother as a jailer and the other sees her as an angel, the lack of consistent images held by family members may result in strong alliances among those with congruent images. A husband and wife are likely to experience conflict if one sees the family as a "nest" involving nurturing, emotion, and protection, and the other sees it as a corporation involving a strong power structure and good organization. Yet, because complete consensus is improbable and change inevitable, the patterns will never become totally predictable; the level of congruence relates to the effectiveness of communication within the family. The family metaphor acts as a perceptual filter and serves as an impetus for future thought and action (Jones 1982, 9).

Family Themes. As well as having images for the family and for every member, each family shares themes—or takes positions in relation to the outer world that affect every aspect of its functioning. A theme may be viewed as a pattern of feelings, motives, fantasies, and conventionalized understandings grouped around a particular locus of concern, which has a particular form in the personalities of individual members (Hess and Handel 1959, 11).

Themes represent a fundamental view of reality and a way of dealing with this view. Through its theme, a family responds to the questions "Who are we?" and "What do we do about it?" Sample theme issues that some families value include the following: physical security, strength, dependability, inclusion, and separation. To demonstrate the viability of themes in a family, we view them as statements that actualize the values more specifically:

Nielsens play to win.
We have responsibility for those less fortunate than we are.
You can sleep when you die.
If God gives much, much is expected in return.
You can only depend on your family.
You can always depend on your family.
Simons never quit.
You can always do better.
Seize the moment.
The Logans are never afraid of hard work.
We are survivors.
God is with us through thick and thin.

Themes relate directly to family actions, thereby allowing us to surmise a family's themes by watching its actions. Living according to a theme necessitates the development of various patterns of behavior that affect (1) how members interact with the outside world, (2) how they interact with each other, and (3) how they develop personally. For example, a family system with the theme "We have responsibility for those less fortunate than we are" might be a flexible system open to helping relationships with nonfamily members, and may accept temporary family members, such as foster children, who have problems. Yet, it may be difficult or impossible for such a family to accept help from an outside source because of its own self-definition as helper. Members may tend to put themselves and other family members second as they deal with outside problems. Following the classic line of the shoemaker's children without shoes, a mother who lives according to this theme may spend hours working at a drop-in center for adolescents in the community and be unaware of the problems her own teenage children are having because of the outward focus of the family life. Young members may grow up learning to minimize their problems and may not have much experience expressing painful feelings. Yet they may learn to self-sacrifice willingly for those less fortunate and may be very empathetic and attuned to the needs of others.

"I grew up with the family theme 'You can sleep when you die.' Ours is a family that values action above all else, especially action pointed toward reaching goals or winning in competition. The task or the goal is the focus, not the person doing the task or reaching the goal. We were expected to be busy. Sitting around and chatting or hanging out with friends was viewed as nonproductive. I learned to hold conversations while cooking, exercising, doing chores, and practicing a musical instrument. Finding that interpersonal time was important to me."

Family themes may be complex and subtle. They may involve worldviews that are not immediately obvious. It is important to identify a family's main theme(s) in order to understand fully the meanings and communication behavior of its members.

Boundaries. In addition to developing images and themes, families create boundaries. The boundary of a system is what separates it from its environment and from all that is nonsystem. In short, the boundary defines the system as an entity (Constantine 1986, 65). We can imagine boundaries as physical or psychological limits that regulate access to people, places, ideas, and values. All families establish some boundaries as they restrict their members from encountering certain physical and psychological forces. Most frequently, family boundaries regulate access to people, places, ideas, and values.

Some family boundaries are permeable, or flexible, and allow movement across them. Others resist movement and are rigid and inflexible (see Figure 2-5). Finally, others are so invisible or diffuse that they are almost nonexistent.

One set of boundaries, external boundaries, distinguish family members from the rest of the world. Another set, internal boundaries, help or keep family members appropriately placed in relationship to each other. Let's look first at how external boundaries function.

Certain families permit or encourage their children to make many different kinds of friends, explore alternative religious ideas, and have access to new ideas through the media; such permeable boundaries permit people, ideas, and values to enter the family. Some families retain rigid control of their children's activities to prevent them from coming into contact with what the family considers "undesirable." Extremes of such behavior result in the creation of rigid boundaries around the family system. Finally, some families provide no sense of identity for members and no control of their contact with people, places, ideas, or values. Members of this type of system experience little sense of "family."

"Although we are close to our parents, my sister and I can do anything that most other young people in our area are allowed to do. My cousins from Greece live in a different world. They are not allowed to date, even though they are sixteen and seventeen. Their parents do not want them to go away to college, and they will be expected to live at home until they are married. They constantly hear that 'good Greek girls would not do that.' There are far stricter boundaries on what they are allowed to experience than what I can do."

Figure 2–5 —————————————————————————————
External Boundaries

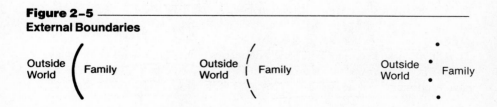

Yet, no matter how set family boundaries are initially, they will vary according to the personalities of the members, the types of experiences to which members are exposed, and the freedom each member has to create his or her own value system.

Although the family unit system may set strong boundaries, a strong, self-assured person may challenge rigid or stereotyped aspects of certain issues and reject the traditional boundaries set for him or her. An intensely emotional or sensitive child may comprehend things never imagined by other family members. This child may push far beyond the geographic limits or aspirational labels held by other family members. Beavers (1982) describes the importance of establishing boundaries indicating optimal family members can "switch hit", that is, identify with the larger world, and yet maintain individual and generational boundaries.

Healthy families establish internal boundaries to protect members' self-identity and the identity of generational groups. If the boundaries between individuals are diffuse or nonexistent, members may experience psychological problems, such as overinvolvement, codependency, or a loss of physical boundaries such as occurs in incest. If the internal boundaries are too rigid and strong, members will feel disengaged and out of touch.

Most families experience boundaries between generations, which establish subsystems of generational hierarchy. Generations establish their boundaries based on behaviors appropriate for that subsystem (Wood and Talmon 1983). For example, parents usually provide nurturance and control for their children. It is unusual for children to extensively nurture or control their parents unless they have become aged and ill. In two-parent families, the marital subsystem represents a critical entity in the functioning of family life. In most families, husbands and wives share unique information and give each other special emotional and physical support. Children are not allowed to share in all aspects of the marital dyad. Many types of conflict may arise if the system's interpersonal boundaries, particularly the marital boundaries, are too permeable and children or others are expected to fulfill part of the spousal role. For example, troubled families, such as those with an alcoholic spouse, may experience shifts in the marital boundary. If an alcoholic husband cannot provide the interpersonal support needed by his wife, she may co-opt one of the children into the marital subsystem by expecting the child to act as an adult confidant and emotional support. When boundaries are inappropriately crossed, roles become confused, and pain may result for all members.

Sometimes boundary issues are played out across a series of generations. A daughter whose mother invaded her life may determine not to act in the same way toward her children and may actually distance herself from them. Her children, in turn, may resolve to develop closeness with their offspring and end up invading their children's lives.

Interpersonally testing or forcing boundaries may involve deep emotional conflicts, which could be resolved through the increased growth of all family members or by the severing of bonds with specific members who eventually leave the system. Each of you has experienced resisting boundaries or having persons challenge your system's boundaries with positive or negative results. Your family relationships may have eventually become stronger or certain relationships may have suffered. Thus, the physical and psychological boundaries set by each family strongly influence the kinds of interpersonal communication that can occur within the system.

Biosocial Issues. All families operate in a larger sphere that provides conventional ways of coping with biosocial issues, but each family creates its own answers within the larger framework. Hess and Handel (1959, 17–18) identify the following as included with biosocial issues: male and female identity, authority and power, shaping and influencing children, and children's rights. Goldner (1989) claims that gender and generation are fundamental, essential organizing principles of family life.

All people are faced with sexual identity issues while growing up and/or while forming their own family systems and raising children. Sexual identity and physical development issues affect styles of interaction and vice versa. A family that assigns responsibilities based on a member's sex operates differently than one that uses interest or preference as the basis for assigning responsibilities. If physical stature automatically determines duties and privileges, the interaction will be different than in a setting where physical development is only one factor among many by which privileges are awarded and duties are assigned as appropriate to males and females.

Other value decisions in the social sphere relate to the use of power within the family structure. To what extent are leadership, decision making, and authority issues resolved according to traditional gender and role configurations? Families negotiate the use of power within the system, and members may find themselves in the renegotiation process for much of their lives. The social sphere also involves attitudinal issues related to roles and responsibilities that may be exemplified in parent-child relationships. Parent-child interactions reflect the mutually held attitudes. If a parent sees a child as a responsibility to be dispensed with at a given age, the interactions will be immensely different than if the parental attitude reflects a prolonged responsibility for his or her offspring, perhaps far beyond the years of adolescence. The extent to which a child is permitted privacy, physical or psychological, also reflects a biosocial orientation.

Hare-Mustin (1989) sees that age, gender, and power interact in complex ways within family systems and argues that women may fall between the male parent and the child in some structures. Thus, the parents versus child hierarchy may be too simple a concept when dealing with power.

"For the first eleven years of his life, my stepson Travis was raised in a household that catered to his every need. He was encouraged to be dependent and to remain a little boy in many ways. His mother, Martha, could not have more children, so she doted on him as her only child. Before he died, her first husband treated Martha and Travis as people who needed to be taken care of. When I married Martha, my two daughters came to live with us. They had been raised to be self-sufficient and independent. I have found myself becoming very impatient with Travis and pushing him to act like my children. Martha and I have had many fights over the children's responsibilities."

The development of images, themes, boundaries, and responses to biosocial issues interacts with the functions of cohesion and adaptability. Flexible families will experience greater variety in images, themes, boundaries, and responses to biosocial issues than will rigid ones. These responses also affect the family's acceptable level of cohesion. For example, a family with fixed boundaries and themes related to total family dependence will develop extremely high cohesion in contrast to the family with themes of service or independence coupled with flexible boundaries. This entire process rests with the communication behaviors of the family members. Communication, then, is the means by which families establish their patterns of cohesion and adaptability, based at least partially on their interactions in the development of images, themes, boundaries, and responses to biosocial issues.

A FRAMEWORK FOR EXAMINING FAMILY COMMUNICATION

There are numerous approaches to analyzing the family as a system, such as looking at a family as an economic, political, or biological system. Because concern lies with the interaction within and around the family, this text centers on the communication aspects of the family system. The following is a framework for examining family communication:

The family is a system in which communication regulates cohesion and adaptability by a flow of message patterns through a network of evolving interdependent relationships located within a defined context.

The family is a system . . .

The family may be viewed as a set of people and the relationships among them that together form a complex whole; changes in one part result in changes in other parts of the system. In short, family members are inextricably tied to each other, and each member and the family as a whole reflect changes in the system.

. . . in which communication regulates cohesion and adaptability . . .

Communication, the symbolic, transactional process by which meanings are exchanged, is the means by which families develop their capacities for emotional bonding and flexibility. Communication facilitates a family's movement on the cohesion/adaptability axis (see Figure 2-3). The way in which people exchange messages influences the form and content of their relationships. Communication and families simultaneously impact each other. Communication affects the way family members relate, and family relationships affect the communication that occurs.

. . . by a flow of message patterns through a network . . .

Based on families-of-origin and other environmental sources, each family develops its own set of meanings that become predictable, because family members interact with one another in the same manner over and over again. Such message patterns move through boundaries that define the relationships along specific networks that determine who interacts with whom.

. . . of evolving interdependent relationships . . .

Family life is not static; both predictable, or developmental, changes and unpredictable changes, or crises, force alteration upon the system. Family relationships evolve over time as members join and leave the system and become closer or farther apart from each other. Yet, because of the family's systemic nature, members remain interdependent, or joined, as they deal with relational issues of intimacy, conflict roles, power, and decision making.

. . . located within a defined context.

In Chapter 1, you encountered some perspectives on family normality, including the view of normality as transactional, or process-oriented. This perspective emphasizes attention to adaptation over the life cycle and adaptation to various contexts. Thus, issues of developmental stages and reaction to change combine with contextual issues such as ethnicity, gender, and socioeconomic status to create a "culture" within which families operate.

Norms and expectations vary greatly across groups of families but may remain relatively similar for families within a given cultural context.

Throughout the following chapters, we will examine the concepts mentioned in this framework in order to demonstrate the powerful role communication plays in family life.

"When you really think about it, family life is extremely complex, and most of us just go through the motions every day without any reflection. I usually take for granted that most families are similar to mine, but the more I look carefully at other family systems the more aware I am of the differences. Perhaps families are like snowflakes; no two are ever exactly alike."

CONCLUSION

This chapter described the process of communication and proposed connection between communication patterns and family functions. The primary functions discussed are cohesion and adaptability, and the supporting functions include family images, themes, boundaries, and biosocial issues. The chapter concluded with a framework for analyzing family interaction: The family is a system in which communication regulates cohesion and adaptability by a flow of message patterns through a defined network of evolving interdependent relationships.

IN REVIEW

1. Using your own family or a fictional one, identify three areas of "meaning" that would have to be explained to an outsider who was going to be a houseguest for a month. For example, what would have to be explained for the houseguest to understand how to interpret the meanings?
2. Describe a recurring interaction pattern in a real or fictional family in terms of the predictable verbal and nonverbal messages. Provide a statement of the effect of this interaction pattern on the persons involved or on the family as a whole.
3. Give three examples of behavior that might characterize an enmeshed family and three examples of behavior that might characterize a disengaged family.
4. Using a real or fictional family, give an example of how the family moved from one point on the adaptability-cohesion grid to another point due to changes in their lives.
5. How might one of the following themes and one of the following images be carried out in family communication patterns?
   Themes:
   • You can always depend on your family.
   • We are survivors.
   • Use your gifts.
   • Take one step at a time.
   • You only live once.
   Images:
   • Circus, army, schoolhouse, rock, corporation, octopus.

CHAPTER 3

The Family as a System

"We live our lives like chips in a kaleidoscope, always part of patterns that are larger than ourselves and somehow more than the sum of their parts" (Minuchin 1984, 2). A systems perspective provides the most valuable insight into a family's communication patterns. Because communication is a symbolic, transactional process, focus must be placed on family relationships, not on individual members. In order to understand the communication patterns of a family, the overall communication context—the family system—must be examined.

"Family life is incredibly subtle and complex. Everything seems tied to everything else, and it's very difficult to sort out what is going on. For example, when our oldest daughter, Marcy, contracted spinal meningitis, the whole family reflected the strain. My second daughter and I fought more, whereas my husband tended to withdraw into himself, which brought me closer to my son. In their own ways, the three children became closer, but our marriage became more distant. As Marcy's recovery progressed, there were more changes, which affected how we relate now, two years later. That one event highlights the difficulty of sorting out what is really going on within a family."

The previous personal statement provides insight into how a family operates systemically and reflects the complexity of the task of examining families from a systems perspective. Everyday systemic patterns are often subtle, buried in predictable patterns yet powerful in their effects. Nonverbal indications of displeasure, avoidance of issues, or ways of expressing affection may dramatically influence how members function. Unless you understand the context, you may not understand the individuals and the messages. In order to understand communication within the family system, this chapter will examine what a system is, how it works, and how it relates to everyday family functioning. We will consider the implications of taking a systems perspective on the family.

CHARACTERISTICS OF HUMAN SYSTEMS

Very simply stated, a system is a set of objects that interrelate with one another to form a whole. A system is characterized by its process of change. If one component of the system changes, the others will change in response, which in turn affects the initial component. Systems may be closed or open. A closed system has no interchange with the environment; this concept applies mainly to physical elements, such as machines, which do not have life-sustaining qualities. An open system engages in interchange with the environment and is oriented toward growth; living, or organic, systems such as family systems fit into this category.

A system consists of four elements: objects, attributes, relationships, and an environment (Littlejohn 1983). The objects are the parts of a system; obviously, in the case of a familial system, these are the family members themselves. The attributes are the qualities, or properties, of the system and its members. Thus, a family or a member has generalized family system attributes, such as goals, energy, health, or ethnic heritage, but each attribute is distinctive to that family or member—attributes such as athletic goals, high energy, ill health, or Polish heritage.

The relationships among parts in the family system are the relationships among family members—the major focus of this book. Such relationships are characterized by communication that affects levels of cohesion and adaptability at any given point in a family's life. Finally, environment is viewed as a system element, because systems are affected by their surroundings, the ecosystems in which they function. Families do not exist in a vacuum; they live within a time period, culture, community, and many other influential systems, such as extended family or educational organizations.

As you read about the family as a system, you may be surprised by some of the technical terminology, which may appear extremely complex at first. Unfortunately, there are no simple ways to talk about these important concepts. It is hoped that you will come to understand the value of a systems approach to family communication and will find the terminology helpful rather than cumbersome.

From a systems perspective, persons are considered as part of an overall context, not as individuals. Decontexted individuals do not exist (Minuchin 1984, 2). Bavelas and Segal (1982) say that when the objects of a system are actually people in relationships with other people, one of the most important attributes of that system is communication behavior (101). In a family systems perspective, one visualizes an image in which the people are in the background and the relationships are in the foreground. A family systems perspective should aid you in analyzing family interaction, predicting future interactions, and creating meaningful changes within the system.

Specifically, we will apply the following systems characteristics to families: interdependence, wholeness, patterns/self-regulation, interactive complexity/punctuation, adaptation, openness, equifinality, hierarchy subsystems, and information processing (Watzlawick, Beavin, and Jackson 1967; Littlejohn 1989; Kantor and Lehr 1976; Kramer 1980; Bavelas and Segal; Constantine 1986; Bochner and Eisenberg 1987).

Relationships among parts in the family system are characterized by communication.

Interdependence

In an essay on systems thinking Noone (1989) asks the question "But how does one come to see oneself as an integral part of a larger whole?" He then answers that the process

> includes observing ourselves as part of an unfolding process rooted in the past and intertwined with larger living systems in the present. It is as mind boggling as gazing into the evening sky and trying to comprehend one's place in the vastness of the universe. (2)

Within any system, the parts are so interrelated as to be dependent upon each other for their functioning. Thus, this related dependence, or interdependence, is critical in describing a system.

The family is a highly interdependent system with a powerful and long-lasting effect on its members. Traditionally, this interdependence has been viewed as the means of maintaining a delicate balance among the system's parts, or members. Family therapist Jackson (1965) was one of the first to describe the process of family homeostasis, the bringing of a changing system back into balance. In Chapter 1, you encountered Satir's image of the family as a mobile in which members respond to changes in each other. As members respond to situations, other members may consciously or unconsciously shift to adjust to the quivering system. Families do not necessarily seek absolute balance; rather, they evolve to, or seek, steady states that are always slightly different from the previous steady state. Current thinkers support an evolutionary model of family systems that incorporates the possibility of spontaneous or kaleidoscopic change (Dell 1982; Hoffman 1980; Bochner and Eisenberg).

No matter what kind of change a family is experiencing, all members are affected due to their interdependence.

You may be able to pinpoint events in your own family that have influenced all members in an identifiable way. Sometimes troublesome behaviors are encouraged, because that individual serves to keep the family relatively balanced by taking the focus off a severe problem. Examples in family therapy literature suggest that parents may use, or focus on, an acting-out child to keep the marriage together; or children may use the parents' overprotectiveness to keep them safely close to home (Hoffman, 54). A behavior that seems problematic to the outside world may serve an important function within the family system. Lerner (1989) describes this exact process as seven-year-old Judy exhibits temper tantrums and obnoxious misbehavior:

> When specifically does Judy act up and act out? From what I can piece together, this occurs when her father's distance and her mother's anxious focus on Judy reach intolerable proportions. And what is the outcome of Judy's troublemaking and tantrums? Distant Dad is roped back into the family (and is helped to become more angry than depressed), and the parents are able to pull together, temporarily united by their shared concern for their child. (13)

Judy's behavior is, in part, an attempt to solve a problem in the family.

Thus, interdependence is a powerful element in understanding family functioning. In a family systems perspective, the behavior of each family member is related to and dependent upon the behavior of the others. When changes occur in family relationships, changes also occur in the individuals, and vice versa (Kramer C., 45).

Wholeness

A family systems approach assumes that the whole is greater than the sum of its parts. The parts, or members, are understood in the context of that whole. Sieburg (1973) provides a commonplace illustration citing the cook who knows that the cake that comes out of the oven is unlike the flour, eggs, and milk that went into the mix (5). A nonsystemic approach to families studies the individual members and "sums up" their personalities and attributes to describe the entire family. Littlejohn suggests that, in the nonsystemic model, the whole is merely a collection with no unique qualities, "like a box of stones" (35). The systems model reflects an integration of parts, whereas overall family images and themes reflect this wholistic quality.

For example, the Riveras, the McCarthys, or the Boyers have a life that characterizes the family as a whole, above and beyond the life of each family member. The Boyer family may be characterized as humorous, religious, warm, and strong, yet these adjectives do not necessarily apply to each family member. Thus, certain group characteristics may not reflect those of each individual member. You may hear whole families referred to as "brainy," "artsy," "driven," "aggressive," "industrious," or "money-hungry," yet you know at least one member who does not fit the label.

In an ongoing human system, the parts, or the people, have importance; but once these parts become interrelated, they take on a life greater than their individual existences. This is called synergy. This occurs when two or more people generate energy greater than the sum of their individual efforts. For example, certain immigrant families rose to power and fame through the single-minded dedication of their members.

Communication patterns between or among family members emerge as a result of this "wholeness." Conflict or affection may become an inherent part of communication between various members. A certain cue may trigger patterns of behavior without members' awareness. Some of these communication patterns will be examined in Chapter 4.

"Something wonderful and funny happens when my sister and I get together. We tend to play off each other and can finish each other's sentences, pick up the same references at the same time and create a dynamic energy that leaves other people out. We don't do it on purpose. Rather we just seem to 'click' with each other and off we go!"

Patterns/Self-Regulation

In your family, what are the appropriate ways to greet other members? What behaviors are acceptable or unacceptable during a family argument? Human beings learn to coordinate their actions in order to create patterns together that could not be created individually. Although coordination of actions varies dramatically across family systems, each system develops communication patterns that make life predictable and manageable.

Although you may not be aware of it, you have learned to live within a family interaction system that is highly reciprocal, patterned, and repetitive. The importance of the system's patterns lies in their ability to put an act into context. The patterns provide data by which to understand acts that may appear confusing or strange when used in isolation. Interaction patterns provide a means of assessing communication behaviors within a system, because they provide the context for understanding specific or isolated behaviors. For example, taken as an isolated pattern, it may be hard to interpret an act such as Mike's regularly hitting his brother, Charles. Yet, if this act is viewed as part of a contextual pattern, it may make sense. If parental fighting and Mike's aggressive acts are related, you may discover patterns in which Mike's parents stop fighting when they focus on his aggression, or you may find that Mike feels guilty for his parents' anger and takes his feelings out on his brother. In a personal example, Lerner (1989) describes how family members can get stuck in a pattern:

My older sister, Susan (a typical firstborn), managed her anxiety by overfunctioning, and I (a typical youngest) managed my anxiety by underfunctioning. Over time our position became polarized and rigidly entrenched. The more my sister overfunctioned the more I underfunctioned, and vice versa. (28)

Patterns provide many more clues for interpreting behavior than do isolated individual actions. A very special type of relationship pattern called communication rules will be explored in detail in Chapter 4.

Rules are relationship agreements that prescribe and limit a family member's behavior over time. Rules serve as generative mechanisms capable of creating regularity out of chaos (Yerby and Buerkel-Rothfuss 1982, 2). Family rules govern all areas of life, including communication behavior. Every human system needs rules and regularity in order to function efficiently over time.

All systems display a need for constancy within a defined range (Watzlawick et al. 147). Thus, a system needs to maintain some type of standard that is reached by noting deviations from the norm and correcting them if they become too significant. The function of maintaining stability in a system is called calibration. Calibration implies monitoring and rectifying a scale. In the case of a family system, it implies checking and, if necessary, rectifying the scale of acceptable behaviors. On occasion, the changes happen too dramatically for a family to exert any control, but everyday life is filled with opportunities to maintain or change family patterns.

Systems generate negative and positive feedback processes, but, in systems language, the terms are used differently than they are in everyday usage. Negative feedback processes imply constancy or maintaining the standard while minimizing change. Positive, or change-promoting, feedback processes result in recalibration of the system at a different level. No value is implied by the labels of negative and positive. You can visualize this process in the following ways. Figure 3-1a represents a system in which negative, or maintenance, feedback prevents change from occurring. For example, this may happen when a teenager swears at a parent for the first time. The parent may threaten, "You swear at me again and I'll ground you for six months"; or the parent may appeal to the family values: "We don't treat family members like that. We show each other respect, even in disagreement." If the teenager becomes frightened by the threat or apologetic for breaking the family value system, swearing may never occur again. Therefore, swearing will not become part of his or her conflict pattern. In another situation, if one partner indicates a desire for new sexual experimentation but the other refuses, the system will be maintained at the original level of sexual intimacy.

Figure 3-1b represents a system in which positive feedback results in change. For example, if a wife cannot stop her husband's initial attempt at physical abuse, hitting may become part of their long-term conflict pattern. In another example, if

Figure 3–1 ————————————————————————————
Feedback Systems

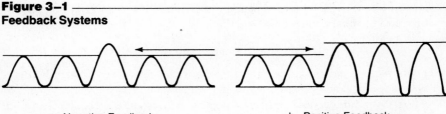

a. Negative Feedback
   (no change)

b. Positive Feedback
   (change occurs)

the partner agrees to some sexual experimentation and both partners find pleasure in it, the system may develop a wider range of sexual intimacy.

According to Olson, Sprenkle, and Russell (1979), positive feedback processes provide the family with "constructive system-enhancing behaviors that enable the system to grow, create, innovate, and change, i.e., system morphogenesis. Conversely, negative feedback processes attempt to maintain the status quo, i.e., system morphostasis" (11). In the following situation, positive feedback processes operate as a father responds to his son's attempts to reach greater physical closeness.

> *"As an adult, I became very aware of the limited physical contact I had with my father. Although he would hug my sister, he never touched his sons, with the exception of a handshake. I determined that I wanted a greater physical closeness with him and consciously set out to change our ways of relating to each other. The first time I hugged my father was when I returned from a trip and I walked in and put my arms around him. I was nervous and tentative; he was startled and stiff, but he didn't resist. From time to time I greeted him with hugs until we reached the point at which both of us could extend our arms to each other. I can now see my brothers developing a greater physical closeness to him also."*

Such attempts to regulate behavior need not occur just between two persons. All members of a family may be part of behavior regulation patterns. Constantine (1986, 61) provides an example of such a family pattern.

For example, when the therapist is interviewing a couple in their home, the woman says, "Dear, the boys are getting awfully noisy down there."

The man goes to the doorway leading to the basement and hollers down, "Okay, you guys! Keep it down to a dull roar." The level of noise drifting up from the basement diminishes somewhat, and the interview continues. A bit later, the woman interrupts her husband.

"Things are pretty quiet down there," she comments. "I wonder what the boys are up to?" Once more he goes to the basement door.

"What are you two doing?" he bellows. "I don't hear the electric train anymore."

"Aw, we're not doing anything, Dad," comes the reply, followed by giggles and the simulated sound of a steam locomotive.

The loop involves (1) the mother, who monitors the level of noise from her sons and signals their father, (2) the father, who takes action intended to reverse deviation from the norm, and (3) the sons, who make the noise. Note that this system reduces deviation in either direction from the desired reference level; it exercises bidirectional control. The mother is not comfortable if the boys are either too quiet or too noisy. (61)

When your family's communication rule has been developed over a period of time, your family is calibrated, or "set," to regulate its behavior in conformity to the rule. If your family or an outside force alters the rule, the family is recalibrated in accordance with the new rule.

The following example demonstrates this process. An unwritten family rule may be that a sick fourteen-year-old is not allowed to hear the truth regarding his illness. If anyone should suggest that he has a blood disease, negative feedback in the form of a nonverbal sign or a change of subject may keep him relatively uninformed. The family is "set" not to discuss the issue with him. Yet the rules may be changed and the system recalibrated through a variety of positive feedback mechanisms. If the young man guesses the severity of his illness, he may confront one or more family members and insist on the truth. Once the truth has been told, he cannot return to his previous naive state, and the system will include some discussion of his illness. Another source of positive feedback may be a doctor who suggests that the young man's condition be discussed with him and may require the family to do so. Again, the system would be recalibrated as family members mature and are considered able to handle certain information or experiences.

Interactive Complexity/Punctuation

A systems perspective implies a move away from thinking about cause and effect to thinking about relationship patterns within contexts (Bochner and Eisenberg, 542). Within a systems perspective, cause and effect are interchangeable. When you function as a member of an ongoing family system, each action serves as both a response to a previous action and a stimulus for a future action. The term *interactive complexity* implies that once a cycle of behavior starts, each act triggers new behavior as well as responds to previous behaviors, rendering pointless any attempts to assign cause and effect. In most families, patterns of behavior develop and take on a life of their own. Thus, it is fruitless to assign a cause to them, because the behaviors are intertwined. Family problems are seen in light of patterns of behavior in which all members have a part. One person does not carry the problems or blame the system.

In order to make sense of the world, human beings tend to "punctuate," or divide up, sequences of behavior. Punctuation refers to the interruption, or breaking into a sequence, of behavior at intervals in order to give it meaning. Punctuation often suggests that "things started here." Interactions, like sentences, must be punctuated, or grouped syntactically, to make sense. Yet punctuation may serve as a trap, forcing persons into thought patterns that assign cause and blame.

Patterns of behavior may be punctuated in various ways. Confusion may occur when people punctuate a communication sequence differently, thereby assigning different meanings to the behaviors. A son may say, "Our trouble started when my mother became depressed," whereas the mother may indicate that the family problems started when her son began staying away from home. Punctuating the cycle according to the son's suggestion would imply a placement of blame on the mother. If the cycle is punctuated according to the mother, the son would be at fault for the family's troubles. The "yes/no" cycle could go on indefinitely. It is fruitless to try to locate the "cause," because even if it could be found, the current pattern is what must be addressed. Working from the idea of circular causality within the system, it seems less important to try to punctuate the system and assign a beginning point than it does to look at the act as a sequence of patterns and try to understand this ongoing process without saying, "It started here." In Figure 3-2, you can imagine the different interpretations that could emerge, depending on how the cycle is punctuated.

Some families try to explain their difficulties by going back through the past and saying, "It started when he took a job requiring travel" or "Things began to fall apart when my wife went back to work." The actions occurring since those blamed behaviors have so altered the system that a job change in either situation would not necessarily resolve the current issues, because the system has long since readjusted. In addition, specific job situations may be a response to a previous unnamed behavior. Only the current behavior is of value in analyzing the family's life and seeking areas for change.

"During marriage counseling it became clear that it did not matter which came first, my wife's sexual distancing or my drinking. They had both become powerful parts of our everyday reality and we needed to address these issues as part of an overall pattern. In short, the problem and the solutions belonged to both of us. It sounds simple but it took us a long time to get over blaming the other and to be able to work together on changing the current pattern."

A classic example of this is found in the "nag-withdraw cycle," which demonstrates the pointless nature of looking for cause and effect. "He withdraws because she nags" versus "She nags because he withdraws" (Dell, 26). An example of such a cycle is found in this analysis of Eugene O'Neill's play *Long Day's Journey into Night:*

The family members watch the mother closely, which makes her visibly nervous, which makes them watch her closely . . . until the circle winds into a spiral leading to the return of her addiction, which they all fear. The above description could also have begun: the mother is visibly nervous, which makes the family watch her closely. (Bavelas and Segal, 104)

Figure 3–2 ———————————————————————————
Circular Causality Within a System

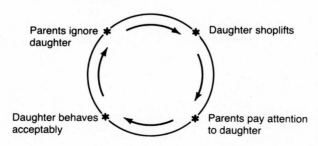

Adaptation

Human systems must change and restructure themselves in order to survive. Families constantly restructure themselves to cope with developmental styles and unpredictable crises. As noted in Chapter 1, change, or adaptation, is a predictable part of the human experience.

Historically, family theorists viewed the family as a system attempting to maintain stability. Yet recent thinking about family systems views the concept of calibration as mechanistic and narrow. To view a human process in a totally mechanistic way is limiting. Hoffman maintains that human systems are capable of sudden leaps to new integrations, which reflect a new evolutionary state (54). In other words, families also experience change through leaps—as random and unpredictable forces propel members into new forms and experiences.

The traditional calibration model needs to be placed within an evolutionary framework, in an attempt to recognize both types of change. Calibration may account for much of the internal system change, whereas evolution may reflect change brought on by outside systems. This will be further developed throughout this book in terms of the system's adaptive quality.

Openness

Just as there are no decontexted individuals, so too, there are no decontexted families. "Human systems are so organized that individuals, families, communities and societies form nested layers of increasing inclusion and complexity" (Walsh 1985, 246). Human systems are open systems that permit interchange with surrounding environments. Whereas closed mechanical systems will break down if they encounter new substances, human systems need interchange with other people, ideas, and institutions in order to remain physically and psychologically functional. The family as a social system maintains an almost continuous interchange, not only within the system but also across the family boundary to the larger ecosystem. Family systems with closed boundaries develop extremely rigid family patterns.

Each family operates within the larger ecosystem, which includes legal, educational, political, health, banking, agricultural, and economic systems, as well as extended family systems. As a small child, you may have depended entirely on your family for all your immediate needs, but as you grew older, you needed to interact with nonfamily members in order to function in society. Such interchange with and adaptation to the environment is critical. Maintaining the bare necessities of life (food, clothing, and shelter) requires a functional relationship with the environment. Education and work provide predictable sources of environmental contact, whereas friends and future spouses must be found outside the narrow limits of the immediate family system.

"As the parent of a hard-of-hearing child, I am constantly managing our family's boundaries and dealing with outside systems. We deal regularly with the medical

community in terms of advances that might affect Melissa's condition. The school system and I monitor which classes we should mainstream Melissa into each year. I need to keep up with legal changes to ensure that our child's rights are protected in terms of access to special programs. Finally, I am constantly aware of the effect of extended family and friends who reach out to support us."

Few families can insulate children as school, medical, and legal systems expose them to a range of values and beliefs, some of which may be contrary to those held by the family. Media such as television, radio, films, and tapes open up worlds that parents may not even comprehend.

Equifinality

An open, adaptive family system demonstrates equifinality; that is, the ability to accomplish a similar final goal or reach a similar state in many different ways and from many different starting points (Littlejohn, 38). In short, there are many ways to reach the same end. For example, two families may achieve a similarly defined "good life" based on a particular income, education, and relationship level through incredibly diverse means. Both families may have the theme "Family members always support each other." Yet each may work differently toward this goal of predictable mutual support. One family may interpret the theme to mean emotional support, whereas the other may view it as an economic issue. The families may differ in their definition of "need" for support and their demands for repayment. In short, there are as many possible ways of reaching a goal as there are families striving for that goal.

In case this appears as a clean linear process of setting a goal and striving toward it, reality is more unpredictable. In Minuchin's words (1984), there is a "humbling conception systems thinking having to do with change." Although you can initiate, you can't entirely predict consequences (88). Hence, a family attempting to reach one goal may find themselves at an entirely different and satisfactory point after six months or six years.

Hierarchy

Human systems develop patterns of order that reflect a hierarchy or the operational pattern of the system. Minuchin (1974) defines family structure as "the invisible set of functional demands that organizes the ways in which family members interact" (71). Historically, a universal rule of family organization establishes parents as more powerful or influential than children. In almost all cultures, authority, respect, and power go to the older generation. Appropriate boundaries separate generations; when these boundaries are blurred, confusion results.

"After my father moved out, I found myself playing surrogate Dad to three younger sisters who needed a lot of support. I moved into the role very easily,

because it seemed to take pressure off my mother who was severely depressed for almost three years. At the time, I just did it without thinking. Now I wish I had not given up my adolescence so easily.''

In recent years, family expectations have represented this notion of family hierarchy and order through the use of a genogram, or a specialized drawing of a family tree that records information about members, events, and relationships over at least three generations (Kramer J. 1985; McGoldrick and Gerson 1985). Complete genograms contain general codes that can be read by a trained eye (see Figures 3-3 and 3-4).

Subsystems

Many subsystems exist within a hierarchy, each crucial to the functioning of the whole. For example, an extended family may include many smaller family units, which in turn contain subsystems.

The complexity of the family system may be seen through the subsystems that contribute to the family's functioning. Each family system contains interpersonal systems and individual or psychobiological subsystems. As noted in the discussion of "wholeness," knowing the family system does not necessarily mean knowing the specific members or their relationships. Using the genogram in Figure 3-3, you can see that to know the Bennett family is not to know totally Tom Bennett or Rose Bennett, nor is it to know Tom and Rose Bennett's particular interpersonal relationship. Therefore, in addition to a total group identity, there is a second level of systemic functioning.

Every family contains a number of small groups, called interpersonal subsystems, that are likely to be made up of two or three persons and the relationships between or among them. Minuchin (1984) identifies subsystems as marital, parenting (involving parent and child), and siblings. Even a three-person system becomes complicated by the interpersonal subsystems within it. A mother, daughter, and

Figure 3–3 ────────────────────────────────
Structure of Family Relationships

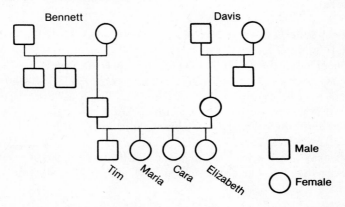

grandson triad represents three such subsystems: the mother and daughter, the daughter and her son, and the grandmother and grandson.

Thus, each of the subsystems has to be considered in order to understand the functioning of the whole. Each subsystem has its own rules, boundaries, and unique characteristics. Consider the Bennett-Davis family. For example, Mom may never tease Maria but may easily kid with Tim. Yet Dad may tease both of them very comfortably and be more affectionate than Mom is able to be. Mom and Tim may spend long hours talking about Tim's future plans, whereas Maria may choose not to discuss this with any immediate family members. Mom, Cara, and Maria may bind together to deal with problems resulting from Tom Bennett's poor health. In most cases, interpersonal subsystems change membership over a period of time. Yet certain subsystems may become so strong or tight that particular members feel either overwhelmed or powerless, or left out.

Coalitions develop when individuals align in joint action against others. For example, in a family with a gambling member, the children and the nongambling spouse may form a tight group as a means of coping with the gambler's unpredictable behavior. The coalition may develop strategies for hiding money, supporting the members in arguments or lying to those outside the system.

The triangle represents a powerful type of coalition. Under stress, two-person relationships may become unstable, so they will draw in a third to stabilize their relationship (McGoldrick and Gerson 1985, 7). Family triangles are characterized by two insiders and one outsider. During periods of stress, the insiders try to rope in the outsider to reduce the stress between them. When tensions are low, the outsider may feel isolated. By observing family triangles, you will see the absurdity of assigning causes or blame to particular events because everyone plays a part (Kerr 1981).

"I saw a dramatic example of a triangle. I grew up in a house where my dad was an alcoholic. My mother and oldest brother formed a tight relationship against him and sometimes against everyone else. They agreed on everything, and my brother became my mother's protector. Even when Dad started to get on the wagon, he could not break up that coalition, and I think that was one of the reasons they got a divorce."

Triangles result in frustration and unhappiness for the "third person." This is especially difficult when the triangle cuts across generations so that appropriate boundaries are violated. This occurs when a parent is aligned with a child against the other parent.

As family systems grow larger, the complexity of the interpersonal subsystems develops accordingly. For example, in the Bennett-Davis family, some subsystems also represent strong coalitions (see Figure 3-4).

To complicate the issue further, each family system reflects the individual or psychobiological system of each member. Each person's unique biological and psychological characteristics are influenced over the years by factors such as gender, age, birth order, and the connections between family developmental stages and individual developmental stages. Therefore, no matter how much three sisters may resemble

Figure 3—4
Relationships Within the Family

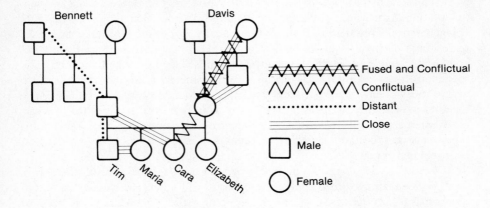

each other, they are psychobiological entities who function partially in an independent manner.

Information Processing

Every system needs a mechanism by which the parts interrelate. Within open systems, adaptation and change are made possible by sophisticated information processing, or message-transmission capabilities. When we talk about human systems such as families, information-processing capacity merges with the communication process so that we are discussing a family's communication function. On the basis of their research in families, Kantor and Lehr assert that "the information processed by the family system is distance-regulation information" (12). Thus, the major information processed by a family system contains the messages that regulate separateness/connectedness, or cohesion. The concept of cohesion was introduced in Chapter 2, and Chapter 4 will discuss messages and meanings further.

Communication as a systems attribute establishes and maintains the relationships between people in a family. Processing information, or coordinating meanings, is integral to family functioning.

A SYSTEMS PERSPECTIVE

What does it mean to take a systems perspective? In this chapter, you have encountered a large number of technical terms applied to a human group, the family. You may be wondering if such a complex terminology is worthwhile. One way to answer this question is to examine the question, What does it mean to look at the family from a systems perspective?

A systems perspective on family functioning gives you a set of lenses through which to view family functioning. If you accept a systems perspective, you need to consider the following assumptions when analyzing family interaction:

- Persons do not live in a vacuum. In order to understand an individual fully, you need to understand how he or she functions within the primary system, the family.
- In established relationships, causes and effects become interchangeable over time. Therefore, to understand interaction, focus on the current patterns. There is little value in finding "the cause" or placing "the blame" because the current pattern is the concern.
- Any human behavior is the result of many variables rather than one cause. Because a change in one part of the system affects all parts of the system, problems must be viewed on many levels; simplistic solutions are questionable.
- Family members operate according to many unrecognized patterns and rules that may be more apparent to outsiders than to the members themselves.
- There are many ways to be a functional family. There is not one right way to get to a certain point or reach a certain goal.
- The whole is greater than the sum of its parts, whether those parts are individuals or subsystems. Viewing the family as a whole demonstrates its communication complexity.

Although this chapter has dealt with a systems perspective primarily in an abstract manner, this view may be applied to everyday family functioning in concrete ways. As Satir (1988) says:

Becoming aware of their system usually opens the way for family members to become searchers and to stop berating themselves and others when things go wrong. People can ask "how" questions instead of "why" questions. Generally speaking, "how" questions lead to information and understanding, and "whys" imply blame and so produce defensiveness. (136)

Understanding the family as a system will alter the way you view families, both academically and personally. For example, an elementary school teacher who holds a systems perspective may try to discover if an acting-out student's unacceptable classroom behavior may be productive behavior within the family system. The teacher would also try to determine how changes in the family system might be reflected in a student's academics or personal school behavior.

A systems approach provides a valuable perspective from which to analyze family interaction. When viewed from this perspective, the focus shifts from individual member's behavior to the family as a whole, with its interdependent relationships and patterns that affect cohesion and adaptability. Looking at the family as a whole brings conceptions of interpersonal communication into greater congruence with the interactional complexity of family life (Bochner and Eisenberg, 541). This perspective allows one to analyze specific behavior patterns in terms of the interpersonal context in which they occur and to understand their meanings in light of the entire family system. A systems perspective has value at an academic level and at a personal level for anyone interested in understanding how families establish and maintain their relationships through communication.

CONCLUSION

This chapter applied a systems perspective to the family. It established that a family system consists of members, relationships among them, family attributes, members' attributes, and an environment in which the family functions. The following systems characteristics were applied to family life: interdependence, wholeness, patterns/self-regulation, interactive complexity/punctuation, adaptation, openness, equifinality, hierarchy, subsystems, and information processing.

IN REVIEW

1. Using Satir's mobile image describe how a change in one member of a real or fictional family affected the other family members.
2. Using a real or fictional family, describe its calibrated level of conflict in terms of acceptable, verbal and nonverbal communication. If applicable, describe attempts to change this calibrated level in terms of positive or negative feedback processes.
3. Draw a three-generation representation (genogram) of a real or fictional family, and indicate and explain the coalitions among certain family members. See Figure 3-4 for a model. Indicate the effect of these coalitions on other family members.
4. How would holding a family systems perspective affect your work as one of the following: a doctor, clergy person, school counselor, office manager, novelist?

CHAPTER 4

Communication Patterns and the Creation of Family Meanings

Every family creates its own identity. Two families may share the same cultural background, uphold similar values and goals, have members of similar ages and abilities, but they can never duplicate the same experience. The interaction of your family members creates an overall experience of family life that cannot be re-created by any other family. This uniqueness reflects the family meanings developed through patterned interactions. The previous chapter examined the family as a system. This chapter will examine the way in which a family develops its view of reality by looking at the formation of family meanings through communication patterns and some sources of those meanings—families-of-origin, rules, and networks.

> *"Christmas holidays represent all the differences in our family backgrounds between my husband and myself. My parents start Christmas preparations in August, and by November a whole holiday scenario is worked out. Gift exchange rituals take place on Christmas morning. In contrast, my husband's mother usually notices the holiday season about December 21. He comes from a family of last-minute shoppers and gift grabbers. In some ways, this represents our different approaches to life; I am a planner and he is the spontaneous one."*

MEANINGS IN RELATIONSHIPS

Communication—the symbolic, transactional process of sharing meanings—undergirds and illuminates the structure of kinship relationships. The form and content of family messages combine to create a family's view of itself and the world. Family members, through their interdependence and mutual influence, create meanings based on their interaction patterns. Yerby and Buerkel-Rothfuss (1982) maintain that "meaning in the family is achieved—behavior is interpreted and evaluated—as

As a family system evolves, family members develop certain meanings within each relationship.

members coordinate their activities through communication" (2). This coordination may be voluntary or involuntary, explicit or implicit.

Communication is not only a simple interchange among people; it also shapes and alters the structure of the family system and the individuals in it. As a family system evolves, the communication among members affects the continuously adapting form of the structure. Over a period of time, family members come to have certain meanings within each relationship. In their classic work, Hess and Handel (1959) suggest that interpersonal ties reflect these meanings, because "the closeness between any two members, for example, or the distance between a group of three closely joined members and a fourth who is apart, derives from the interlocking meanings which obtain among them" (18–19). This can be seen in the following example:

"Our communication patterns tend to separate family members from each other, although Mom and Amy are really joined against Dad. Here's a typical example of the family in action:

Mom: *Sam, let's go to the zoo. The kids would love to see the animals.*
Dad: *I'm tired of doing what the kids want. Let's just sit around the house.*
Sister: *Damn, Dad, you never want to do anything that we like!*
Mom: *Amy, watch your language! Now, apologize to your father!*
Amy: *No, he doesn't care about us.*

Dad: *That's correct. I don't care!* (Very serious facial expression.)
Scott: *We always have these fights. Why do we bother being a family?* (Scott storms to his room.)

"By now we are so used to the moves that we hear the opening line and go through the predictable scene."

The Creation of Meanings

Each of you learns to interpret and evaluate behaviors within your family system and create a set of meanings that may not be understood by an outsider. Each family system creates a worldview, or "a library of framing assumptions," that organizes shared beliefs and meanings (Reiss 1981; Stephen 1986; Brighton-Cleghorn 1987). This view of reality undergirds all communication.

In order to see this more closely, consider the behaviors of a couple as they begin to form a family system. Family therapist Minuchin (1974) suggests that each young couple must undergo a process of mutual accommodation through which the partners develop a set of patterned transactions; that is, "ways in which each spouse triggers and monitors the behavior of the other and is, in turn, influenced by the previous behavioral sequence. These transactional patterns form an invisible web of complementary demands that regulate many family situations" (17). In order to form a marital system, a couple must negotiate a set of common meanings through mutual accommodation so that, eventually, the meanings for one are linked through conjoint action with the meanings of the other. The negotiation process is both subtle and complex; some couples never accomplish this task.

A couple strives to create mutually meaningful language. General similarities in their physical and social processes assure some generalized common meanings. However, the intent of some behaviors, if not discussed, may be misinterpreted; yet these behaviors and their interpretations will become part of the couple's meaning pattern. Usually, the more similar their backgrounds, the less negotiation is needed. With the entire realm of verbal and nonverbal behavior available, they must negotiate a set of common meanings that reflect their physical, social, and individual processes for viewing the world. When behaviors are interpreted in the same way or interpretations are discussed and clarified, similar meanings emerge and communication becomes clear.

In an attempt to distinguish between distressed and nondistressed couples, Gottman, Markham, and Notarius (1977) concluded that nonverbal behavior was an important key. They found that distressed couples were more likely to "express their feelings about a problem, to mind read, and to disagree, all with negative nonverbal behavior" (467–468). Thus, the use of verbal and nonverbal messages and their eventual patterns plays a significant role in a family's existence. However, you will always find an exception to the norm because of a system's equifinality, or ability to reach the same point differently. There will always be examples of the unique, happily married couple or satisfied family that break all the rules.

When couples create mutually meaningful language, communication becomes clear.

Coordinated meanings do not emerge early or quickly within relationships. Partners may struggle for years to gain similarity in interpreting and responding to each other's behaviors. Parents and children may live with serious misunderstandings and mistaken assumptions throughout most of their shared lives as a result of communication breakdowns. For example, both may consciously avoid a subject, one may resist the other's attempt to explore the subject, or one may remain unaware of a difficulty the other is reluctant to address directly.

A sense of self and family worldviews are analogous "symbolic blueprints" that guide behavior (Brighton-Cleghorn). Family disorder occurs when great differences occur among individuals' worldviews, such that there is no longer a family set of common meanings.

Meanings in Highly Developed Relationships

There is a family story that attempts to describe the intense marital relationship between Pierre and Marie Curie, the scientists who discovered radium. Pierre Curie died while lecturing to his university class. When his widow appeared to carry on his teaching, she began by completing the sentence her husband had started before his heart attack and continuing the lecture from that point. Such a story serves two purposes. First, it stands as an example of how family meanings—in this case, the intense marital bond—are transmitted. Second, it reflects the unusual level of connectedness that characterizes highly developed family relationships. Highly developed, or close, committed relationships display certain characteristics reflecting the coordination of meaning between, and sometimes among, family members. Stephen suggests that communication between members of ongoing relationships generates a shared view of the world that bonds relationship members, a bond that unites symbolic interdependence.

There are numerous ways to examine highly developed relationships. Altman and Taylor (1973) suggest that characteristics that appear in committed and close relationships include richness, efficiency, uniqueness, substitutability, pacing, openness, spontaneity, and evaluation (129). The following description of the way each of these characteristics relates to communication depicts how relationships function when meanings are shared effectively.

Richness refers to the ability to convey the same message accurately in a variety of ways. Siblings and spouses have many ways of sharing displeasure, delight, or other feelings. Affection may be shared in words, either in a teasing or serious manner, or through looks, hugs, or kisses. "I always thought it was neat that my mother would sit on my father's lap in front of us kids." Spouses report that sexual experimentation helps keep a marriage vital. A relationship without richness remains in a very predictable and limited pattern of "the same old thing."

Efficiency refers to accuracy, speed, and sensitivity in the transmission and reception of communication. In highly developed relationships, meanings are shared rapidly, accurately, and with great sensitivity. Family shorthand abounds in which the raised eyebrow conveys more than words. The comment "I don't want another Thanksgiving scene" may conjure up similar images in everyone's head of late arrivals, a charred bird, and angry words. Only members of the family can code and decode the messages' meanings with such efficiency.

Uniqueness, or the development of idiosyncratic message systems, reflects the meanings created within family boundaries. Verbal expressions may take on new meanings; words may be created or used in unusual ways. Certain vocal tones, facial expressions, or body movements may have special meanings understood only by members of the system. If a family member claims a need for "puddle time," other members may willingly withdraw, whereas an outsider would not associate a pool of rainwater with time to relax alone. In their study of the world of intimate talk and communication uniqueness, Hopper, Knapp, and Scott (1981) reported interviewing 112 cohabiting couples about their personal idioms. The results included eight types of idioms: teasing insults, confrontations, expressions of affection, sexual invitation, sexual references and euphemisms, requests and routines, partner nicknames, and names for other persons (28).

Substitutability refers to the ability to convey the same message in alternative fashions when necessary. For example, one need not wait for the last guest to leave the party to convey anger through a yelling match, because nonverbal signs such as a glare, "meaningful" silence, or a specific hand or foot movement will alert one member to the other's anger. Persons in a close relationship understand the meaning of the substituted behavior just as easily as they would the usual expression.

Altman and Taylor suggest that these four characteristics of richness, efficiency, uniqueness, and substitutability probably overlap. However, together they reflect the dynamics of a close relationship that involves multiple levels of functioning, including rich, complex communication patterns and a better understanding of the meaning of transactions (132).

> "My mother and father have been married for thirty-two years, and it's amazing to watch them together. They stay in tune with each other, even though many other people may be around, by relating on two levels. Words or gestures that have ordinary meanings also have special meaning for them. Even I can feel like an 'outsider,' recognizing that I'll never really understand what's going on between them. I'd like to have such a marriage someday."

Pacing, or synchronization, refers to the coordination and meshing of interpersonal actions as people work into mutual roles and behave in complementary ways. A common metaphor for this coordination is that of a free and fluid dance (Rogers 1984). There is a sense of apparently effortless teamwork demonstrated by the members of the relationship. Members seem to know when to joke, when to pull back, how to support another, and when to stop a particular verbal or nonverbal move.

Openness in a highly developed relationship implies verbal and nonverbal accessibility to each other. On one level, openness occurs when personal, private information is expressed or received (Montgomery 1981). Yet it is not just intimate interactions that characterize openness, but also the individuals' ability to move in and out of private areas of communication in a quick and facile way.

Spontaneity grows as relationships deepen. The informality and comfort of strong relationships allow members to break patterns. Quick or unexpected lovemaking, surprise trips, unpredictable comments, and changed plans all have their places as a couple develops a life together. Family members may take chances with each other that they would avoid with others.

Evaluation, or the sharing of negative and positive judgments about one another, reflects the security that the relationship will not end if negative feelings are discussed. Family members may express their true feelings in hopes of finding resolution. Alternately, praise need not be threatening or viewed as "moving too fast." Thus, positive feelings are aired that might otherwise be unspoken.

As a group, these eight characteristics provide the backdrop for communication patterns that emerge within particular family systems. Adaptability and cohesion are central to the development of such committed relationships. Adaptation is a core feature of efficiency, substitutability, pacing, and spontaneity, whereas cohesion underlies the development of uniqueness, richness, openness, and evaluation. The security of relationships characterized by these factors allows the widest range of interpersonal behaviors to occur and fosters the continued growth of the individuals and their relationship. Thus, each family develops particular message behaviors that are understood by other members of the system.

When one enters an unfamiliar home as a guest, he or she has to try to adapt to the message systems within that environment. The baby may walk around carrying her "doe," which serves as a blanket and psychological comforter; Grandpa may continually refer to four-year-old Neal as the "heir to the throne"; and the hall closet may be known as the "pit." A visitor must make decisions about the emotions behind the parent's tone of voice that first calls "Matthew" and later "Matthew Noel Wilkinson." Although the father's manner may not appear to change, the visitor learns to respect the whispers of the other family members to "leave him alone right now," because they are reading nonverbal messages unavailable to the untrained eye. "In" jokes and past references abound. Family members may scream and shout in ways that make the visitor most uncomfortable, but no one else appears bothered. On the other hand, the visitor may be hugged and kissed every time he or she arrives and leaves, which could be pleasant or very disconcerting.

On a more subtle level, the family functions give a sense of underlying meaning. If a teenager's invitation to spend a year abroad challenges the family's meaning of closeness, the invitation will be rejected. The meaning of having children varies across families. If the family image is a rock, economic reversals may create a strong sense of danger because the family greatly values self-reliance. A theme of service to others will give certain meaning to how one responds to local tornado damage. Over a period of time, family responses form predictable patterns that both respond to and create family meanings.

COMMUNICATION PATTERNS THAT INFLUENCE FAMILY MEANINGS

Meanings emerge through the continuous interpretation of and response to messages. These interactions become predictable and form patterns or complex sets of "moves" that have been established through repetition and have become so automatic as to continue without conscious awareness. A communication pattern is distinguished by seven characteristics:

1. It is verbal and nonverbal.
2. It is specific to the relationship within the system.
3. It is recurring and predictable.
4. It is reciprocal and interactive.
5. It is relationship defining.
6. It is emergent.
7. It may be changed by forces within the ecosystem, or it may influence changes in that system (Yerby and Buerkel-Rothfuss, 7).

Over time these patterns serve to create meanings or symbolic interdependence in relationships, rather than just reflect the interaction. To understand freely how these family meanings emerge, the following areas must be explored: (1) family-of-origin influences, (2) family communication rules, and (3) family communication networks.

Family-of-Origin Influences

"My son's a Kaplan, all right. He'll walk up and talk to anyone without a trace of shyness." "My family always fought by yelling at each other and then forgetting about it. My grandparents and my parents were great shouters. My wife doesn't understand this." These typical sayings reflect perceptions of intergenerational influence. They highlight the potential family-of-origin influence in communication patterns that form as new systems are created. Family-of-origin refers to the family or families in which a person is raised and is generally thought to be the earliest and most powerful source of influence in one's personality (Bochner and Eisenberg 1987). Thus, the family in which you grew up is your family-of-origin. Many of you still function primarily within your family-of-origin system. Others of you have already formed new family systems.

The term *family-of-origin influences* refers to the specific experiences one encounters while growing up, which reflect both a unique combination of (1) multigenerational transmissions and (2) the ethnic/cultural heritages represented within the family-of-origin. Although the mutual accommodation and development of common meanings within a marital relationship depend on the physical, social, and individual filters of each person, the multigenerational and ethnic background that each spouse brings to a relationship is also a significant social influence. Many of you may desire a family life different from the one in which you grew up, yet you find yourself re-creating the familiar in a new relationship. The socialization by parents serves as a major factor in determining children's family-formation behavior (McLanahan and Bumpass 1988). "People often work out marriages similar to their own parents' not because of heredity; they are simply following a family pattern" (Satir 1972, 127).

Multigenerational Transmissions. Families-of-origin may provide blueprints for the communication of future generations. Initially, communication is learned in the home; and throughout life, the family setting provides a major testing ground for communication behavior. Each young person who leaves the family-of-origin to form a new system takes with him or her a set of conscious and unconscious ways of relating to people. For example, the idiosyncrasies and culturally based communication patterns of the O'Briens may be passed on to generations of children in combination with the patterns gained from in-laws' families-of-origin. Most families develop "family words" that are understood only by a small circle, words that can be traced back to a child or a grandparent and that may be passed down from generation to generation (Dickson 1988).

"My mother said my grandmother referred to ice cream as 'I-box' when she was little. My mother called it that for me, and I have taught it to my son. I hadn't thought about it for years, but it just came back when Steven was old enough to ask for it."

Just as simple language terms travel across the generations, more significant attitudes and rule-bound behaviors move from a family-of-origin to a newly emerging family system. For example, in their examination of male and female expressiveness, Balswick and Averett (1977) tested the following hypothesis: Persons whose parents were expressive to them will be more expressive. They reported: "Our evidence suggests the expressive children come from expressive parents, or at the very least, from parents who are perceived as expressive" (126).

Wide differences in family-of-origin behaviors can lead to communication breakdowns in a couple's system. In the following example, a young wife describes the differences in nonverbal communication in her family-of-origin from that of her husband.

"It was not until I became closely involved with a second family that I became conscious of the fact that the amount and type of contact can differ greatly. Rarely, in Rob's home, will another person reach for someone else's hand, walk arm in arm, or kiss for no special reason; hugs are reserved for comfort. When people filter into the den to watch television, one person will sit on the couch, the next on the floor, a third on a chair, and finally the last person is forced to sit on the couch. And always at the opposite end! Touching, in my home, was a natural, everyday occurrence. Usually, the family breakfast began with 'good morning' hugs and kisses. After meals, we often would sit on our parents' laps rocking, talking, and just relaxing. While watching television, we usually congregated on and around someone else as we sat facing the set. Even as adults, no one ever hesitated to cuddle up next to someone else, run their hands through another person's hair, or start tickling whoever happens to be in reaching distance."

This example illustrates the extent to which each member of the couple was raised differently and how that can affect the communication behavior in the new system. When you consider your parents' marriage or your own, you can find instances in which the rules or networks affect how and what communication occurs. For instance, if you have lived in a stepfamily, you may have witnessed the stress of negotiation involved in integrating your stepparent's family-of-origin influences into a system with communication patterns that already reflected two families-of-origin.

Although family-of-origin issues may be discussed as parent-to child transmissions, recently greater emphasis has been placed on transmission across generations. You were introduced to this idea in Chapter 3 through the genograms. In recent years, family scholars and researchers have focused more directly on the effect of multigenerational systems. The basic assumptions inherent in such an approach are synthesized as follows:

Multigenerational systems—

- influence, and are influenced by, individuals who are born into them.
- are similar to, but more complex than, any multiperson ecosystem.
- are developmental in nature, witnessing changes in individuals and subsystems.
- contain patterns that are shared, transformed, and manifested through intergenerational transmission.
- impact nuclear families as the husband's and wife's heritages reflect crossgenerational influences.
- contain issues that may appear only in certain contexts and that may be at unconscious levels.

- have boundaries that are hierarchical in nature.
- develop functional and dysfunctional patterns based on the legacy of previous generations and here-and-now happenings. (Hoopes 1987, 198–204)

As a way to envision some of these influences, consider the genogram in Figure 4-1, which contains examples of powerful parent-child relationships, themes of service, and flexible boundaries. In it, you can see he power of multigenerational transmission that is part of a puzzle that is unfolding. In the following passage, a young woman reflects on her painful experiences and insights:

> *"I have come to learn that my problem of behavior was a reaction to my mother's alcoholism and to her emotional distance during my infancy and childhood. Likewise, my mother's behaviors had a similar origin. Handicapped by her own mother's chronic depression, my mother never received the affirmation she needed and desired. Yet having been reared by an alcoholic mother, my grandmother was in no better position to be an effective mother or role model for intimacy. With such unavailable models, the women in my family were perpetually unable to develop this essential capacity. Consequently, my own mother had to build our relationship from a faulty blueprint."*

Ethnicity. The communication patterns of diverse ethnic heritages may bring partners into regular conflict until the source of the misperceptions can be identified and addressed. For example, the contrast between a strong Italian heritage and a strong British heritage may serve as the key to unlocking marital confusion between marital partners from these backgrounds (Lerner 1989). Ital-

Figure 4—1
Multigenerational System

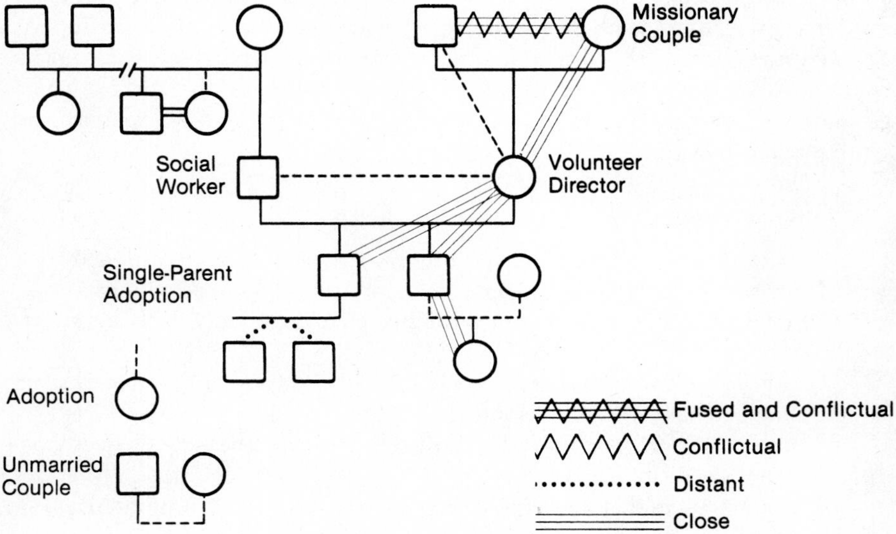

ian families place strongest emphasis on togetherness and absorbing new members into the family. In contrast, a strong British tradition emphasizes the family as a collection of individuals who place a high premium on launching self-reliant, competent young adults. Any combination of strong ethnic heritages will cause marital issues to surface.

The role of ethnicity often is overlooked, yet its influence can be powerful because ethnic values and identification are retained for many generations after immigration. Ethnic family issues may be reflected in issues such as age, gender, roles, expressiveness, birth order, separation/individuation (McGoldrick et al. 1989b; McGoldrick, Pearce, and Giordano 1982). In their examination of Italian families, Rotunno and McGoldrick (1982) highlight the families' cultural enjoyment of celebrating, loving, and fighting, and their orientation toward social skills, including cleverness, charm, and graciousness. These behaviors exist within an orientation to values that places heavy emphasis on how actions affect the family, especially its honor. In addition, Italian families function within a network of significant-other relatives, *gumbares* (old friends), and godparents from whom mutual support is expected. This orientation stresses parental role distinction, with the father as the undisputed head of the family, and the mother as the heart, or the family's emotional sustenance. This generalization about the Italian heritage comes into sharp contrast with descriptions of Scandinavian family patterns, which generally stress the importance of emotional control and the avoidance of open confrontation (Midelfort and Midelfort 1982). Within the Norwegian family, words are likely to be used sparingly; inner weaknesses are kept secret; aggression is channeled into teasing, ignoring, or silence. In terms of male/female roles the man serves as head of the family and exacts discipline, whereas the woman is the communication center, establishing the social network among kin (438–443). The marriage of persons reflecting these two ethnic backgrounds has the potential for misunderstanding unless differences are addressed. Strong conflicts may develop as each person plays out behaviors appropriate to his or her family-of-origin. Such differences may never be resolved because of the strength of the family pattern, or compromises may be necessary as the whole family is influenced by social forces.

A family's ethnic heritage may dictate norms for communication that are maintained for generations. For example an emphasis on keeping things "in the family," the acceptability of discussing certain subjects, or the way such subjects are discussed may pass from generation to generation, reflecting individual and cultural influences. An examination of communication patterns through three generations of an extended Irish-American family revealed great similarities across generations in terms of culturally predictable communication patterns (Galvin 1982). Respondents from each generation reported their variations on the theme of privacy stated in expressions such as: "What you see and hear in this house goes no further," "Don't advertise your business. Handle it on the q.t.," "This information doesn't leave this table." Whereas the Irish family set strong boundaries, the following description of Arabic family life portrays a different picture:

"Growing up in an Arab household our immediate family and our extended family reflected the strong patriarchal influence and a theme of 'family is family,' which

implied active support of many relatives. We lived by the Arabic proverb 'A small house has enough room for one hundred people who love each other,' and we shared joys, sorrows, money, and things among and across generations.''

The importance of a family-of-origin is summarized well by Kramer (1985) in her description of its influence on a child's view of the world:

> He observes the environment he inhabits, partakes of its ambiance. He forms values and beliefs; develops assumptions about how marriages and families are and should be; learns about life cycle, including how to handle the changes of maturation and of aging and death. He learns about power and control and about the consequences of emotions, both his own and others. He is schooled in patterns of communication: what role to take in triangles; how to handle secrets; how to respond to pressure. (9)

Family Communication Rules

"Both my grandfathers are alcoholic. The adults talk about my paternal grandfather's drunkenness as 'acting bad,' or 'he is on one of his sprees again.' My two cousins, 10 and 11, refer to him as 'Mac' whenever he gets drunk.

"On the other hand my other grandfather's 'sickness' was never allowed to be discussed. It was ignored. He was referred to as 'Herbie,' a phrase my mother and sisters created to deal with his actions when they were younger. The rule is—no one ever uses the words alcoholic *or* drunk *in reference to him."*

This example reflects a very common family experience — the family communication rule.

Every family develops rules for interaction and transmits them to new members. As noted in Chapter 3, rules are relationship agreements that prescribe and limit a family's behavior over a period of time. A family acts as a rule-governed system: family members interact with each other in an organized, redundant fashion, creating patterns that direct family life. Rules serve as generative mechanisms capable of creating regularity where none exists. In most cases, rules reflect patterns that have become "oughts" or "shoulds." Rules exist in social situations because social behavior depends on regularities, even though some individuals may act in unpredictable ways. Persons judge each other and hold each other accountable for their actions. Because of their regularities, rules serve a powerful function in coordinating meanings among people (Cronen, Pearce, and Harris 1979). Through rules, family members gain a sense of shared reality and mutual understanding.

Although individuals may follow personal rules such as "I never discuss my religion with strangers," and although society may promote standardized usage rules such as "Tell the truth if under oath," these rules do not reflect an interpersonal generative function. The term refers to the tendency of people in relationships to "develop rules unique to a specific interaction situation and to repeat them until they become reflected in patterns of behavior" (Yerby and Buerkel-Rothfuss, 3).

Rules vary on a continuum of awareness, ranging from very direct, explicit, conscious relationship agreements that may have been negotiated actively to the implicit, unspoken, unconscious rules emerging from repeated interactions. Whereas the former are rather straightforward, the latter are extremely complex and convoluted. Because of this complexity, much of this discussion will center on rules that can be recognized, even if they are not named or negotiated.

Development of Rules.   Since birth, you have learned to adjust to social and personal regulation, and you have expected others to do the same in a predictable way. You were raised in a world of rules, particularly communication rules, but how did you learn them? You learned some rules through conscious discussion, but you learned most through redundancy—repeated interactions.

Family rule development varies from conscious direct negotiation among members to unconscious, unspoken repetition. In some families, particular rules are negotiated directly, such as "We will never go to bed without kissing goodnight" or "We will openly discuss with the children." But most rules develop as a result of multiple interactions. One person's behavior becomes a powerful force capable of evoking a predictable response from the other person. In most cases, these rules are both influential and invisible. They are so much a part of the family's way of life that they are not recognized or named.

"Family rules are very implicit in the Marshall household. For example, when I bring up a subject that is taboo, and we are around other people, my mother gives me the cold stare, although she would deny it. When we are engaged in a one-on-one conversation, she ignores me or changes the subject. We've never talked about these topics or rules directly. I doubt we ever will."

Many rules reflect the couples' families-of-origin rules, which, if not questioned, pass from generation to generation. Spouses from families with dissimilar rules experience greater struggles than those from similar families-of-origin.

Persons who form a system must be sensitive to the relational consequences of their acts. Consider the difficulties if two people bring to their marriage the following individual rules for behavior during a family argument:

Person 1:   If one person discloses a very negative emotion, the other should leave the room to consider it carefully and refrain from spontaneous response.

Person 2:   If one person discloses a very negative emotion, the other should respond with emotional supportiveness. To avoid responding would indicate total rejection.

You can imagine the process of rule negotiation that would have to occur in order for these two people to achieve a communication pattern with which both of them feel comfortable.

Analysis of any rule-bound system requires an understanding of the mutual influence pattern within which the rules function. Because of the transactional nature of communication, the mutual influence process will result in new relational patterns. This process has been described as follows:

> No matter how well one knows the rules of communicator A, one cannot predict the logic of his/her communication with B without knowing B's rules and how they will mesh. The responsibility for good and bad communication is thus transactive with neither A nor B alone deserving praise or blame. (Cronen et al. 36)

Once rules are established, changing them may be complicated and time-consuming unless the family has a flexible adaptation process and can recognize the rule for what it is. When a family rule has been developed over a period of time and members are accustomed to certain "acceptable" behaviors, the family regulates its behavior in accordance with the rule.

"Now that we are adults, our rules have changed considerably, and we talk about issues that were taboo in earlier years. Money, sexuality, and religion are issues of discussion, although sometimes this will spark some feeling of discomfort where our father is concerned. He feels that he has already taken a big step by realizing that we have feelings and thoughts of our own, as well as by relinquishing his major authoritative role. Asking him to talk about issues would really be asking too much. Mother, on the other hand, enjoys the open discussions and appreciates our company and advice on personal matters."

Rules are maintained or changed through negative (maintenance) or positive (growth) feedback processes. Limits can be recalibrated unconsciously or consciously. For example, rules may be renegotiated as family members pass through certain developmental stages. A child of twelve may not be allowed to disagree with his parents' decisions, but when he reaches seventeen, his parents may listen to his arguments. This recalibration may not be a totally conscious process but one that evolves as the child matures toward adulthood. On the other hand, rules about what is acceptable may be openly negotiated or changed as the result of various factors, such as member dissatisfaction or feedback from outside sources like teachers or ministers. Comments such as "Encourage Michael to make more decisions" or "Encourage Patrick to state his own opinions" may affect a parent's behavior.

Most rules exist within a hierarchy. The Parsons and the Coopers may each abide by the rule "You do not swear." In the Parson family, it may be a primary concern, more important than any issue, whereas with the Coopers it is not at the top of the hierarchy. Once you learn the family rules, you then have to figure out the importance placed on each of them.

Rules involve prescriptions that can be followed and that specify appropriate behavior according to context (Shimanoff 1980; Pearson 1989). You have lived with certain rules without discussing them for years but they are adhered to as closely as if they were printed as a list of shoulds on your refrigerator door. As a family insider, you make subtle adjustments to context with ease and limited awareness. The power of patterns emerges as you adjust your language in front of an older relative, refrain from raising a certain topic at the dinner table, or assess your partner's mood before discussing money.

Yet sometimes a member of a family system operates according to rules unknown to the others. A major source of conflict centers around the breaking of rules that one member of the pair may not even know exist. "You should know enough not to open my mail"; "Don't listen to my phone calls." Such conflicts frequently arise as stepfamilies form. The more conscious the prescriptions, the greater the possibility of their renegotiation at appropriate times.

Importance of Rules. Rules are important for many reasons because they support (1) family self-definition, (2) relational development, and (3) family satisfaction (Pearson, 34). Through rule-bound interaction, families establish their primary and secondary family functions. Rules set the limits of cohesion and adaptability within a family. In some families, one may learn that everything is to be kept within the family, intimate physical and verbal behavior is expected, and friends are to be kept at a distance. In others, one may encounter a lack of concern for protecting the privacy of family issues, suggestions that problems be taken elsewhere, and injunctions against changing one's position on a controversial point. Rules help form a family's images, themes, boundaries, and positions on biosocial issues such as power and gender. These in turn guide further rule development. The interaction of rules and functions supports the development of self-definition.

As individuals come together to form relationships they create an increasingly unique pattern of interaction until in some cases they exhibit the characteristics of the highly developed relationships discussed earlier. The higher the relational knowledge between partners, the greater their ability to predict interaction patterns. Rules provide a major means of coordinating meaning in such a developing relationship.

Finally, rules contribute to a family's sense of satisfaction. Imagine trying to function in your family without a large number of rules. You would live in chaos! Rules provide predictability and stability in interactions and serve a socialization, or teaching, function for younger members. If every time a "hot" topic such as death or sex arose, a family had to discover each member's response to the subject, there would be constant confusion. Predictable communication patterns allow a family to carry on its functional day-to-day interactions smoothly. Members know whom to approach about what under which circumstances. There is security and satisfaction in such knowledge.

Types of Communication Rules. Three questions provide a framework for looking at types of communication rules: (1) What can be talked about? (2) How can it be talked about? and (3) To whom can it be talked about? (Satir, 98-99).

The first set of rules relates to what one is allowed to talk about. Can death, sex, salaries, drugs, and serious health problems be talked about in the family? Are there family skeletons or current relatives who are never mentioned? Most families have topics that are taboo either all the time or under certain circumstances.

Sometimes family members may openly agree not to raise a particular topic, but usually they realize it is inappropriate because of the verbal or nonverbal feedback they receive if they mention it.

"At my father's house, there are lots of unspoken rules that dictate unsafe topics of conversation. It's clear that I should never mention (1) my mother, (2) the way we used to celebrate holidays, (3) my need for money, (4) my mother, (5) old family vacations, (6) my mother's relatives, (7) (8) (9) (10) my mother!"

Although topics may not be restricted, many families restrict the feelings that can be shared, especially negative feelings that should be denied. Emotions such as anger, sadness, or rage may be avoided at all costs and not shared with other family members.

Decision making often provides a fertile field for family rules. Does the system allow children to question parental decisions, or are they "the law" that cannot be challenged? In some families, the inability to question decisions appears very clear, whereas in other cases, the same message is sent with subtlety.

In some families, children may hear such words as "We're moving and that's final. I don't want to hear another word about it." Other families have rules that allow joint decision making through discussions, persuasion, or voting. In such cases, all members are allowed to question the decision.

The next question to explore relates to how you can talk about a topic. Within your family, can you talk about things directly, really leveling about feelings on a particular issue, or must you hedge the topic or sneak it in with another idea? For example, in some families with an alcoholic member, the other family members may say, "Mom's under the weather," but no one says, "Mom is an alcoholic." There is a tacit agreement never to deal with the real issue. In dealing with death, children learn that "Grandpa's gone to a better world," but the reality of death is not discussed. Many couples have never drawn up a will because they cannot find a way to talk directly to each other about the death of one of them. Some parents prevent the treatment of their handicapped child by referring to the child as "different" and ignoring the reality of the child's disability. Thus, the "how" may involve allusions to the topic or euphemisms for certain subjects.

Most families have rules that lead to strategies for communication—for breaking bad news, asking for money, or expressing anger. Such strategies may involve a change in both verbal and nonverbal communication behavior. A competent woman may suddenly revert to childish mannerisms to express disapproval acceptably. Her husband may respond with corresponding parental behavior.

Strategy involves the timing of conversations, such as "Don't bother your father with that while he's eating," or the timing of discussion on a particular issue, such as "We won't tell Bobby that he's adopted until he's seven years old." It also involves selecting a place for communication. Many married couples agree not to fight in the bedroom, preventing the room from having associations of anger and conflict. Some families have a place, such as a kitchen table, where the "real" talking gets done. For some people, the car serves as the place for really good conversations. In a family's communication system, the verbal and nonverbal strategies, including the issues of time and place, indicate how members may talk about things.

The final question is, With whom can you talk about it? Consider the following: "Don't tell Grandma; she'll have a stroke." "Don't you think Jenny is too young to hear about custody battles?" Often the rules for "who" relate to the age of family members. For example, while children are small, they may not hear much about family finances, but as they grow older, they are brought into the discussion of how money is earned and spent. Remember the ways your family changed rules as members grew older and the family adapted to developmental or situational events.

Sometimes unforeseen circumstances, such as death or divorce, move a child into a conversation circle that would have been denied otherwise. A fourteen-year-old and a single-parent family may discuss topics that only the other parent typically would have heard. A widow may discuss previously undisclosed financial matters with close relatives.

"Lately my father has taken to discussing his dating and even his sex life with me. He seems to think this is a way for us to get closer, but I wish he could find a friend instead. My mother died only a year ago and it's hard for me to imagine Dad with other women."

Family myths or stories dictate the directions of many conversations. The message "Don't tell so and so; she can't take it" sets up myths that may prevail for years. Consider these statements: "Don't tell your grandfather; he'll have a fit." "Don't talk to your sister; she'll just get sad." Often in such instances, no one ever attempts to see if Grandpa will be outraged or Alice will cry. It is assumed, and communication proceeds accordingly.

In order to appreciate fully the what, how, and who of a family's communication rules, it is necessary to analyze the system to see which rules are enforced in what contexts. The following set of communication rules developed within one young woman's family indicates the interpersonal nature of rules:

- Don't talk back to Dad unless he's in a good mood.
- When Mother is hassled, don't discuss school problems.
- Tell the truth at all times unless it involves a happy surprise.
- Do not fight except with Mom about your appearance.
- Don't talk about the family's worth outside the family.
- Do not discuss politics or religion.
- Do not discuss sex.
- Don't ask Sally about her boyfriend.
- Kiss Mom when coming and going. Kiss Dad at night.
- Share feelings with Mom.
- Don't talk about Granddad's two remarriages.
- Never mention Aunt Bea's cancer.
- Tim's hearing problem is not to be discussed.
- Family deaths are discussed only in terms of religion.
- Mother's pregnancy at marriage is not admitted.

The author of these rules concluded that she had learned to distinguish among people and circumstances but had not experienced very direct, open communication in her family. The factors of what, how, and who provided her with a way for looking at such basic issues within her family's communication rules.

Communication rules are affected by cultural or ethnic backgrounds. In discussing problems in doing therapy with multigenerational Irish families, McGoldrick (1982) suggests that family members may "clam up," because there are particularly strong rules about sharing personal information with those of the opposite sex or different generations. In contrast, members of Jewish families value direct verbal expressions of feelings (Herz and Rosen 1982). Each ethnic or cultural group reflects its own rules. Breaking the rules may result in the creation of a new set as the system recalibrates itself to accept a wider variety of behavior. Old patterns may shift. For example, one may hear "I have broken the rule about not discussing sex by openly discussing my living arrangement with my mother. She is now completely vulnerable, because she can no longer use the familiar pattern of communication." Although a period of chaos may precede the emergence of a new set of rules, the new system may be more open and flexible as a result.

The process of forming new systems through marriage or remarriage provides fertile ground for renegotiating existing rules and requires adaptation skills. For example, the rules become even more complicated in blended families, where people come together having learned sets of communication rules in other systems. When widowed or divorced persons remarry, they may involve each of their immediate families in a large recalibration process as the new family system is formed.

Metarules. In addition to ordinary rules, there are metarules, or rules about rules. As Laing (1972) aptly states: "There are rules against seeing the rules, and hence against seeing all the issues that arise from complying with or breaking them" (106). When a couple does not make a will because of the difficulty of dealing with death, there may also be a rule that they not talk about their rule about ignoring death. Each pretends they are too busy or too poor to meet with a lawyer. The following thoughtful analysis of the rules in the family of the young woman referred to earlier indicates this meta level of rule-bound behavior.

"Sex may be a topic that is never mentioned and so becomes one of those topics you should forget. In order to forget it, you must make the rule that forbids mentioning the rule that forbids the discussion of sex. In this way, you can pretend it isn't forbidden and that deep levels of communication actually exist. We may laugh at a guest's dirty joke, or my mother will set a very strict curfew for my younger sister, but no one ever directly discusses sex. Yet we pretend we can."

Perceiving the metarules of your own system is very difficult because you may be used to thinking about the basic rules, not the metarules. All family members live with powerful rule-bound patterns, giving little conscious attention to most of them. Yet they give meaning to each relationship. Although rules serve the practical function of getting us from day to day without renegotiating every interaction, they can stifle interaction unless you remain aware of their function and become flexible to change. According to Perlmutter (1988) as each child is born into the family, the family map changes and its metarules and the rules themselves evolve. The birth of each child increases the communication complexity.

Family Communication Networks

Family members establish patterned channels for transmitting information called family networks. By definition, a network determines the two-way flow of messages from one family member to one or more other members or significant others outside the family. Family members regulate the direction of message flow up, down, or across the lines of the network. Horizontal communication occurs when the persons involved represent perceived equal status or power, as when siblings pass messages, or when parents and children sit down and work out problems together. In such cases, all persons have an equal say, and status or role differences are minimized. The communication is vertical when real or imagined power differences are reflected in the interaction. For example, although the Turner children may share in many family decisions, they know that certain things are not negotiable. Mrs. Turner sets curfew and limits on the car, which means she hands down information on these topics in a vertical manner. An older sibling may serve as the babysitter and, therefore, disciplinarian.

Over time, families develop communication networks to deal with the general issue of cohesion, and with specific issues such as carrying out instructions, organizing activities, regulating time and space, and sharing resources. Family adaptability may be seen through the degree of flexibility in forming and reforming networks. Families with high adaptability and flexible rules may use a wide variety of network arrangements; families with low adaptability and rigid rules may consistently use the same networks for all concerns.

Although two-generation networks are complicated, most current family systems are part of multigenerational networks of greater complexity. By the year 2000, the parents of the baby boomers may be members of four- and five-generation families (Neugarten 1975; Giordano 1988). Such networks are staggering in their complexity, yet only key persons will relate regularly across generations.

Networks are a vital part of the decision-making process and relate to the power dynamics operating within the family. Certain networks facilitate dominance, whereas others promote more shared communication. Networks also play an integral part in maintaining the roles and rules operating within the family system. Thus, networks and rules operate with mutual influence: rules may dictate the use of certain networks; networks create certain rule patterns.

Types of Networks. To develop awareness of networks, observe the usual flow of verbal and universal exchanges between members of a family. Who talks to whom about what? Who exerts nonverbal control? This processing of communication may be horizontal or vertical and may be one of several types: a chain, Y, wheel, or all-channel. The choice of network types indicates much about family relationships.

> *"There are four girls in our family, and we have a very set pattern for requesting things from our mother or father. Gina tells Angela, who tells Celeste; Celeste tells me, and I talk to Mom. Usually, things stop there, because she makes most of the decisions. If it is something really important, she will discuss it with Dad and tell me their decision. Then I relay the message down the line."*

This example describes an operating chain network. It has a hierarchy built into it whereby messages proceed up through the links or down from an authority source. Quite often, a father or mother controls the chain network and passes out orders to children. For example, in male-dominated families, the father may control the flow of messages on vital family issues. As in all of these networks, there are times when the chain has definite advantages. All busy families tend to rely on a chain network when certain members do not experience much direct conflict.

Sometimes chains keep certain family members separated. If Annemarie always avoids dealing with her stepfather, communicating all her desires or concerns through her mother, she and he will remain distant. A child may honor the communication rule forbidding direct discussion of a topic with Dad by relaying such messages through Mom. In a chain network, a two-way exchange of information may occur between all persons except those on the end. They have only one member with whom to communicate (see Figure 4-2).

In the Y network, one key person channels messages from one or more persons on a chain to one or more other family members. In blended families with a new stepparent, the biological parent may consciously or unconsciously set up a Y network, separating the stepparent from the children (see Figure 4-3). For example, a stepfamily may have a rule that only the biological parent can discipline the children.

The wheel network (see Figure 4-4) depends upon one family member to channel all messages to other members, a position that carries with it power or control. This central figure can filter and adapt messages positively or negatively, or enforce the rules about how to communicate within the family. He or she can balance tensions in the family system effectively or ineffectively. Because only one person communicates with all the others, this person becomes critical to the ongoing family functioning and may experience dominance or exhaustion as a result. When the communication load is heavy and concentrated, as it can be when all family members

Figure 4–2 ————————————————————————
Chain Network

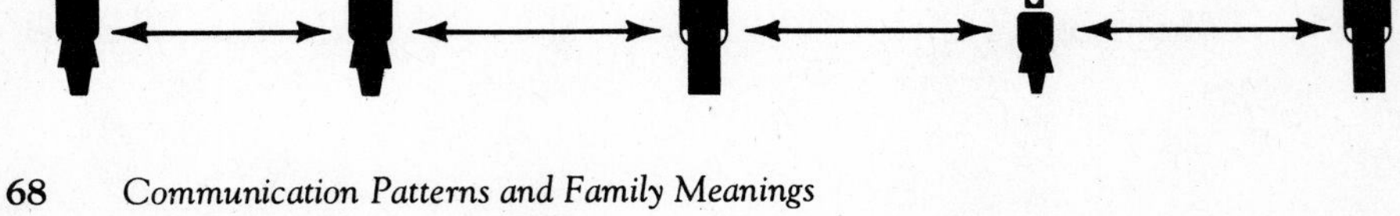

| Grandma | Mother | Son | Daughter | Son |

Y Network

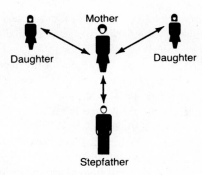

want to get off to work or school, the talents and patience of the central family member in the wheel network can be severely taxed. In some families, the central member of the wheel network can be quite nurturing and effective in holding a family together.

> *"My mother was the hub of the wheel in our family. When we were children, we expected her to settle our problems with other family members. She always knew what everyone was doing and how they felt. When we left home, we always let Mom know what we were doing. Mom digested the family news and relayed the information about what each of us was doing. For several years after her death, we children had little contact. Now, seven years later, we have formed a new subsystem in which four of us stay in contact with each other. One sister, Mary Alice, is the new hub."*

Messages in chain, Y, and wheel networks are filtered, so they may become distorted as they pass from one person to another. A family member can selectively

Figure 4—4
Wheel Network

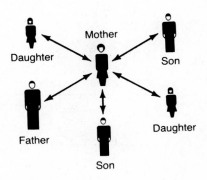

change parts of a message. This may help to defuse some family conflicts, but misinformation could escalate others.

The all-channel network (see Figure 4-5) provides two-way exchange between or among all family members. Communication flows in all directions, and effective decisions can be made because all members have an equal chance to discuss family issues and respond to them. This network provides for the maximum use of feedback. All interaction can be direct. No family member serves as a go-between, and each participates freely in the process of sharing information or deciding issues. Yet, if the rules say that certain subjects should not be raised, access will have little effect. Although this network allows equal participation, it can be the most disorganized and chaotic because messages flow in all directions. Each family member may compete for "air time" to ventilate his or her views.

Variations of these networks occur under certain circumstances. The ends of the chain may link forming a circle; chains may lead toward the central figure in the wheel. Most families use a variety of networks as they progress through daily life. Special issues arise that may cause a family to change the usual network patterns and adopt new ones to solve the issues. In daily life, for example, a family may operate essentially in the chain and wheel networks, but when vacations are planned, the network used is all-channel. Multigenerational networks may add more variations when they are operational.

Subgroups and coalitions directly affect the family networks. The two people on one end of the chain may become very close and support each other in all situations. The key person in the Y formation may conspire with another member to keep certain information from the others, or control certain information. Some family members may never relate directly as the parts of the network form small groups that support or relate to each other. Often the family rules about "who one may talk to" determine the access of persons in a network. If you learn never to raise sensitive topics with your father, the family may develop a strong Y network in which only Mom talks to him about such topics, and only when absolutely necessary!

Most functional families have the capacity to use more than one network pattern, shifting to meet the needs of a particular situation. Even families with very predictable network patterns make alterations from time to time. As children grow

Figure 4-5
All-Channel Network

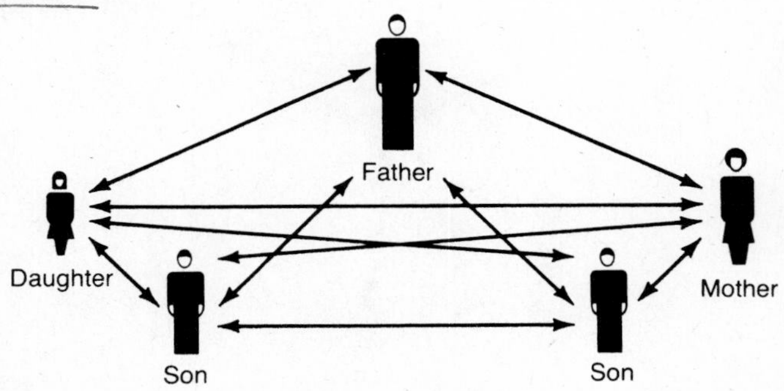

up and increasingly take over the direction of their own lives, adaptive families often move from the chain or wheel network to the all-channel. The wheel and chain networks facilitate order and discipline but may no longer be needed when children become autonomous and capable of directing their own decision making. Parents may signal their recognition of these changes by permitting more issues to be discussed via an all-channel network. As parents enter later life stages, they may lose their central places in a network. The loss of a member can send the system into chaos. When a key member dies or leaves, entire systems may fragment. After a divorce, family members must establish new networks, often involving additional members, in order to maintain certain types of contact.

Extended Networks. Because each family functions within the larger ecosystem, it becomes involved in a wide variety of informal and formal nonfamily networks. The definition of networks includes the possibility that significant others outside the family may have an influence upon the communication patterns within it if the boundaries are permeable. A significant other is a person who has an intimate relationship with one or more of the family members. This may be a godparent, close family friend, lover, or a child's fiancé. In long-term defined relationships, such a person's place in a network may become predictable and clear. For example, a parent's long-term partner must be included in decisions about vacations and holidays, whereas a godmother must be consulted about the college or wedding plans of her godchild. In some cases, the family member with ties to a significant other outside the family may very well make decisions within the network that were determined by this relationship.

Extended networks serve to alleviate stress and encourage well-being during life transitions and crises (Cooke et al. 1988). Families experiencing divorce or remarriage report a high need for friendship and community support. Yet only a few friendships really manage to sustain these transitions (Wallerstein and Blakeslee 1989). In addition to friendship networks, family members become involved in formal networks created by educational, religious, and health institutions. Members must exchange information with representatives of these institutions in order to survive in our interdependent society.

Thus, networks serve a very important function within families. They determine who talks to whom, who is included or excluded, who gets full or partial information, and who controls certain information. Yet the rules for what, how, and to whom to communicate exist within each style of network.

CONCLUSION

This chapter explored how a family creates its own identity. You examined the importance of coordinated meanings between family members and how those meanings are developed through repeated interpretation and evaluation. You discovered how meaning functions within close relationships, using the categories of richness, uniqueness, efficiency, substitutability, pacing, openness, spontaneity, and evaluation.

You also examined the patterns that family systems need to provide order and predictability for their members, focusing specifically on (1) family-of-origin influences, including multigenerational transmissions and ethnic/cultural heritages, (2) communication rules, and (3) family networks. Each contributes to unique family meanings and each factor influences the others. As you will see throughout this book, patterns serve as the skeletal structure for family life, both reflecting and determining relationships.

IN REVIEW

1. Analyze a two-person family relationship, giving examples of verbal and nonverbal communication that are representative of Altman and Taylor's characteristics of developed relationships.
2. Take a position and discuss the extent to which the family-of-origin influences the communication patterns of future generations.
3. What communication patterns have been passed down from your family-of-origin that you believe reflect a multigenerational transmission?
4. Describe three incidents in a real or fictional family's development that demonstrate specific communication rules by which the members live.
5. Using a real or fictional family, describe how the most frequently used communication networks have changed over a period of time because of developmental change or family crisis.

CHAPTER 5

Communication of Intimacy Within Families

What keeps a husband and wife attracted to each other for years? How do young people move from being "the kids" to being adult friends to a parent? Why do members of one family drift apart, whereas members of another remain connected and caring throughout a lifetime? Family intimacy depends, in part, on the members' use of communication to maintain nurturing relationships.

Every family must engage in the kinds of communication that keep the home running, children fed, clothes washed, and bills paid. Life revolves around day-by-day patterns and routines, and functional communication must support such task-oriented interactions. Yet all families have the opportunity to provide their members with different kinds of communication experiences, including those that nurture the relationships involved. Nurturing communication carries messages of recognition and caring that indicate that "I'm aware of you" and "I care about you" (Wilkinson 1989). Such communication contributes to intimacy among family members.

This chapter will focus on how communication influences the development of intimacy among family members. Developing intimate relationships requires effort and risk-taking behaviors but provides rewards for the persons who desire such closeness. In order to understand intimacy within the family realm, you need to explore (1) the development of marital and family intimacy, (2) relationship development and the communication of intimacy, (3) barriers to intimacy, and (4) commitment of effort.

DEVELOPMENT OF INTIMACY

Intimate relationships may be characterized by mutual devotion and committed love involving intellectual, emotional, and physical capacities. According to Lerner (1989), intimacy means that "we can be who we are in a relationship and allow the other person to do the same" (3).

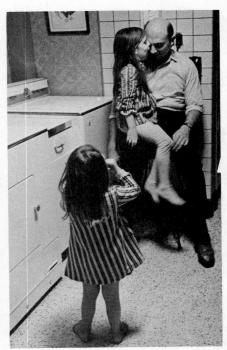

Marital and family intimacy reflect many similarities.

In response to the question, What does intimacy mean to you? people from a variety of backgrounds provide answers reflecting four themes (Waring et al. 1980). These are (1) sharing private thoughts, dreams, and beliefs, (2) sexuality, with emphasis on affection and commitment, (3) having a personal stable sense of self-identity, and (4) the absence of anger, resentment, and criticism.

Marital and family intimacy reflect many similarities. Feldman (1979) suggests that marital intimacy involves the following characteristics: (1) a close, familiar, and usually affectionate or loving personal relationship; (2) a detailed and deep knowledge and understanding from close personal connection or familiar experience; and (3) sexual relations (70). With the exception of sexual relations, these characteristics may be applied to all family relationships if one understands that intimacy is "a much different order of business among siblings than between children and parents" (Perlmutter 1988, 34). Family intimacy involves mutual devotion and intellectual, emotional, and physical dimensions demonstrated by (1) shared knowledge and understanding and (2) close loving relationships, both of which are reflective of developmental stage and culture. Such a concept of intimacy translates into reality through the communication patterns of family systems and subsystems.

Acceptable levels of family intimacy are calibrated through the interaction of family members. The level established for a particular relationship reflects a meshing of each member's past intimate experiences, need for intimacy, perception of the other, and desire for increasing predictability within a relationship. Feldman suggests that when one member of a couple feels that the intimacy is becoming too great, he or she will initiate some type of conflictual behavior to decrease the amount of interpersonal closeness. The same concept may be applied to other family relationships. Each two-person subsystem sets its limits for acceptable intimacy. A small son and his mother may cuddle, tickle, kiss, and hug. A teenager and stepmother may discuss important events, hopes, or dreams and exchange kisses on occasion. A husband and wife develop limits for acceptable and unacceptable sexual intimacy as well as ways of sharing feelings and showing affection. These acceptable limits of intimacy reflect the family's ways of showing affection, and the depth of the particular relationship.

Relational Currencies

"Since as early as I remember, affection has been displayed openly in my household. I remember as a young child sitting on my father's lap every Sunday to read the comic strips with him. I always hugged my father and mother, and still do. 'I love you,' is still the last thing said by my parents and by me when we talk on the telephone."

Family members develop a set of behaviors that have meaning within their relationships, a point made in Chapter 4. Thus, a wife may cook beef stew to please her husband, or a grandfather may rock a grandchild for an hour while telling him stories of years gone by. Each of these instances represents an attempt to share affection, but the meaning depends on a shared perception. The husband may devour the stew and interpret the message of affection, or he may wish his wife had made lasagna; the grandchild may "snuggle in" or long for escape.

Communication behaviors that carry meaning about the affection or caring dimension of human relationships can be viewed as *relational currency*. Although some of the relational currency literature portrays it according to an economic model of investing time or money and trading goods, within a communication framework the currencies can be seen as a symbolic exchange process. As partners share currencies, they will form agreements about the meanings of things and either strengthen or limit their relationship worldview (Stephen, 1984).

Types of Currencies

Relational currencies may be thought of as intimate or economic (Villard and Whipple, 1976). Intimate currencies are personal verbal and nonverbal ways of sending relationship messages. For example, one can smile, hug, engage in intercourse, and exchange secrets as ways of sharing affection. Thus, physical or psychological identity is shared with another. Intimate currencies make a direct statement. The act is the message: a hug means "I'm glad to see you" or "I'm sorry you are leaving." Usually, the sender's intent is clear and easily interpreted. Economic currencies may involve loaning money or possessions, doing favors, giving gifts, or sharing things or time with one another. Economic currencies permit a greater range of interpretation. Exactly what is the message contained within the act of sending a bouquet of flowers? After a family quarrel, does the arrival of flowers mean "I'm sorry," "Let's keep the peace," or "I still love you even if we don't agree on one issue"? The message of such a relational currency may not be as direct as the message sent through a smile, hug, or words of endearment. There are many possible relational currencies. Table 5-1 lists some of the common ways family members use to share affection.

Each of the following currencies represents one way of sharing affection. The use of each currency must be considered within the contexts of gender, culture, and developmental stage (McGoldrick, Pearce, and Giordano 1982; McGoldrick, Anderson, and Walsh 1989).

Positive Verbal Statements.   Such statements include oral and written messages that indicate love, caring, praise, or support. In some households, people express affection easily, saying "I love you" directly and frequently. Other families view such directness as unacceptable, preferring to save such words for unusual situations. Within families, age, gender, and role affect this currency. For example, a study of statements of love within birthday cards reveals that the recipients of such affectionate messages are more likely to be female relatives (Mooney and Brabant 1988).

Self-Disclosure.   Disclosure about self, or voluntarily telling another things about yourself that the other is unlikely to discover from other sources, serves as a means of deepening understanding between people. As a currency, self-disclosure is intentionally used to show caring and investment in a relationship. This currency is discussed in detail later in the chapter.

Listening.   An often overlooked activity, listening carries a message of involvement with and attention to another person. Empathic listening requires focused energy and practice. "It's a mental habit at which one has to work" (Ryan and Ryan 1982, 44). Listening may be taken for granted easily and the effort discounted unless the speaker is sensitive to the listener's careful attention.

Table 5–1 ————————————————————————————
Sample Relational Currencies

Positive verbal statements	Gifts
Self-disclosure	Money
Listening	Food
Facial expressions	Favors
Touch	Service
Sexuality	Time together
Aggression	Access rights

Facial Expressions. Affect displays are spontaneous displays of affection best characterized as "love in that 'eyes lighting up' sense." (Malone and Malone 1987, 14). These displays of affect indicate joy at the other's presence.

Touch. Touch is the language of physical intimacy. Positive physical contact carries a range of messages about friendship, concern, love, or sexual interest. Touch varies greatly across genders and cultures, and so may be easily misinterpreted.

Sexuality. For adult partners, sexuality provides a unique opportunity for intimacy. The discourse of intercourse and the act itself combine to create a powerful currency. Sexuality is discussed in detail later in the chapter.

Aggression. Aggression connotes actions usually thought to be incompatible with affection. Yet aggressive actions may serve as the primary emotional connection between members of certain families. Persons who are afraid to express intimacy directly but who wish to feel connected may use verbal or physical aggression as a sign of caring. Children may find teasing or poking a way of staying connected to a sibling. When adults do not know how to express intimacy in positive ways, children may experience hitting, sarcasm, or belittling as the only means of parental contact. Some conflictual couples may maintain their contact through screaming and hitting, which have become relational currencies within that family system.

Gifts. Gifts are symbols of affection that may be complicated by issues of cost, appropriateness, and reciprocity. They may be read as signals of a person's intentions about future investment in a relationship (Camerer 1988). "Gifts become containers for the being of the donor" (Csikszentmihalyi and Rochberg-Halton 1981, 37). The process of identifying, selecting, and presenting the gift serves as part of the currency.

Money. Dollars and cents symbolize the economic nature of an exchange of currencies. In order for it to serve as a currency, money must be given or loaned as a sign of affection and not as a parental or spousal obligation.

Food. A symbol of nurturing in many cultures, food has emerged as an important currency in romantic and immediate family relationships, in addition to its historical place in intergenerational methods of affection. Preparing and serving food for another serves as a major sign of affection in many relationships.

Favors. Performing helpful acts for another may be complicated by norms of reciprocity and equality. Favors, to be considered currencies, must be performed willingly rather than in response to a spousal or parental order. The underlying message of an action may be missed if the effort of the favor is not appreciated.

Service. Service implies that a favor has evolved into a habitual behavior. Driving the carpool to athletic events, making the coffee in the morning, or maintaining the checkbook may have begun as favors and moved into routines. Such services frequently go unnoticed or are taken for granted, thus negating the underlying message of affection.

Time Together. Being together, whether it's just "hanging out" or voluntarily accompanying a person on a trip or errand, carries the message "I want to be with you." This is a subtle currency with potential for being overlooked.

Access Rights. Allowing another person to use or borrow things you value is a currency when the permission is intended as a sign of affection. This currency is not at work when you let "just anyone" use your things. What makes this a currency is the exclusive nature of the permission, which is given only to persons you care about.

This list of currencies does not represent the last word on the subject. You may identify unnamed currencies that you exchange or that you have observed in family systems.

Meanings and Currencies

The meanings attached to relational currencies have a direct impact on relationship development. Stephen hypothesizes a framework in which interaction may be viewed as an exchange process in which actors are invested in trading and meanings. He suggests that when meanings are shared, rewards are experienced; when meanings are missed, costs are experienced. Therefore, over a period of time intimate partners will create common assumptions about the importance of currencies and develop high levels of symbolic interdependence.

Although relational currencies may be exchanged with the best intentions, accurate interpretation occurs only when both parties agree upon the meaning of the act. Usually, the meaning you give to another's currencies you would use in a similar situation. For example:

> Each of us tends to identify as *loving* those expressions of love that are similar to our own. I may express my love . . . by touching you, being wonderfully careless with you, or simply contentedly sitting near you without speaking. You may express an equally deep love feeling by buying me a gift, cooking the veal, working longer hours to bring us more monetary freedom, or simply fixing the broken faucet. These are obviously different ways of loving. (Malone and Malone, 74)

In the previous example, the question remains, Does the contented silent partner know that a veal dinner or a fixed faucet is a way of showing love, and vice versa? When you think about your relationships, you may find that you are apt to see others as more loving if they express their love the way you do. Such similarity adds to a growing sense of symbolic interdependence.

Misunderstanding may be more frequent when two family systems attempt to blend into a new one. For example, in the man's family, gifts may be given often for no special occasion as a way of saying "I care." If the woman comes from a family where gifts were not highly valued, she may be delighted to start a new tradition and give and receive gifts on nonspecial occasions, or she may have difficulty adapting to this type of relational message. She might think it is a waste of money to buy nonholiday gifts, or she may never think to reciprocate on ordinary days, leaving her husband feeling unappreciated.

Relational currencies that are repeated regularly may come to be taken for granted and lose their meaning. The service of an early riser who puts on coffee, although she drinks tea, may be a service that becomes expected. Even greetings with hugs and kisses can become routine and lose their meaning in the hassles of everyday life.

Without common meanings for relational currencies, family members may feel hurt or rejected. For example, one spouse may consider sex to be the ultimate currency in married life and place a high value on sexual relations. This partner may assume that sexual relations will be exclusive and sex will be engaged in only when both people are satisfied in the relationship and desirous of sex. If the other partner holds similar views, the sexual currency will be appropriately exchanged. Yet, if the other partner does not share those meanings, these two people will have difficulty with the communication of affection through this currency. Such differences are very common.

"After I became a parent of a teenager, I realized how many ways my father had shown love—through waiting up for me at night, driving me around, sliding a five dollar bill into my pocket. I hope he understood that I was a bit too self-centered to be grateful in those years."

What happens if family members want to share affection but seem unable to exchange the currencies desired by others? After interviewing married couples, Villard and Whipple concluded that spouses with similar affection exchange behaviors were more likely to report (a) high levels of perceived equity and (b) high levels of relationship satisfaction. Thus, they experienced greater relationship rewards. It is interesting to note that accuracy in predicting (i.e., understanding) how the other spouse used currencies did not raise satisfaction levels. Just knowing that your husband sends love messages through flowers does not mean that you will be more positive toward this currency if you prefer intimate currencies. Persons who were very accurate at predicting how their spouses would respond to certain items still reported low marital satisfaction levels if the couple was dissimilar in their affection behaviors (Millar, Rogers-Millar, and Villard 1978, 15). Unfortunately, this finding, coupled with the finding that wives are more likely to use intimate currencies, suggests that many marriages may face "unhappiness, unfulfillment, conflict and/or divorce because of socialized differences between men and women in how they share 'who they are' and how they manifest 'affection' " (15).

"When my wife went through a very bad time in her work, we bumped into our differences. My caring solution was to give advice, try to help more around the

house, and leave some little gifts for her. These were not what was desired at the time. Cybele wanted someone to listen to her—empathic listening—not a bunch of suggestions. She wanted to be held. She needed verbal reassurance. Fortunately, Cybele let her needs and wants be known, and in the midst of that self-disclosure, a crisis was turned into an opportunity for growth. Since that time, I have worked to provide listening, compliments, and hugs, and the bond between us has grown stronger."

A family's level of cohesion and its adaptability interact with its communication of affection. Highly cohesive families may demand large amounts of affection displayed with regularity, whereas low-cohesion families may not provide enough affection for certain members. Systems near the chaotic end of the adaptability continuum frequently may change the type of currencies used and valued, whereas more rigid systems may require the consistent and exclusive use of a particular currency. Family themes may dictate the amount or type of currencies used. "The Hatfields will stick by each other through thick and thin" may set the expectation that family caring will be supported by providing money for hard-pressed members. Boundaries may establish which members or outsiders may receive more personal types of affection.

Because the family system evolves constantly, personal meaning placed on intimate or economic currencies changes over time. As relationships mature, members may change their ways of sharing affection because of new experiences, pressures, or expectations. For example, certain beliefs about gender roles may hinder a man from displaying affection at first, but as he becomes comfortable as a father and husband, he may be open to using more intimate currencies. Economic conditions also affect how certain currencies are exchanged. A lost job may result in fewer gifts but more sharing and favors within a family. Such changes may affect the levels of relationships attained by family members. For example, if an unemployed executive is able to share his feelings and frustrations, the self-disclosure may deepen his relationship with his wife. Once employed, he may not have the time or inclination to continue their sharing sessions, and the relationship may return to its previous level of intimacy.

The process of exchanging relational currencies significantly affects the level of intimacy attained by the family members. The more similarity in the exchange process, the higher the levels of symbolic interdependence and relational satisfaction. The following sections will discuss how the depth of a relationship is influenced by the exchange of currencies and will expand the discussion of selected currencies.

RELATIONSHIP DEVELOPMENT AND COMMUNICATION OF INTIMACY

Carl Sandburg once said, "Life is like an onion. You peel off one layer at a time and sometimes you weep." People in relationships share their layers, smiling or weeping, at different points in the process. Interpersonal ties develop incrementally as you discover other people or share layers of yourself through communication. This interpersonal exchange gradually progresses from superficial, nonintimate areas to deeper layers of the self. The following discussion excludes small children from this process, because relationship development models assume direct and conscious effort on the part of the persons involved. Family development is discussed in Chapter 10.

Stages of Relationship Development

All developing intimate relationships reflect a history-building process that includes initiation, maintenance, and possible dissolution (Wilmot 1987). Numerous scholars have proposed models of relationship development based on stages through which the partners move as they draw closer (Knapp 1984; Altman and Taylor 1973; Lewis 1973; McWhirter and Mattison 1984). Psychologists Altman and Taylor created such a model, called "social penetration," which captures the stages of relational development. They hypothesize that interpersonal exchange gradually progresses from superficial, nonintimate areas to more intimate, deeper layers of the self. Along the way, people assess interpersonal costs and rewards gained from interaction. The future development of a relationship depends on their perception of these rewards and costs. These psychologists propose a four-stage model of relational movement based on the eight characteristics of a developed relationship discussed in Chapter 4: richness, uniqueness, efficiency, substitutability, pacing, openness, spontaneity, and evaluation. The extent to which these dimensions exist in a relationship is reflected by the communication that occurs between the persons involved; each dimension becomes more apparent as the relationship moves through the stages toward the highest point. Movement through the stages also depends on the perceived costly or rewarding interactions as estimated by each person in the relationship.

The model is best understood by picturing a continuum (Figure 5-1) with guidelines for movement through the stages. The levels represent where the relationship is at a given time, even if one or the other persons involved wishes it were different. Although we talk about relationship within the system, each relationship reflects the connectedness or distance between two system members. For example, three sisters would not move through the stages as one relationship. There would be three separate dyadic relationships that might be very similar and overlap, but each relationship belongs to a dyad.

The *orientation stage* represents the first meetings when strangers tend to follow traditional social rules, try to make a good first impression, and attempt to avoid conflict. In short, they try to reduce uncertainty about the other person and increase their ability to imagine future reactions. Except for situations involving babies or small children, all family relationships start at this point, although some previous information may have been known about the "other." Future spouses may have been co-workers or classmates who met at the watercooler or in geology class. Future stepfathers and stepchildren may have skirted around countless unpleasant topics as they tried to be polite "for Mom's sake."

Figure 5–1
Stages of Relationship Development

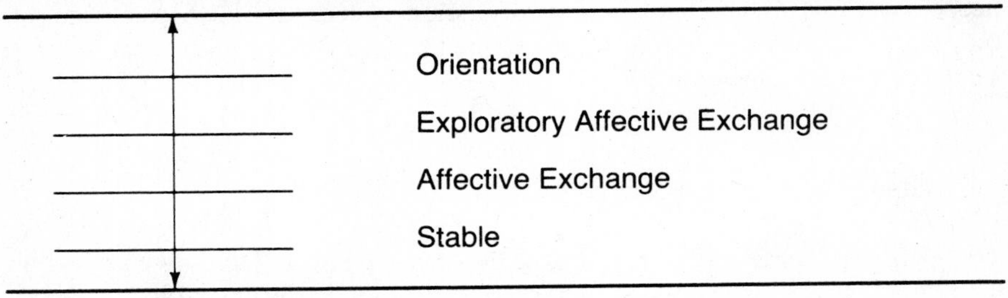

Orientation

Exploratory Affective Exchange

Affective Exchange

Stable

The second stage, *exploratory affective exchange,* is characterized by the relationship between casual acquaintances or friendly neighbors. By this point, the relationship contains some honest sharing of opinions or feelings that are not too personal, but no real sense of commitment exists. Most relationships do not go beyond this second casual exploratory stage.

Countless family relationships remain indefinitely at this stage. Uncle Ned may be delightful, but you do not seek him out beyond the annual Christmas get-together. Siblings may find friends with whom they have stronger bonds than they have with one another. Some parent-child or husband-wife relationships function at an acquaintance level, with little sense of commitment or deep involvement.

The third stage, *affective exchange,* is characterized by close friendships or courtship relationships in which people know each other well and reflect a fairly extensive history of association based on reciprocity. This association may be built over a long period of time or through intense short meetings. Communication includes sharing positive and negative messages, including evaluations. By this stage, members of the relationship enjoy richness and uniqueness. There are private references, shared in-jokes, and mutually understood gestures or glances. Communication sensitivity increases. People outside the relationship may be able to recognize close friends by displays of open affection that range from touching to teasing. Although very intimate areas of personality may still remain closed, high levels of self-disclosure occur and a strong trust develops. By the time a relationship reaches the affective exchange level, a real commitment exists, and the relationship itself is likely to be the subject of conversation.

"My relationship with my daughter in college has developed into a friendship. Karen and I went through some rough times when she was in high school, but in the past two years we have developed a closeness I never thought possible. We can sit down and share some very personal thoughts. I am learning to let her be an adult and have stopped trying to impose my way of life on her. I think because of that she is willing to tell me more about her life. There are certain parts of my life I may never be able to tell my daughter about, but it is such a pleasure to have an adult female friend who is also my child."

Some family relationships may exist at this level for long periods of time, whereas others will remain at lower areas of the continuum. As children mature, they develop the empathy needed to participate in the transactional process needed to reach the affective exchange level. Often, such abilities reflect the communication modeled by older family members and the relational currencies they demonstrate.

Affective exchange level relationships are likely to occur in families with themes that support close interactions and interpersonal boundaries that permit extensive sharing. This stage is the highest relational level that many people will ever experience. Many marriages exist at the affective exchange level, and partners remain either satisfied or frustrated, depending on their spouses. Many people find this level of intimacy sufficient.

Finally, some relationships enter the *stable stage,* which is characterized most often by committed, intimate friendships or familial relationships. Openness, richness, and spontaneity abound. In a relationship at this level, you are likely to experience your highest levels of self-disclosure. Both negative and positive aspects of personality are shared and accepted. At the stable level, communication is efficient, verbal and nonverbal cues are easily interchanged, and predictions are made with accuracy. In addition to verbal sharing, there is a freedom of access to each other's personal belongings that may not have been available before. This stage is characterized by high symbolic interdependence and a strong relationship worldview.

Yet even these unique relationships require extensive effort if they are to be maintained. Partners who share a stable relationship are very aware of each other's needs and the ways in which each is changing. They are willing to engage in intense risk-taking behavior to maintain their relationship.

"After twenty-six years of marriage, my parents seem to have an incredibly close relationship that I haven't seen in other people. They often hold hands. They share a great deal of common interest in music and will play together. They just can't get enough of each other. Life hasn't been all that easy for them, either. But they have coped with these things together; they almost sound alike. They finish each other's sentences and seem to have a shorthand by which they understand each other. I'm very grateful to them for what they have taught me about loving another person."

Such relationships usually require a high investment of time, energy, and sensitivity, but participants find great rewards from their interactions. Again, family themes, images, and boundaries influence the ability of a relationship to move to, or remain at, such an intense level of sharing. The participants have to reach mutually acceptable levels of adaptation and cohesion.

Relationships do not move through the four stages easily and simply. Some relationships may speed through certain stages; others may remain at one stage for years. Other relationships may move through the levels as the partners' lives change. Relationships that proceed too quickly to core areas may have to retrace steps through beginning stages.

Altman and Taylor suggest that the process can be reversed when considering the dissolution of a relationship. For example, a couple may have moved toward the stable stage before the birth of their children, but attending to the children may have taken so much time and energy that the couple's relationship moved to the lower level of affective exchange. Relationship deterioration will be explored further in Chapter 11.

Other models provide variations on the theme. For example, in his extension of Altman and Taylor's work, Knapp proposes a model of interaction stages in relationships that details five coming-together stages. Table 5-2 illustrates representative communication of each stage. This model appears more heavily oriented toward male-female romantic relationships.

Knapp's final coming-together stage, *bonding,* is unique. It occurs when the partners undergo a public ritual announcing to the world a contract of commitments. In essence, bonding institutionalizes the relationship. Traditionally, this involves going steady, engagement, and/or marriage. Knapp sees bonding as a way of gaining social or institutional support for the relationship. Whereas ritual events, such as baptism, circumcision, or legal adoption, should be viewed as examples of family bonding, it is more difficult to imagine traditionally accepted bonding experiences for homosexual pairs, stepchildren and stepparents, or long-term foster families.

All stage models assume voluntary relationships. There has been little careful study of nonvoluntary relationships, such as those experienced within some stepfamilies. Such relationships may begin with stages characteristic of deterioration relationships, such as low self-disclosure, conflict, and resentment (Galvin and Cooper 1990).

You should be able to see how some of the previously described stages relate to your own life. Perhaps you developed a deep relationship with an older brother or stepsister as you grew into a young adult. Perhaps you watched parental relationships suffer and deteriorate. Such movement affects not only the participants in the specific relationship but all members of the systems to which they are connected.

Table 5–2
A Model of Interaction Stages

Process	Stage	Representative Dialogue
	Initiating	"Hi, how ya doin'?"
		"Fine, you?"
	Experimenting	"Oh, so you like to ski . . . so do I."
		"You do? Great! Where do you go?"
Coming	Intensifying	"I . . . think I love you."
Together		"I love you too."
	Integrating	"I feel so much a part of you."
		"Yeah, we are like one person. What happens to you happens to me."
	Bonding	"I want to be with you always."
		"Let's get married."

Variations Across Systems.   In his discussion of relationships in the future, Toffler (1971) raises the issue of expected relationship turnover and suggests that family relationships are expected to last longer than what he considers "medium duration relationships" (relationships with friends, neighbors, job associates, and comembers of voluntary organizations). He suggests that "we expect ties with immediate family and to a lesser extent with other kin, to extend throughout the lifetime of the people involved" (100). However, people involved in long-term relationships cannot remain at a peak level of communication. They cannot center all their time and energy on the relationship.

Although all humans seem to have intimacy needs—to be loved, held, touched, and nurtured—there may also be fear of intimacy; that is, a fear of being controlled by another, loved and left by another, or possessed by another, all of which keep relationships from reaching high stages of involvement. Thus, the needs and fears, rewards and costs become calibrated as the balance of the intimacy scale is set, at least for a certain period of time.

Each family system is influenced by its overall themes, images, and boundaries that indicate some acceptable intimacy limits for family members. Family themes that stress verbal sharing, such as "There are no secrets in this family," may promote honest disclosure if a sense of community and support exists. Otherwise, such themes may promote painful secrets. You may take risks with someone you perceive to be friendly rather than with another you view as an unfeeling "computer." Family boundaries influence how much intimacy is shared among family subsystems and how much intimacy may be developed with those outside the immediate family. Gender-related attitudes support or restrict the capacity of members in certain roles or power positions to develop certain levels of intimacy. The belief that a father has to remain slightly aloof from his children to be respected in a "head of the household" position limits the level of intimacy he will reach with his children. Knowledge about another family member is not sufficient to develop intimacy. Relational growth depends on communication of and about that knowledge (Duck, Miell, and Miell 1984).

COMMUNICATION FOUNDATION OF INTIMACY

The basis for all relationships lies in the members' abilities to share meanings through communication. Three major factors serve to undergird the development of intimacy within family systems and reflect the use of many of the relational currencies described earlier. These are confirmation, self-disclosure, and sexuality.

Confirmation

Confirming messages communicate acceptance of another human being—a fundamental precondition to intimacy. Remember the distinction between the content and relationship levels in a message. The relationship level comments on the bond between people. In other words, "on the relationship level people do not communicate about facts outside their relationship, but offer each other definitions of that relationship and, by implication, of themselves" (Watzlawick, Beavin, and Jackson 1967, 83–84). Sieburg (1973) provides four criteria for confirming messages. A confirming message (1) recognizes the other person's existence, (2) acknowledges the other's communication by responding relevantly to it, (3) reflects and accepts the other's self-experience, and (4) suggests a willingness to become involved with the other.

Confirming responses may be contrasted with two alternative responses, rejecting and disconfirming. Whereas confirming responses imply an acceptance of the other person, rejecting responses imply that the other is wrong or unacceptable. Rejecting messages might include such statements as "You don't know anything," "That's really dumb," "You're a real pain," and "Don't act like a two-year-old." Disconfirming responses send the message "You don't exist." Disconfirming responses occur when a person is ignored, talked about as if he or she is invisible, or excluded from a conversation.

"When my sister remarried, she and her new husband tried to pretend they did not have her twelve-year-old son living with them because her new husband did not really want him. They would eat meals and forget to call him, plan trips and drop him with us at the last minute, and never check on his work in school. The kid was a nonentity in that house. Finally, his father took him, and Derrick seems much happier now."

Sometimes certain family members get the feeling they are invisible. People talk about them in front of them, ignore or interrupt them, or refrain from affectionate physical contact with them. How often have your requests for help, your questions or your statements about feelings been met with no response? People who care about each other acknowledge that they are listening and give feedback to indicate that they have heard the messages. This responsiveness keeps a spouse, parent, or child from saying "I feel like I'm talking to a wall—nothing comes back."

Confirming communication is characterized by messages of recognition, dialogue and acceptance that indicate a willingness to be involved (Sieburg, Barbour, and Goldberg 1974.) Each is described below.

Recognition. Verbally, one can confirm another's personal existence by using the individual's names, including him or her in conversations, or just acknowledging his or her presence. Comments such as "I missed you" and "I'm glad to see you" serve to confirm another. In their work on communication skills related to marital satisfaction, Boyd and Roach (1977) suggest that a spouse's comments such as "I listen and attend when my spouse expresses a point of view" is characteristic of desirable behavior (541).

Nonverbal confirmation has more subtle but equal importance in the recognition process. From earliest infancy, tactile recognition serves as the basis for relationships. A child develops his or her earliest sense of recognition through touch, a critical factor in the development of healthy emotional relationships (Montagu 1978). Direct eye contact and gestures also may serve to confirm another person. Confirming relationships develop from a base of mutual recognition.

Dialogue.   When family members say things in front of each other "without actually responding in an honest and spontaneous way to each other's ideas and feelings, their interaction might be described as a series of monologues rather than a dialogue" (Barbour and Goldberg, 31). Dialogue implies an interactive involvement between two people. Husbands and wives, siblings, and parents and children must be able to share attitudes, beliefs, opinions, and feelings, and work at resolving their differences. Comments such as "Because I said so" and "You'll do it my way or not at all" do not reflect a dialogical attitude, whereas "What do you think?" or "I'm upset! Can we talk about it?" open the door to dialogue and rewarding interactions. Boyd and Roach found comments such as "I 'check out' or ask for clarification so that I will understand my spouse's feelings and thoughts" and "I ask honest, direct questions without hidden messages" to be associated with marital satisfaction (541). Nonverbal dialogue occurs in families where hugs, kisses, and affectionate displays are mutually shared and enjoyed, and where hugs of consolation or sorrow are exchanged.

Acceptance.   Acceptance gives a powerful sense of being all right. "When we feel acceptance, even though disagreed with, we do not feel tolerated; we feel love" (Malone and Malone, 73). Acceptance avoids interpreting or judging another, rather it lets another *be,* even if in that being the other is different from yourself.

From a communication perspective, acceptance occurs when "we respond to the statements of another person by genuinely trying to understand the thought and feeling he or she has expressed, and by reflecting that understanding in our responses" (Barbour and Goldberg, 31). This may involve allowing yourself to hear things you really do not want to hear and acknowledging that you understand. Although a mother may find it painful to hear that her son is leaving college because he has failing grades, she should not insist on a more socially acceptable explanation such as "You just need some time to find yourself."

Nonverbal messages such as a wink, smile, and barely perceptible nod that says "I agree" or "Keep up the good work" reinforce and confirm another family member. Comments or looks that tell a third party "She doesn't mean that" or "What he really means is . . ." undermine a partner or loved one.

Confirming behavior often reflects the specific roles and cultural backgrounds of one's family-of-origin. Persons who grew up in a nonexpressive family may have trouble satisfying the reassurance/recognition needs of a spouse. Cultural differences in the use of eye contact or touch may create disconfirming feelings for one partner.

Confirmation's role in developing intimate relationships cannot be underestimated. If such behaviors are viewed as rewarding and are met with an equal response, a mutually rewarding relationship will result. Family intimacy depends on each member's sense of acceptance and care. Children learn such behaviors by watching other family members and by experiencing the confirmation and affection directed at them. If one learns to love by being loved, then one learns to confirm by being confirmed.

Self-Disclosure

The most powerful and profound awareness of ourselves occurs with our simultaneous opening up to another human. . . . It is the most meaningful and courageous of human experiences. (Malone and Malone, 20)

In addition to feeling confirmed, persons in intimate relationships need to experience openness in their communication. Such openness is experienced through sharing and receiving self-disclosure.

"I'm always fascinated by all the letters to the advice columnists that say 'Should I tell my spouse about . . .?' and then they mention some secret. I will be married in eight months, and, although my fiance and I have a very special relationship, there are some things he does not know about me, and, I imagine, he has some secrets, too. I wonder about the value of total honesty, especially when it could hurt the other person. There are some things I don't think I'd want to hear from him."

Self-disclosure occurs when one person voluntarily tells another things about himself or herself that the other is unable to discern in a different manner (Pearce and Sharp 1973). Thus, you participate in acts of self-disclosure when you voluntarily tell someone personal, private things about yourself. It involves a willingness to accept such information or feelings from another. Self-disclosure allows a person to reduce uncertainty about the discloser's personality in terms of similarity, competence, and believability (Berger and Bradac 1982, 93).

Within intimate relationships, the purpose of self-disclosure is to deepen or enhance the relationship. As discussed earlier, when people move from the orientation stage to higher levels of a relationship, the process usually involves extensive mutual self-disclosure, starting with positive or neutral information. You make predictions about how others will deal with your disclosures and usually attempt to build up a series of positive experiences before engaging in strong negative self-disclosure.

Trust, the essence of which is emotional safety, serves as the foundation for self-disclosure. "Trust enables you to put your deepest feelings and fears in the palm of your partner's hand, knowing they will be handled with care" (Avery 1989, 27). In her examination of family self-disclosure, Gilbert (1976a) links self-disclosure and intimacy. High mutual self-disclosure is usually associated with voluntary relationships that have reached the affective exchange or stable exchange level and that are characterized by trust, confirmation, and affection. Yet high levels of negative self-disclosure may occur in nonvoluntary relationships characterized by conflict and anger.

Traditionally, self-disclosure has been considered a skill for fostering intimate communication within families. Jourard (1971) describes the optimum marriage relationship as one "where each partner discloses himself without reserve" (46). Many current marriage and family enrichment programs support self-disclosing behavior (Galvin 1985), as do popular texts on the subject of marital or parent-child interaction. Premarital counseling often focuses on revealing areas of feelings or information not yet shared by the couple.

Yet, as you will see in the next section, some cautions about unrestrained self-disclosure need to be considered. In order to understand the importance of exchange in self-disclosure within the family system, you need to review some relevant issues and examine the practice of self-disclosure in developing family intimacy.

Variables in Self-Disclosure. Much of the research in self-disclosure has been conducted through questionnaires and self-reports collected from family members, usually couples. The actual self-disclosing behavior is not easily observed or measured. What family material exists focuses on marital couples or parent-child interactions; entire family systems have not received attention. Yet even this limited research raises issues and implications for family relationships.

Some generalizations can be made about self-disclosure in family relationships, but much of the original research in the area is under review due to more sophisticated follow-up studies. Littlejohn (1989) has summarized the findings of research in self-disclosure as follows:

(1) Disclosure increases with increased relational intimacy. (2) Disclosure increases when rewarded. (3) Disclosure increases with the need to reduce uncertainty in a relationship. (4) Disclosure tends to be reciprocal (dyadic effect). (5) Women tend to be higher disclosers than men. (6) Women disclose more with individuals they like; men disclose more with people they trust. (7) Disclosure is regulated by norms of appropriateness. (8) Attraction is related to positive disclosure but not to negative disclosure. (9) Positive disclosure is more likely in nonintimate or moderately intimate relationships. (10) Negative disclosure occurs with greater frequency in highly intimate settings rather than in less intimate ones. (11) Satisfaction and disclosure have a curvilinear relationship; that is, relational satisfaction is greatest at moderate levels of disclosure. (161)

Family Background. Family-of-origin, cultural heritage, gender, and socioeconomic status set expectations that may influence self-disclosing behavior. Hurvitz and Komarovsky (1977) report a comparison of marital studies done with middle-class high-school graduates in the Los Angeles area and a working-class urban community called Glenton. The middle-class respondents were more likely to view spouses as companions to each other, with expectations of sharing activities, leisure time, and thoughts. Marriage, as seen by members of the Glenton community, was more likely to include sexual union, complementary duties, and mutual devotion, but not friendship. Two-thirds of the wives confided in mothers, sisters, or friends.

Ethnic heritage may influence the amount and type of disclosure. For example, the Mexican-American society appears to be relatively more open than the Anglo-American society when it comes to discussions of death (Falicov and Karrer 1980, 423). Whereas Jewish families exhibit verbal skill and a willingness to talk about trouble and feelings, Irish families may find themselves at a loss to describe inner feelings (McGoldrick 1982b).

Although the research on gender and disclosure is inconclusive, female pairs tend to be more disclosive than male pairs (Cline 1989). Generally, women tend to be higher disclosers than men; they disclose more negative information; they provide less honest information; and they disclose more intimate information (Pearson 1989, 246). These differences reflect differences in socialization between females and males.

Marital Status. Marital self-disclosure studies reveal consistent findings across groups. According to Fitzpatrick's self-report, studies show a positive correlation between the self-disclosures of husbands and wives and between self-disclosure and marital satisfaction (1987, 585–586). Yet a high disclosure of negative feelings is negatively related to marital satisfaction. In addition, dual career couples appear to be more able to disclose to one another. The effect of age or length of marriage on spouse self-disclosure is unclear, because the content of discussion may vary over a period of time (Waterman 1979, 226–227). Married men are less likely to disclose to friends than married women, although of married men and women who reported high self-disclosure within the marriage, only the women reported moderate to high disclosure to a friend (Tschann 1988, 6).

Parent-Child Relationships. Parent-child disclosure has received some attention, revealing that self-disclosure does not involve all family members equally. From her review of research, Waterman suggests that most mothers receive more self-disclosure than fathers. Parents perceived as nurturing and supportive elicit more disclosure from children who find those encounters rewarding. In her study of families with adolescents, Abelman (1975) reports that mutual self-disclosure exists mainly between parents and children of the same sex, and adolescent self-disclosure correlates more highly with self-image than with parental self-disclosure.

College students are more likely to disclose more information more honestly to same-sex best friends than to either parent (Tardy, Hosman, and Bradac 1981). In her summary of research, Pearson suggests:

> In general, mothers receive a greater amount of information, more intimate information, more accurate information, and more information about a child's social life than fathers do. (247)

Such a brief review only highlights certain issues but indicates the complexity of a subject that some popular writers tend to treat simplistically as they encourage unrestrained "open" communication in family relationships.

Satisfaction. The positive effect of self-disclosure on intimate relationships has been described extensively. Clearly shared and accepted personal information or feelings enhance intimacy in a relationship. Yet such sharing and acceptance is not the norm. In fact, high self-disclosure is not necessarily linked with relational satisfaction (Sillars et al. 1987).

In exploring the relationship between self-disclosure and marital satisfaction, Levinger and Senn (1967) found that satisfied couples disclosed more than unsatisfied couples. However, unsatisfied couples disclosed more unpleasant feelings than satisfied couples. A later study found similar patterns of satisfaction (Burke, Weir, and Harrison 1976). Recent studies highlight the value of "selective disclosure" (Sillars et al.; Schumm et al. 1986). In general, marital self-disclosure is rewarding because it signals to the listener the speaker's willingness to trust and share (Fitzpatrick, 585).

In your family experiences, you may have discovered that when you were least satisfied with certain relationships, you tended to engage in more negative self-disclosure.

Related Issues. Factors that influence disclosure include content (what is said about what topic), valence (whether statements are positive or negative), honesty, and self-esteem.

The valence, or positive or negative position toward a particular issue, relates directly to how comments will be received. Most people appreciate receiving positive self-disclosure, although such positive self-disclosure represents one of the most "neglected areas of communication between partners" (O'Neill and O'Neill 1972, 11). More frequently, self-disclosure is considered "dirty laundry," the misdeeds or negative feelings that are likely to cause pain for the listener. Some of the studies cited earlier report that higher self-disclosure levels are more characteristic of happily married couples, but that unhappily married couples are higher in disclosure of a negative valence. Families characterized by pleasant self-disclosure content can experience intimacy at higher levels more easily than those trying to discuss painful, negative-laden issues. For example, talking about a desire for continued sexual experimentation within a generally satisfactory relationship has a much greater possibility of leading to further intimacy than a revelation of severe sexual dissatisfaction.

Although your communication patterns are usually built on the assumption that you are sharing "the truth" with another person, some people are dishonest or inaccurate in their disclosures (Berger and Bradac, 87). These inauthentic disclosures may be difficult to detect but, once discovered, may interfere with future believability and mutual self-disclosure. In marriage, partners may be caught between desires for openness and protectiveness. A husband may be dismayed by his wife's weight gain, but he knows that bringing up his feelings would feed her low self-esteem. An adult daughter may wish to share her incest experience with her mother but questions destroying her mother's image of her husband.

Satir (1988) views high self-esteem as the basis for all positive communication within families. According to her, integrity, honesty, responsibility, compassion, and love flow easily from persons with high self-esteem because they feel they matter. Such people are willing to take risks, whereas persons with low self-esteem constantly feel they have to defend themselves. Satir places the responsibility for building self-esteem on families, which have the almost exclusive responsibility for young children's esteem. Abelman found that the self-disclosures of adolescents to their parents seemed more closely tied to their own self-esteem than to the amount of self-disclosure received from the parents. Gilbert supports the relationships between self-disclosure and esteem, maintaining: "Research literature relating self-disclosure to esteem, within the context of interaction in family systems, reveals that often people refrain from expressing their feelings because they are insecure about their marriage" (225). Because self-disclosure requires risk taking, it appears more likely that persons who feel good about themselves would be more willing to take such risks than would persons who have low self-esteem.

A Model for Self-Disclosure. Based on a review of self-disclosure research, Gilbert suggests a curvilinear relationship between self-disclosure and satisfaction in relationship maintenance, holding that a moderate degree of disclosure appears to be most conducive to maintaining a relationship over time. This position contrasts sharply with that of Jourard (1971) and Lederer and Jackson (1968), advocates of full self-disclosure within relationships. The following diagrams will help you visualize the differences (see Figure 5-2).

According to diagram (a), as relationships become more disclosing, satisfaction moves from a growth pattern to a decline; whereas according to diagram (b), increased self-disclosure is directly related to increased satisfaction. Let us look further at the underlying claims of each position. The research based on a curvilinear view holds as follows: "As disclosures accumulate through the history of a relationship and as the nature of the relationship itself changes, then the connection between disclosure and relational satisfaction reverses from a positive to a negative association. . . . [T]his is the way disclosure functions for most relationships" (Gilbert, 211). When you think of many of your friends or relatives, you may realize that you do not discuss the particularly negative aspects of yourself, or discuss theirs, because this may begin the decline of the relationship. Perhaps you have been in a relationship in which very unpleasant disclosures seemed to diminish or end it. Family members may not have been able to cope with the negative information they received about themselves or other family members.

Figure 5-2 ——————————————————————————
Relationships Between Self-Disclosure and Satisfaction

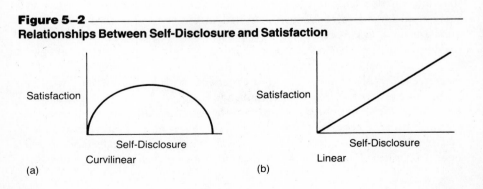

"As a child, I never fully understood what happened, but there was a big change in the relationships in our house, and there seemed to be a dark secret that no one would talk about. Fifteen years later, I found out from my oldest brother that my father had a short affair with someone at the office, and after it was over he told my mother. She was devastated. It changed their relationship for many years."

The linear point of view, suggesting that self-disclosure "may and should remain a positive source of relational satisfaction throughout the history of the relationship," clearly describes an "optimum state of affairs" rather than how things usually are (Gilbert, 211).

Yet the linear relationship and its positive outcome may occur in special cases when a mutual capacity to handle positive and negative deep self-disclosure exists. Such cases, though, are uncommon. Gilbert suggests that for a linear pattern of disclosure to work in intimate relationships, both persons need healthy selves, including high self-esteem, a willingness to risk a commitment to the relationship and to push it to higher levels of intimacy, and reciprocal confirmation. The diagram in Figure 5-3 presents the possible combinations of approaches to self-disclosure and satisfaction found in the different types of relationships.

Figure 5-3 illustrates that as relationships move from being nonintimate to intimate, the initial high positive self-disclosure gains in importance. In order to handle this and remain satisfied with the relationship, both of the individuals involved must be characterized by high self-disclosure because of the amount of trust and risk involved (Pilkington and Richardson 1988).

Because family life involves long-term involvements during which people grow and change, it would be ideal if members could handle the negative and positive

Figure 5–3 ————————————————————————————
Disclosure Processes in Relationship Development: A Linear Versus a Curvilinear Schemata

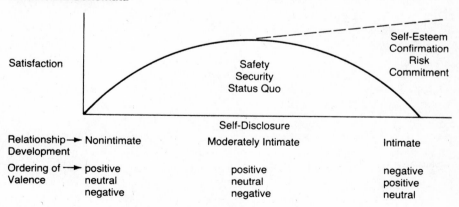

From Shirley Gilbert, "Empirical and Theoretical Extension of Self-Disclosure," pp. 210, 211–212 in *Explorations in Interpersonal Communication*, edited by Gerald R. Miller. Copyright © 1976 by Sage Publications, Inc. Reprinted by permission of Sage Publications, Inc.

aspects of each other's development, permitting total honesty within a supportive context. Yet many negative self-disclosures are necessarily painful for one or both members of the relationship, and each individual's capacity for, and willingness to endure, pain varies. Thus, in many relationships, high levels of self-disclosure result in low levels of satisfaction.

Self-disclosure serves as a powerful tool in relationship development, not just as a by-product of deepening relationships. Researchers are only now carefully investigating why and how persons in a relationship use self-disclosure to reach certain goals (Duck et al. 1984).

The Practice of Self-Disclosure. Now that you have received some of the research and thinking in the area of marital or family self-disclosure, you can think about your own family relationships according to the following general characteristics of self-disclosure:

1. Relatively few communication transactions involve high levels of disclosure.
2. Self-disclosure involves verbal and nonverbal signals.
3. Self-disclosure usually occurs in dyads.
4. Self-disclosure tends to be reciprocal.
5. Self-disclosure increases when rewarded.
6. Self-disclosure occurs in the context of positive, trusting relationships.
7. Self-disclosure usually occurs incremental with increased intimacy. (Pearce and Sharp; Littlejohn; Duck et al.)

If you think about family relationships in terms of these characteristics, you can see ways in which family systems tend to encourage or discourage self-disclosure. Considering the time it takes to do the functional things in families, you can understand that little time or energy may be available for nurturing communication, including self-disclosure. Additionally, with the exception of new couples or newly blended families, there is less need to spend much time revealing past history, because family members have already shared many of those issues. Hence, risk-taking communication is not likely to occur frequently within family life, but certain developmental or unpredictable stresses may trigger extensive amounts of personal discussion.

The self-disclosure process has a nonverbal component. A sequence of appropriate nonverbal signals occurring in the context of verbal disclosure also contributes significantly to mutual understanding. For example, nonverbal signals may tell a husband that his wife is surprised that he is unaware of her feelings about a topic (Duck et al., 305). Duck proposes the term *intimation sequences* for these signals in which both partners intimate new levels of evolving awareness within a discussion. Thus, verbal self-disclosure and nonverbal intimation sequences are bound together in face-to face interaction.

If high levels of disclosure occur mainly in dyads, how often do two-person systems spend time together? How often does a parent of four children get time alone with each one of them? When do a stepparent and stepchild make time alone for themselves? Many family members never spend one-to-one time with each other, yet such time is important for openness to develop in their relationships.

Reciprocity of self-disclosure is critical in dyadic relationships. Many couples report a serious imbalance of openness; traditionally, the female partner discloses more and desires more disclosure, becoming frustrated with the lower male response. Avery suggests the more trusting you are, the more likely you are to be trusted by others. In parent-child situations, it is more likely that parents provide the initial impetus and model for self-disclosing behavior. As children grow older, they may begin to share in reciprocal ways with the adults in their lives, depending on what they have experienced, just as the adults depend upon reciprocity to build their own relationships.

Families create unique opportunities for self-disclosure. Joint living experiences provide needed time and space for such interaction. Yet this can take place only where positive social relationships, including trust, exist. Parents may find that they have unwittingly halted the development of self-disclosure with a child because they discussed the child's concern with another adult, not recognizing the child's desire for privacy. Unless disclosers indicate how private certain information is to them, another person may accidentally reveal that information to others and destroy the relationship.

> *"I have stopped discussing anything important with my mother because she cannot keep her mouth shut. She has told my aunt and some friends at work all about my relationship with my boyfriend, my use of birth control pills, and some of my health problems. Well, she doesn't have much to tell them now because she doesn't hear about my real concerns anymore."*

In some nonvoluntary family relationships, especially those involving stepfamilies, the bases of trust and liking may be missing, thereby reducing the likelihood of openness developing in the first two to five years (Galvin and Cooper). In a family in which the trust level remains high, relatively few moments of high disclosure occur without unhappy repercussions, and, over a period of time, the pattern of sharing develops among members.

In self-disclosure, as in many other areas of life, one is likely to repeat behaviors that are rewarded, or are met with positive response. In a family that indicates pleasure at knowing what the members are thinking or feeling, even if the information itself is not necessarily pleasant, the likelihood of continued self-disclosure is great. If self-disclosure is met with rejecting or disconfirming messages, the level of sharing will drop significantly.

Although self-disclosure enhances intimacy development, it can be used to manipulate or control another family member. Partial or dishonest disclosures can undermine trust in a relationship. Sometimes young persons or immature adults engage in pseudo self-disclosure to see how it works or to gain something else from the relationship. In this process, they take advantage of the other by betraying a trust. Therefore, the motives underlying disclosure need to be considered when examining its effects on intimacy.

Self-disclosure bears a direct relationship to family levels of cohesion and adaptation. Extremely cohesive families may reject negative self-disclosure, because it would threaten their connectedness, particularly if the family has a low capacity for adaptation. For example, a highly cohesive family with the theme "We can only depend on each other" would resist negative disclosures that might threaten their security and cause internal conflict. Such a theme might be accompanied by rigid boundaries that would resist self-disclosures to outsiders.

Families with very low cohesion may tolerate negative self-disclosure but have difficulty with positive self-disclosure, which might lead to greater cohesion. Families with moderate to high adaptation and cohesion capacities may cope relatively well with the effects of high levels of positive or negative self-disclosure. As you have discovered through these pages, self-disclosure is a complicated process that may result in intimacy when two people make the effort to share with each other. In short, self-disclosure, or "sharing what's inside—even if what's inside isn't pretty—is the supreme act of faith in another" (Avery, 31).

Sexuality and Communication

How would you describe sexuality within the marital relationship? As a series of isolated physical encounters? As an integral part of a growing relationship? Do you see marital sexuality as restricted to "being good in bed"? For most partners, sexuality within a marital relationship involves far more than just physical performance; it involves the partners' sexual identities, their history of sexual issues, their mutual perceptions of each other's needs, and the messages contained within sexual expression.

Feldman stresses the importance of sexual relations to marital intimacy, yet the quality of the sexual relationship affects, and is affected by, the other characteristics of intimacy—the affectionate/loving relationship and a deep, detailed mutual knowledge of the two partners. In their study of over six thousand couples, Blumstein and Schwartz (1983) report, "Our findings lead to the overwhelming conclusion that a good sex life is central to a good relationship" (201).

How would you describe sexuality within the family relationship? As an important dimension of family life? As unrelated to family issues or scary within the family context? For family members, healthy sexuality reflects the balanced expression of sexuality in family structures and functions that enhances the personal identity and sexual health of members and the system as a whole (Maddock 1989).

At both the marital and family level, sexual issues directly impact communication. Sexuality, including sexual attitudes and behavior, may be viewed as a topic of communication, as a form of communication, and as a contributing factor to overall relationship intimacy and satisfaction. In this section, sexuality will be explored in terms of socialization, parent-child communication, partner communication, and communication breakdowns.

Socialization and Sexuality. The basis for a mutually intimate sexual relationship reflects the development of each of the partners, particularly in the family-of-origin. An individual's sexuality remains closely intertwined with his or her intrapersonal, interpersonal, and environmental systems—systems that interlock yet vary in importance according to an individual's age. According to Greene (1970):

> The sexual feelings (intrapersonal) and behavior of a person are a reaction to the parental attitudes (interpersonal) in which he was raised. These attitudes, in turn, were handed down by their parents and were largely molded by broad cultural viewpoints specific to their social class (environmental forces). (57)

The sexual dimensions of family life are tied strongly to developing gender identities, setting boundaries, and handling developmental change. Much of your sexual conduct was originally learned, coded, and performed on the basis of biosocial beliefs regarding gender identity, beliefs learned originally in your family-of-origin. Parents possess a set of gender-specific ideas about males and females learned from their childhood experiences and from "typical" behaviors of girls or boys of ages similar to those of their children. Based on these and their personal experiences, parents transmit a gender identity from earliest infancy; this results in children's establishing gender identities at a very young age. This identity is so strong that efforts to alter such socialization patterns must be presented to children before age 3 or they will have little impact (Gagnon 1977, 68). Your personal identities include sexual/gender identity as a core component, which influences your later sexual experience. According to Gagnon:

> When we do begin having sex in our society, our beliefs about woman/man strongly influence whom we have sex with, what sexual things we do, where and when we will have sex, the reasons we agree, and the feelings we have. (59)

An overall sense of personal identity, with a core sexual identity, is a "prerequisite for intimacy in marriage and sexual relationship" and is also "strengthened and affirmed by experiences of interacting constructively with a person of the complementary sex" (Clinebell and Clinebell 1970, 139). Sexual experiences contain powerful confirming or disconfirming messages that affect sexual interactions.

Parent-Child Communication. Many of today's adults grew up in a home atmosphere of sexual silence and now live in a world of open sexual discussion (Ryan and Ryan). Much of what you learned about sexuality took place within the rule-bound context of your family. In the earlier discussion of communication rules, you may recall that many sex-related rules are negative directives: "Do not . . ." Often, communication about sexual issues remains indirect, resulting in confusion, misinformation, or heightened curiosity. Recall how your sexuality was explained to you. Who talked with you? If your genitals were talked about, how were they talked about? What attitudes did you pick up regarding your gender and sexuality? You may remember much mystery and confusion as you tried to sort things out.

Families differ greatly in their approach to sexuality. Maddock (1989) has described communication behaviors of sexually neglectful, sexually abusive, and sexually healthy families. In some "sexually neglectful" families, sex is discussed little or not at all. If it must be addressed, sexual communication occurs on an abstract level; therefore, direct connection is not made between the topic and the personal experience of family members (133).

"My mother explained the act of sex in the most cold, mechanical, scientific, factual way she could. I was embarrassed, and I couldn't look at her face after she finished. I know it was very difficult for her. Her mother had not told her anything at all, and she had let her get married and go on a honeymoon without any knowledge of what was going to happen. She made a point of saying throughout, 'After marriage . . .' "

Such messages communicate an underlying attitude of anxiety or displeasure, but the direct issue remains hidden. Veiled messages often continue through adolescence and into adulthood. According to Satir (1988):

Most families employ the rule, "Don't enjoy sex—yours or anyone else's—in any form." The common beginning for this rule is the denial of the genitals except as necessary nasty objects. "Keep them clean and out of sight and touch. Use them only when necessary and sparingly at that." (124–125)

In many families, the marital boundary remains so tight around the area of sexuality that children never see their parents as sexual beings—no playful swats, hugging, or tickling occurs in view of the children. Children may perceive adults who are cool or distant and who appear to associate sexuality with shame or guilt.

Yet, in other families, the marital boundary is so diffuse that children encounter incestuous behaviors as they are co-opted into spousal roles. This "sexually abusive" family is typically a closed rigid system with boundary confusion between individuals and between generations. Communication reflects a perpetrator-victim interaction pattern, especially in cross-gender relationships, resulting in marital conflict and lack of emotional intimacy (Maddock, 134). Yet, in both the sexually neglectful and sexually abusive families, sexual attitudes and sexual behavior are seldom addressed directly.

According to Maddock, sexually healthy families are characterized by (1) respect for both genders, (2) boundaries that are developmentally appropriate and support gender identities, (3) effective and flexible communication patterns that support intimacy, including appropriate erotic expression, and (4) a shared system of culturally relevant sexual values and meanings.

Sexually healthy families communicate effectively about sex, "using language that can accurately cover sexual information, reflect feelings and attitudes of members, and facilitate decision making and problem solving regarding sexual issues" (135). Sex education is accurate and set in a context of family values transmitted across generations.

"I grew up in a family where sex was a comfortable part of everyday life. My grandparents were affectionate even in their eighties, and my parents used to put

a 'Do Not Disturb' sign on their room every Saturday morning. The family joke was that they were 'working on the bills.' The kids would tease each other about their romantic lives, and it was no big deal."

Today, direct parent-child communication about sexuality is not only important for healthy family functioning but for the long-term physical health of family members. Pressing issues, such as AIDS, sexually transmitted diseases, and a high percentage of unwanted pregnancies necessitate such discussions. Parents need to be able to address issues of safe sex practices and ways of talking about sex with their children.

"In our family we did not discuss sexuality openly. When I left for college, my mother (totally unprovoked) told me that if I ever decided to go on birth control I was never to tell her, and NOT to get it through our family doctor, but through the school health service. By doing so, she made sure she separated herself from ever discussing the topic—so much so that she did not even ask me if I had ever thought of it. This is how much she wanted to avoid the subject."

The family represents the first but not the only source of sexual information. As children mature, they gain additional information about sexuality from peers, church, school, and the media. When you look back over your childhood and adolescence, what were your major sources of sexual information? What attitudes were communicated to you about your own sexuality? What could have improved the messages you received?

Partner Communication. As an individual embarks upon sexual experiences, his or her sexual identity influences the encounters, as does the partner's sexual identity. Open communication becomes critical for both individuals, because a good sexual relationship depends on what is satisfying to each partner. Ryan and Ryan describe the mutuality involved in sexual experience:

Having sex with someone is a semi-private act. It begins with an invitation, often unspoken by one, and the acceptance, often tacit but clear, by the other. It is semi-private in that the pleasure of sex is one's own, but the quality of the pleasure depends on what the other does. In sex, one is both a giver and receiver of pleasure. (75)

This sense of mutuality is enhanced by direct and honest communication between partners. In discussing marital sex, Scoresby (1977) maintains:

Sexual expression needs to consist of clear messages that effectively communicate the feelings of both partners. Sexual pleasure that is freely given, in an honest and mutually intimate way, can draw two people together into a loving and passionate bond that is continually strengthened, enhancing the marriage. (45–46)

Some understanding comes only through a combination of self-disclosure and sensitivity as spouses reveal their needs and desires while learning to give pleasure to the other. For some spouses, this involves working on "signal clarification" to minimize miscommunication. From another perspective, we can distinguish between monological and dialogical sex—the former being sexual experiences in which one or both partners "talk to themselves" or attempt to satisfy only personal needs. Dialogical sex is characterized by mutual concern and sharing of pleasure (Wilkinson 1990).

Yet many partners find it difficult to talk about their sexual relationship. Adelman (1988) defines the discourse of intercourse as that "sexual conversation which occurs between two people prior to, during, and after sex" (1). She maintains that the vocabulary for sex talk is impoverished and thus ineffective in many relationships. Thus, impoverished language and parental socialization may conspire to restrict the adult sexual experiences, preventing husbands and wives from communicating freely about or through their sexual encounters. The following vividly portrays the euphemistic language characteristic of even long-term marriages:

> Consider the kinds of talk that occur before intercourse in most households. In some, the husband or wife may say, "Let's go do it," but such directness is rare. What usually happens is that the husband may say, "I think I will take a shower." What that really says is "I am going to be clean for you.". . . The wife then says, "I will be upstairs in a few minutes." That is a "yes." Or she says, "I am too tired today; I have a headache; I have been to the hairdresser; the kids might wake up." Those are all "no." A man will say, "I am tired; I have got to get up early in the morning; I have some reading I have to do." There is a whole indirect language which people use to say "yes" or "no." (Gagnon, 208)

Sexual discussions are rife with euphemisms that may serve to romanticize or confuse the message (Bell 1987; Hopper, Knapp, and Scott 1981). Euphemisms serve partners well when they promote the desired erotic reality, but may serve to create disappointments or anger.

Satisfied couples report their ability to discuss directly issues of feelings about sex, desired frequency of intercourse, who initiates sex, desired foreplay, sexual techniques or positions. They avoid mind reading such as "If she really loved me, she'd know I would like . . ." or "If he really loved me, he would . . ."

Because of their taboos regarding a discussion of sexual behavior, many couples rely solely on nonverbal communication to gain mutual satisfaction. For some, this may be acceptable, but for others, unclear messages result in frustration as partners misinterpret the degree or kind of sexual expression desired by the other. Some partners report a fear of using any affectionate gesture because the other spouse always sees it as an invitation to intercourse; others say their partners never initiate any sexual activity, whereas the partners report being ignored or rebuffed at such attempts. Mutual satisfaction at any level of sexual involvement depends upon open communication between spouses; yet intercourse, according to

Lederer and Jackson is special "in that it requires a higher degree of collaborative communication than any other kind of behavior exchanged between the spouses" (117).

The current AIDS crisis has brought about a new consciousness of the need for clear discourse about intercourse (Michal-Johnson and Bowen 1989). The following vignette (Adelman 1988, 1) from an interview about safe sex talk illustrates the depth of the problem:

> She spoke openly about her sexual practices, describing in candid terms her preferences for foreplay and certain positions. When she had finished her graphic description I asked her, "So what do you *say* to your partner during sex?" She laughed nervously and replied, "Oh, *now* you're getting personal."

Given the dangers, "partners can no longer remain silent about their sexual pasts, nor fear to voice their concerns about a mutual sexual future" (Adelman, 3). The need for safe sex talk and practice becomes more apparent daily. Thus, for couples engaged in an intimate relationship, open and direct communication about sexuality may deepen the intimacy and provide tremendous pleasure to both spouses.

Sexuality and Communication Breakdowns. Although sex as a form of communication has the potential for conveying messages of love and affection, many spouses use their sexual encounters to carry messages of anger, domination, disappointment, or self-rejection. Often, nonsexual conflicts are played out in the bedroom because one partner believes it is the only way to wage a war. Unexpressed anger may appear as a "headache," great "tiredness," roughness, or violence during a sexual encounter.

Blumstein and Schwartz found that married couples who report fighting a lot about housekeeping, income, expenditures, and whether both should work are less happy with their sexual relationship (202). If partners experience unsatisfying sexual encounters early in their relationship, their "mutual disappointment and embarrassment can easily lead to sensitivity and reluctance to talk about what has been happening to them" (Ryan and Ryan, 80).

As more information is gathered about sexuality through the life cycle, it becomes clear that sexual expectations are altered over time due to developmental changes and unpredictable stresses. Couples interviewed about the history of their sex lives report that they have experienced dramatic changes in sexual interest, depending on other pressures in their lives (Ryan and Ryan, 89). There are indications that sexuality may become more pleasurable in later life when a couple's child-rearing burdens cease.

Based on his work in the area of sexual communication, Scoresby developed a chart indicating areas of sexual breakdown. Table 5-3 indicates the possible areas of breakdown related to communication and possible ways to address them.

Scoresby also describes the advantages of thinking of sex as communication:

1. We become more aware of its complexities and intricacies as opposed to focusing on physical or mechanical procedures.

Table 5–3 ───────────────────────────────────
Signs of Difficulty in Sexual Communication

Common Symptoms	Possible Solutions
1. Failure to talk openly with each other.	1. Increase each person's ability to self-disclose feelings.
2. Repeated lack of orgasm by female.	
3. Tension and lack of relaxation.	2. Spend increased positive time alone together.
4. One demanding the other to perform.	3. Avoid threatening to dissolve the marriage.
5. Excessive shyness or embarrassment.	4. Check for angry conflict and reduce if possible.
6. Hurried and ungentle performance.	
7. Absence of frequent touching, embracing, and exchanges of intimacy.	

2. We conclude that we'll never utilize all its potential, and this leads us to more fully exploring its possibilities.
3. We view the sexual relationship as a continuous process instead of as a series of isolated events. (46)

The area of sexuality and communication within the family realm has received less attention than other, less sensitive types. Yet the emotional and physical health of family members depends in part on their ability to communicate about sexuality.

BARRIERS TO INTIMACY

Marital or familial intimacy depends on confirmation, self-disclosure, and sexual communication and commitment. However, because of the perceived risks involved in intimate communication, drawing close to another person can be frightening. For many people, it is much more comfortable to maintain a number of pleasant or close relationships, none of which involve true intimacy, than to become intensely involved with a spouse or child. Low risk takers establish barriers to relationship development to protect themselves from possible pain or loss. Whitehead and Whitehead (1981) address this directly when they say, "The central threat of any close intimacy encounter . . . is the threat of injury and loss" (223).

There are many reasons for a fear of intimacy, including the following discussed by Feldman: merger, exposure, attack, and abandonment (71–72). People may fear a *merger* with the loved one, resulting in the loss of personal boundaries or identity. This occurs when the "sense of self" is poorly developed or when the sense of "other" is very powerful. Comments such as "I'll disappear altogether" or "I have to fight to keep my identity" indicate struggles with merger. You will recall the discussion in Chapter 3 of enmeshed systems in which members experience fused or poorly differentiated relationships. Such lack of boundaries leads to great anxiety and dysfunctional interaction. People may fear interpersonal *exposure*, because individuals with low self-esteem or low self-acceptance may be threatened by being revealed as weak, inadequate, or undesirable. If you don't feel good about yourself, it's scary to share that self with another person for fear of rejection. Persons who fear exposure avoid engaging in self-disclosure that prevents them from experiencing intimacy.

People may fear *attack* if their basic sense of trust in themselves and the world is low. If you have shared personal private parts of your life with another and that person has turned against you, it may take a while to be able to risk trusting another person. These persons also choose to avoid self-disclosure as a self-protective mechanism. People may fear *abandonment*, the feeling of being overwhelmed and helpless when the love object is gone. For those who have experienced excessive traumatic separations or broken relationships, the way to prevent such helplessness is to remain distant. Once one has taken the risk to be intimate, rejection can be devastating, resulting in reluctance to be hurt again.

For most people, fear of intimacy is tied directly to issues of boundary management. Sometimes intimacy becomes confused with an unhealthy togetherness or extreme cohesion, resulting in a loss of personal boundaries and identity. As you remember, boundaries serve as regulatory factors to help one see differences and similarities within systems and subsystems, thereby providing certain limits and rights.

In families with unclear boundaries, one person's business is everyone's business. Much communication occurs across family subsystem boundaries, and members may feel obligated to engage in high self-disclosure and even seek disclosure inappropriate to the subsystem or role. An adolescent may feel obligated to discuss all of his or her dating behavior with a parent. A mother may discuss marital problems with a teenage son. Yet the pressuring person requires the other to "be like me; be one with me." He or she suggests, "You are bad if you disagree with me. Reality and your differentness are unimportant" (Satir 1967, 13), demonstrating the difficulty of negative self-disclosure. Members may require, or sense a demand for, constant confirmation to serve as a reassurance that they are cared for. Yet intimacy becomes smothering if people are fused.

"My father thinks we all experience life as he does, because he treats us as extensions of himself. He expects us to love and hate what he does. He assumes when he's cold, tired, or hungry, we are cold, tired, or hungry. He's like a whale swallowing little fish."

In some families, the parents may be so afraid of sharing both good and bad things with each other that they establish a united front for themselves and displace any anger onto a child. Thus, the child serves as a scapegoat, whereas the parents convince themselves that they are experiencing intimacy. Such false togetherness becomes a barrier to true marital intimacy while seriously harming the scapegoated child.

Within disengaged, or very low cohesive families, individuals do not get through the rigid boundaries to each other, and the members may not receive necessary affection or support. Each person is a psychological subsystem with few links to the surrounding family members. Intimacy is undeveloped or at a low intensity level in households where each family member is concerned solely with personal affairs, remains constantly busy, and spends time away from the home. Yet, even if persons spend time together, unless their communication goes beyond the task-oriented type, they may remain generally disengaged. Both types of families set up barriers to true intimacy by smothering or ignoring individual family members.

One of the challenges of life is to learn how to be yourself while you are in a relationship to another person. In a truly intimate relationship, the "I" and the "we" coexist to the joy of both persons.

COMMITMENT OF EFFORT

"If you have to work at a relationship, there's something wrong with it. A relationship is either good or it's not." These words capture a rather common belief about marital and family relationships. How often have you heard people argue that relationships should not require effort and that "working at a relationship is phony"? Such a position is naive; relationships need care and attention. It is only through effort and commitment that a loving relationship remains a vital part of one's life. The investment creates its own rewards. For example, "Trust is inspired when both partners communicate that the relationship is a priority; something they want to invest in for their own benefit and their partner's" (Avery, 30).

Many factors compete for attention in your life. Meeting home, work, school, friendship, and community responsibilities takes tremendous time and effort. The nurturing of marital or family relationships often gets the time and energy that is left over, a minimal amount at best. In most cases, this limited attention spells relational disaster. Unless familial ties receive high priority, relationships will "go on automatic pilot" and eventually stagnate or deteriorate. The individuals involved will exhibit behaviors representative of those on the lower levels of Altman and Taylor's stages or in the dissolution stages of other models.

"After our separation, the hardest thing we faced was regaining our sense of intimacy. We had hurt each other so badly that we had to rebuild a whole new sense of trust and sharing. It was an effort to say personal things, to touch each other lovingly, to discuss our feelings. We have been back together for over a year, and only now is our sexual life coming around. It had been so important to us before, but we were scared of allowing ourselves to be free, truly free, in that area. Each small risk has been a victory, but it has been a very painful, slow process."

Because the family operates within the larger ecosystem, including such areas as work and school, decisions in family and in other arenas impact on each other. In describing the tensions between work and home obligations, Blumstein and Schwartz refer to the interaction between "where people put their emotional energy (home versus work) and their commitment to their relationship" (173). In this era of dual-career couples and families, commuter marriages, and high technology and subsequent job loss or relocation, family intimacy can be lost in the shuffle.

Only a conscious and shared commitment to focus on the relationship can keep marital and family ties high on one's list of priorities. As you will see in Chapter 14, many couples and families seek out opportunities to enrich their lives, to reaffirm their commitment to work on their relationships. According to Avery, the way a couple demonstrates their commitment is personal and nonverbal.

> It can be willingness to do things for each other, spending time together, making personal sacrifices on the other's behalf, being consistent. Self-disclosure is part of it too, because sharing what's inside—even if what's inside isn't pretty—is the supreme act of faith in another. (31)

Thus, only conscious commitment and dedication to working at relationships, particularly through communication, can preserve or heighten intimacy. Lerner captures the link between the development of intimacy and communication. Her words serve as a fine conclusion to this chapter.

> "Being who we are" requires that we can talk openly about things that are important to us, that we take a clear position on where we stand on important emotional issues, and that we clarify the limits of what is acceptable and tolerable to us in a relationship. "Allowing the other person to do the same" means that we can stay emotionally connected to that other party who thinks, feels, and believes differently, without needing to change, convince, or fix the other.
>
> An intimate relationship is one in which neither party silences, sacrifices, or betrays the self and each party expresses strength and vulnerability, weakness and competence in a balanced way. (3)

CONCLUSION

This chapter explored the close relationship between intimacy and communication. After describing the relational currencies and stages in relationship development, the chapter focused on specific communication behaviors that encourage intimacy within marital and family systems: confirmation, self-disclosure, sexual communication, and commitment effort. Confirming behaviors communicate acceptance of another person. Self-disclosure provides a means for mutual sharing of personal information and feelings. Sexuality serves as a means of communicating affection within a marital relationship. Family intimacy cannot be achieved unless members nurture their relationships through care, effort, and risk.

Think about the kinds of interactions you see in the families around you. Is most of their communication strictly functional? Do you see attempts at intimacy through confirmation or self-disclosure? Are these people able to demonstrate an ability to touch each other comfortably? If you think back to Gilbert's model of curvilinear versus linear development of self-disclosure, you can imagine the model applied to all relationships, knowing that only a few are likely to have the mutual acceptance, risk-taking capacity, and commitment to move toward true intimacy.

All human beings long for intimacy, but it is a rare relationship in which the partners (spouses, parents and children, siblings) consciously strive for greater sharing over long periods of time. Such mutual commitment provides rewards known only to those in intimate relationships.

IN REVIEW

1. Create your own definition of intimacy and provide two examples of a marital and a family relationship characterized by intimate communication. Discuss some specific communication behaviors.
2. Trace the development of a real or fictional couple through some of the stages of relationship development, citing representative examples of their communication patterns at each stage.
3. Using a real or fictional family, describe the relational currencies most commonly used. Indicate any family-of-origin influences you see in the current pattern.
4. Describe some confirming behaviors that can become patterned into a family's way of life.
5. Take a position and discuss whether and under what circumstances, if any, you would recommend withholding complete self-disclosure in a marital and/or family relationship.
6. Take a position and discuss the axiom: If you have to work at a relationship, there's something wrong with it.

CHAPTER 6

Communication and Family Roles and Types

As the American family undergoes rapid and dramatic changes, family roles receive extensive attention from the media, family researchers and therapists, and individual family members struggling to manage everyday life. Family life is not as predictable as it once was; the opportunity to shape a family life involves challenges and excitement. There are no easy answers regarding what it means to be a step-mother, grandfather, single father, half-sibling or mother. There is tremendous variability across families as members develop roles through interaction with each other. In order to explore these issues, this chapter will discuss role development, role functions, role conflict, and couple/family typologies, relating each topic to communication across life stages.

ROLE DEVELOPMENT

Within families, roles are established, grown into, grown through, discussed, negotiated, worked on, and accepted or rejected. As family members mature or outside forces impact the family, roles emerge, shift, or disappear. The term *role* is so widely used that it can mean very different things to different persons. In order to understand role development, you need to consider first the definitions of roles and then examine role expectations and role performance.

Role Definitions

Role theorists frequently disagree on the definition of family roles (Heiss 1968; Hood 1986; Linton 1945). This text supports the view that "family roles are defined as repetitive patterns of behavior by which family members fulfill family functions" (Epstein, Bishop, and Baldwin 1982, 124). This position contrasts with some theories

Part of learning roles occurs by observing and imitating role models.

that present a fixed, or unchanging, view of roles. For example, some theories maintain that family members hold specific expectations toward the occupant of a given social position, such as "father" or "grandmother." These expectations carry beliefs about how a role can and should be enacted, no matter what the circumstances.

Rather than take a fixed view of the position of a child or a parent in a family, most theorists prefer an *interactive perspective,* emphasizing the emerging aspects of roles and the behavioral regularities that develop out of social interaction. This approach takes into account the transactional nature of the encounters experienced by persons with labels such as "father" or "wife" and reflects the reciprocal nature of roles. According to this interactive philosophy, you cannot be a stepfather without a stepchild, or a wife without a husband; in fact, you cannot be a companionable stepfather to a child who rejects you or be a confrontive wife to a man who avoids conflict.

Over a period of time, family members negotiate their mutual expectations of one another, and gradually family members fulfill those expectations in specific situations. Family members acquire role attachments and make an emotional investment in carrying out, for example, the roles of provider or nurturer. In addition, as circumstances change, members may have to give up roles, a process called role relinquishment (Hood 1986). Yet roles do not emerge solely through interaction. Part of learning roles occurs by observing and imitating *role models,* persons whose behavior serves as a guide for others.

The interactive role reflects (1) the personality and background of a person who occupies a social position, such as oldest son or stepmother, (2) the relationships in which a person interacts, (3) the changes as each family member moves through his or her life cycle, (4) the effects of role performance upon the family system, and (5) the extent to which a person's social/psychological identity is defined and enhanced by a particular role. For example, a woman's behavior in the social position of wife may have been very different in her first marriage than in her second, due to her own personal growth and the actions of each husband.

The distinction between interactive and fixed roles has many implications for communication. In his classic work, British sociologist Bernstein (1970) identifies two primary forms of communication that contrast and typify families—the position-oriented type and the person-oriented type. Position-oriented families usually maintain strict boundaries along the lines of age, sex, and age-related family roles. Thus, the behaviors attached to the roles of grandparent, mother, and son become carefully defined and delineated. In a position-oriented family, aunts do X, mothers do Y, and husbands do Z. Person-oriented families center more on the unique individuals occupying each label and have fewer boundaries or exacting rules for appropriate behavior. Johnson (1978) describes the communication differences between these two approaches by discussing a hypothetical child—Allison—as she might develop in either family.

> If she develops in a position-oriented family, she learns that her role as a child is very communalized; she learns that mother and father can direct and prohibit behavior because they are mother and father and as such need only provide general rule statements as directives of behavior: "You're not to leave the table until you drink your milk," "Apologize to your father," "Be quiet, I'm on the phone." If, on the other hand, Allison develops in a person-oriented family, she will probably be asked to drink her milk, apologize to her father, and be quiet, but these directives are less likely to stand on their own. Allison's parents will provide reasons for the desired behaviors that go beyond mother and father's rights to direct. (5–6)

A child raised in a position-oriented family learns that what can be said and done in relation to others depends on the roles one has relative to others, whereas a child raised in a person-oriented family learns that, although role relationships are important, what constitutes appropriate or inappropriate behaviors depends on reasons that transcend role relationships and depends upon the personal nature of the family members.

"I feel strongly that in my family my children need to be flexible, and I always try to encourage their direct participation in all decisions and events. I try to raise them in a nonsexist manner, giving equal responsibilities to them in the home and outside, regardless of their age and sex. My daughter cooks, gardens, and dances. So does my son. They also have to help me fix things. Sometimes I feel that I am lucky to be their only role model, so they will learn to be full and open individuals with a sense of self-worth."

Roles are inextricably bound to the communication process. Family roles are developed and maintained through communication. One learns how to assume his or her place within a family from the feedback provided by other family members: "Such a good girl, helping Mommy like that." "I don't think either of us should argue in front of the children." Individuals talk about what they expect from another as they enter a marital relationship. In-laws are verbally or nonverbally informed about what is considered appropriate behavior; children are given direct instructions about being a son or daughter in a particular household. In general, adults tend to use their family-of-origin history as a base from which to negotiate particular mutual roles as they form a family system; children develop their communicative roles through a combination of their cognitive skills, family experiences, and society's norms and expectations.

Family roles and communication rules are strongly interrelated, as each contributes to the maintenance or change of the other. Rules may structure certain role relationships, whereas particular role relationships may foster the development of certain rules. For example, such rules as "Children should not hear about family finances" or "School problems are to be settled with Mother" reinforce a position-oriented structure; in turn, such a structure contributes to the creation of this type of rule.

Current literature on family roles often centers on terms such as *dual-career couples* or *dual-earner couples*. These terms also need to be clarified. The term *dual-career couple* refers to a pair in which each pursues full-time career advancements. Each spouse feels committed to achieve professional growth as well as marital satisfaction. By contrast, in a *dual-earner couple*, both spouses have taken a "job" in the labor force primarily for economic reasons. This couple cannot "make ends meet" on one salary, but the issue of career growth is not of major importance. Clearly there are many variations of these two spousal arrangements.

In order to understand family roles more fully, you need to examine (1) the sources of role expectations and (2) the determinants of role performance. Many of you no doubt remember making such comments as "When I'm a parent, I'll listen to my kids" or "I'd want my wife to go out and work." Probably each of you has spent time planning how you will perform a specific future role based on your expectations. Most of you have experienced situations in which your role expectations did not match reality.

Role Expectations

Society provides models and norms for how certain family roles should be assumed. Currently, the media are an important societal source of family role expectations. Look at any newsstand and you will see articles on how to be a good parent, grandparent, stepparent, and so forth. Television has provided many family role models, from the time of "Father Knows Best" to Bill Cosby's or Roseanne Barr's show. Advertising reinforces stereotypes of how family members should act.

Daily life within a community also serves as a source of role expectations. As you were growing up, the neighbors and your friends all knew who were the "good" mothers or the "bad" kids on the block or in the community. Ministers, priests, and rabbis presented exhortations for the "good family life." School personnel influenced adult expectations of what "good" parents should do for their children. Each of you has grown up with expectations of how people should function in family roles.

"My mother grew up on a ranch in the Great Uinta Basin in Utah. The women in her family were extremely strong and accustomed to doing 'men's work.' Again, whatever had to be done would be done by whoever was available. It didn't matter whether one was a girl or boy, all hands were necessary and looked upon as being equal in her family."

Cultural groups hold beliefs about parenting or spousal roles, which are learned by members of their community. For example, in the Jewish tradition, the role of mother is associated with the transmission of culture and, as such, carries a particular significance and implies certain expectations. Mexican-American children, in a comparative study with Anglo children, described fathers significantly more as rule makers but sensed both mothers and fathers as rule enforcers. Anglo children depicted fathers more often both as rule makers and enforcers (Jaramillo and Zapata 1987). In their study of the physical and psychological health of middle-aged and older black women, Coleman and colleagues (1987) found an expectation of parenting and providing. Black women did not separate the behavior of providing from parenting or the marriage from providing. They sensed these behaviors, interconnected with the providing role function, as primary to their well-being.

Role expectations also arise from significant others and complementary others. *Significant others* are those persons whom you view as important and who provide you with models from which you develop role expectations. Your mother may greatly influence your expectations of motherhood or your father of fatherhood. You may have had a grandmother who taught you caring behaviors that parents should exhibit. A young couple expecting a child watches another couple with small children to learn to deal with their impending role. Most people tend to seek models for particular lifestyles.

Complementary others are those who fulfill reciprocal role functions that directly impact on your role. Their expectations of your behavior influence your expectations. A husband has expectations for a wife, a parent for a child. During early stages of romantic relationships, men and women spend long periods of time discussing their expectations for what being a complementary other, a husband or wife, will be like. "I want my wife to be home with the children until they go to school" or "I need a husband who will parent my children from my first marriage." As families blend, prospective spouses may talk with their future stepchildren about what they think the relationship should be like. If one partner's expectations are more position-oriented, the partners are more likely to clash than if both hold similar orientations.

Additional expectations come from each person's self-understanding. A person who expects to fulfill the role of spouse or parent has certain ideas about what such a role entails and how he or she thinks a "fit" between the role and the person can be created. You may find that you relied on a role model, or you decided that with your skills or personality you would like to be a certain kind of spouse, parent, or lover. Although society and others greatly influence your expectations, you put your own special identity into your final expectations of how you will assume a role. Sometimes expectations lead one to decide not to assume a role.

"Leah and I have arguments with our parents. They expect us to 'produce' grandchildren, but neither of us wants the responsibility of children. It has taken each of us over a decade to finish our education by paying for it on our own and working full-time. We love our dog, but that doesn't guarantee we would be nurturing parents!"

Although many expectations develop prior to assuming a role, persons may develop new expectations for that role. For example, a young mother may watch her boss take his teenage daughters out to lunch every second Saturday and develop new expectations for parenting of older children.

Role expectations are influenced by an imaginative view of yourself—the way you like to think of yourself being and acting. A mother may picture her friends' looks of envy at her ability to juggle a career and home life. A father may imagine himself telling his child about the "facts of life." Such imaginings are not just daydreams; they serve as a primary source of plans of action or as rehearsal for actual performance. No matter what you imagine, until you enact your role with others, you are dealing with role expectations.

Role Performance and Accountability

Role performance is the actual interactive behavior that defines how the role is enacted. As with role expectations, role performance is influenced by such factors as societal or cultural norms, reactions and role performances of significant and complementary others, and the individual's capacity for enacting the role. *Role accountability* requires a family mechanism for seeing that role functions are accomplished. This may come through family members' development of a sense of responsibility for carrying out their role functions, including the creation of monitoring and corrective mechanisms (Epstein et al.). Without role accountability, the family system becomes dysfunctional.

Churches may influence whom their members can marry and how parents and children should act. School and community organizations may give feedback as to how well people are carrying out their family roles. The extent to which you respond to this feedback determines its influence upon you. You may choose to "keep up with the Joneses," or you may decide that the Joneses do not know much about how to live.

The actions of important persons in your life affect role performance. Most of you have experienced the influence of feedback from significant others. Perhaps a friend told you he is not as disrespectful to his mother as you are to yours, and you changed your behavior toward your mother. Or someone told you what a good stepparent you are, and you began trying even harder to be responsive to your stepchildren.

Persons in complementary roles have direct bearing on how you assume your role. Have you ever tried to reason with a parent who sulks, pamper an independent grandparent, or order a willful child? You were probably frustrated in enacting your role. On the other hand, if two complementary persons see things in similar ways, it enhances role performance. A college student who believes that she should no longer have to answer for her evening whereabouts will be reinforced by a mother who no longer asks. Thus, the way others assume their roles and comment on our roles affects how we enact our roles.

Additionally, your background influences your behavior. The range of behaviors allowed by one's background limits what he or she can do. For example, if certain communication behaviors are not part of your repertoire, they cannot appear by magic in a particular situation. A father may wish he could talk with his son instead of yelling at him or giving orders, but he may not know how to discuss controversial subjects with his child. Self-confidence in attempting to fulfill a role may affect behavior. A shy stepmother may not be able to express affection for her new stepchildren for many months. The role aspects that you emphasize affect your behavior. If you view the major function of fatherhood as providing for your children, you are probably more likely to take a second job than to take the family on Saturday picnics.

Sometimes individual expectations do not match the realities. A woman who had planned to mother many children may find herself comfortable with the role of mother to one. On occasion, people discover that they can function well in a role they did not expect or desire.

"I was really furious when my husband quit his sales job to finish his degree. I didn't choose the role of provider, and I didn't like being conscripted. But after a while, I got to feeling very professional and adult. Here I was supporting myself and a husband. I didn't know I had it in me. But I look forward to the possibility of working part-time in the future."

As you will see in later chapters, predictable and unpredictable life crises affect the roles you assume and how you function in them. Thus, although role behavior functions as a result of expectations and interpersonal interactions, unforeseen circumstances may alter life in such a way that roles change drastically from those first planned or enacted. The next section discusses the role functions that adults assume in families. The extent to which each adult assumes certain functions affects both the way roles are enacted and the type of communication that occurs within the family.

SPECIFIC ROLE FUNCTIONS

The concept of the family as a mobile can be applied to roles, using the McMaster's model of family functioning. In this model, role functioning is examined by discovering how the family allocates responsibilities and handles accountability for them (Epstein et al.). In a well-functioning family, allocation of tasks is perceived as fair and reasonable, and accountability is clear. According to this model, five essential family functions serve as a basis for needed family roles: (1) providing for adult sexual fulfillment and gender modeling for children, (2) providing nurturing and emotional support, (3) providing for individual development, (4) providing kinship maintenance and family management, and (5) providing basic resources. These family functions can be categorized as instrumental (providing the resources for the family), affective (support and nurturing, adult sexual needs), and mixed (life-skill development and system upkeep). Within each family system, the existing themes, images, boundaries, and biosocial beliefs affect the way these functions are carried out. This chapter places a greater emphasis on those related to sexual identity, child socialization, nurturing behavior, and maintenance of the family system because these have stronger implications for communication. As you look at Figure 6-1, imagine a mobile with the systemic parts balanced by the multiple roles operating within the family, such as providing maintenance, or adult sexual fulfillment. These role functions become attached or superimposed on the family system characteristics, because the ways in which the family survives financially or the children behave affect all parts of the system.

Providing for Gender Socialization and Sexual Needs

Gender Socialization.   In a culture that provides multiple possibilities and few clear distinctions, males and females face a dilemma in trying to be both nurturing and strong, both independent and interdependent in family dynamics (Leonard 1982). For example, men today can receive a double message from women who want

Figure 6–1 _____
Family Role Functions

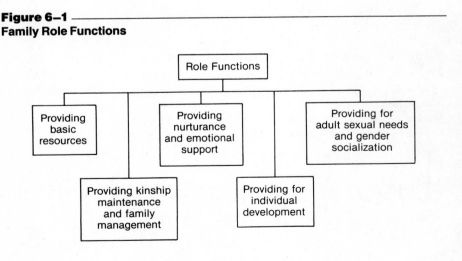

Table 6-1

Psychological Dimensions of the Female and Male Roles

The Female Role. Women are expected to be (or allowed to be) the following:
1. Home oriented, child(ren) oriented.
2. Warm, affectionate, gentle, tender.
3. Aware of feelings of others, considerate, tactful, compassionate.
4. Moody, high-strung, temperamental, excitable, emotional, subjective, illogical.
5. Complaining, nagging.
6. Weak, helpless, fragile, easily emotionally hurt.
7. Submissive, yielding, dependent.

The Male Role. Men are expected to be (or allowed to be) the following:
1. Ambitious, competitive, enterprising, worldly.
2. Calm, stable, unemotional, realistic.
3. Strong, tough, powerful.
4. Aggressive, forceful, decisive, dominant.
5. Independent, self-reliant.
6. Harsh, severe, stern, cruel.
7. Autocratic, rigid, arrogant.

a man who is expressive, gentle, nurturing, and vulnerable, yet must be successful, wealthy financially, and capable of taking charge (Hayes 1988). Women can receive similar conflicting messages.

The process of learning what it means to be male or female begins at birth. Even as newborns, males and females are handled differently and may be provided with "sex-appropriate" toys. Males and females learn expected behaviors at an early age. Studies of kindergarten children show that boys are keenly aware of the masculine behaviors expected of them; therefore, they restrict their interests and activities to avoid what might be judged feminine. Girls continue to develop feminine expectations gradually over five more years. Some people believe that separate male and female behaviors are necessary for the continuation of the family as they have known it. Certain religious or political groups and cultural traditions support strong male-female distinctions, seeing such practices as necessary for continued family existence and development. Some of you may believe that men and women should fulfill certain family functions on the basis of sex. For others, such sexually bound distinctions appear repressive. The generalized dimensions of male and female roles are found in Table 6-1 (Feldman 1982, 355).

These characteristics are important because of the ways they can affect family communication. Feldman concluded that the culturally defined characteristics of what was appropriate or inappropriate in sex roles indicate that "men are not supposed to act like women, and women are not supposed to act like men" (355). Further verification of differences between mothers and fathers can be found in a study of full-time employed couples who revealed their perceptions of major parental role responsibilities in raising children. Parents agreed highly on role responsibilities for a male child but significantly less regarding those for a female child. Fathers placed greater emphasis on girls' acquiring emotional skills and boys' acquiring instrumental skills and attitudes for working in the future. They wanted sons more than daughters

Gender distinctions affect communication within the family.

to be taught cognitive development skills, such as reading and writing, assertiveness skills to deal with peer pressure, and questioning skills to evaluate rules and standards (Gilbert, Hanson, and Davis 1982). These and other studies indicate that many men reinforce stereotypical attitudes about how male and female children should be raised. These attitudes restrict children's development and affect their communication within the family.

Children imitate behaviors that reflect the family communication rules pertaining to gender distinctions. Gender-bound rules may determine who can perform or respond to such communication behaviors as crying, swearing, asking for money, hitting, or hugging. The gender-based communication directives you received as a child come into play when you form your own family system. For example, look at the area of self-disclosure. Traditionally, men are thought to disclose less about themselves than women and keep more secrets. Compared with women, men relate more impersonally to others and see themselves as the embodiment of their roles rather than as humans enacting roles. Jourard (1974) believes that men do not express the entire breadth and depth of their inner experience, either to themselves or to others. Shimanoff (1983) discovered that men do not trust other men and prefer to express their emotions to women, whom they perceive to be more nurturing. Men fear that talking about emotions reduces their competitive edge. Self-disclosure and openness are critical to communication and sharing love within families; if men accept a very restrictive definition of their nurturing communication, they may deprive themselves and their family members of desired intimacy. Women may suffer when female role prescriptions prohibit spontaneous, assertive, or independent communication. Yet each family member's behavior is constantly modified by the other members with whom he or she interacts.

> *"I recently received a letter from my son that reminded me of how his young adulthood is so very different from mine. He wrote about his week as a 'single parent' while his wife was in Los Angeles on business and how he survived the carpools and cooking. Their lifestyle amazes me, but I love to see Brian act as such a caring and active parent to the boys."*

The concept of androgyny has possible applications to roles for communication within families. Androgyny refers to "the human capacity for members of both sexes to be masculine and feminine in their behaviors—both dominant and submissive, active and passive, tough and tender" (DeFrain 1979, 237). Androgyny means that family members evaluate all types of issues on the merits or demerits of those issues without reference to the gender of the persons involved. The androgynous person is flexible, adaptive, and capable of being both instrumental (assertive, competent, forceful, and independent) and expressive (nurturing, warm, supportive, and compassionate) depending upon the demands of the situation.

An androgynous communication style appears in a family system with a person orientation. A position orientation, operating with fixed expectations, maintains strong gender distinctions. An androgynous orientation prizes flexibility and interchangeable gender expectations.

Androgynous married partners demonstrate more understanding of their spouses. They perceive emotional messages much more accurately and listen more empathically (Indvik and Fitzpatrick 1982, 43). This orientation has been shown to be an important psychological resource for women in high stress situations (Patterson and McCubbin 1984).

Sexual Activity as Communication. Another aspect of the sexual identity function relates to engaging in adult sexual activity. Sexual behavior is a form of communication that has a powerful effect on the quality of a marital relationship.

> *"If there is anything I would wish for my daughter as she enters marriage, it would be the ability to talk to her husband about sex. It was unthinkable to me that men and women could really talk about what gave them pleasure in sexual activity. My husband and I spent years in troubled silence. It took an affair, a separation, and counseling for us to be able to begin to talk about our sexual life."*

Even in today's more open society, many communication breakdowns stem from an inability of couples to communicate honestly about their sexual relationship. In Carlson's study of the sexual expectations of married couples, 80 percent of both spouses indicated that the husband initiates sexual activity more than the wife, but

45 percent of the husbands felt that both should have equal responsibility. Wives responded differently; only one-fourth thought it should be an equal responsibility, and an equal number saw no duty involved (1976b, 103).

As you discovered in Chapter 5, many partners do not feel comfortable discussing this intimate part of their relationship. Childhood socialization and the rules of their current system may inhibit adult discussion, which may result in frustration or anger. Feldman (1982) observes that a woman's inhibitions against sexual assertiveness prevent her from being active in meeting her needs. This behavior reinforces the man's expectations that she is not interested but goes along with satisfying his needs. This response blocks his empathic understanding of her needs, and the circle of poor communication continues.

In relationships between couples, unsolved problems in other aspects of their lives can be carried into the sexual relationship. A kind of sexual politics game dominates the relationship and one or the other spouse uses power, excuses, pressure, or ignoring tactics instead of direct communication. Some couples reach a stalemate and miss the potential joys and rewards of intimacy. Others learn to communicate about their sexual behaviors and needs.

Providing Nurturing and Support

In a family, members need mutual admiration, support, and reassurance. Marcy needs a hug from her husband, Joe, when she comes home from a hard day's work. Their children—Jeff, Debbie, Cheryl—all need to know that their parents enjoy their presence and willingly provide for their needs. In all of these functions, children influence the role satisfaction parents receive. Cheryl's perception of her mother's willingness to listen to her problems affects their communication. Transactionally, family happiness develops when each member meets the needs and expectations of the others. Children are socialized by their parents, peers, and the environment, which, in turn, affect children's capabilities to nurture and be supportive.

Nurturing Children. Nurturing incorporates communication because it is the chief process used to transmit parental caring, values, and a sense of community to the children. Through advice, directives, and answers to questions, children learn what parents and society expect of them. The parent who carries out most of the responsibilities of the childcare function has the potential for a greater socializing influence. Until recently, mothers had greater amounts of contact with their children and were most likely to contribute to their nurturing. Children usually experienced their fathers as more distant, less empathic, and less caring, especially in verbal and nonverbal signs of love (Slevin and Balswick 1980; Shepard 1980). Perhaps these differences are because men spend less time in childcare, regardless of their work schedules. In one large study, men whose wives worked full-time spend 2.3 hours per day in childcare compared with 4 hours for mothers (Moen and Dempster-McClain 1987, 579). Yet men are becoming more active nurturers of young children, and children are finding nurturing from other significant adults, ranging from childcare providers, to stepparents, and so forth.

Socialization for nurturing can specify acceptable or unacceptable communication behaviors, such as yelling, lying, crying, hugging, directness, and silence. Each person experiences communication socialization through a family-of-origin and social institutions that influence childhood and adult communication competence. For example, children who never make decisions, defend a point of view, or negotiate for something will not automatically develop such communication skills when they leave their childhood home.

In keeping with the interactive nature of roles, children can resist socialization messages. This frustrates parents, especially those in an extremely rigid family system who cannot be flexible enough to present other options. Communications between parents can also become confused if the mother feels threatened when the father demonstrates to relatives and neighbors that he is capable of childcare. Likewise, the father can feel undermined in his providing role when the wife demonstrates her capabilities in a career and puts pressure on him to take more responsibility for the children (Feldman, 370).

Providing Support and Empathy. This function, sometimes called the therapeutic function, implies a willingness to listen to problems of another and provide emotional support. The listening must be empathic in order to give the other the understanding needed or the chance to ventilate pent-up feelings of rage, frustration, or exhaustion. Adults should do it for one another, and should be aware that children require the same kind of listening.

"My father's way is to be very calm and patient with his children. When he helped me with my homework, he would never leave until he knew I understood it completely. He would recall how hard it was to deal with math and science assignments. Now, when I explain something, I try to see that my children understand, because I remember the good feelings that I had when I finally understood my homework."

Empathy implies nonjudgmental understanding of another person. In addition to having someone available in times of crisis or to hear about a problem, family members need someone to give them a sense of belonging—a sense of occasional refuge from the realities of the world they want to ignore or gain time to cope with. If the communication channels between family members encourage and permit the expression of open feelings, various individuals in the family can function therapeutically by offering advice and questioning motives. For example, one brother can serve as a sounding board for another.

Providing for Individual Development

This role function includes those tasks that each individual must fulfill in order to become self-sufficient. Although each family member is part of a system, each must develop his or her own personality in order to take pride in his or her self-concept.

A sense of individual achievement in meeting physical, intellectual, emotional, and social needs is necessary in order to survive meaningfully both in the outside world and within the family. Family members who do not develop this role function can easily become dependent or enmeshed in the system. A "take care of me" attitude on the part of any member diminishes the wholeness and interdependence aspects of the family system. Babies begin life with the need for constant care to survive but must progress toward self-care.

Family members must facilitate for one another opportunities for self-discovery and development of talents. Parents do the majority of this task in their children's formative years, but from an early age, children influence one another's talents. Competition for grades, positions on sports teams or musical groups, and membership in organizations all create options for self-growth. In many cases, children's activities require the family to communicate regularly with outside persons and institutions, such as coaches or music teachers.

Adults need to be aware of their own continuing development needs and those of other adult family members. Persons may claim time to pursue interests, or partners may make time to share with each other apart from other family members.

Providing for Maintenance and Management

Kinship Maintenance. One important maintenance function involves kin-ship ties with the extended family network, as well as ties with neighbors and friends. The kinship maintenance function has direct implications for family communication. Kinship involves sharing, participating in, and promoting the family's welfare as contacts are maintained with relatives outside the family home. In short, it involves boundary management. Parents, children, sisters, brothers, uncles, aunts, step-relatives are all involved in maintaining a family network. Whether or not one is included or excluded from family events or hears the latest family gossip signifies one's place within the family system. While fulfilling the kinship function, family members may operate within their own rules or rituals, and outsiders may not feel welcome or included in the unique family communication patterns.

Holidays are a special time for family communication. In some families, particularly highly cohesive ones, attendance at get-togethers is mandatory, and only illness or great distances may be acceptable excuses. Exchange through intimate and economic currencies occurs as part of a ritual. In some households the events are painful, because "cut-off" members may be excluded, or members of low cohesive families may feel they are missing something. In blended families, holidays may serve as a background for custody issues or as a time of competition between former spouses for their children's affection.

Women do most of the communicating with relatives (Hagestad 1985). One study found that husbands maintained fewer kinship contacts with their relatives and actually had more contact with their wive's relatives. Ninety percent of interaction with the kin was concentrated in three areas: visiting, recreation, and communication by letter and telephone (Rollins and Bahr 1976; Berardo, Shehan, and Leslie 1987).

The single-parent and blended family systems encounter special kinship concerns. For example, in divorced families, there may be special problems in communicating with the ex-spouse and his or her new family. One of the ex-partners may refuse to communicate with the other; children may become pawns and resent forced separations from legitimate kinship ties. One study indicates that remarried families' kinship issues differed for spouses. The husband placed the spousal relationship as the most important, and that influenced his relationships with his, hers, or their children. Men were less affected by problems their wives had with their children. Wives were affected more by problems with their stepchildren and former husbands. This resulted in the father curtailing his kinship ties with prior-marriage children (Hobart 1988, 660).

Family networking in order to maintain kinship also varies according to family-of-origin and ethnicity. For example, in a large study of New York City Puerto Rican families, both men and women had equally strong relationships with their relatives. However, Puerto Rican men networked more with other persons outside their families, whereas the women formed their strongest relationship ties within families (Rogler and Procidano 1986)

Because a family consists of persons who consider themselves to be a family, kinship ties often include extended family members bound together by caring. Such groups engage in kinship behaviors similar to those previously mentioned. Alternative lifestyle couples experience additional systemic pressures because of societal biases that make communication more difficult, even with their families-of-origin.

"Because my immediate family is dead and any other distant relatives on my husband's side or my side live thousands of miles away, we have worked at creating a 'local family.' Over the years, we have developed close friends who serve as honorary aunts and uncles for the children. The highlight of our Christmas is our annual dinner, when we all get together to decorate the tree and the children get to see Uncle Bernard or Aunt Lois within a family context. I feel closer to these people than I do to many blood family members."

Such activities represent a special way to communicate the message that kinship is important. In this mobile age, where families often live great distances from their kin or have few relatives, this idea has merit.

When family members feel safe in sharing their problems, joys, and family celebrations, they reap the benefits of the kinship function. The immediate system experiences the extra security, protection, and warmth of the larger unit of relatives. Ideally, communication can flow from kin outside the immediate family, back and forth with members inside the family, and be enriched and deepened by the support and sharing that occurs. The kinship circle can provide a ring of insulation around the family, with communication serving as the vehicle for support and comfort.

Management of Daily Needs. Other role maintenance and management functions include decision making to facilitate housekeeping, childcare, recreation, and taking care of family budgets, bills, income taxes, and savings/investments.

Discussions of decision making occur in a later chapter. Housekeeping, childcare, and recreational aspects of family roles will be noted briefly.

The housekeeping function traditionally has meant that the wife performs the cooking, cleaning, and maintenance of the home, but this is changing slowly. Although surveys show that men believe housekeeping should be shared, they held that it was more the responsibility of women. In spite of the fact that most women are working full-time or part-time and are involved in careers, the cooking, cleaning, laundry, and childcare duties are seldom shared equally (Berardo, Shehan, and Leslie 1987; Rexcoat and Shehan 1987). Another study of the division of household labor among older couples indicated that when both worked, the wives did most of the domestic work. The same result was true of a comparative group of older couples where both had retired (Lee 1988). Yet wives whose spouses help with household work report far less depression than those with men who do not (Shamir 1986). Couples who accepted nontraditional gender role values also shared a joint housekeeping role (Secombe 1986). The changes in this area reflect active negotiation between partners, because most are creating a housekeeping system different from that in their families-of-origin. In many single-parent or dual-career homes, children are taking on increasing responsibility for housekeeping functions.

Childcare management, or the keeping of the child physically and psychologically safe, is also changing. For the child, management means being bathed, dressed, fed, housed adequately, and protected from terrifying experiences. In a society of smaller families and couples who are child-free by choice, childcare has diminished in importance for some families. Yet, even in small families, the arrival of children requires parents to assume childcare responsibilities for a long period of time.

Even when the children leave home, certain aspects of childcare continue. You can have an ex-wife or ex-husband but never an ex-child! Also, more young, single mothers are opting to raise their children, and more single-parents are taking full responsibility for childcare—making it an enormous task in some cases. Parents are under tremendous financial pressure, because it takes tens of thousands of dollars to raise a child. Caring for children involves continual adaptation to their changes, especially as they move through developmental stages, and involves decisions about whether to, and how best to, keep a child physically and psychologically safe.

Children have a strong impact on the way couples organize all of their family roles. The addition of children often necessitates the mother's moving into the typical domestic role. The mother's time and energy for adult interactions become drastically reduced, including the number of activities the couple can share together. When young children arrive, if the wife's parents are available, a kinship and role study revealed that they gave a significant amount of help. This help, however, resulted in a decrease in the husband's participation (Hill 1988). In many three- or four-generational single-parent systems, the grandmother takes on the primary childcare responsibility.

Recreation management implies coordinating those things you do for relaxation, entertainment, or personal development. Families vary as to who is responsible for carrying out the recreational function, but research indicates that it is considered important (Carlson, 137). More husbands than wives value family recreation activities. Yet, with the rise of dual-career families and increased opportunities in sports for women, this may change.

Family recreation can be complicated, because individual members have their own interests as well as the desire or obligation to participate in family activities. Extremely cohesive families encourage much group activity, whereas families with low cohesion may not.

Although the recreational function provides opportunities for nurturing communication, in some families people perform the role in isolation or nonfamilial settings. Stereotypically, men have found a recreational niche in strong, masculine athletic behaviors. Parental behavior telegraphs to children what is expected recreational behavior, and conflicts may result if a child does not measure up. Most of you have seen parents yelling at a Little League umpire or at their eight-year-old batter who has struck out. In some families, recreation, such as bowling or bridge, provides a means to escape from the family. If all recreation is separate, important communication opportunities may be missed.

Providing Basic Resources

Traditionally, men are expected to be major providers in families (by a ratio of three to one in most studies), and laws and customs help to carry out these expectations. Women have been limited in terms of the providing function, which historically has affected their decision-making power within the family system. Due to inflation, increasing educational and career opportunities for women, improvements in day care and nursery schools, smaller families, greater numbers of female-headed single-parent families, and automation in the home, increased numbers of women have gone to work; today, women comprise over 55 percent of the work force (1988 Bureau of Labor Statistics Report). Thus, the providing function is being shared and in many families assumed by a single parent. As more couples share responsibility for providing resources, greater potential for shared power and decision making results. Stepfamilies often face conflicts as the stepparent may feel he or she has lost control of resources that go toward the stepchildren. Single parents often feel that providing economic stability has become their primary role, when they would wish for a greater balance with nurturing or recreation.

Each family combines these five role functions in unique ways. For example, in the Kondelis family, child rearing and child socialization may no longer be important functions, although recreation may be highly valued and organized by the husband/father. If finances permit, most housekeeping functions may be provided by a cleaning service, whereas providing may be done by both husband and wife. In the Rosenthal family the single mother may engage primarily in the providing and therapeutic functions, delegating childcare and socialization functions to the two older children. Recreation may be more individually oriented, whereas kinship functions may receive limited attention. Again, ethnicity influences role function. For example, research on two-parent black families indicates that there is more role flexibility between black partners and that black fathers play a larger part in housekeeping, child rearing, and nurturing than do white fathers (Broman 1988).

As children mature, they participate more actively in many functions. Yet, in some single-parent, dual-career, or dual-earner families, children may be inappropriately required to engage in a type or amount of activity usually reserved for a spouse. For example, an older child may assume total childcare or housekeeping responsibilities in a busy dual-career household. In a single-parent system, children may be expected to provide therapeutic listening that might be expected of a spouse in a two-parent household. Members of highly adaptable families may find themselves fulfilling numerous functions on an unpredictable schedule; whereas in highly rigid families, specific functions may be associated with the same individual indefinitely.

ROLE CONFLICT

"I have had a great deal of experience with role conflict in my marriage. I spend most of the time with my in-laws wearing the mask of the 'wonderful little woman-wife' who does all the traditional things while they act like guests in my home. I feel such a sense of relief when our visits are over, because we each know this is a big fake, but no one will remove the mask."

Family roles emerge from the repetitive pattern of behaviors that members use to carry out family functions. If not analyzed or planned, these patterns can cause interpersonal and individual conflicts. Repetition can be boring and confining to individuals who find themselves expected to behave in certain role functions in certain ways. Much negotiation occurs as system members attempt to work out their own definitions of the role interchange. Role conflicts can be divided into (1) interpersonal conflicts over roles, and (2) intrapersonal conflicts over roles.

Interpersonal Conflicts

Although individuals may know what is expected of them in a family, not all members perform the expected behaviors. For example, a husband may relinquish the provider function and decide to write "the great American novel," or he may suffer a fall that prevents him from returning to work. Consequently, his wife may be thrust into providing for the family, with resulting potential conflict. When this happens, the organizational structure in the system changes; a new kind of interdependence must evolve. Family messages are punctuated differently; equifinality is achieved by new means. Role changes, especially by parents, upset the balance in the system.

If complementary or significant others have different expectations of the way a person should be performing a role, conflict may occur. A child or adolescent may expect far more nurturing from a parent and complain about the lack of emphasis on it. A wife may expect her husband to assume half the provider responsibility and resent his limited attention to what she considers his duty. The reverse can be true if the wife refuses to work outside the home and the husband feels all the responsibility is unfairly his.

If the priorities or goals of system members are not congruent with each other, role conflict occurs. If money is critical to one spouse and recreation has a high priority for the other, there may be major fights over providing resources versus playing. For many couples, the addition of the first baby signals a whole set of role changes, which are often accompanied by conflict. One spouse may suddenly devote extensive time to the childcare function, thereby neglecting the therapeutic or kinship functions that the other spouse expects and values.

Feelings for the other person may affect the extent to which conflict occurs. A parent may react differently to each child by basing his or her actions on the child's behavior. For example, a mother with extensive childcare responsibilities may abuse one child and not another. A child of a single parent may be co-opted to serve as a surrogate spouse to provide emotional support. Other family members often resent the favored status given to the co-opted brother or sister. Usually, such actions lead to later conflict as individuals struggle to maintain roles that are not appropriate to their ages or relationship.

"As the oldest daughter, I ended up with a great deal of responsibility and feel as if I lost part of my own childhood. My mother was an alcoholic, and my father and I almost became the 'adult partners' in the house. He expected me to take care of the younger kids and to fix meals when Mom was 'drying out.' I hated all the work I had to do and all the responsibility. He didn't even want me to get married because he didn't know how he would cope."

These behaviors affect all parts of any family system. Although these and other issues lead to interpersonal role conflict, some people experience role conflict within themselves.

Intrapersonal Conflicts

Occasionally, people find themselves performing role functions that do not fit their self-concepts, which leads to internal conflict. Some new parents experience difficulty adjusting to childcare responsibilities expected of them. Others find that they did not expect to be breadwinners or do not see themselves as integral members of an extensive kinship network. Such differences between how you see yourself and how you act may lead to intense intrapersonal struggles. In multigenerational systemic terms, Bradt (1980) suggests that the idea of primacy of the mother developed because fathers and extended family members failed to participate as co-parents, grandfathers, godfathers, and uncles. He feels that too often the two-parent biological family is isolated, and the economic system operates so that fathers work outside the home, resulting in mother-baby bonds, creating an "omnipotent system" called "Momism" (129).

People sometimes find themselves in roles that they expected to assume comfortably but which they cannot perform adequately. Although the new "supermom" is pictured as balancing a career, household duties, and child-rearing duties with equanimity, many young women have discovered that there are not enough hours in a day to maintain such a schedule, and they cannot fulfill their ideal wife/mother role. This often leads to disappointment and anger at themselves for not fulfilling expectations. Even men who believe in equality experience difficulty in returning the emotional backing and encouragement they receive from their wives. Too many men have not been socialized to assume nurturing roles (Elman and Gilbert 1984).

In Cahn's study of the stages in a relationship, he found in married partners that acceptance and appreciation functioned as a self-concept support. Some communication behaviors that enhance a relationship are the desire to participate in a number of social activities with each other, the willingness to share many interests with each other and respect for one another (1987). Certainly, increasing each partner's sense of worth would affect the couple's role performance and lessen conflicts.

Such interpersonal and individual role conflicts necessitate sensitive and extensive communication among members of a family system if it is to be recalibrated to fit the needs of individual members. Role performance constitutes an important way of regulating family life. Yet, if roles are viewed as "set in stone," they will limit personal and system growth. Thus, roles should be seen as reflections of the individual and his or her interpersonal encounters, a conception that implies a transactional growth process.

COUPLE/FAMILY TYPOLOGIES

Couple or family typologies represent another way to explore family interaction. Many family researchers and therapists believe family behavior and organization can be classified into various typologies, or family types, depending upon the patterns of its interactions. When these types emerge, some predictability is possible. If typologies can open doors to predictable communication patterns, these would be very valuable information for researchers and therapists. Although much of this research is recent and ongoing, some typologies are emerging. A few typology systems will be developed in detail.

Couple-Oriented Research

The most extensive work done in classifying couple types is found in Fitzpatrick's research (Fitzpatrick, Fallis, and Vance 1982). In her early work, influenced by Kantor and Lehr, Fitzpatrick (1977a; 1977b; 1988) tested a large number of characteristics to find out which made a difference in maintaining couple relationships. She isolated eight significant factors: conflict avoidance, assertiveness, sharing, the ideology of traditionalism, the ideology of uncertainty and change, temporal (time) regularity, undifferentiated space, and autonomy. Individuals and couples fit a type when their answers indicate that they possess a number of characteristics. Fitzpatrick designated relational definitions of traditionals, separates, and independents, plus six mixed-couple types wherein the husband and wife described their relationship differently. She found that 20 percent are traditionals, 17 percent are separates, and 22 percent are independents (1988, 79). Thus, 59 percent can be classified as pure types and 40 percent as mixed.

Independent types accept uncertainty and change; they pay limited attention to schedules and traditional values. Independents represent the most autonomous of the types but do considerable sharing and negotiate autonomy. They do not avoid conflict. Independents are more likely to support an androgynous and flexible sex role (Fitzpatrick 1988, 76).

Separates differ from independents in greater conflict avoidance, more differentiated space needs, fairly regular schedules, and less sharing. In relationships, separates maintain a distance from people, even their spouses; they experience little sense of togetherness or autonomy. Separates usually oppose an androgynous sexual orientation and tend to avoid conflict.

Traditionals uphold a fairly conventional belief system and resist change or uncertainty because it threatens their routines. Physical and psychological sharing characterize the traditional type. This leads to a high degree of interdependence and low autonomy. Few boundaries exist in the couples' use of physical and emotional space. They will engage in conflict but would rather avoid it. Uncertainty and change in values upset them. Traditionals, like separates, demonstrate strong sex-typed roles and oppose an androgynous orientation.

The other six mixed types (approximately 40 percent) included traditional/separate, separate/traditional, independent/separate, separate/independent, traditional/independent, and independent/ traditional (Fitzpatrick 1988). In mixed types, the husband is designated by the first term.

Which relational type experiences the greater satisfaction? Which couples are the most cohesive? The answers follow and have implications for role enactment. In their summary of the research, Fitzpatrick and Best (1979) reported traditional couples significantly higher than the other three types on consensus, cohesion, relational satisfaction, and expressing affection. Independents were lower on consensus, open affection to one another, and dyadic satisfaction; however, their lack of agreement on issues regarding dyadic interactions did not impair their cohesiveness. Separates were the least cohesive, but on relational issues appeared high on consensus. Separates demonstrated few expressions of affection toward their spouses and rated lower on dyadic satisfaction. In the separate (husband)/traditional (wife) category, couples had low consensus on a number of relational issues, but they were moderately cohesive. These couples claimed high satisfaction for their relationship and outwardly expressed much affection.

Further findings indicated that couples who agreed on relational definitions agreed with one another on a greater number of issues in their relationship. Those who agreed were also more cohesive. It is interesting to note that couples who disagreed on typing themselves were as satisfied with their marriages as couples who agreed on their definitions. Enduring relationships were characterized by more variety in the modes of communication used by partners (Fitzpatrick and Best, 167).

Table 6-2 summarizes the ways in which couple types responded to a variety of relationship measures, including sex roles and gender perceptions. In predicting communication, you might expect that traditional families would demonstrate affection and sharing of the role functions discussed earlier in this chapter, with males and females remaining in defined positions. You could expect male dominance in attitudes and values regarding the providing, recreational, housekeeping, sex, and kinship functions, because the traditional type resists change. Because independents are more open to change, they might be more open to dual-career marriages and sharing the providing and housekeeping functions. Because independents value autonomy and avoid interdependence, individual couple members may be freer in their role functions. This self-reliance might better equip independents to handle the unknown and accept the inevitable changes that occur in roles and life.

The potential for problems when communicating about role functions relates especially to the separates who have not resolved the interdependence/autonomy issue in their marriage. Fitzpatrick uses the label "emotionally divorced" for this type, because separates are least likely to express their feelings to their partners. Thus, if a partner is dissatisfied with the role expectations of the other spouse yet cannot freely express these feelings, the relationship suffers.

Other academic and popular writers have proposed couple types. Burgess, Locke, and Thomas (1963) distinguished between institutional and companionship marriages. In institutional marriages, roles are sex differentiated along traditional lines. Husbands are more instrumental and rigid in their roles, and wives are more expressive and flexible. Couples in a companionship marriage place an emphasis upon their personalities interacting and the affective aspects of their relationship. Sexual enjoyment, companionship, and communication are expected to follow love. Burgess believes that the family is in transition from an institutional to a companionship type of relationship.

Table 6–2
Couple Type Differences on Relational Measures

Couple Types	Marital Satisfaction	Cohesion	Consensus	Affectional Expression	Sex Roles	Psychological Gender States (Wives Only)
Traditionals	High	High	High	Moderately high	Conventional	Feminine
Independents	Low	Moderately high	Low	Low	Nonconventional	Sex-typed androgynous
Separates	Low	Low	Moderately high	Low	Conventional	Feminine sex-typed
Separates/ traditionals	Moderately high	Moderately high	Moderately high	High	Conventional	Feminine sex-typed
Other mixed types	Moderately high	Low	Low	Moderately high	Depends on mixed type	Depends on mixed type

Family Typologies

Kantor and Lehr's work *Inside the Family* (1976) serves as the touchstone study of family types. Relying on intensive study of nineteen families, researchers Kantor and Lehr developed a descriptive theory of family process. They identified basic component parts of family process and how these parts affected members' behavior.

As a means of dealing with the basic family issue of separateness and connectedness, or what Kantor and Lehr called "distance regulation," they developed a six-dimensional social space grid on which family communication takes place (70–78, 221). All communication represents efforts by family members to gain access to targets, that is, things or ideas members want or need. Specifically, family members use two sets of dimensions. One set reaches targets of affect, power, and meaning through the way they regulate the other—the access dimensions of space, time, and energy. Thus, families regulate the activities of people, objects, and events.

In carrying out the functions in any role, all family members have a target, or goal, of gaining some degree of affect, power, or meaning. Affect means achieving some kind of intimacy or connectedness with the members of the family and receiving some reward in the form of nurturing behavior in their verbal and nonverbal communication. Power implies that a member has the independence to select what he or she wants and the ability to get the money, skills, or goods desired. This freedom to choose what an individual wants gives a family member power and the separateness needed to develop autonomy. The third target is meaning. Each family member in the system seeks some philosophical rationale that offers reasons for what happens to them in the family and outside world. The acquisition of meaning by each member develops a stronger self-concept and provides an explanation of why members live as they do. When family members collectively find meaning in their interactions, cohesion develops.

Kantor and Lehr provide descriptions of the access dimensions (space, time, and energy) from an analogical as well as physical point of view. The spatial dimensions include the way a family handles its physical surroundings (exterior and interior) and the ways in which the members' communication regulates their psychological distance from each other. The time dimension includes a consideration of clock time and calendar time in order to understand a family's basic rhythmic patterns. The energy dimension deals with the storing and expending of physical and psychological energy. Each of these dimensions would affect role enactment because they regulate behavior. Family communication usually involves at least one access dimension and one target dimension. For example, a wife moves physically closer (space) to her husband in order to gain more affection (target) from him.

Using these six dimensions, the authors have created a typology for viewing families, consisting of open, closed, and random types, acknowledging that actual families may consist of mixtures of types. The ways in which these three family types maintain their boundaries, or regulate distance through access and target dimensions, account for their differences.

Closed families tend to regulate functions predictably with fixed boundaries. Such families interact less with the outside world. They require members to fulfill their needs and spend their time and energies within the family. Usually, there are emphases on authority and the continuation of family values. Events in closed families tend to be tightly scheduled and predictable. Family members often focus on the preservation of the past or plan for the future. Energy is controlled, used to maintain the system, and dispersed at a steady rate. Moderation, rather than excess, prevails.

In the open family, boundaries tend to remain flexible as members are encouraged to seek experiences in the outside space and return to the family with ideas the family may use if group consensus develops. Open families seldom use censorship, force, or coercion because they believe family goals will vary, change, and be subject to negotiation. They carry these characteristics into intimacy and conflict situations. Members are more likely to concern themselves with the present, and energy in this type is quite flexible. Family members do not have total freedom because they cannot use methods of refueling their energy that cause excess harm or discomfort to other family members. For example, a teenager cannot play tapes at the loudest level after eleven o'clock at night when other family members want to sleep.

Unpredictability and "do-your-own-thing" aptly describe the random family. The boundaries of space surrounding this family are dispersed. Family members and outsiders join in the living space based on interest or desire, or they voluntarily separate from one another without censure. Social appropriateness holds little importance for such members. Time is spent on an irregular basis. Each individual functions according to his or her own rhythm, resulting in high levels of spontaneity. People may change their minds and their plans at any time. Energy in the random family fluctuates. No one source for refueling has been predetermined by the family. Members may rapidly spend high levels of energy and then need long refueling periods.

"I think we must have been a random family during the first ten years of my life. I am next to last of eleven children, and by the time I came along, the family was in chaos. The younger kids lived with different relatives off and on until we were almost adolescents. When we did live at home, things were always unpredictable. Every morning my mother would put a big pot of cereal on the stove, and people would eat when they wanted. You never knew exactly who was going to be sleeping where each night. When I was about ten, my parents got their own life straightened out, and enough older kids were gone so that we could live a more 'normal' life, although I found it hard to suddenly have rules that were enforced and times when I had to be places."

Table 6-3 summarizes the characteristics that Kantor and Lehr delineated for each of these family types. You may identify more closely with one of the types, or you may find that your family incorporates two of the types. You may also realize your family has shifted in typology over the years.

Table 6-3
Characteristics of Family Types

Type of Family	Use of Space	Use of Time	Use of Energy
Closed	Fixed	Regular	Steady
Open	Movable	Variable	Flexible
Random	Dispersed	Irregular	Fluctuating

"As I grew up, my family could be described as a closed family. My parents kept a watchful eye over my three sisters' activities by scrutinizing friends, watching phone calls, keeping strict curfews, chaperoning dates, and generally isolating our family from 'them,' that is, the rest of the South Bronx community. Dad and Mom knew where you were going and whom you were with and told you what time to return. The communication pattern, mostly nonverbal, was also simple: the better you behaved, the more privileges you were allowed.

"Then things changed. When my father died, I found myself closer to my mother, and vice versa. My sisters also found themselves closer, not only to my mother but to each other. My family has gradually progressed to being a more open family. A general rule in our current family is that any requests for either joining or separating are viewed as reasonable and legitimate."

A speculative comparison can be made between Fitzpatrick's and Kantor and Lehr's research. Olson's model of cohesion and adaptability (see Chapter 2) can also be integrated into their thinking. Fitzpatrick's and Olson's early work was greatly influenced by Kantor and Lehr. The terminology each theorist uses can be clarified by remembering that Fitzpatrick's autonomy/interdependence is similar to Olson's cohesion dimension, and in Kantor and Lehr is affect. Adaptability as used by Olson, is similar to power (measured behaviorally) in Fitzpatrick and Kantor and Lehr. Fitzpatrick's "ideology" refers to "meaning" in Kantor and Lehr's thinking and does not appear in Olson's work. Communication is included in the behavioral data collected by Fitzpatrick. In Olson's model, communication appears as an enabling dimension, and in Kantor and Lehr as distance regulation.

Although Fitzpatrick and Kantor and Lehr do not take a strict systems approach in their typology research, these studies provide insights into how roles operate in families. Kantor and Lehr's "open" families would differ greatly in role performance from "closed" families. Whatever the family or couple type, the adults use communication strategies that maintain their type and that are important socializing information for children.

CONCLUSION

This chapter takes a transactional approach to roles, stressing the effect of family interaction on role performance. The distinction between position-oriented and person-oriented roles was developed and applied to communication. The development of roles takes part in a two-step process—role expectations and role performance—each of which has communication components. The five role functions were presented in a mobile model and explained in detail. These are (1) providing gender models and adult sexual fulfillment, (2) providing nurturing and emotional support, (3) providing for individual development, (4) providing kinship maintenance and family management, and (5) providing basic resources. Finally, the couple and family typologies, with their predictability, are viewed as sources of communication understanding.

A major consideration in examining roles or couple/family types is their dynamic nature, which is viewed in accordance with the personal developments and unpredictable circumstances faced by the people involved. Each role or type is assumed and maintained on the basis of personal choice and adaptation to the overall family system.

IN REVIEW

1. Take a position and discuss whether a family needs to be more position-oriented than person-oriented in order to function through crises over time.
2. To what extent are role models actually teachers of communication?
3. Compare and contrast the communication tasks required in carrying out the role functions involved in providing resources and nurturance for the family. Describe these functions in a family with whom you are familiar.
4. Identify a real or fictional family that has changed over a period of time. Note the role changes and give your reasons for these changes. What has been the effect on the system?
5. Give examples of partners you know who fit Fitzpatrick's couple types. Describe sample communication strategies they use.
6. Analyze your family or another real or fictional family and explain why it is an open, closed, or random family type. Cite examples of communication patterns.

CHAPTER 7

Power

Power, a central factor in all human life, has a unique influence on family dynamics. In family systems, the issue of power surfaces in the interactions among members. Family members engage in power maneuvers in an attempt to control their lives (Dell 1989). Therapist Jay Haley believes that "the struggle for status and the question of who is going to be in charge is basic to human relationships" (Simon 1982, 33).

Yet, as you will see throughout the chapter, power does not operate in a simple, linear way. It is not a thing belonging to one or two and sought by many. It is easy to talk about power as a tangible or easily observed "thing," but relational power cannot be classified simply. Power resides in a relationship; it does not reside with one or the other person in the relationship.

"I see my family power image as a three-ring circus. There are always three or four things going on at once. My mother is the ringmaster! She stands center stage and calls the shots. My father is the promoter and the producer. He keeps everything ready for the arena. My sisters and I are the performers. We compete for the spotlight, and each of us thinks her act is the star attraction. Because I'm the oldest, my name always comes first! However, it's hard to say one person has more power than another because we are so very interdependent. I'm sure Ringling Brothers had a much easier time getting the show on the road than my parents had!"

Power serves as a subtle and persuasive aspect of family life. McAdams (1985) suggests that each family member constructs stories that become organized around two general life themes, power and intimacy. Haley sees interpersonal power struggles as the central issue in human life (Simon).

In order to begin to understand the complexity of power and its communication dynamics within family systems, you need to examine (1) the concept of power, (2) the various aspects of power that influence family systems, (3) the development of power in family systems, and (4) communication strategies that affect power.

THE CONCEPT OF POWER

When exploring the issue of power in families, power must be understood within a systems context. Power has been defined frequently as the ability or potential to influence others (Manz and Gioia 1983), but this definition is too limited for application to the family. Power does not belong to an individual; rather, it is a property of a relationship between two or more persons. Thus, the following definition evolves: "Power, a system property, is the ability, potential or actual, of an individual(s) to change the behavior of other members in a social system" (Cromwell and Olson 1975, 5). It follows, then, that family power is the ability of individuals to participate in changing behavior within the family. You must not think of power in a family as static, or fixed. The power dimension in a family system may vary greatly over time, depending upon a host of factors: the family structure, the developmental stages of the children or parents; the predictable and unpredictable stress encountered by the family; and the economic, cultural, or intellectual resources and opportunities of the family. Power operates transactionally in a family, and any power maneuvers within it have a systemwide effect. One member cannot assert independence or dependence on an issue without affecting other members. As one or more members exert power or acquiesce to others' power moves, the whole system may be recalibrated. You may recall from Chapter 3 that a human system has properties of interdependence and wholeness. The transactional nature of power within a family reflects the members' interdependence. Each child or parent has the power to affect the relationships of any other person within the family and to be affected in return. The total potential power in the family system, or wholeness, is greater than the sum of all the individual members' power. The system, through its adaptability mechanisms, reacts to all pressures and maintains balance between the power plays and players.

Power has both perceptual and behavioral properties. The way in which one family member perceives the power dynamics helps determine and explain the reasons for that member's actions. However, the same power issue may be perceived differently by every other family member.

Think of family power as a way of examining the process by which group activity is accomplished. The family, collectively as a group, interacts about an end or goal that one or more family members desire. This specific goal sometimes conflicts with group or family goals. Power is the ability of one or more family members to prevail in a family setting of conflicting ends so that goals are achieved. To understand power, one must identify the pattern of verbal and nonverbal interaction the family goes through to accomplish a goal.

"When my parents separated and Father left the house, my grandmother became the ruling force. She was very domineering and wanted everything done her way. My mother would go along, out of respect for Grandma's age, even though Mom would disagree many times and secretly do what she wanted.

"Grandma would yell and scream if something wasn't done the way she wanted. She could not accept our opinion. We had no voice in her rulings. Each of us left home sooner than we might have to escape her control attempts."

ASPECTS OF POWER IN FAMILY SYSTEMS

McDonald's model of the interrelatedness of units of analysis and dimensions of power (Figure 7-1) helps to depict the complexity of power issues visually (1980a, 844). The model begins with social power found in the environment, including the laws, customs, and traditions surrounding any family in the culture/community in which it operates. This model demonstrates how the family is influenced by other systems in the social sphere, such as government, education, business or religious organizations. Family power is tied directly to the family system's interactions with this ecosystem or larger social system. Family power is a system property, which

Figure 7—1 —————————————————————————————
Units of Analysis and Dimensions of Power

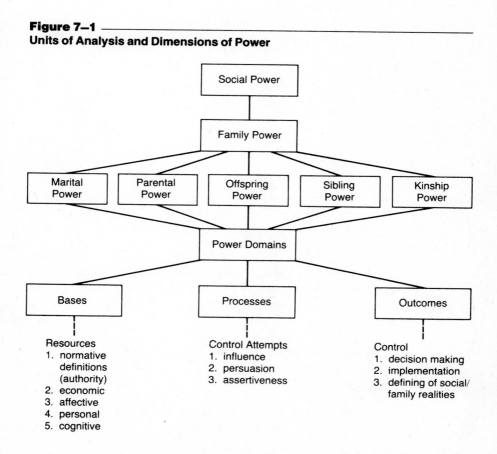

McDonald divides into marital power (husband/wife), parental power (mother/father), offspring power (children/parent), sibling power (brother/sister or combinations of sister/sister and brother/brother), and kinship power (grandparent/aunts/uncles/stepfamily members). When you consider the large percentage of stepfamilies in today's society, you can imagine some of the complex power issues that are included under the term *kinship power*. The power domains include the areas along which power develops, ranging from the bases of power, through the strategies or processes of control to the outcomes. However, in real life this is a dynamic rather than a linear experience. The following discussion attempts to clarify the concept of power by discussing three family power domains: (1) power bases, (2) power processes, and (3) power outcomes.

Power Bases

The bases of family power are the sources of power or resources family members can use to increase their chances of exerting control in a specific situation. Resources consist of whatever is rewarding to an individual or a relationship. Thus, a resource is anything that one partner makes available to the other to satisfy needs or attain goals. No two family members within a system utilize exactly the same resources to achieve their ends. You may exert power because of your education or assertiveness. Your sister's power may come from her strong personality, whereas your mother may have the authority to veto decisions. Yet, unless others respond to these power positions, no power can be exerted. If your brother does not respond to your assertiveness, you are powerless in relation to him. There are many models from which to develop bases or resources of power (McDonald 1981; French and Raven 1962). McDonald's five resources serve as bases from which persons may derive power. They include normative, economic, affective, personal, and cognitive resources.

1. *Normative resources* refer to the family's values and to the cultural or societal definitions of where the authority lies. The expectations of how power is generated and later used depend upon cultural factors that often go back to the families-of-origin. Some families have norms that expect the father to do the providing, whereas other families expect power to emerge based on individual strengths or talents. Normative definitions represent the culturally internalized expectations of the nature of the marriage relationship and perceived role expectations and obligations of the parents and/or the children of the family (McDonald 1981, 827).

2. *Economic resources* refer to the monetary control exerted by the breadwinner and/or persons designated to make financial decisions. Economic power comes from wages earned, money saved, wealth inherited, and so forth. The ability of each partner or family member to earn a living affects power.

3. *Affective resources* refer to the level of involvement with and degree of dependence on others. Affective resources reflect who in the family nurtures others and how each member in the family meets his or her needs for

feeling loved or belonging to the system. These resources can be seen in the use of relational currencies.

4. *Personal resources* refer to each family member's personality, physical appearance and role competence—interpersonal factors that may cause the individual to be perceived as attractive or competent and therefore, accorded power. One's self-perception of attractiveness or personality strengths relates to self-concept and in turn to perceptions of powerfulness or powerlessness.

5. *Cognitive resources* refer to the insight family members have of how their power influences their own actions and affects others. It deals with using intelligence to sense logically what power options are available. Not all family members cognitively achieve the same level of awareness, especially when under stress or conflict. McDonald's bases of power go beyond the earlier work of French and Raven (1975, 218–19). They listed six resource bases of power: (1) punishment or coercive power, (2) positive reinforcement or reward power, (3) expertise or knowledge power, (4) legitimacy or power gained through a position, (5) identification or referent power gained through affiliation, and (6) persuasion or information power. McDonald (1980) suggests that French and Raven's bases of social power could be viewed as resources according to his model.

Although not a perfect match, French and Raven's work can be integrated with McDonald's model if you think of punishment and positive reinforcement as related both to what is normative in a family and who has the authority or who is expected to enforce the rules. Reinforcement or reward power often has an economic tie or may be affective in the forms of hugs or messages of praise. Expertise relates to McDonald's personal and cognitive bases of power. When you believe another family member knows more about a subject than you do, you defer to that person and grant him or her the power to use his or her skill or knowledge. Identification may relate to both McDonald's personal and cognitive resources as affiliation may add to one's self-concept and knowledge. These speculative linkages demonstrate how such approaches complement each other.

Note that these power terms are defined by the way in which the situation is perceived by others. In a family relationship, no member possesses all five of these power sources equally or uses all of them in a given situation. Some may never be used and others may be used in combination. It is possible for a husband to use normative and economic power resources extensively in his interactions, and simultaneously for his wife to use cognitive and affective resources in her interactions. Children in the same family might use affective and personal power resources, especially when they are younger.

"It drives me crazy to watch my little sister get whatever she wants from my mother, because she can cuddle up and make a big deal out of her size and how cute she is. As the oldest, I am expected to be rational and logical, to have few feelings, especially negative ones. If I get upset, no one listens; if she gets upset, she gets her way."

Power becomes a resource base wherein family members perceive ways in which they can use communication in order to establish their status in various family situations. Family members accumulate power options in attempts to define their relationships (Barge 1984).

Power bases are related to many factors such as income and culture. According to Blumstein and Schwartz (1983), discovering how money bestows power reveals crucial things about a relationship (53). In their study of American couples, money established the balance of power in all couple types except lesbians. According to Blumstein and Schwartz, money represents identity and power to men, and to women it represents security and autonomy. Within various cultures power may reflect age and family position. Whereas parents in Jewish families tend to have democratic relationships with their children, in Italian families the father tends to be an authoritarian and the undisputed head of the household (McGoldrick 1982a).

"I can influence Ryan. I simply have to go about it the right way! There are times he sets rules and expects the rest of us to follow them. Then I form power alliances with my daughters, and together we skillfully seek ways to go around the rules; we bend them little by little out of shape."

Power Processes

The ways in which power operates in a family are revealed by its power processes, or by studying ongoing interactions among family members. These processes affect interactions in family discussions, arguments, problem solving, decision making, and especially in times of crises. McDonald refers in his model (Figure 7-1) to these processes as control attempts through influence, persuasion, and assertiveness. Power processes include the interactional techniques individual family members use in their attempts to control the negotiation on decision making. Because each family member exercises different degrees of influence, persuasion, or assertiveness, the power process is unique for each family system. No two can be alike.

These power processes reflect the internal resources that each family member accumulates by living interpersonally together. The internal resources are the amount and types of information family members process from one another within the family. When Dad wants a positive response from Mom or a daughter, he must use an appropriate message stimulus. The effectiveness of the message depends upon Dad's abilities to perceive how Mom or the daughter will react to different message strategies. Family members learn how to discriminate in the selection of the right stimulus message to achieve their goals. In other words, Randy could have ample economic or affective resource power and still fail to gain his son's compliance to accept a curfew if he doesn't select the right message. Power is transmitted through the use of messages that discriminate in specific situations how best to implement an idea to meet a need or goal. Over time, each family member accumulates a knowledge of what internal resources will communicate better in different situations, both positive and negative ones (deTurck and Miller 1986).

Researchers have examined the number of times people talk, how long they talk, to whom they address their comments, and how long a talk session lasts. They have also analyzed questioning, interrupting, and silence patterns, and have concluded that family members who talk most frequently and for the longest periods of time are dominant, and those who receive the most communication are the most powerful (Berger 1980, 217).

Yet, as you know from your own experience, the longest or loudest talker may not hold the power in each situation. One must distinguish between the power attempts a person makes and the final outcomes. Assertiveness and control maneuvers affect family power. Assertiveness means the number of attempts, for example, that Debra makes to change the behavior of her sister. Control represents the influence or number of effective attempts that Debra made that changed the behavior of her husband or sister.

Chapter 3 examined the complexities of messages and described how all messages in a family are co-defined by the senders and receivers. Thus, family members may send mixed messages, which are difficult to analyze accurately. When an individual says one thing but means and wants something else, confusion results. Contradiction often appears in the nonverbal aspects of a message. In analyzing power messages, both the content and relationship dimensions must be analyzed carefully to understand family communication. A family member who acts helpless attempts to control the behavior in a relationship just as effectively as another who dominates and insists on specific behavior.

"My sister, I think, has a great deal of power in my family because she positions herself as dependent and helpless. Everyone is supposed to help Charmaine because 'she can't cope.' I think she is highly capable, deliberately or not, of manipulating everyone to meet her needs. She has always possessed this quality. She preferred to remain unemployed while she was single! And, now that she has a kid, she has a very good reason to not work and to need help in every way—money, childcare, home, car. My mother falls for it all the time."

Some studies indicate that wives evidence "powerless" language in that they use two and one-half times more tag questions and five times more hedges than their spouses. However, closer analysis reveals that although men use fewer of them, they do indeed also use them to get complete attention and more detailed answers. In addition, women use tag questions and hedges creatively and assertively to accomplish their communication goals and improve interpersonal relationships (Giles and Wisemann 1987; Bradac and Mulac 1984).

Messages created by ill or dysfunctional members can influence family power. Families with an alcoholic member have learned just how powerful that member can be. Everyone may learn to tiptoe around the drinker and develop a reactive way of living—planning personal moves in order to minimize the alcoholic's verbal abuse. This places the alcoholic into a central and powerful position in the family, although he or she may be talked about as weak or helpless.

"My sister and I would meet at the front door to our house after school to report to each other on our father's mood. He was either in a 'good' mood (sober) or a 'bad' mood (drinking), and Robin and I tailored our actions and plans to his mood. We learned to adapt to whatever mood and situation came our way."

Power Outcomes

The final area, family power outcomes, focuses upon those issues involving who makes decisions and who wins. In this aspect, one or more family members get their way or receive rights or privileges of leadership. McDonald's model also equates power outcomes with control through decision making, implementation activities, and further defining the social/family context in which the power is carried out. In this last item, which is number three under "outcomes" in his model, McDonald cautions readers to remember that what becomes a power outcome depends on who controls the family in specific situations, and determines the range of possible decisions. Also who in the family, or what alliance of members, decides which decisions to make or which to ignore? If the decision is also to delegate authority, who in the family can decide who will or who will not do something?

More research has been done on power outcomes, especially on decision making, than on power bases or power processes. Some of the findings in this area are reported in Chapter 8. Researchers have studied whose ideas are accepted by family groups, who in the family went along with whom, and whose influence counted in which situations. It is easier to measure power outcomes than to measure power processes. However, in many cases, predictions made from the processes are not accurate. The loudest, longest talker may not have his ideas accepted. The most persuasive adult may lose to an angry child.

Conflict can function as a necessary condition for power. Through conflict, family members attempt to settle their differences. However, power resources can influence outcomes by suppressing potentially conflictual situations. Power hierarchies in the family system also establish guidelines for power processes that avoid conflicts yet affect power outcomes (McDonald 1980a, 843). Family members have orchestration power and implementation power. Orchestration power means that a family member usually makes decisions that do not infringe upon his or her time but determine the family lifestyle and major aspects of the system. The one with orchestration power can delegate unimportant and time-consuming decisions to the spouse or older child who derives implementation power by carrying out these decisions. In the model of power, Figure 7-1, orchestration (related to decision making) and implementation appear under outcomes as controls.

Power bases influence power outcomes. Family members who hold normative positions of authority may have the greatest power. Often, the balance of power rests with the partner who contributes the greatest economic resources to the marriage. Sources of power may be tied to rewards, which affect outcomes. It may be rewarding to receive praise, to gain information, to learn from an expert, to identify with another person, to be persuaded, or, of most importance, to be confirmed by others.

Family power outcomes focus on the issues involving who makes the decisions and who wins.

Some family members who give much to others, both emotionally and economically, expect much in return. The family member who suffers a real or perceived abuse of power or an injustice caused by one or more members may become upset, and this upsets the family system's balance. A family member who cannot achieve harmony within the system because he or she feels powerless may in extreme circumstances resort to separation, divorce, desertion, suicide, murder, or beating. The exit act may be an important power play to a family member, but it can create new problems. Children may feel trapped and have to wait until legal age to exercise their power to reject a defective family system. Family members consciously and unconsciously obtain certain outcomes from the actions they use in a power struggle. In many well-functioning families, members attempt to provide resources for each other in order to maintain a certain level of harmony.

In his review of power in families, Berger suggests that, although Blood and Wolfe (1960) found a positive relationship between the income, educational level, and occupational prestige of the husband and the extent of his power, "the absolute number of resources a person brings to the marriage does not determine his or her power, but rather the relative contribution of resources to the relationship" (210). He maintains that most of the studies he reviewed provide support for the resource theory, but he found notable exceptions, particularly in studies of other cultures. Berger concludes that resources have been defined narrowly—mainly as economic contributions and social prestige—and suggests that family research should include an analysis of resources such as interpersonal skills, and personality orientations such as dominance, physical attractiveness, and sense of humor (214).

Power in the conjugal dyad involves an examination of the extent to which one spouse loves and needs the other. Safilios-Rothschild's (1970) extension of Waller's important research on the "principles of least interest" suggests that the spouse with the strongest feelings puts himself or herself in a less powerful position, because the person with less interest can more easily control the one more involved. She also suggests that the existence of an alternative relationship provides power to one or another family member.

> "One of the ways I was finally able to live at home with some degree of peace was to make it clear to my father that I could and would go and live with his sister if he kept hitting me. My mother agreed with my position although she didn't like it, and he finally realized I was serious. Once he understood that I had somewhere else to go, he began to treat me better."

In discussing options for couples, Berger states: "The mere existence of alternatives does not ensure increased power for the spouse who has them; in addition, the other spouse must have some degree of commitment to the relationship so that the alternatives of the other spouse represent a real threat" (215). If Pat does not care deeply about Chris anymore, he may not become terribly upset by Chris's affair with another man, and Chris may not be able to use this new interest in a power play to win Pat back. According to systems theory, this change of feelings will affect the mutual influence and punctuation of messages. Remaining in the relationship requires system recalibration if the affair continues.

Couples may enter a relationship with unequal power, but the relationship can achieve balance over time. One family member may have most of the power in one area, and both may perceive their power as balanced. Also, the sharing of decisions and tasks causes the systemic balancing principle to operate. Many couples may attempt to develop family themes that stress equality of power, and those with children may encourage sharing of power with them. Finally, themes such as "Each person is an individual" or "We respect all opinions" may lead to shared power.

> "In the beginning of our relationship, Jack, who is older, tended to dominate. He had a lover for several years, and when that commitment ended, he made up his mind to be more autonomous in any future relationship. I resented his treating me as if I were his former partner and assuming that we would conflict in similar situations in the same way. His behavior limited my trust in our relationship. Now that we have been together over five years, he realizes that the past is not the present. We can make joint decisions, and both of us are much happier. Power flows more equally between us."

Each family uses a variety of power sources relevant to its needs and the personalities involved. In some families, traditional roles, including the biosocial issue of male dominance, are clearly defined, and because no one challenges them, the family operates as if that were the only way to function. In other families, negotiation has resulted in mutually acceptable compromises on power issues. The following section considers the development of power within marital and family systems.

DEVELOPMENT OF POWER IN FAMILY SYSTEMS

Because of the systemic nature of a family relationship, power occurs in a transactional manner. An alcoholic cannot control a spouse unless the nonalcoholic spouse permits it. A mother relinquishes her own personal control when she gives an "acting-out" child power over her. Only the small child, who has limited means of resisting power moves, must accept certain power outcomes; for example, an abused toddler has few means of resisting punishment. Women have argued that they also have limited means of resisting power, because in our culture, power outcomes have been largely, and sometimes unfairly, managed by men. Society has affected the development of power within families.

These thoughts about power relationships relate to family boundaries, themes, and biosocial issues. If a family decides that each member, regardless of sex, should develop his or her potential in order to be self-sufficient, the power process and outcomes will differ from a family that believes men should take care of women. This belief limits the boundaries and possible future power options of female members. If, however, the family cultivates a theme of achievement for every member—"The Nicholsens rank at the top of their classes" or "The Jones family will be active in politics and public service"—the power dimensions will reflect these goals. Over time, the family system creates patterns of power that reveal to outsiders how these themes operate.

Types of Power Patterns

Spousal authority may be examined by the number and type of areas over which each spouse exercises authority. The spouse with the greatest range of authority has the highest relative authority. Spouses may have shared authority, where there are areas of life jointly managed. There are four authority types: wife-dominant, husband-dominant, syncratic, and autonomic. In husband- or wife-dominated families, major areas of activity are influenced and controlled by the dominant one.

"Mother decides things and gets her way by using her temper, yelling, screaming, and crying if Dad or any of us strongly object. Father determines when to cut the grass, the time for sons to get haircuts, how long my sisters can wear their hair, where to eat or go for entertainment or groceries, and when any of us kids can leave the house after supper. I wait and wait—until he finally decides when he

wants to eat dinner, which determines when I can get ready to go out, and so on. I never get anywhere on time."

Dominance by one spouse permeates all areas of family power: the use of resources or bases, power processes, and power outcomes. One spouse demonstrates control of power in the system, and the other accepts such control. Thus, one spouse often orchestrates and the other implements the power. However, the type of power that families use depends upon the mutual activity or inactivity of all members of the family. Support groups for families with addicted members recognize how power transactionally affects all members. In these groups, family members learn how to cope with some of the power maneuvers they encounter. This includes learning how to ignore power moves that hook family members into nonproductive behaviors. Highly skewed relationships, such as extreme husband or wife dominance, have greater violence (Allen and Straus 1979).

A further finding indicates that the lower a husband's economic and prestige resources were relative to his wife's, the more likely he would use physical violence (coercive power) to maintain a dominant male power position (85).

The amount of violence or abuse each parent experienced in his or her family-of-origin relates directly to the use of coercive power in families. The frequent observation of abuse in the family-of-origin consistently indicated a risk for wife abuse (Marshall and Rose 1988, 414).

In couples with more equally divided power, the structure can be described as either syncratic or autonomic. A syncratic relationship, characterized by much shared authority and joint decision making, implies that each spouse has a strong say in all important areas.

"When Jim and I married, we agreed never to make big decisions alone, and we've been able to live with that. This way we share the risks and the joys of whatever happens. It just works out best between us if we wait on deciding all important matters until we sound out each other's opinions. Neither of us wants to force the other to accept something disliked. It's when we decide over the little things that I know that each of us respects the rights of the other and wants equal consideration."

In the autonomic power structure, the couple divides authority; that is, the husband and wife have relatively equal authority but in different areas. Each spouse is completely responsible for specific matters. The division of areas usually coincides closely with role expectations.

Shared power situations reflect specific agreements or role definitions about who controls what situations. The wife might have more power over the budget, vacation plans, and choice of new home and the husband more power over the selection of schools, buying anything with a motor in it, and whether the family moves to another state.

Power and Marital Satisfaction

As you might imagine, certain power arrangements can increase marital satisfaction. High levels of marital satisfaction occur most frequently among equalitarian (syncratic or autonomic) couples, followed by husband-dominated couples, and least among wife-dominated couples (Corrales 1975, 198). In a study of 776 couples in the Los Angeles area, over two-thirds of husband-dominant, syncratic, and autonomic couples reported themselves "very satisfied"; however, only 20 percent of wife-dominant couples were "very satisfied" (Raven, Centers, and Rodriges 1975, 234).

Research by Corrales also suggests that women do not seem satisfied when dominating a marriage. In a study in which the wives indicated they dominated, they gave themselves low satisfaction scores. This outcome suggests that wives exercise power by default to compensate for a weak or ignoring husband (211). In this same investigation, one-quarter of the systems were wife-dominant; these same wives had only 10 percent of the authority regarding final decision making. Corrales explained this discrepancy as follows: "The spouse with little authority may seek less visible ways to make her or his power felt. Interactive control appears to be one such way" (208). One sidelight is that husbands in wife-dominant marriages indicated they were not as dissatisfied as their wives. Kolb and Straus (1974) explained this outcome with their "role incapacity" theory, which posits that when a man relinquishes his traditional leadership role or fails to carry out his part of an equalitarian relationship, the wife becomes dissatisfied because she feels she married a less competent man.

Wives and husbands react differently to dissatisfaction in marriage (White 1989). Men tend to take a coercive stance toward their partners, whereas women take an affiliative position that uses communication strategies such as reconciling, resolving, and appealing to fairness. Men's coercive power was expressed in strategies that indicate rejecting, blaming, or using guilt. If the question arises, Do men or women have more power? remember that historically research has indicated that men overestimate and women underestimate their power in the family. Self-reports reveal that individuals may underestimate their power and overestimate their partner's.

DeTurck and Miller found that husbands and wives who carefully discriminated and then adapted messages to their partner's individualistic beliefs, attitudes, needs, and desires experienced greater marital satisfaction and better conjugal power outcomes than those couples who communicated using more stereotyped cultural, social, and role expectations. Both husbands and wives were happier when they had the abilities to exert social control over their partner. This kind of conjugal power, however, influenced greatly wives' self-esteem, but not their husbands'. An interesting sidelight of their research using the Conjugal Understanding Measure, is that adaptability frequently determines the quality of marital relationships. Although earlier research indicated that the circumplex model of family systems viewed cohesion and adaptability as independent family functions, researchers found that cohesion was a consequence of the couples' adaptability (Olson, Sprenkle, and Russell 1979).

Wives' successful use of coercive control enhanced their self-esteem and confidence so that other family members appreciated their company. This research and other studies indicated that as women adopt more male-oriented persuasion tactics, they equalize the power between the spouses and now suffer less from the challenge (deTurck 1985; Burgoon, Dillard, and Doran 1984). Males used more coercive power in resolving conflict if either they or their wives were dissatisfied. Although women had higher rates of coercive behavior overall than their spouses, the use of this kind of power was not related to their marital satisfaction with partners or their self-esteem (White 1989, 101).

The type of power processes used by couples can often be traced to their experience in their respective families-of-origin. Growing up in a family in which people were physically controlled may lead a person to adopt the same method, particularly when other alternatives are not immediately available. A son who had a dominant father may find it very difficult to visualize himself in an equal-dominance relationship with his wife.

"My German father and my Irish mother both exercised power over us in different ways. My father used to beat us whenever we got out of line, and that power move was very obvious. On the other hand, my mother never touched us, but she probably exercised greater power through her use of silence. Whenever we did something she did not approve of, she just stopped talking to us. It was as if we did not exist. Most of the time, the silent treatment lasted for a few hours, but sometimes it would last for a few days. My brother used to say it was so quiet 'you could hear a mouse pee on a cotton ball.' I hated the silence worse than the beatings."

A family-of-origin serves as the first power base in which a child learns to function. The strategies used there are often repeated later in the child's adult life. Certain types of power strategies, such as silence, seem to move from generation to generation, because such control was learned at an early age and often not questioned.

Children and Power

Children have great influence on family power situations. Early studies often ignored them, possibly on the assumption that parents controlled decisions and that children had to follow their directions. Traditionally, parents are expected to control and be responsible for their children's behavior. The law also supports the idea of power in the parents' hands. In no other relationship within a family system does a person have such complete power over another as parents do over young children. Children need to be included in any study of power because of their influence on making the family system more than the sum of its parts. Parents replying to questionnaires indicated that they possessed power, but when trained observers used behavioral methods to measure power, they found that children definitely exercised power in a family (Turk and Bell 1972, 220).

A whole new power scheme emerges when two family members become three, or four, or more. Alliances can form between and among family members, upsetting the original balance of power. The door is open for two-against-one power plays and all other possible combinations. In an era of smaller families, an only child or two siblings may have four living grandparents who divert many resources to the grand-children or the parental generation to support them in child rearing. Thus, the children gain resources for themselves and the system.

The number of children definitely affects power because couples who have been married fewer years and had fewer children were more satisfied with their marriage than those couples married longer and with more children (White, 95).

"When I was growing up, I was very close to my father and we usually agreed on things, so my mother began to see it as 'the two of you against me.' I thought it was silly because we enjoyed being together, and we did not mean to be against her, but as I've grown older, I can understand that she felt left out. Now, I often feel outmatched when my son and my husband agree on things and I do not."

Power Interactions and Alliances.   Often, children influence the interaction and outcomes of power struggles in families by using power plays such as interruptions or illness. Adolescents identify with the parent who has the most power over their behaviors; they see the father as holding more outcome-control power (McDonald 1980b). They seemed to identify more closely with their same-sex parent, making for power alliances (Adcock and Yang 1984). However, daughters identify with the father when they perceive that he has more legitimate power than the mother. Sons identify with the mother only to the degree that she controls outcomes and has referent power.

In many families, one spouse consciously or unconsciously co-opts a child into an ally position in order to increase the strength of his or her position. Similarly, children become adept at playing one parent against the other. "Daddy said I could do it" or "If Mom was here she'd let me" has echoed through most homes as new alliances form. Blended families are especially vulnerable as children quote ex-spouse's ideas and unsolicited opinions.

Alliances take varied forms. Many alliances often follow a same-sex bias, and boys and girls are expected to be like their respective parents. "My mother and I stick up for each other against the men" represents such a power move.

"I couldn't believe it when I heard my four-year-old grandson announce to his mother and two-year-old sister, 'The men will go to the store; the women will stay home.' He then turned and followed me out to the car. When I asked him about it, he replied, 'Men do things together.' "

Parents may form an alliance against the children, establishing an inflexible boundary that prevents negotiation or discussion. The extended family can become a part of the power block to be used in both everyday and crisis situations. Single-parent families display unique power alliances, due to the presence of one adult. A potential advantage for a child in a single-parent family is that the child may negotiate directly with the parent for immediate answers and have direct personal power (Wieting and McLaren 1975, 97). A single mother cannot say, "I'll let you know after I talk it over with your father." However, the same child cannot form a parent-child alliance to try to change a decision the way a child can in a two-parent family. Yet either the parent or the child can create an alliance with a grandparent. Blended families often contend with children's playing one side of the family against the other. "She can't tell me what to do, she's not my real mother" is the kind of communication that may cause years of pain as new roles are negotiated.

Some alliances continue in families over a period of time; others exist only for reaching a specific decision. The results of past alliances can obligate family members to feel they must support another on an issue to repay a debt; for example: "Roy helped me convince Dad to let me buy a new ten-speed bike. Now I ought to help him argue with Dad to get his own car." Wives and husbands can also form alliances with one another or their children and behave in this way. Alliances in some families demand loyalty and "pay-offs" that affect a fair use of power in the family system. It is also a way members of families adapt to the needs and frustrations of living together in the same system. Alliance members are able to pool their individual assets so as to increase their chances of dominance. Parents should not ignore their adult power responsibilities, and no child should feel persuaded to assume premature responsibilities (Beavers 1982).

Power Development. Although young children exercise power, they develop more independent power as they grow older when they demand and can handle more power within the family structure. Whereas a six-year-old may fight for a later bedtime, a sixteen-year-old fights for independence. A school-age child may begin to have expertise in some areas unknown to his or her parents, thereby gaining power. Each of you has seen a small child explain computers, metrics, or a board game to a confused adult. Parents often provide their children with educational opportunities and material advantages they never had. The resulting knowledge and prestige can give children an additional advantage over their parents in power struggles. Adolescence is a difficult time in certain families as sons and daughters rebel against normative parental power, yet for adaptable systems the adolescent's talents and skills may be welcome.

As families change, the original power relationship of a couple undergoes enormous modification as the family network increases, fragments, or solidifies. In addition to developmental issues, many other forces, such as separation from the family-of-origin, affect changes in family power. Outside influences that affect the family—vary from inflation and environmental factors to changing cultural norms. Parents' competency in relating their needs and desires, first to one another and then to their children, affects power. Spouses' or children's acceptance or rejection of these requests influences power outcomes. The increasing or decreasing independence or interdependence of the couple alters power in the entire family system. If a spouse leaves, or falls ill or dies, the remaining parent may return to the family-of-origin seeking everything from shelter to advice. The single parent left with children must modify family power processes. Power structures are not static. The family power structure changes constantly as members achieve or change goals.

COMMUNICATION STRATEGIES AND POWER

Many families develop predictable communication strategies for addressing power issues, yet any given strategy is effective only if it is met with a response that engages it. Such is the transactional nature of communication.

Sample Strategies

Confirming, disconfirming, and rejecting behaviors are strategies that affect power. These three strategies can become a part of power messages as family members attempt to separate and connect in one-up, one-down subsystems. In a one-up position, one family member attempts to exercise more power control over one or more other members. The one-down member accepts from the one-up member the control implied in the messages.

Confirming implies acknowledgment and may be used to gain power as one tries to get another to identify with him or her, or as one tries to give rewards in order to gain power. The careful, nonjudgmental listener may wittingly or unwittingly gain power through the identification or information learned by such behavior. A highly complimentary father may be given power by a child who needs positive support. Such approaches to marital power are found in certain self-help books that exhort wives to use positive, confirming approaches as a way to gain power in the marital relationship.

The "silent treatment" probably represents the most powerful and most often used disconfirming behavior—a behavior that does not acknowledge the other person's existence. One family member can put another in a one-down power position through the punishment strategy of disconfirmation. "I ignore him; he'll come around" represents such an effort. On the other hand, disconfirming a power message can serve as an effective method of rejecting power. The child who pretends not to hear "clean up your room" messages effectively deflects the parental power, at least for a while.

Rejecting messages tie directly to punishment messages and are often used as control in family power plays. "I hate you" or "I don't care what you say" may effectively halt control attempts, just as "If you don't behave, you can't go" may serve to pull a reluctant family member into line. The negative conflict behaviors of displacement, denial, disqualification, distancing, and sexual withholding can also be used as rejecting power moves.

Self-disclosure serves as a major means of gaining intimacy within a relationship, but it can also be used as a power strategy as one attempts to control the other through the "information power" gained by self-disclosure. For example, when a self-disclosure is thrown back at a spouse during a fight, that person loses power. "Well, you had an affair, so how can you talk?"

Self-disclosure may be used as a means of offering power to a loved one in an intimate relationship. The disclosure gives power to the listener in an effort to gain connectedness. Such sharing involves risk and gives the listener "information power," which he or she could use to cause pain or separation in the relationship. In such cases, the more knowledgeable person has the capacity to control the relationship.

"One of the most meaningful times in my life occurred when my teenage daughter and I had an all-night session about love, sex, and growing-up problems. It was the first time I honestly told her about what I went through growing up and how we faced some of the same things. I had always kept those things to myself, but I suddenly realized that she shouldn't feel like she was different or bad because of her feelings. It's scary to tell your daughter your faults or fears, but it certainly resulted in a closer relationship between us."

Power Transactions

According to a transactional view of relationships, power must be given as well as taken. In short, it is negotiated between/among family members. This transactional quality can be seen in the research of Rogers-Millar and Millar (1979), in which they examine the distinction between dominance and domineering behavior. They defined domineering as the sending of "one-up messages," or verbal statements claiming the right to dominate; for example, "Be sure to have my supper ready at 6:00 P.M." Domineeringness comes from an individual's behavior, whereas dominance relates to dyadic relational behavior (Courtright, Millar, and Rogers-Millar 1979, 181). Courtright and colleagues' research focused on the area of power processes; they studied the messages exchanged between spouses as they accepted or rejected one another's statements. Pure dominance meant that all one-up remarks made by an individual were followed by a one-down response from the other.

Correlating domineering behavior to self-report data, Rogers-Millar and Millar found that "higher rates of wife domineeringness related to lower marital and communication satisfaction for both partners and higher role strain" (244). They found some further important results when they analyzed the interaction data, or messages between the spouses. The dominance of one spouse correlated positively to the number of support statements (i.e., agreement, acceptance, approval remarks) and negatively to the number of nonsupport statements made by the other spouses. Nonsupport statements were in the form of rejections, disagreements, or demands. Talk-overs, defined as verbal interruptions or intrusions that succeed in taking over the communication while another is speaking, occurred more frequently in couples who used the domineering style.

Ken: "I've got to tell you about this wonderful movie I saw last . . ."
Kim: "You won't believe who I saw in the bar last night."

Ken: "This movie has such beautiful . . ."

Kim: "He came over to me, acting as if nothing happened and tried to buy me a beer."

In both wife-domineering and wife-dominant interactions, the discussions were longer. The reverse was true of husbands. A second study provided additional conclusions: the more domineering one spouse was, the more domineering the partner became. This indicated a more defensive or combative style of conversation developed from a domineering style (Courtright et al.). Frequent question asking characterized the wife's style of interaction when the husband dominated (Rogers-Millar and Millar). The more domineering the husband, the less accurate were both spouses' predictions about the other's satisfaction with the marriage. The same held true for domineering wives in predicting their mates' satisfaction. The researchers suggested that if you do not want to be dominated, you should increase your domineeringness. However, they added that if you do so, be prepared to accept the possibility that both your satisfaction and your partner's will decrease.

Other aspects of one-up, one-down communication have been described by Haley (1974) as dysfunctional communication strategies. He suggests that helplessness will influence another person's behavior as much as, if not more than, direct authoritarian demands. One who acts helplessly defines the relationship as one in which he or she wants the other to take care of him or her (371). This kind of behavior in a relationship can be avoided by using qualifications in part of the message that indicate that an individual takes responsibility for his or her decisions. For example, Carlos might say to his brother, "I want your opinion, but I know it's my problem to solve." This approach to communication lessens the likelihood of control by another, thus giving persons possession of their own powers. Thus, the communication strategies used to enhance relationships or to increase intimacy also may be used to gain power.

In order to achieve cohesion, each family has to work out a communication pattern that allows intimacy without overpowering certain members. Corrales states, "In this culture, behavior that is more conducive to building self and other esteem seems to be more effectively communicated in an equalitarian interaction structure than in either type of dominant structure" (216). The equalitarian structure includes the syncratic and autonomic types of power sharing. In either of these family types, individuals can deal honestly with their feelings and aspirations. Their more open nature encourages freer communication exchanges than either the husband- or wife-dominant types.

Steinor (1978) distinguished between "gentle power" and "control power." Gentle power sends the message: "I can give you what I feel and think. You can understand it and you can compare and decide." This makes people powerful. Ideally, to use communication effectively to counteract the negative aspects of power, there can be no power plays between the persons involved. Steinor suggests that power should not be used to rescue others from solving their own problems. When parents take over their children's problems, they also assume power that is not rightfully theirs. Husbands, wives, or lovers who, through power plays, make decisions for the other, reduce that partner's power potential. An equalitarian family relationship requires that each member have the power to solve the problems he or she encounters.

All human beings find themselves in power struggles in all areas of their lives. Just as power struggles in the larger social system affect the family, so too, family struggles influence how one functions at work or school. Individuals and families can operate more effectively when they can identify power issues and develop a repertoire of communication strategies to address these issues.

CONCLUSION

This chapter presented an application of power issues to the family. It discussed power bases, power processes, and power outcomes as described by McDonald's model and indicated how they affect cohesion and adaptability in family systems. The research has indicated that a rigid power structure, characterized by dominance and little sharing, restricts family flexibility, reduces cohesion, and adversely affects satisfaction in families. Power in the system changes as the family system grows and develops. Spouses create power patterns such as wife-dominant, husband-dominant, syncratic, and autonomic. Children wield power, often through power plays that gain attention. Families often involve member alliances that make certain issues predictable. Each family serves as a context for certain predictable communication strategies that fail or succeed only as they function within the transactional context. All power maneuvers take place within the boundaries the family has established; thus, all communication and activities that take place affect the images, themes, and degree of unity, or cohesion, the family desires. Power operates within a dynamic, growing, interdependent, transactional family system. The sum total of family power is greater than the individual power of each member.

IN REVIEW

1. How may power affect a family's cohesion and adaptability?
2. Describe how cultural and gender patterns influence the basis of power used in family systems.
3. List ways in which power might be effectively shared in an equalitarian family.
4. Analyze the power resources used regularly by members of a real or fictional family. Indicate how members use communication to convey their use of these resources.
5. Describe the type of power exhibited by a real or literary couple. If power has changed over time, what accounts for the change?

CHAPTER 8

Decision Making

Decisions, large and small, test a family's adaptability. Decisions enable a family to change behaviors that harm members or to create opportunities for members. However, decisions require cooperation, insight, and communication skills that family members do not equally possess or practice. Families experience a constant struggle between individual members' needs to assert their independence and yet remain interdependent and achieve a sense of wholeness in the system. Although families often fear change because it introduces uncertainty into the system, families cannot not change (Bochner and Eisenberg 1987). Families adjust to stresses by finding ways through decision making to hang on to a sense of stability.

> *"Both Mom and Dad work overtime. The oldest one home is in charge of decisions that involve those in the house. For example, when my older brother is home, he makes decisions on who can go somewhere or what friend can come over. If he's at work, I take over. My next younger sister does the same when I have something after school."*

In McDonald's model of power (Chapter 7, Figure 7-1), decision making appears under power outcomes. Decisions carried out by family members become the way power is implemented. Decisions implement not only power but reinforce the family rules, themes, images, and roles.

Decision making, like power, is a process that belongs to the family system, not to an individual. Therefore, decision making varies greatly among families because each family processes its interactions and resources into roles and power domains differently. Keeping McDonald's model in mind will help you understand how complicated decision making can be in families. Power dimensions permeate decision making. According to Scanzoni and Polonko (1980), decision making means getting things done in a family when one or more family members need to agree with others to accomplish something.

Family decisions require cooperation, insight, and communication skills.

Many decisions have a moral component, involving a sense of what is right or wrong, that affects family behavior. Kohlberg (1969) and Gilligan (1982) stated that moral development progresses through a series of stages, from meeting individual desires, to societal norms, to universal ethical principles. Kohlberg believed morality centers around concepts of justice, but Gilligan found care and responsibility more important in decision making, especially for women (Evans 1987). These differences highlight the inherent complexity of the decision-making process.

Your family differs from a small group that comes together merely for the purpose of doing a particular task. Your family has a history of continuous interaction and consists of a combination of interdependent individuals. Even if the decision-making process results in turmoil, your family remains a unit, although sometimes a factional and unhappy one. This is not true of outside groups. If the members cannot reach a decision, they usually disband rather easily. Short of death, divorce, or moving out, families tend to remain together even if members disagree.

Family decisions can be either instrumental or affective. Instrumental decisions require solving rather mechanical issues, such as getting a job to pay the family bills or providing transportation. Affective decisions relate to emotions or feelings. Epstein, Bishop, and Baldwin (1982) concluded that "families whose functioning is disrupted by instrumental problems rarely, if ever, deal effectively with affective problems. However, families whose functioning is disrupted by affective problems may deal adequately with instrumental problems" (119). Feldman (1982) indicates that women who adopt a traditional role experience difficulty with instrumental problem-solving skills.

The location of a family along the cohesion and adaptability continuum affects their decision-making behavior. Highly enmeshed, rigid families may pressure members to reach predictable and low-risk decisions, because change or separation would be threatening. Disengaged systems may have trouble sharing enough information to make reasonable decisions, whereas families characterized by chaos probably experience few real decisions that stand.

In order to understand the family as a decision-making system, you need to examine (1) a model of decision making, (2) types of family decision making, (3) modes of family governance, (4) steps in decision making, and (5) factors that influence decision making. This chapter extends the study of power to look in greater detail at decision making as a negotiation process that influences power outcomes. Who influences the decision, and how is the influence felt? Who decides what, when, and how certain necessary aspects of family life are resolved? The answers will vary according to how communication is used to maintain the way rules, roles, and power operate within a given family.

"My brother, Tim, a very dominant personality, has always needed to be heard! This was particularly difficult for his youngest brother, Denny. If Denny disagreed with Tim, Tim would put Denny down and call him an idiot—especially if Denny would make a different decision, not necessarily a 'wrong' decision. Tim was older and assumed he made the rules and knew more information on all subjects."

DECISION-MAKING MODEL

The ways in which decisions are made differ greatly within families. Wood and Talmon (1983) present the idea that decision making represents a type of territory that a family develops. In this "decision space," the family allows some decisions to be made by individuals, whereas other decisions require approval from certain subsystems or the whole family. For example, Marissa may ask the whole family's opinion of her Girl Scout project, whereas her parents' decision to go on a trip without the children may not be submitted to the whole family for approval. Sometimes family members take over another's decision space. For example, a father may offer suggestions and persuasions that are not needed or welcomed yet pressure the person or subsystem making the decision. The following model should help clarify the decision-making process.

This model supports the idea that marital negotiations that lead to decisions can be analyzed in terms of social contexts, processes, and outcomes. In drawing upon earlier work by Straus (1979), Scanzoni and Polonko devised this model to demonstrate the ongoing nature of process and outcome in decision making. They divided family social context dimensions into four areas:

1. *Composition,* meaning ages of spouses, cohabitors, or lovers; length of marriage, ages and number of children; and time available before deadline.
2. *Resources,* including amount of education, salary, job status, amount of work each year, and experience negotiating decisions.
3. *Orientations,* including self-esteem, sex-role attitudes, amount of concern about the outcome, and importance of the issue.
4. *Actor's orientations,* referring to each partner's past bargaining experience and how the actor (spouse) perceives that his or her partner will negotiate. This includes perceptions the couple has about how hard each will bargain, how fairly, and how cooperatively. It also includes how much each partner can be trusted to follow through on decisions.

The main part of Figure 8-1 indicates how the "one-shot" negotiation works. For example, Emily and Carmen negotiate a problem, making use of various strategies and tactics and modifying their respective positions as necessary. The vertical arrow at the bottom of the model represents the interaction that takes place in the course of the bargaining process. The outcome that results is labeled "a" on the time line at the bottom of the model. Once this outcome has been reached, it becomes a part of the social context within which additional decision-making negotiations occur, affecting the future outcome "b." Outcome "b," in turn, provides context for outcome "c," and so on.

This model emphasizes the importance of bargaining as a mediator of power. Scanzoni and Polonko state that this idea "sensitizes us to the notion that power is intrinsically associated with ongoing movement, or process, rather than outcome" (33). This model makes us aware that outcomes often do not end issues. Family members are not always equally satisfied with decisions. The model provides for repeated series of negotiations occurring over varied periods of time before true consensus happens. Power resides in each partner's or child's shifts or changes in bargaining position. The degree of flexibility, or willingness to compromise, enhances the probability of reaching consensus.

Figure 7–1 _____
A Model of Explicit Marital Negotiation

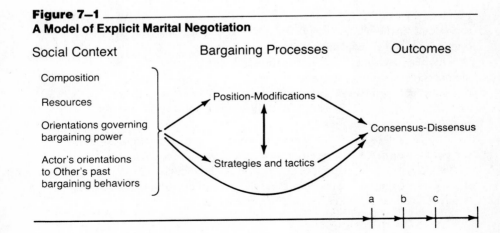

Social context variables—such as disparity in tangible resources (schooling or salary), differences in intangible variables (self-concept or sex roles), and insights into a family's decision-making history—usually have significant impact on process and outcomes variables (Hill and Scanzoni 1982). Research indicates that the greater the education disparity, the larger the amount of disparity will be on three other dimensions: income, self-esteem, and perceptions of past bargaining. Income and self-esteem positively correlate, as do self-esteem and perceptions of past decisions. Other findings show that style of communication has a powerful pervasive effect in determining spouses' responses. A defensive style increases the number of disagreements, as do verbal strategies that are ego centered and evoke memories of past decisions. Decision making is a multifaceted process. Understanding the process helps us determine the meaning of an outcome. Other aspects of this model will be discussed later in this chapter.

TYPES OF DECISION MAKING

Each family has its own way of reaching decisions on issues. In his early study of family decision-making patterns, Turner (1970) differentiates decision-making outcomes according to the degree of acceptance and commitment of family members. He identifies three kinds of decision making that remain valid categories: (1) consensus, (2) accommodation, and (3) de facto decisions (98–100).

Consensus

In consensus decision making, discussion continues until agreement is reached. This may require compromise and flexibility, but the desired goal is a solution acceptable to all involved. Because all family members have a part in the decision and a chance to influence it, they share the responsibility for carrying it out. In some families, all major purchases are decided on the basis of group consensus. This type of decision making does not occur as frequently as the other two.

"Every Tuesday night is family night, and everyone must be present from 7:00 P.M. until 8:30 P.M. This is the time when we make certain family decisions that affect all of us. We may make a joint decision about vacations and try to find a plan that will please everyone. Sometimes Dad will let us decide on a big item to buy with his bonus. Each of the six of us has to finally agree for us to go ahead with the decision."

Accommodation

Accommodation occurs when some family members consent to a decision, not because they totally agree, but because they believe that further discussion will be unproductive. They may give their consent with a smile or with bitterness. The accommodation decision may represent a great deal of give-and-take, but no one really achieves what he or she desires. For example, you may want to go to church family camp, whereas someone else may want to play in three ball games that weekend. Eventually, the family may agree to go on a picnic, and the baseball player gets to play one game in the schedule. No one's wants have really been satisfied with the decision; individual wants have been merely placated or postponed to some future time. This kind of decision making tends to leave some or all family members disappointed. When decisions are made this way, factions may emerge, and one family member may feel obligated to repay the others who argued for his or her goals. This type of decision making may occur in families that pressure for high cohesiveness by maintaining their themes and boundaries.

"It's just easier to agree with Dad and let him think his ideas are what we all want than to argue with him. He's bound to win anyway, because he controls the money. Sometimes when we humor his wishes, Mom, my sister, and I can then get our way on what we want to do—sort of a trade-off!"

Sometimes accommodation results from voting as family members line up on one side of an issue and the majority wins. The minority views held by losing family members might have genuine merit, but the losers accept majority rule rather than cause trouble. Anyone who loses consistently finds this to be an unacceptable way to make decisions.

One danger of accommodation is that it encourages dominance behavior. Too often, decisions favor those who dominate, and less aggressive family members develop a pattern of submitting to their wishes. Accommodation may appear to be a decision-making approach that furthers family cohesion and adaptability, but this is not the case. The results are temporary at best, because the communication that goes into accommodative decisions represents compromises made by members out of fear or lack of equal power. Such decisions over time accent separateness and lessen connectedness among family members. Accommodative decision making can also enforce negative family themes and images while implementing stereotyped thinking on biosocial issues, especially in cases of male dominance.

De Facto Decisions

What happens when the family makes no decision or when the discussion reaches an impasse? Usually, one member will go ahead and act in the absence of a clear-cut decision. This is a de facto decision—one made without direct family approval but nevertheless made to keep the family functioning. A fight over which model of television to buy while televisions are on sale may be continued until the sale nears an end and Dad finally buys one by himself.

De facto decisions encourage family members to complain about the results, because they played either no part or a passive part in the decisions. The family member who acts in a vacuum created by the lack of a clear-cut decision has to endure the harassment or lack of enthusiasm of those who must accept the decision. Again, dominant family members can easily emerge victorious in too many decisions; their wishes are carried out, whereas those of others are unfairly suppressed.

"We talked about doing something together as a family last Sunday afternoon. I wanted to bowl. Mom wanted to see a movie. My sister wanted to go to the amusement park. Dad thought a ball game or ride in the country would be OK. No one pulled us together. Finally, it got too late to do anything. Dad took a nap, Mom read, I went over to Chuck's house, and my sister went swimming with a friend."

Although many families, particularly rigid ones, seem to use only one type of decision making, more flexible families vary their styles according to the issues. Critical issues may require consensus, whereas less important concerns can be resolved by a vote or a de facto decision. As we will see later, the style of decision making experienced in a couple's families-of-origin has a great effect on the decision-making styles adopted when the partners form their own system.

STYLES OF GOVERNANCE

In an interesting approach that combines ideas about family power and decision making, Broderick (1975) set up three styles of governance based upon Kohlberg's (1964) study of children in different cultures and the universal steps in reasoning that they go through to reach moral maturity. The lowest level of reasoning for decisions was hedonistic self-interest, or zero-sum; the next was based on conventionality and obedience to rules; the third was based on social contract and principles of conscience (118).

Zero-Sum Decisions

Applied to decision making in conflict situations, the first and most primitive way to reach a decision is simply to insist upon your own way. Broderick labeled this approach a hedonistic, "zero-sum" power confrontation. This means that in an argument, one person wins and one loses. The sum of their wins (+) and losses (-) is always zero. You have seen this operate between small children who refuse to share. Instead, they shout, "That's mine, you can't have it." Unfortunately, such behavior does not always stop as family members move beyond the toddler stage. In this kind of decision making, each family member insists upon his or her own way without compromise. This approach can lead to threats, yelling, browbeating, and slanting of the truth.

Broderick suggests only two circumstances in which families could survive using zero-sum confrontations. For example, if the wife and husband are closely matched, with each getting an equal number of wins and losses, the relationship could continue. Also, if the consistently losing partner feels there are no alternatives and lacks the emotional or financial resources to leave, he or she may remain in the relationship in spite of the heavy psychological cost of lower self-esteem. Children can be victims in this kind of household, because they have no way to escape. Young people caught in this kind of family make such statements as "I can't wait until I graduate and can get out of here" or "I don't like it, but it's not worth fighting over." In time, the losers either leave the family or define their role as second class. In zero-sum governance, decisions are static and predictable.

The maintenance of a zero-sum relationship requires coercive power, or punishment, especially the use of fear and threat. Information is of little use, because too much evidence might weaken the position of the hedonist family member who insists upon his or her views. Of even less use is reward power, because the "winner" does not usually sense the need to give anything in return for acceptance of the decision.

"In our house you went along with parental decisions or you were punished—it was as simple as that. I had one brother who was a rebel, and my father would beat him. My mother usually went along with whatever my father said because I think she was scared of him, too."

Some family members use force in decision making. Violence is a problem-solving method learned in a family setting; this reflects society's attitude toward permitting the use of physical force in intimate relationships (Steinmetz 1977; Ford 1983). The method parents use to solve their problems becomes the method usually employed to solve parent-and-child and child-and-child problems. Thus, the parental approach to decision making becomes the model for other family interactions. When verbal aggression and physical force characterize the parents' attempts to make decisions, the same behavior appears in that of a parent with his or her children or between the children when they disagree. As unfortunate as it seems, many people use fists rather than words to settle family problems.

According to the process model of decision making, to be a constant winner requires defensive behaviors and putting up with the loser's submissive behaviors. To lose constantly requires a person to live with low self-esteem and continually try to subvert the more powerful person. The images maintained in zero-sum family relationships foster separateness and reduce the chance for much cohesion. The pattern of adaptability required to maintain zero-sum relationships does too little to develop positive self-esteem for individual members within the family system. In many families, victories are hollow because they curb or destroy ideas and limit decision-making skills in others that might lead to better and more meaningful solutions.

Decisions Based on Rules

A second mode of governance involves the creation and enforcement of rules. A family may live most of its life according to the rules and avoid certain power clashes, as well as certain opportunities for growth. Rules affect decision making because, over a period of time, they become accepted ways to operate when problems arise. Rules evolve from the social contexts of the family members plus repeated family interactions. Broderick distinguished among three types of rules used in family decision making: (1) rules of direct distribution, (2) rules of designated authority, and (3) rules for negotiation.

> *"After almost twenty years of working in banking, I decided to return to graduate school to make an eventual career change. My wife worked part-time, and we used up much of our savings. As part of the process, we decided ahead of time how much money could be spent for different necessities, and we stuck to it. The children were given a clothing allowance, and they had to live within it or use their babysitting money. Although there was some grumbling, most of us stuck to the rules, and we were able to get through a rough period."*

Rules of Direct Distribution. Rules of direct distribution imply the dividing of family resources directly among members. This includes the distribution of family income into the amounts available for food, housing, tuition, vacation, and entertainment. Similar distribution can be made of living space—which child gets which room or has to share a bedroom; which shelves belong to each child or parent; and where personal items are to be kept. These rules function to avoid confrontations and reduce power plays in the family through the presolution of possible problems. Rules of this kind require that family members carry around in their heads a whole series of predetermined decisions about matters of family living.

Rules of Designated Authority. Designated authority rules indicate who has the authority over certain areas. For example, Mother pays the bills and, thus, collects the checks and does the budgeting. Dad does the painting and refinishing and, thus, decides on the materials to use. Lois plays in the band and, thus, does not need to explain her absence for practice after school or help with housework on weekends when the band travels. Sometimes rules allocating authority contain a series of steps. For example, either Dad or Mom can go out for an evening with friends if the other knows who is going and where. Either can veto such a decision if his or her job requires overtime work and the children will be home alone. This type of rule, dispersing authority, often relates closely to roles in the family. Whoever controls the kitchen and all of the activities that take place there has the authority to make the decisions in that area.

> *"As an immigrant Assyrian family living in the United States, my family is quite different. I would describe our family as 'closed' because we have learned that this works better if we are to keep our culture, language, religion, and traditions. My father makes all important decisions. Thus, we don't make decisions like other families in our neighborhood."*

Rules of designated authority tend to set clear boundaries for who may get involved with what. Certain people may have far more decision-making power than others. Yet children can also have areas of decision making assigned to them. For example, if they do their expected tasks, they can make decisions about their free time. If a son likes to bake and does all of the buying and preparation of baked goods, he may be given the authority over the oven and that part of the kitchen. The autonomic family described in the previous chapter quite often operates its decision making in accordance with this rule.

Rules for Negotiation. The third type of rule is based on negotiation. Over time, families can establish rules that govern the process decision making will follow when conflict occurs. Rules of this type imply greater family input in settling differences. It may mean placing a limit on the amount of force or threat one member can use against another. Certain tactics, such as yelling and hitting, can be outlawed and negotiation done only when all involved agree not to interrupt. This approach implies that the decision reached may require compromise or sacrifice on one or more family members' part. Many current marital or family enrichment programs stress how to negotiate differences according to rules that allow all members of the system some input.

In some families, each person has a right to decide what is negotiable and what is nonnegotiable for himself or herself. Others intimately involved have a right to know what is nonnegotiable and can question or evaluate it, but the final decision is up to the individual and is respected. For example, in some interfaith marriages, couples agree that each partner has the right to continue his or her religion. Thus, the choice to attend church or synagogue services is nonnegotiable.

> *"Ever since the children have grown older, I have declared Saturday as my day to do whatever I desire. It is sacred to me, and I do only what I want on that day, even if somebody else will be disappointed. I am wife or mother to four people during six days of the week. I really need some scheduled time to myself, and Saturday's it!"*

Thus, the third type of rule involves potential negotiation about what is not negotiable. This approach has the potential to increase family cohesion and provide a method for adaptability. To be successful, family members have to communicate their wishes directly to all other members and take responsibility for their comments. Negotiation implies change and flexibility. If this expectancy of later possible change is recognized by the family, its members realize that negotiation can be another communication skill to use to gain adaptability within their system. It can help keep a system open and flexible.

Decisions Based on Principle

Broderick's third mode involves governance by contract or principle. As you might imagine, few families actively operate at this high a level, and those that do usually include older children and adults. It is based on a belief in the basic human goodness of the family members and their desire to put the family's welfare above their own. Individual family members operate on principles of fairness and concern. For example, if either Dad or Mother works late, he or she calls the other and explains. The operating principle is that neither partner unnecessarily inconveniences the other. Both respect the other's right to make overtime decisions, but fair play motivates each of them to inform the other. This prevents one from preparing food that is not eaten or planning activities that later must be cancelled. In this, there is no rule about hours to come and go, but a principle operating that neither will waste the time of the other.

This type of governance works in families with children if the parents have taught them how to use good judgment and value the rights, strengths, and limitations of one another. It requires harmony and cooperation. Disharmony can be handled as a temporary condition that will be resolved by fair decisions that restore balance to a family system. Children realize that they play an integral part in the successful operation of their system. A family might have a contract in which areas of work and play are shared; each member has duties assigned so that time remains for individual and joint family activities. Compromise is a part of this form of governance so that all members' legitimate needs are met.

You have examined both Turner's and Broderick's ways of viewing family decision making. The former relates to the actual behavior, whereas the latter takes more complex issues into consideration because it involves a level of moral reasoning reached by the members. This last approach also carries out Kohlberg's and Gilligan's emphasis upon the importance of justice, care, and responsibility in all decision making. Another way to combine approaches would be to divide them into either policy-guided or non–policy-guided choices. If family policy has been established on a given matter, decision making would then be guided by that policy. This would involve the rules established to deal with similar situations. Non–policy-guided choices could require either accommodation, consensus, or some form of negotiation to reach decisions.

In conflict situations people make decisions by coalitions, judications, and negotiations (Littlejohn 1989, 192) Coalition decisions base outcomes on numbers, with the majority of family members winning and the others losing. This kind of decision making equates to the zero-sum type. In judication, a family member with authority makes the decision, probably a mother or a father. Other family members may be heard, but the outcome is determined by the family member with the power to judge. Negotiation in family decision making would involve two or more family members' making proposals and counterproposals in order to find a solution to a problem. The important feature of negotiation is that its outcome aims to achieve a joint solution that pleases the involved family members, rather than one based on an authoritative (judicial) or numerical (coalition) decision.

STEPS IN DECISION MAKING

No steps in problem solving work in families until members sense that their input in decision making has any chance of support. In dysfunctional families, change through effective decision making gets blocked via maintaining rigid rules and images that protect the status quo. In order for any decision making to take place, it has to be a priority. If it isn't important or the risks involved are perceived to be too great, the process never gets underway. In some families, procrastination avoids decision making until crises occur or deadlines prevent the parents or children from having enough time to negotiate decisions.

Steps are never as simple as they appear. In examining the five problem-solving steps in decision making, it is important to realize that the process may be short-circuited at any point by a family member or subsystem alliance that does not agree with certain choices. Or the family group may reach a decision by skipping some steps.

The first step requires definition of the problem, including isolating the parts of it that family members agree need attention. At this stage it is helpful to make sure everyone understands the problem's key terms in the same way or to establish that the definitions differ. Sometimes differences in meaning cause part of the problem and delay in decision making.

The second step includes an exploration of the problem and analysis of the differences. At this stage, all pros and cons should be debated, with every involved family member's having a chance to be heard.

The third step involves setting up criteria that any solution or decision should meet. Sample criteria might be the following: the family can afford the money to do it; there will be enough time available to do it; the decision will be equitable and not take advantage of any member; the advantages will outweigh possible disadvantages. This important step tends to be overlooked, yet it can help clarify the family's goals and lead to better decisions. It is a listing of what is needed to be fair and just in making a decision that will solve a problem.

The fourth step focuses on listing possible solutions that might solve the problem. In this phase of decision making, alternative ways to solve a problem are brought out. If democracy prevails in the discussion, this step gives submissive family members a chance to express their ideas. All participants should be encouraged to contribute suggestions. In this way, if they have a part in the process and are later outvoted, they can feel that their ideas were at least considered.

The last step requires selecting the best solution for this family at this particular time. The decision made should represent the members' best combined thinking and meet the criteria agreed upon in the third step.

Finally, a plan of action for implementing the decision needs to be agreed upon—a plan that will strengthen and enhance the operation of the family system, because a problem that had reduced the efficiency of the system has been solved. Note the steps followed by the family in this example:

"My two brothers and I and our wives actually went through a formal decision-making process as we decided how to take care of our elderly mother after she was unable to live alone. We went through all kinds of hassles regarding nursing homes, residential facilities, and social security benefits. We had to set a monetary criterion for any solution based on a percentage of our salaries and based on a location that everyone could reach. Mother had to agree to the solution also. We

agreed we could not force our solution on her. Each couple investigated different options, such as specific senior citizen housing options, live-in nurses, nursing homes, and specialized group homes. Then we all sat around and hashed ideas over. We finally reached two options that we could live with—a particular senior citizen facility or a nursing home that accepted people who were not severely ill. We discussed these with my mother, who rejected the nursing home instantly but who agreed to the senior citizen housing facility."

This planned approach to decision making does not just happen in families. In fact, left to their own ways, most families do not solve their problems in an organized way. Many families become bogged down and never get beyond the first or second step.

No matter how decision making occurs, whatever style or type of governance is used, the actual process involves many factors. Unfortunately, it is not a very predictable and streamlined process. In order to understand the complexity of the process, we need to examine what affects family decision making.

FACTORS THAT AFFECT FAMILY DECISION MAKING

Over the years, each family evolves some patterned ways of solving problems. The decision-making process is more than trial and error, although that may be a part of it. Family decisions relate to a variety of factors that explain the actions taken. In this section, we will discuss: (1) how children affect decisions, (2) how gender influences modify outcomes, (3) how the individual's involvement and resources influence decisions, and (4) how time available and quality of communication skills affect family decision making.

The Role of Children in Decision Making

By now, you are fully aware that your family-of-origin experiences affect all areas of your life; thus, your decision-making experiences as a child partially determine your approach to adult decision-making situations. On the other hand, your children may have some interesting effects on family decision-making processes. The arrival of the first child opens the door for the formation of triangles or alliances in the family and provides the first opportunity for a chain network by which decisions may be relayed.

Children often influence decisions by forming alliances with one or the other parent or by presenting a united front to a certain proposed decision. In some families, permanent alliances seem to exist. For example, "Dad, Debbie, and Brad always form an alliance to stick together on issues, and that often leaves Mom and me on the other side."

> *"A trite axiom the two of us share is 'together we stand, divided we fall.' My brother and I took tremendous advantage of the concept of joint pressure throughout our college years. My brother and I dreamed up strategies to combat my parents in order to achieve our ends. At times, we add complexity to the tension-filled situations by pairing one parent off against the other. Sometimes it works, but sometimes we end up losing."*

In certain circumstances, children share the leadership in making decisions. Russell (1979) found that this happened in a family atmosphere in which a child or spouse felt support from other members. This atmosphere also made it easier for a less assertive member to risk taking charge of a problem and trying to solve it (42). Through observations of family members during problem-solving sessions, Kolb and Straus (1974) found children exercising leadership in directing outcomes, but "high child power" was associated with low marital happiness. They thought this result might have been caused by the societal expectation of father leadership, and when he was not the leader, the children felt deprived of leadership. On the other hand, certain parents consciously plan to allow their children opportunities to lead or influence decision making as a way of preparing them for future responsibilities.

In family problem solving, children respond best to positive emotional patterns of communication and perform less effectively when parents express negative emotions. Although negative feelings need to come out in decision making, the way in which they are treated affects the outcomes. The "let it all hang out" philosophy hinders family problem solving (Forgatch 1989). When too many negative feelings surface during decision making, the focus shifts from problem solving to personalities. This triggers more emotional responses, which fuel each other. Children can withdraw or manipulate these situations, both undesirable responses.

Gender Influences

The ways husbands and wives define their roles and responsibilities directly affect family decision making. In a study of couple allocation of responsibility for eighteen family decisions and thirteen tasks, Douglas and Wind (1978) asked husbands and wives to group decisions and tasks into areas of responsibility in their families. The findings revealed basic spousal agreement with a group of wife-dominated activities, including washing and drying the dishes, laundry chores, food budgeting, and buying. Other decisions were joint decisions, such as places to go on vacations, who is invited to dinner, which movie to see, the amount to spend on appliances, what furniture to buy or replace, and if the wife should work.

Couples differed on other decision areas. Wives made more distinctions than did husbands. Certain tasks were perceived as male dominated: getting the car repaired, choosing the liquor, maintaining the yard. The same held true on family financial decisions, such as investments and insurance. On financial decisions, some wives indicated more competence and joint participation and involvement. On clothing decisions, wives indicated they often acted as influencer or consultant.

It is interesting to note that in this study and several earlier ones, the couples had a harder time identifying who made a decision than who performed a task. For example, a husband could not recall who influenced what in the decision to buy a new sofa, or whether he or his wife asked friends over for a barbeque, but he knew who did the dishes regularly and who balanced the checkbook. In talking about how they make decisions, Krueger (1983) concluded that "both spouses tend to avoid singular responsibility" (99). White (1989) found that men use coercion to distance, analyze a situation, and take charge of a problem before it escalates. Women, by contrast, sought affiliation to maintain connections long enough to find a solution, thus maintaining their relatedness (104).

A family's role ideology determines who carries out certain decisions and tasks. Thus, in male-dominant households, the husband will take over the financial decisions and the wife the household operation. Egalitarian couples will make more joint decisions. However, Douglas and Wind found little systemic relationship between couples' role attitudes and responsibility patterns (42). These findings indicate that responsibility in families for various decision areas and tasks seldom demonstrates a dominant authority pattern.

Floyd (1988) conducted a study of couples in problem-solving discussions and found, in decision making, men more often than women misinterpret their partner's communication behaviors, especially nonverbal expressions. This insensitivity results in what Weiss (1984) defined as a "sentiment-override." If the men felt positively toward their partners, they interpreted their communication behaviors positively in spite of the fact that the women were indicating reservations in the decision making. Fitzpatrick (1988) also found wives more accurate in predicting their spouse's feelings. Her separates were the least accurate. In casual conversations, she discovered both independents and mixed couples employed challenges and justifications to assert control over spouses, whereas traditionals used orders in decision making (133).

Spitze concluded from a number of studies that employed women had more power than their husbands in decisions about money matters (1988). However, women who didn't work outside the home, but indeed did work on family farms, had no more and possibly less influence on decision making (Lyson 1985; Rosenfeld 1986). Doherty (1981) discovered that newlywed wives attributed events to causes differently than did their husbands. Wives who attributed other couples' marital problems to negative personality traits and attitudes were more likely to use verbal criticism of their husbands in problem-solving discussions. The same was not true of husbands, suggesting that an attributional style, which requires assigning causes to events, affects men less in marital problem solving. This finding relates to an earlier review of one hundred bargaining and negotiation studies that concluded that women negotiate in a reactive, non–task-oriented manner that decreases their skills in problem solving. Women had greater difficulty ignoring provocations and frequently overreacted to situations (Rubin and Brown 1975). Decisions may appear final at one moment and then be reconsidered at a later time. What seemed to be the best decision may upon experience be proven otherwise and necessitate a new search for a better one. In a viable, open family system, this would be a healthy state—all decisions subject to reevaluation and study whenever new information or changes seem important to any family member.

The role functions carried out in a family affect the decision-making process. These roles vary greatly from family to family, so each family's decision making must be studied to see whether it fits the generalizations from the research presented.

Individual Involvement and Resources

How many times have you dropped out of or avoided a family decision-making session because you did not care about the result? If you do not see how things affect you, you are not likely to get involved, even though, as a system member, you will be affected. Not all family members care equally about the outcome of decisions. Antonio's desire to go to college away from home may not be a major concern for his little brothers. Mom's desire and need for a new refrigerator may not be perceived as important to a teenager. If money or any other shared resource is scarce, decision making can become a competitive process for the limited resources. Decisions may be unimportant to some individuals in families; even if relevant, the decisions may not be points of disagreement.

Communication in making decisions changes greatly as children grow and develop their own sense of self-sufficiency. The same holds true for parents who also go through great changes and growth. Network formations reflect these changes, as do rule adjustments. As parents grow accustomed to problem solving and encounter different situations demanding solutions, they cannot replicate previous decisions, even if they so desired. The real world does not hold constant. Their personal investment in decisions varies over time with the degree of separateness or connectedness within the family system. The dependence-independence of the members fluctuates as children become adults and leave home. Parents learn from their decision successes and failures with older children, and, as a result, the communication going into decision making with younger children may be quite different from what it was with older children. In a highly cohesive family, all members are more likely to invest time in important decisions that affect the whole family. However, in decisions that do not jeopardize unity, members may invest little interest and trust the others to be fair.

Empathy, an important element in effective communication, relates to power and decision making. Empathy may be operationalized as the individual's ability to predict the decision of another family member about a problem. The greater the empathy regarding a particular decision, the greater the agreement between the measures of predicted and actual power.

Because the family is never static, individual members can also be involved in several decision making matters simultaneously, both within and outside the family. Matters requiring decisions, depending upon their importance, affect the members involved and determine their degree of active or passive commitment to new decisions.

> "My brother has more decision-making skills as a result of not only living but also working with my dad in a contracting business. My dad is dependent on him to assist him directly. My brother has the technical computer ability to pull the rug out from under my dad, which would 'disable' my dad from maintaining his livelihood, home, car, and girlfriend. My brother and father have a love-hate relationship, and their continual contact, both night and day, frequently tests their relationship."

If one member of a family exerts too much power in the form of coercion, control, or suppression over another, decision making falters. Problem solving requires an equalization of power. You can achieve a favorable power balance by employing problem-solving methods, but if family members sense that you don't care about them, they hesitate to get involved.

> "Both parents (especially Mom) taught John and me that listening is essential when trying to make decisions. Dad wanted his children to be good listeners, but he never was. He always interrupted before you were able to finish, or he jumped to conclusions. He would make his own mind up about a situation before we could explain. Later, when we would tell him that we did say such and such, he would deny it."

Outside Influences

Because each family is one permeable subsystem among many, all sorts of outside factors affect how a family makes decisions. Mom's salary, BJ's friends, and Mary Frances's teacher may all affect how a decision is resolved.

Decisions within a family system often represent compromises or adaptations to other societal systems. School, corporate, and government systems impinge upon families and influence decisions. The interface between any other system and the family can make problem solving easier or more difficult. Other systems also have rules, images, and boundaries that require maintenance and a change process that helps them continue as viable systems. For example, think of how a business where one parent works affects decision making. If the mother must travel, work overtime, or take customers out in the evening, the family makes decisions differently than if this were not necessary. The school/home interface requires other adjustments in decision making, particularly if both parents work or a single parent has chief responsibility for providing income and childcare and nurturance. Latchkey children, filling time between the end of the school day and the time a parent arrives home, make different decisions than children greeted by a parent at the door.

Government, business, and education are deeply and permanently involved in policies that influence families. Decisions forced upon a family by outside agencies restrict individual members' choices and require flexibility and adjustments, sometimes for poor reasons, often resulting in more tension in families.

"In this age of 'experts,' our family was almost ripped apart as my parents tried to make decisions about how to raise my younger brother, who has a serious attention deficit disorder. My mother was always wanting to follow the advice of a doctor or teacher; my father wanted the family to make the decisions about Robert's care. My parents were constantly disagreeing with each other and the medical and educational experts."

According to Sporakowski (1988), "Decision-making processes used in previous generations may not work under the conditions in which families find themselves functioning" (367).

COMMUNICATION IN DECISION MAKING

Keep in mind the discussion of these family decision-making factors as you read the following results of a comparison of communication and decision-making systems between married couples and unrelated single couples. Note how communication differs in decision making because a couple operates within its own system, whereas unrelated single individuals do not have those systemic ties to consider before deciding. Winter, Ferreira, and Bowers (1973) measured seven aspects of communication: spontaneous agreement (the shared values and like preferences that exist prior to the decision-making process); decision time; choice fulfillment (the number of times a positive or negative choice by one agrees with that of the partner); silence (the length of time no one communicates); interruptions; explicit information (a definite statement of a liked or disliked choice); and politeness (overall impression of how couples treat one another, e.g., tone of voice, asking questions, listening quietly, and being supportive). The results indicated that married couples had more spontaneous agreement, were less polite, made more interruptions, and exchanged less explicit information. A higher degree of spontaneous agreement would be expected, because a married couple has learned the values and wishes of one another, and each partner has a history of sharing these values. Married and unmarried couples took about the same amount of time to reach a decision and were almost equally effective in reaching mutually satisfying decisions. Unrelated stranger pairs listened more respectfully to one another than did married couples, a sad commentary on marital communication.

In another study, Krueger found that disagreements serve as a functional part of the decision-making process, particularly when each partner uses positive communication strategies to express his or her differences. She found this was true except when a sequence began with a disagreement, followed too rapidly by another disagreement, which signaled the beginning of conflict escalation. She also noted that partners change subjects sometimes as a transition and at other times to avoid conflict. These changes indicate that couples do not focus for long periods of time on a single issue, thus demonstrating a cyclical model of decision making, with the couple taking up a topic and leaving it but later returning to reach a decision (114).

Throughout this chapter, you have seen that communication plays a key role in determining the outcomes of family decision making. The way in which family members use verbal and nonverbal communication determines decision-making outcomes. The sending of mixed messages by one or more members affects decisions and may alter the cohesion and balance of the family system. Thomas (1977) listed the following communication difficulties that hinder decision making:

> . . . overtalk, overresponsiveness, quibbling, overgeneralization, presumptive attribution, misrepresentation of fact or evaluation, content avoidance, content shifting, content persistence, poor referent specification, temporal remoteness, opinion surfeit, opinion deficit, excessive agreement, excessive disagreement, too little information, too much information, illogical talk, and negative talk surfeit. There are some others that are potentially less serious, but if extreme, may interfere to some extent, also. These are affective talk, obtrusions, excessive question asking, excessive cueing, and acknowledgment deficit. (123)

Researchers have argued over whether the dominant authority structure in a family can be determined from the manner in which decision-making responsibilities have been allocated or from studying the decision outcomes. The conclusion is that family authority and decision making operate together as a dynamic, interactive system, requiring give-and-take among family members.

The following principles, based on Kohlberg's and Gilligan's concerns for justice, care, and responsibility, could help guide family members in their decision making: (1) create a sense of justice by treating family members equally, regardless of sex or power resources, (2) create a sense of autonomy by respecting each family member's rights to free choices in order to carry out actions that enhance his or her life, (3) create a sense of caring by helping other family members achieve their goals, (4) create an awareness of which decisions lead to actions and behaviors that harm family members or place them at risk, (5) create a sense of loyalty by keeping promises and carrying out decisions mutually agreed upon. These principles should enhance the self-concepts of each family member. Of more importance, the use of these ethical guidelines in decision making should enable family members to self-disclose more easily and achieve greater intimacy. This complex process of decision making can be streamlined by experiences of a life of shared communication.

"For fifty years, Lambert and I have always tried to make decisions together. We try to spend our money as we both see fit and discuss what is important to us. We usually shop together: groceries, machinery, cars, and so on. Even on buying our tombstone, we looked them over and decided on one we both liked. We've had our differences, but we always tried to see things from the other point of view, and eventually we'd resolve the problem."

CONCLUSION

This chapter discussed, with the help of a model, a process-oriented approach to understanding decision making. Through communication interactions, power is used and decisions made often using consensus, accommodation or de facto decisions. These decisions may occur in families that govern their systems by styles such as zero-sum confrontations, by the creation and maintenance of various types of rules, or by guiding principles of fairness based on conscience.

There are five decision-making steps that families often use to communicate differences yet solve their problems: establishing definitions, exploring and analyzing the problem, establishing solution criteria, listing possible solutions, and selecting a solution. Although compromise may be required, this problem-solving approach has the potential to strengthen cohesion in the family. The chapter concluded with a variety of factors that affect communication in decision making.

IN REVIEW

1. Give an example of a decision that was made in a real or fictional family that illustrates one of the types of decision making.
2. Give specific examples of how factors such as gender, age, individual interests, or resources affected a family's decision-making process.
3. To what extent should children be part of the family's decision-making process? How can they be guided to develop the communication skills necessary to participate effectively in such discussions?
4. Decide and explain the kinds of decisions the family members in a television sitcom usually make under a variety of situations.
5. If you wanted to improve your decision-making skills and make decisions easily with a significant other person in your life, what communication behaviors would you try to demonstrate? Make a list of suggestions based upon your understanding of ideas in this and other chapters.

CHAPTER 9

Communication and Family Conflict

Normal families fight! Controversies in families enable the systems to grow and change. The mere absence of conflict does not make a family function well. Both functional and dysfunctional families conflict, but the functional family processes conflict more positively. In the functional family system, members adapt to the stress in arguments and seek ways to overcome conflict. In spite of the best decision-making strategies, individual family members can feel cheated or misunderstood as they attempt to meet their needs within the family system. The way a family agrees is important, and the more grounds for agreement shared by its members, the less is the likelihood of disastrous conflict. The way a family disagrees is equally important. When in agreement, the family continues to function, but, with too much disagreement, effective functioning ceases.

One strong parent or sibling can suppress or avoid conflicts and can provide necessary stability so that other members can take coordinated actions that make the family system appear to be balanced. Over time, however, such suppression or avoidance can have negative effects. Dysfunctional families may get stuck in a powerful conflict cycle and devastate one or more members.

Conflict affects and is affected by all areas of family life. Family members use rules that serve either to help solve problems through communication strategies or to escalate or avoid conflict. Conflict may create boundaries, yet boundaries may serve to reduce potential conflicts. A family's themes or images will influence the amount and the type of conflict that develops.

"In our family we were not allowed to fight. My mother wouldn't tolerate it! She would say, 'God only gave me two little girls, and they are not going to kill one another.' Arguments were cut off or we were sent to our rooms. After she died, we fought most of the next ten years! We each had so many old resentments—scores to settle. For over two years we didn't speak! Fortunately, we relearned how to relate to one another and now conflict only when necessary."

This chapter will examine the conflictual process, a model of conflict styles, factors related to the conflict process, and communication strategies for managing inevitable family conflicts.

THE CONFLICTUAL PROCESS

Family members who confront their differences can improve their relationships and accomplish joint benefits that increase love and caring. Conflict can provide opportunities for effective feedback that leads to innovations that enhance adaptability and cohesiveness. Think of conflict and communication as interdependent. Each affects the other. Communication either helps or hinders conflict, verbally and nonverbally indicates the symptoms of it, and serves as a way to resolve conflicts or continue them (Hocker and Wilmot 1985). The intensity of the conflict determines the kinds of messages produced, the patterns the confrontations follow, and the interpretations placed on the communication cues (Roloff 1987, 486).

Conflict Defined

Conflict is a process in which two or more members of a family believe that their desires are incompatible with those of the others. It may be a matter of perception, as when Jose believes that the degree of intimacy expected of him is too threatening or requires more of him than he is willing to deliver. Conflict may also develop over a difference in attitudes or values. Maria does not enjoy cooking and would rather the family went out to eat pizza than expect her to fix dinner. Conflict may also emerge when one person's self-esteem is threatened. If each person can reach his or her own goals, there is no conflict. Conflict occurs when one person's behavior or desire blocks the goals of another, resulting in "a struggle over values, behaviors, powers, and resources in which each opponent seeks to achieve his goals usually at some expense to the other" (Scanzoni and Polonko 1980, 31). From a communication perspective, conflict may be viewed as "an expressed struggle between at least two interdependent parties, who perceive incompatible goals, scarce rewards, and interference from the other party in achieving their goals" (Wilmot and Wilmot 1978, 9).

The conflictual process is very complex. Conflict has an individual dimension. The conflicts going on within an individual family member often can cause trouble with others in the family, such as when a father or daughter senses an incompatibility or inconsistency within his or her own cognitive elements (Roloff, 486). A frustrated family member who doesn't like his or her job and feels inadequate about his or her coping skills has individual issues that affect his or her behavior within the family's conflict situations.

Sometimes persons initiate conflict with a safe substitute rather than with the real object of difference. For example, Dan may have a fight with his boss; because he cannot take out his anger at work, he comes home and explodes about eating dinner late. Midge and Ben may have a fight just when things seem to be working well—when they have really gotten into a pattern of sharing and affection. Some families never experience a real fight. Life just seems to go on without much feeling; there is no feeling and not much loving.

Change may trigger uneasiness and conflict. A new family member, the acquiring of a new job, and the trauma of a divorce, death, or loss of income all have an influence within the family system. Because change causes strain and conflict, disturbances in equilibrium lead to conditions in which groups or individuals no longer do willingly what they are expected to do. Family systems experience a constant level of friction, because they continually change to survive and cope with conflict, either realistically or unrealistically. In his classic work, Coser defined *realistic conflicts* as those that result from frustration of one family member wanting something from another member who does not see the necessity of granting the request or meeting the need (1967, 98). *Nonrealistic conflicts* are those characterized by at least one antagonist's need for tension release. Within family systems, conflict directed toward members for the improvement of conditions and rights is realistic. Nonrealistic conflicts may result from frustrations caused by persons other than those against whom the conflict is waged. Such behavior may result in misdirected anger or scapegoating. For conflict to be realistic, the communication must be between the family members directly involved in the matter.

If a couple or family plans to share experiences and realizes the advantages of family solidarity, conflict will be an inevitable and valuable part of the process. Too often, family conflict evolves into a stalemate or bitter fight, and no members emerge happily. By exploring the process of conflict and how it can develop realistically or nonrealistically, plus becoming aware of better communication practices to use during conflict, you can better understand the development and management of family conflict situations.

Several studies have concluded that conflicts are present in successfully functioning marriages as well as in dysfunctional marriages (Yelsma 1984; Schaeffer 1989; Argyle, Henderson, and Furnham 1985). Although all relationships have problems, the successful ones have partners who learn how to negotiate conflicts. In addition, conflict outside the home in jobs, social groups, or friendships can cause unrealistic conflicts within the family. Individuals who live together in a close and intimate relationship cannot expect a conflict-free existence. For some couples in certain stages of courtship, there is little conflict, but conflicts develop as the relationship progresses.

In his early important work on measuring intrafamily conflict, Straus (1979) states that conflict is an inevitable part of all human association and keeps social units, such as nations or families, from collapse. "If conflict is suppressed, it can result in stagnation and failure to adapt to changed circumstances and/or erode the bond of group solidarity because of an accumulation of hostility" (75). Most people, especially those in close relationships, fear conflict and seek ways to avoid it. But avoiding conflict can lead to further difficulties because the underlying problems causing it have not been solved.

Model of Conflict Styles

Every family member has a distinct conflict style. Each conflicts differently with every other member. Your personality in conflict changes from one family member to another. For example, your mother and brother have a conflict style that is not exactly the same as the way each of them conflicts with you. You also conflict differently with Mom than you do with your brother. In addition, your experiences within your extended family, plus your perceptions of conflict in other social systems, affect your conflict style. As you grew up, you learned how to survive conflicts; this learning influenced the conflict strategies you tend to use.

Killmann and Thomas (1975) developed a model (Figure 9-1) to demonstrate that conflict style consists of two partially competing goals: concern for others and concern for self. Conflicts contain elements of both cooperation and assertiveness as well as needs for interdependence.

Each of these styles warrants discussion. Avoidance implies that you are nonassertive and not particularly interested in cooperation; therefore, you avoid conflicts. You will not participate. The storm brews but you seek cover. However, remember that although you might behave this way in a dispute with your older sister, you might be more assertive, and hence competitive, with a younger brother on the same issue. This conflict style particularly hampers communication about intimate matters in cases where one partner simply ignores such topics.

At the lower right of the model is accommodation. This style of conflict happens when you are nonassertive but cooperative. It is the opposite of competition, because you meet the demands or needs of the other person but deny your own.

"My father left my mother last year to live with someone else. I have become my mother's main support. She calls me at college almost every day and demands I come home for all kinds of silly reasons. Right now I can't seem to tell her to back off, so I do whatever she wants and hope this stage will pass."

Figure 9—1
Conflict Styles

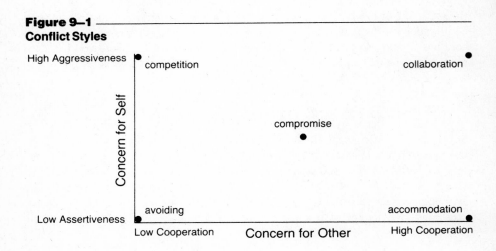

Competition and collaboration are at the top of the model. Competitiveness requires aggressiveness and going after what you want. Your concern for self is high, and, thus, you see conflict as a way to get what you need, regardless of the concerns of others. Competition can be quite selfish if it is your only style of conflict. It can mean "I win; you lose" too often and can destroy cohesion within a family. The challenge is to compete to achieve personal goals without taking unfair advantage of other family members. Wilmot and Wilmot changed the term in Killmann and Thomas's model from high assertiveness to a highly competitive condition. Assertiveness, a more positive term, recognizes the rights of others to disagree (29).

Collaboration occurs when you show concern for those other family members. Collaboration requires that conflicting members seek a solution that enables all parties to feel they have won without compromising issues vital to their needs. Again, remember that your collaboration style varies from member to member. You use your personality differently in conflict, depending upon the family members involved and your closeness to them.

Compromise occupies the middle ground of this model. A compromise represents a solution that partially meets the needs of each member in the conflict. It is an adjustment to the differences that all can accept. In some families, the motto is "Be wise and compromise." Such a family theme recognizes that too much independence detracts from family cohesion and that adaptability via compromise enables more intimacy and tasks to be accomplished in a family.

This model of conflict style provides a way of sensing how one family member's fights affect another's counterarguments through feedback. This feedback varies between parents and also between parents and each of their children. For example, you are not permanently competitive; it depends upon whom you are fighting. You may carefully watch your conflict style with your stepfather because of his high blood pressure, but not with your mother, who enjoys—even encourages—speaking out.

Stages of the Conflictual Process

Conflict develops in stages with a source, beginning, middle, end, and aftermath (Vuchinich 1987; Gottman 1977; Filley 1975). Understanding how conflict develops permits you to unravel some of the complexity and places a point of anger or blowup into a larger context. The following six stages (see Figure 9-2) provide a model for analyzing the conflictual process:

1. Prior Conditions Stage
2. Frustration Awareness Stage
3. Active Conflict Stage
4. Solution or Nonsolution Stage
5. Follow-Up Stage
6. Resolved Stage

As these stages are explained, think about a recent conflict in your family. Did each of these stages emerge as a distinct entity, or was it difficult to know when one ended and the next began?

Prior Conditions Stage.   Conflict does not occur without a prior reason or without a connection of the present event to the past experiences in the family. It does not emerge out of a vacuum but has a beginning in the background of the relationship of the people conflicting. The family system or its context establishes a framework out of which conflicts arise. The participants are aware of the family's rules, themes, boundaries, biosocial beliefs, and accepted patterns of communication.

In conflict, at least one member perceives that the rules, themes, boundaries, or beliefs have been violated or that they have been threatened by something inside or outside the family. Prior conditions are present in the absence of conflict but, under pressure, come into play. Prior conditions that may affect a new conflict situation include ambiguous limits on each family member's responsibilities and role expectations, competition over scarce resources such as money or affection, unhealthy dependency of one person upon another, negative decision-making experiences shared by those involved in the conflict, necessity for consensus and agreement by all on one decision, and the memory of previously unresolved family conflicts (Filley, 8–12). Thus, past experiences set the groundwork for new tension.

Frustration Awareness Stage.   The second conflict stage involves one or more family members becoming frustrated because a person or group is blocking them from satisfying a need or concern. This leads to an awareness of being attacked or threatened by something they have seen or heard, which may be a nonverbal message in the form of a stern look or avoidance of eye contact. If you closely monitor any developing conflict, usually nonverbal cues of conflict appear before verbal ones. As you become aware of the conflict, you may ask: "What's wrong?" "What's his problem?" "Why am I not being understood?" This frustration depends upon the mutual perceptions of the individuals involved. Such perceptions then determine their judgments of the issues in conflict. Inaccurate perceptions can create conflict where none exists. Frustration is affected by whether members are having an isolated disagreement or if they are functioning in a general state of disagreement at a particular time (Schaeffer). Perceptions also affect the degree to which the participants feel they will be threatened or will lose if the conflict continues. Conflict may end at this stage if one party perceives that the negative consequences outweigh the possible advantages. In families, this happens when one of the members shows signs of power and expects compliance or else. Backing off from the issue ends the conflict but does not remove the causes or satisfy the needs that provoked it. This kind of unrealistic conflict can be avoided through self-disclosure: "I'm really just upset about the test tomorrow and I'm taking it out on you" or "You're right—I was selfish and I'm sorry."

It is during this stage, which Gottman labeled "agenda building," that cross-complaining occurs via a series of negative messages that the involved family members are unwilling to stop. They also refuse to recognize nonverbal signals asking for affection or cooperation. In this stage, each family member defends his or her view (Brandt 1982).

Active Conflict Stage.   In this stage, the conflict manifests itself in a series of verbal and nonverbal messages. This symbolic interchange can either be like a

Figure 9–2
Stages of Family Conflict

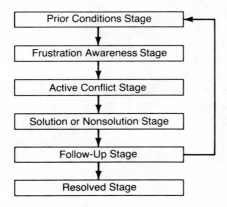

Prior Conditions Stage

Frustration Awareness Stage

Active Conflict Stage

Solution or Nonsolution Stage

Follow-Up Stage

Resolved Stage

battleground or be relatively calm, depending upon the family's rules and style of fighting. In some families, yelling and screaming signal the fight of the decade, whereas others exercise their lungs weekly over minor issues.

> *"Unfortunately, my husband is the type who would rather yell. He is not always a fair fighter. When I want to talk and explain my feelings, and then give him a chance to explain his, he either goes into moody silence or explodes. I find both approaches useless."*

Typically, conflict escalates from initial statements and queries to bargaining or an ultimatum. More will be said later in this chapter about ways to fight fairly and unfairly in families. In the active conflict stage, there is a discernible strategy, or game plan, as one or more family members try to maneuver and convince others of the merits of an issue. The longer the conflict continues, the more the participants' behavior may create new frustrations, reasons for disliking, and continued resistance. During the conflict, sides may be taken as family subsystems and alliances come into action.

Solution or Nonsolution Stage. The active conflict stage evolves into either a solution or nonsolution stage. The solution may be creative, constructive, and satisfactory to all involved, or it may be destructive, nonproductive, and disappointing. The solution may represent a compromise or adjustment of previously held positions. In this stage, how the conflict is managed or solved determines the outcomes and whether positive or negative results follow.

Some conflicts progress into the nonsolution stage. Family members may not have the resources or talents to solve the problem; or after going this far into the conflict process, they may recognize that they do not want the responsibility of carrying out what they demanded. Perhaps they decide they do not want to pay the trade-off costs of accepting a change they earlier demanded. This nonsolution brings the conflict to an agreed-upon impasse. Obviously, communication problems can develop if too many conflicts end with nonsolutions. However, every family lives with some unresolved conflicts, because the costs of an acceptable solution outweigh the disadvantage to one or more family members.

"My sister and I are thirteen months apart. We fought like cats through our teens. Jamie would always keep at me until I would reach the breaking point. I would say that my anger was rising. Naturally, that was the red flag, and we would end up with my crying and her goading me on. It's ridiculous now when I think about how she manipulated me into crying."

Follow-Up Stage. The follow-up stage could also be called the aftermath, because it includes the later reactions that follow the conflict and affect future interactions, such as repeats of the same conflict, avoidance, or conciliation without acceptance. Grudges, hurt feelings, or physical scars may fester until they lead to the beginning stage of another conflict. The outcomes may be positive, such as increased intimacy and self-esteem or honest explorations of family values or concerns. This aftermath stage is linked by a feedback chain to the initial stage, because each conflict in a family is stored in the prior conditions "bank" of the family and comes into operation in determining the pattern of future conflicts.

Resolved Stage. This stage occurs when conflicts move out of the family system; they simply no longer affect its balance. For example, a husband and wife may conflict over priorities on bills to be paid. They negotiate and compromise on demands, and then stick to their agreement. Time and developmental stages of each family member affect solutions to conflicts. For example, parental conflicts over who will take Steve to school decrease or disappear after he becomes old enough to walk there by himself; the same will be true of parental conflicts over dating rules and curfews when he becomes a young adult. Conflicts over space and territory among six children competing for three bedrooms no longer require a solution when all have left home and the "empty nest" remains.

It is important to remember that in the model (Figure 9-2) participants may "exit" at any stage. A drop-in visitor may interrupt during the frustration awareness stage and actually defuse the tension. One or the other party may disengage from the issue, give in, or shift the focus. Gottman (1982) found in analyzing the sequential nature of conflicts that an essential difference between distressed and adjusted couples was the ability of happy couples to de-escalate verbally potential negative effects. Vuchinich discovered in his study of conflicts at the family dinner table that 61 percent ended in standoffs that were used as the easiest way to get out of conflicts. The different family members involved most frequently used submission and compromise to close off conflicts.

The Conflict Model in Action

To demonstrate the operation of this model of conflict, follow the example of the Hanrahan family: Dad (45), Mom (45), Frank (21), Louie (19), and Nellie (17).

The boys attend the local junior college because the family's funds are limited. At an evening meal in January, Nellie asks her mother if she can apply to a distant four-year college to major in her specialty, marine biology. Mom responds positively, because Nellie has high grades and has been promised financial help on her degree. Frank frowns, because he assumes that Nellie's request means that he cannot go away to college; he silently begins to react. He thinks about the other family hassles and recalls other encounters between himself and his sister when Mom took Nellie's side. Frank wonders if Dad or Louie would agree with him that his education was more important than Nellie's. In the past, the men in the family have banded together. All of these prior conditions are important to the outcome of this conflict.

Communication shifts into the second stage. Louie clears his throat and nonverbally gains his mother's attention by waving his fork. He enters the frustration stage, because he too wants to go away to school and fears that planning between Nellie and Mom will move fast. He thinks there is no way Frank or he can go away to finish their degrees if Nellie insists. Louie announces, "I was going away myself next year." Both his mother and Nellie cease talking and nonverbally check out Louie, their eyes asking the question "Are you serious?" They discover he is and also that he looks angry enough to fight. They check out Frank, and he looks equally agitated. The sons eye one another for support. The women look at one another as if to say "Where do we go from here?" This leads to the third stage—active conflict.

"I asked Dad on Wednesday if I could go to the university," Frank declares. The women exchange glances again, and then each looks at Dad, who nods in agreement. "Also, I checked with Louie, and he didn't disagree." Louie nods to confirm this.

"I never get to do what I want in this family," Nellie says in a defeated voice. "When all of you [looking at each of the men] get through planning, there is nothing left for what I want." Her voice begins to rise as she pushes back her chair and noisily begins to pile up her dishes. "The junior college doesn't even have one course in my field, and I will lose credits when I transfer."

Mom anxiously glances at all the children and then at her husband, who catches her eye and then looks toward Nellie and Frank. His silent message seems to be "How are we going to solve this?" This scene of conflict could continue in countless ways. The parents could remain silent, and Frank and Nellie could escalate the conflict into a series of harsh remarks, including charges of favoritism or wasting family money, thus repeating unsolved family brawls. The development of the controversy will depend upon what the prior conditions "bank" includes and the family's problem-solving style. What rules does it follow in conflict situations? What rules do the father and mother assume in such disputes? If Mom is the peacemaker, she will smooth things over. If Father is dominant, he will negotiate a settlement— fair or otherwise.

The solution stage of the conflict starts as Dad speaks up: "Wait a minute! Perhaps Mom and I can help this argument." Mom smiles at Dad to let him know she likes this approach. In this family's conflicts, the parents present a unified position, and the father usually asserts that "he and Mom" will be the arbitrators. Dad asks, "Can Nellie go another time?" Nellie shakes her head "No." Dad then looks at Frank with an unstated question, inquiring if he has any flexibility and could change his plans. Frank sends back a "no compromise" message. So does Louie. "Well, what can we do?" Dad asks. "Are there any other options?"

This leads to a series of possible solutions. "Couldn't Nellie go to the junior college like we did?" Frank volunteers. "It might take her longer, but by that time Frank and I would be through school and there would be more money for her," Louie suggests.

"Would that work?" Mom asks Nellie. She shrugs, for she does not really prefer that solution. This leads to a discussion of how much money each of the children thinks he or she will need in the next few years for college expenses. Because education has been a high priority theme in this family, all participants have a vested interest. Both parents want all of their children to have the degrees that they themselves were unable to obtain. Another theme has been to "pay as you go," and, thus, loans have not been considered.

In this family, a compromise solution works. Mom agrees to accept a full-time position she has been offered and use the income to help pay the increased expenses when Frank and Nellie go away to school. Because this discussion occurs in January, she has nine months before tuition is due.

Dad agrees to increase his credit union savings by 15 percent. Frank and Nellie agree to secure loans and to work part-time. Louie stays at the community college because it has an excellent pre-engineering program, but he receives assurances that he could have additional future support. The family reaches the decision that each child receives the same amount of money from the parents and that each would have to earn or secure loans for the rest.

The follow-up stage continues the conflict process. The family will store in their "prior conditions" computer the positive aspects of this experience. Louie may feel Nellie owes him a favor, and Nellie may be more willing to agree in a future encounter because Louie accommodated her. They will also store the amount of self-worth and self-confidence each family member has received in this conflict. That is why the feedback link from this follow-up stage back to the first conflict stage is so important. Future conflicts are affected by the positive or negative aspects of the current conflict: this family may one day have to renegotiate the allocation of resources for college educations.

If the compromise works effectively, eventually the conflict moves into the resolved stage, a kind of "They lived happily ever after" stage. The family comes to closure with this conflict over resources. However, disagreements or favoritism can lead to the cycle of conflict all over again. The reaching of this resolution stage is a major goal of effective family communication. Otherwise, years later, family bitterness develops, as in the next example.

"I wanted a degree, and my father kept insisting on my being a farmer. When it came time to go to college, no money was ever offered. Yet my brothers received livestock, equipment, and loans to start farming with my dad. My sisters didn't

Family members fight with one another in different ways.

receive any encouragement or support either for further education. If we wanted to leave, fine, but we couldn't expect any help. I still resent it."

FACTORS IN FAMILY CONFLICT

You fight with each member of your family in different ways. Over time, most families develop their rules for conflictual situations, and each member stays within the calibrated levels, except for unique situations when he or she may go beyond acceptable fighting levels or reconciling behaviors. A tearful embrace may jolt the family pattern far more than a flying frying pan. A family's systemic nature affects its conflictual patterns, which emerge and maintain themselves. As the system's architects, any type of couple within a family sets the stage for its style of conflict.

Scanzoni (1972) classified couple conflicts into two major types: those that concern the basis of the relationship and those that concern less central issues (73). In the first type, basic values and goals held by one family member are ignored or challenged by another. Conflict over such values as religion, having children, or the need for education can become quite painful or have a dysfunctional effect upon the family system. Unresolved, these conflicts could result in separation or termination of the relationship. The second type occurs when family members seek ways "to change or maintain some part of the distribution of rights and privileges in the relationship" (76). Such conflicts might deal with problems over which bills to pay first or where the family should go for vacation.

Patterns of Family Conflict

In their major study of conflict in early marriage, Raush and colleagues (1974) found that "whatever the contributions of the specific partners, the marital relationship forms a unit, and the couple can be thought of as a system." Their analysis revealed that the marital unit was the "most powerful source in determining interactive events" (201). Couples developed their own styles of conflict, which were unique to them. Soon after marriage, the system had its own fight style.

How does a fight style form so quickly? Do yellers marry yellers, apologizers pair with apologizers? Common sense says this is not always the case; yet within a short time, a couple appears to acquire a set of characteristic conflictual behaviors. Raush and his colleagues found similar responses to be one of the major determinants of interaction; that is, certain conflictual behaviors of one partner were more likely to elicit similar responses from the other (198). The same reciprocal pattern held for negative behaviors, such as coercive tactics or personal attacks. The only exception occurred when one partner rejected the other. Rejection is usually met with either coercion or emotional appeals. If each partner rejected the other, communication ended. Family members' use of appeals, whether to fair fighting, justice, promises, or future favors, kept the communication process going. Thus, partners were more likely to send similar reciprocal messages than they were to shift to a new message style.

Such reciprocity is a tendency, not an absolute; conflict does not function as a totally predictable ritual with foregone conclusions. Certain partners may have such different approaches to fighting that reciprocity does not emerge. As you saw in the Fitzpatrick typologies, separates, traditionals, and independents each display particular conflict styles, and it may be more difficult to create reciprocity when different types marry than when similar types marry. Rosenblatt, Titus, and Cunningham (1979) have found that when one or both partners use disrespect, coercion, and other abrasive factors in their communication, conflicts escalate and couples spend less time together. Before togetherness, or cohesiveness, can be increased and conflicts settled amicably, couples "must first deal with abrasive aspects of the relationship" (54).

Who starts conflicts? Do family members in their roles as father, mother, son, or daughter initiate more fights? No consistent pattern has developed. According to Vuchinich, parents started 47.6 percent of the conflicts, and children began 52.4 percent of them. Of more importance, the father had less conflict initiated against him. Mothers, sons, and daughters shared about the same number of conflict attacks. Children started conflicts twice as often against the mother. Sons initiated conflicts three times more frequently against the mother. Fathers started disagreements with their daughters three times more frequently than against their sons. Mothers countered this by starting conflicts twice as often against their sons.

Another pattern appears in the closing of conflicts, with mothers most frequently involved in working out compromises or standoffs in which the family members agree to disagree and no one really wins. Daughters more readily than sons or fathers participated in the above ways of closing conflicts. In solving conflicts via submission, children acquiesced three times more frequently than did parents. After standoffs occurred, females initiated nonconflict activities twice as often.

Feldman (1979) views a couple's conflictual behavior as part of an intimacy-conflict cycle. Couples move from a state of intimacy as one member becomes anxious or fearful, which leads to conflict and separation. Eventually, one partner makes an attempt to patch up the differences. The desire for intimacy draws them back together. The human need to be touched, reaffirmed, comforted, and nourished is a powerful conciliatory force in conflicts. At first, one partner might reject attempts to resume more positive communication, but the need for intimacy provides the motivation for repeated efforts to achieve it (69–70). This research relates to our emphasis upon the element of cohesion in all families.

The couple's coming back together does not mean that the problem between them has been resolved. Quite often, the issue has not been satisfactorily discussed or even fairly treated in the best interests of one or the other. This means that future communications on the same issue will take up where the old conflict leaves off. Intimacy will again evolve into conflict when one partner feels threatened by the issue or aggressive enough to challenge. Have you heard people fighting and had the feeling you were hearing a rerun or rehearsed battle? Communication reaches the conflict stage because some rules in the relationship have been violated; the system tries to recalibrate itself. The degree and limits of acceptable intimacy and acceptable conflict are important dimensions of a marital system's calibration. When these limits are violated, the intimacy-conflict cycle starts over again. It ends when the couple learns how to listen to one another's problems, needs, and fears, and finds answers to these demands so that each can return the support and nurturing the other desires.

Rules for Family Conflict

Members of family systems develop implicit and explicit rules governing the communication of conflictual messages. Jones and Gallois (1989), in their study of rules used in conflicts, found that couples generated or implied the use of four kinds of rules in resolving their differences. They identified (1) rules governing consideration (e.g., don't belittle me; don't blame each other unfairly; don't make me feel guilty); (2) rules governing rationality (e.g., don't raise your voice; don't get me angry; don't be so aggressive); (3) rules governing specific self-expression (e.g., let's keep to the point; let's be honest; don't exaggerate); and (4) rules governing conflict resolution (e.g., explore alternatives; make joint decisions; give reasons for your views) (961–962). These researchers found that rules governing conflicts differed when couples were in public or in private. The rationality rules were used more in public settings than in private. They were also more important to husbands than wives; however, both agreed rationality rules were the least important. These results agreed with Schaap, Buunke, and Kenkstra (1987), who discovered that in conflicts husbands tended to use rational arguments and distance themselves, whereas their wives used more emotional strategies.

Rules relating to conflict resolution were more important to both husbands and wives in private conflict. Rules governing consideration helped prohibit behaviors that would hurt others and helped maintain intimacy. Self-expression rules operated in conflicts to regulate the process of communication and helped maintain intimacy by encouraging the exchange of opinions and enhancing a problem-solving style of discussion. Couples rated respect for self expression rules second in importance in conflict resolution rules (Jones and Gallois, 963).

"As a child, I remember my parents referring to their rules for fighting, such as 'Never go to bed mad' or 'Never call the other person names.' It seemed a bit silly at the time, but after the kinds of fighting I experienced in my first marriage, I made sure that my fiance and I discussed fighting and set some rules for disagreeing before I would consider a second marriage."

Costs and Rewards

Part of a family's systemic function relates to how costs and rewards are negotiated. Conflict may result if a teenager believes the costs of living in a family (rules, obligations, and pressures) outweigh the rewards (emotional and/or economic). Partners stay together as long as the rewards for remaining in a system outweigh the pain or costs of leaving it. Caring for children may be part of a reward and responsibility component in a marriage and may hold a family together for a time; but eventually, if serious conflicts continue, one of the partners will leave. To avoid constant conflicts there must be sufficient rewards in the family system to justify remaining together.

Conflicts may follow when these expectations are not met. When one family member does something special for another, a debt is owed. If the other fails to reciprocate, especially after several requests, conflict will start. Reciprocity becomes, or is a part of, the exchange of costs and rewards in the family. For the family to operate emotionally as a system, this reciprocity does not need to be equal either in amount or kind. Most family members do not keep an inventory up to date, but they know generally who owes them favors. "This reciprocity," according to Scanzoni, "helps to account for marital stability because it sets up a chain of enduring obligations and repayments within a system of roles in which each role contains both rights and duties" (64). To ignore these obligations and repayments creates conflict in families.

Roles in Family Conflict

Role expectations affect conflict. Position-oriented parents may require their children to ask them for what they want, whereas person-oriented parents look for consensus among the members and share leadership roles, especially with their children. Conflict may begin when role demands do not coincide with a family member's desires or abilities. He or she may not be prepared to fulfill certain functions. The expectancy that the individual can fulfill the present role causes anxiety and unhappiness. Young husbands raised in households where men never entered the kitchen to help with household chores will find difficulty in doing so, even if they are willing to change. In conflict, family rules determine who can do what, where, when, and how, and for what length of time (Jones and Gallois; Miller, Corrales, and Wackman 1975).

Stereotyped sex-role conditioning hampers effective decision making and heightens marital conflict. Many men in our society receive training that inhibits emotional feelings and the expression of empathy but permits physical violence as a way to defend oneself. Many women receive countertraining that encourages over-expressiveness of feelings and inhibits constructive assertiveness and negotiation. This lack of expressiveness in husbands during conflicts causes "an emotional overreaction in wives which interferes with their rational problem-solving skills and leads to pressuring and coercion" (Feldman 1982, 356). Other researchers have found that women repress or suppress conscious reactions to threatening, unpleasant messages (Watson and Remer 1984). In a comparative study, men could identify with confrontation only to a moderate degree, and they had difficulty with empathy and seeing themselves accurately in conflict situations (Remer 1984). Fitzpatrick's independent-type couples have little commitment to traditional sex roles, and thus they will more readily negotiate and bargain with their spouse. This can lead to more conflict because independents won't tolerate stereotyping.

Men react differently in conflict, especially in unhappy marriages. In one study, wives reacted to small affective changes in their partners, but their husbands seldom responded to large emotional changes in their wives (Giles and Wiemann 1987). In discussing conflict topics, satisfied wives used higher proportions of supportive and informational behaviors, whereas dissatisfied wives used more competitive behaviors and individualistic utterances. Husbands responded similarly. However, in general, both satisfied and dissatisfied husbands used many more neutral communication cues, whereas satisfied and dissatisfied wives needed a higher ratio of positive cues (Maxwell and Weider-Hatfield 1987, 19).

In a study of sex-role socialization, Arntson and Turner (1989) found that kindergarten children have different role expectations for fathers than for mothers. Children in role playing would allow fathers to talk more and exert more power. They also would argue or conflict more with the mother.

Family members' ties to kinship networks also influence conflicts. For example, in a study of urban families moving to the suburbs, Anderson (1982) found that working-class women who moved felt more isolation and experienced more marital conflict than middle-class women who had more resources in solving transition problems, including staying in contact with kin and friends. In addition, research has shown that couples who disagree about a wife's desire to work conflict more. They also argue more about how the children should be raised (Blumstein and Schwartz 1983).

Family and Couple Types and Conflict

Family types and structures can affect their conflict patterns. As a family evolves, the system develops conflictual behaviors, which characterize the group if not the individuals. Using Kantor and Lehr's (1976) types, one can predict how open, closed, or random families will behave in crises or conflict situations. These researchers hypothesized that closed families in conflicts frequently suppress the individual. This type of family operates successfully in conflict if members agree on solutions or accept those handed down to them. However, rebellion results when a member differs, and a permanent schism develops if one or more members refuse to comply with a major decision. Conflict in open families is usually resolved via group consensus in a meeting in which decisions are reviewed and modified. Conflicts are expected and welcomed if they make family living more meaningful. In decision making, every family member can reveal his or her feelings about an issue. This openness means that promises made in family conferences are kept. The random family demonstrates no set way to solve conflicts. No one person's views dominate, and ambiguity characterizes the negotiations. Emotional impasses occur when no solutions can be agreed upon. Solutions come spontaneously and creatively. Crises are not taken as seriously as in the other two family types and are viewed more as an interruption of day-to-day events.

The Fitzpatrick (1988) couple types demonstrate distinctive conflict behaviors. Traditional couples seek stability and resist change by confronting rather than avoiding conflict. However, they may avoid conflicts more than they realize. Traditionals more often collude with one another to avoid conflicts. Independents more readily accept uncertainty and change by confronting societal views on marriage in a much more direct communication style than do traditionals. Independents do not run from conflicts. They resent a spouse who withdraws. Separates stress autonomy, especially by keeping their own space and distance as a strategy to avoid conflict. They hope to keep conflicts neutral and to a minimum. Separates appear angry toward a spouse who pushes conflict but withdraws when confronted. In conflict situations, independents receive satisfaction from self-disclosure, description, and questioning to receive further disclosure (Sillars et al. 1983).

Family Developmental Stages

Conflict patterns change over the years because the issues to be resolved in families vary greatly over the years. During the early years of marriage, a couple develops a fight style that may be modified as a family grows. In their analysis of couples who had a child within the first two years of marriage, Raush and colleagues identified three stages of development (newlywed, pregnancy, parenthood) that were characterized by varying conflict behaviors, including rejection. They compared these "developmental" couples to couples who did not have a child during those years. During the newlywed stage, the developmental couples behaved more coercively than the matched couples, which may indicate greater stress due to parenting responsibilities.

Finally, during the parenthood stage, four months after the child's birth, both members of the couple appeared to handle conflict less emotionally and more cognitively than their matched counterparts. Yet the reconciling behavior of the husbands returned to prepregnancy levels. The early stage of being a threesome may lead to difficulties, because roles need to be reworked when a new person begins to compete for affection, often causing one of the adults to feel left out. Although a joyful time in most families, early parenthood provides great stress that can lead to significant conflicts.

In the early childhood stage, parents often make the decisions and solve conflicts by offering few options. As the child's ability to reason increases with age, the resolution of conflict relates closely to the type of family structure previously outlined. The adolescence period usually presents a greater number of family conflicts as young people search for independence and test rules and role expectancies. Intense peer pressure heightens conflict as family beliefs and practices are questioned. Teenagers make space and privacy demands, which may also cause conflict. Conflicts occur when adolescents question the patterns, images, and rules in their families. When dating starts, mothers especially have more conflicts with children, especially daughters (Silverberg and Steinberg 1987).

"When I decided to go to New York for a 'cattle call' for a possible movie part, it was the first time I actually argued with both my parents. During most of the argument, my father would not agree that we were in the midst of an argument. 'We're just raising our voices,' he insisted. This was his way of handling the conflict. He didn't want his little boy to grow up and leave. Finally, I stopped arguing about New York and argued about how he always denied we were fighting. Finally he admitted we were fighting. Two weeks later I went to New York City."

If families undergo separation and divorce, children witness a recalibration of the system that usually involves a wider range of conflict behavior. One study of family conflict and children's self-concepts found no significant differences in self-concept scores of children from intact, single-parent, reconstituted, and other types of families. However, "self-concept scores were significantly lower for children who reported higher levels of family conflict" (Raschke and Raschke 1979, 367). A later study clearly revealed the same, that if high parental conflict before and after the divorce continued, adolescents performed less well on both social and cognitive functions (Forehand et al. 1988). The stress and depression reported by single mothers (Webster-Stratton 1989) can create a conflictual climate for children at home. Broken homes did not yield broken lives, but excessive family conflict was definitely detrimental.

The "empty nest" stage, defined as the period when the youngest child leaves home, presents fewer problems in flexible families than in rigid types. Parents' loneliness, uncertainty, or worry over capabilities of young adult "children" to care for themselves largely disappears after two years. In fact, this stage has positive effects upon the psychological well-being of some parents, because their child has been successful in making it on his or her own merits. Conflicts develop when the youngest lingers and takes extra years to leave (West, Zarski, and Harvil 1988; Suitor and Pillemer 1987).

Older married couples report significantly less conflict and greater happiness and life satisfaction than do younger couples. Morale increases over time, and older couples evaluate their marriages in a positive manner and describe the quality of their marriages as improving (Steinberg and Silverberg 1987).

DESTRUCTIVE CONFLICT

"One member of our family, a stepson twenty years old, enters the house with a barrel full of hostilities and problems. He overwhelms my wife with yelling and screaming and a string of obscenities. My reaction is to tell him to shut up and not to have anything to do with him—certainly not to do anything for him. My wife seethes until she can no longer cope; then she explodes. After a litany of verbal attacks, she retreats behind a closed bedroom door—sealing herself off from the problem."

You have probably been involved in a variety of conflict situations, some of which were difficult but resolved themselves well, and others that caused great pain or increased anger. On other occasions, you may have discovered that you were upset but could not put your finger on the exact cause of the problem. Conflict styles may range from the very overt (pots, words, or fists flying) to the very covert (the burned dinner, late appearance, or cutting joke). Although all overt conflict cannot be labeled constructive, it does let you know where you stand. Covert conflict, on the other hand, places you in a guerrilla warfare situation: "Is she really angry?" "Am I reading things into his behavior?" "Are those mixed messages?" In almost all cases, covert conflict falls into the destructive category.

Covert Destructive Conflict

Covert, or hidden, conflict usually relies on one of the following five communication strategies: denial, disqualification, displacement, disengagement, and pseudomutuality. You experience the *denial* strategy most directly when you hear such words as "No problem; I'm not upset" or "That's OK; I'm fine" accompanied by contradictory nonverbal signals. *Disqualification* occurs when a person expresses anger and then discounts, or disqualifies, the angry reaction: "I'm sorry, I was upset about the money and got carried away" or "I wouldn't have gotten so upset except that the baby kept me awake all night." Admittedly, some of these messages are valid in certain settings, but they become a disqualification when the person intends to cover the emotion rather than admit to it.

Everyone has heard the story about the man whose boss yelled at him, but he could not express his anger at the boss. When he arrived home, he yelled at his wife, who grounded the teenager, who hit the fourth-grader, who tripped the baby, who kicked the dog. In some families, this type of incident is not just a story. When you believe you cannot express anger directly, you may find another route through which to vent the strong emotions. Thus, *displacement* occurs. One type of displacement happens when a couple who cannot deal emotionally with their own differences turn a child into a scapegoat for their pent-up anger. Many families tend to single out one person who appears to be the "acting-out" child but who, in many cases, receives covert negative messages with such regularity that he or she finds it necessary to act-out to release the feelings (Minuchin 1974; Gurman and Kniskern 1981). Dogs, children, in-laws, friends, and spouses all may bear the brunt of displaced anger.

The *disengaged* couple or family lives within the hollow shell of relationships that used to be. Disengaged members avoid each other and express their hostility through their lack of interaction. Instead of dealing with conflict, they keep it from surfacing, but below-the-surface anger seethes and adds immeasurably to the already tense situation.

"My wife and I should have separated ten years before we did because we hardly had any relationship. I was able to arrange my work schedule so that I came home after eleven o'clock and slept until Norma and the kids had left in the morning. That was the only way I could remain in the relationship. We agreed to stay together until Nick graduated from high school. Now I feel as if we both lost ten years of life, and I'm not sure the kids were any better off because we all ate and slept in the same house."

Pseudomutuality represents the other side of the coin. This style of anger characterizes family members who appear to be perfect and delighted with each other because no hint of discord is ever allowed to drop the image of perfection. Only when one member of the perfect group develops ulcers, nervous disorders, or acts in a bizarre manner does the crack in the armor begin to show. Anger in this situation remains below the surface to the point that family members lose all ability to deal with it directly. Pretense remains the only possibility.

Very frequently, sexual behavior is tied to these covert strategies. For many couples, sex is a weapon in the guerrilla warfare. Demands for, or avoidance of, sexual activity may be the most effective way of covertly expressing hostility. Sexual abuse, put-downs, excuses, and direct rejection wound others without the risk of exposing one's own strong anger. Such expressions of covert anger destroy rather than strengthen relationships.

Often covert behavior is a rejection of family themes that discourage conflict or independence. Themes such as "We can only depend on each other" or "United we stand; divided we fall" encourage conflict to occur.

Overt Destructive Conflict

In the first of the following pair of quotations, a daughter states her views on the way conflicts are handled in her family. She reveals how her expectations of her mother in the parent role function differ from the mother's actions. In the second quotation, written independently, her mother perceives the siblings' conflicts from a different vantage point.

> *"In my family, conflict is settled by the laissez-faire method. My single-parent mother refuses to negotiate conflicts between her four daughters. We fight but with mixed results. I believe this is bad because it brings out the worst in each of us at times. We never learn from one another; it's more like survival of the fittest."*

> *"I used to get involved in my daughters' conflicts, especially arguments over borrowing clothes without asking one another's permission. I now try to divorce myself totally from these conflicts when they try to get me to intervene on their side. I let them handle it themselves."*

Each of you could list overt forms of destructive conflict that you have participated in or lived through. The following are some commonly used negative behaviors.

Verbal Attack. In all conflicts, the language used by family members has a great impact on the outcome. Word choice reflects the degree of emotion and reveals the amount of respect the conflicting individuals have for one another. Emotional hate terms ("You idiot!" "Geek," or "Liar") quickly escalate conflicts. In some families, swearing is an integral part of venting rage. In others, the rules do not permit swearing, but name calling replaces it. Each generation has its own slang terms used to put down opponents. Put-downs heighten conflicts and slow the solution process by selecting words that describe and intensify bad feelings. These attacks are usually accompanied by screaming or other negative nonverbal cues. Families handle verbal attacks in special ways, such as gunnysacking and game playing.

Gunnysacking. A gunnysack is a burlap bag; but according to some family members, a gunnysack is a deadly weapon that implies storing up grievances against someone and then dumping the whole sack of anger on that person when he or she piles on the "last straw." In some conflicting families, members store resentments instead of dealing with them as they occur. Eventually, those members dump out the gunnysack when a spouse, sibling, or parent does that "one more thing." The offender usually responds by attacking back, and the war escalates.

Game Playing. In many family conflicts, there is a great deal of game playing. Games are nonproductive ways of solving conflicts. In their classic work on couple conflict, Bach and Wyden (1966) suggest that most couples would love to stop playing games, because these players never know where they stand. "The more skillful they are, the less they know, because their objective is to cover up motives and try to trick their partners into doing things" (19). Games end when one player refuses to play and be trapped. An essential test of game players is to ask "How does this solve the conflict on a more permanent basis?"

> *"I don't remember seeing my parents ever hit one another before they divorced. I do remember arguments. We were hit as children by Dad. Mom rarely spanked us; she just threatened that Dad would do it. It seemed as if the longer they were married, the more overadequate Dad became and the more underadequate Mom*

became. He had a take-charge personality and a hair-trigger temper. She complained to us and seemed like a martyr. She had ways of aggravating Dad. She always covered up for us and did our chores, or they didn't get done until he came roaring home.''

Physical Attack.   Hitting, screaming, kicking, teasing, grabbing, and throwing objects characterize some family conflicts. In one study of persons between the ages of eighteen and thirty in families with more than one child, physical aggression was used in 70 percent of the families to settle conflicts between parents and their children and by the children to settle disputes among themselves. Thirty percent of the husbands and wives used physical means to resolve their conflicts (Steinmetz 1977). Instead of solving conflicts, violence led to more violence. A related study also confirmed previous findings that physical punishment increased rather than decreased aggressive behavior in children (Burnett and Daniels 1985, 169). Further evidence has indicated that child abusers are likely to have been abused children (Straus 1974; McClelland and Caroll 1984). Aggressive nonverbal abuse as a way to manage conflicts causes more harm than good.

"My mother always seemed to think that my father had some type of 'problem.' Every once in a while she would give him the shopping list to pick up a few things. Every time when he would return home, my mother would find something that he did 'wrong.' For example, my dad did not get the exact meat that was on sale; he got four bags of grapefruit instead of three, or he bought the wrong brand of napkins. Comments such as 'Can't you follow simple directions?' served as a spark to really set him off.''

A large national study of marital aggression has revealed that teenagers who observe their parents hitting one another are likely to beat their own spouses in later years. This has a greater influence on future behavior than the children's being hit by their parents. Further, seeing the father hit the mother increases the chances that their children will be both victims of such abuse and instigators of it. This means that aggression can be transmitted across generations and is not sex specific (Kalmuss 1984).

The research on family violence indicates that parent-parent and parent-child abuse becomes a part of role relationships. In physically combative families, such behaviors occur frequently enough for children, husbands, wives, or lovers to become accustomed to it. Kalmuss maintains that "exposure to aggression between specific family members teaches children the appropriateness of such behaviors between inhabitants of those family roles" (17). Children grow up accepting beatings as part of parents' rights in governing them but not accepting their parents' hitting one another. Children know about other neighborhood children receiving physical punishment, but they also know Mom's hitting Dad or vice versa violates a societal norm. Burnett found that young men from violent families-of-origin differed significantly in their conflict resolution skills, especially when under stress, when compared with young men from nonviolent families-of-origin.

Because abuse in conflicts occurs intermittently, children learn to live with it, because they also see periods of affection and love between conflicts (Burgess and Conger 1979). The mixed message of love followed by hate and violence causes children mentally to seek ways to avoid getting hurt themselves. They adopt a "wait and see" attitude and hope the conflicts will not lead to additional violence.

Incest is the most extreme form of family violence. The increasing evidence of this problem has led some researchers to warn that incest occurs in families that are not classified as pathological or perceived as dysfunctional. Incest is related to family stress, and poor management of conflict certainly heightens stress. It is important to note that extreme male dominance of the family, plus weakness in the mother caused by illness, disability, or eventual death, correlates highly with rates of incest. Further, women who have been abused both in their families-of-origin and by their husbands are more likely to be forced to accept abuse, resulting in submissiveness. This fear toward male assailants increases the likelihood of incest also happening to their children (Breines and Gordon 1983).

How a couple feels about their relationship influences their complaint behavior. Functional couples made behavioral complaints, used more positive verbal and nonverbal cues, and replied more frequently with agreement responses. Dysfunctional couples made more personal character complaints, used more negative communication cues, and responded more often with countercomplaints (Alberts 1988).

CONSTRUCTIVE CONFLICT

Constructive conflict provides a learning experience for future conflicts. As noted earlier, a couple's manner of dealing with conflict is probably established during the first two years of marriage and remains quite consistent. Therefore, partners may create a fight style in the first twenty-four months of marriage that will characterize the next fifty years. Raush and colleagues have discovered that harmonious couples consist of two types: "those who manage to exhibit constructive conflict and those who deal with conflict constructively" (204). Those who exhibit constructive conflict show "even within the space of a single scene, sequential communication exchange, growth, development, and sometimes even creativity" (203–204). Both types of harmonious couples can avoid conflict escalation.

Elements of Constructive Conflict

Recall the example of conflict over college expenses presented earlier as you review the process of constructive conflict.

The following characterize successful conflict management:

1. A sequential communication exchange takes place in which each participant has equal time to express his or her point of view.
2. Feelings are brought out and not suppressed.

3. People listen to one another with empathy and without constant interruption.
4. The conflict remains focused on the issue and does not get sidetracked into other previously unsolved conflicts.
5. Family members respect differences in one another's opinions, values, and wishes.
6. Members believe that solutions are possible and that growth and development will take place.
7. Some semblance of rules has evolved from past conflicts.
8. Members have experience with problem solving as a process to settle differences.
9. Little power or control is exercised by one or more family members over the action of others.

These goals are not achieved in families in which young people fail to learn these communication and problem-solving skills, because their parents either shield them from conflict or typically make the decisions.

In successful conflict management, happy couples or children go through validation sequences (Gottman). They know they can either agree or disagree in arguments and bring out their ideas and feelings. If family members can listen to one another, they can better understand motives, opinions, and feelings. Happy families believe that solutions can be found for problems and they reach agreements more readily. Members can give in to one another or compromise without resentment (Brandt).

"One of the things that characterize both my parents is their willingness and ability to listen. They may not always agree with us or let us do the things we want, but no one feels like they don't care. At least we feel like they heard us, and usually they explain their responses pretty carefully if they don't agree with us. As a teenager, I was always testing my limits. I can remember arguing for hours to go on a coed camping trip. Mother really understood what I wanted and why I wanted to go, but she made it clear that she could not permit such a move at that time. Yet I really felt that she shared my disappointment, although she stuck to her guns."

In a comparative study of the communication patterns of couples who had problems and sought counseling and couples who did not, Gottman, Markham, and Notarius (1977) found that in conflict situations, the happier couples began with remarks that told the partner that, although they disagreed on an issue, the other party was a decent human being. They also avoided negative exchanges and ended discussions with some sort of verbal contract to solve the conflict. Other studies reveal that satisfied family members often overlook conflicts or choose communication behaviors that decrease the chance of escalation (Roloff 1987), and families that control negative emotional behaviors have an easier time of solving problems (Forgatch 1989).

Families seem to be able to manage conflict creatively by recognizing that they have a twofold responsibility: to meet their individual needs and wants and to enrich further the family system. This requires give-and-take, resulting in compromise. The attitude behind this view enhances flexibility and helps avoid conflicts that result from being too rigid and assuming that one family member's views must be followed. A conflict that presents something new to the family system, requiring accommodation or assimilation, tests the strengths and capacities of the system. If the system is flexible and differentiated, family members can more readily accommodate one another, learn new ideas from other members and themselves, and change. Undifferentiated family members become enmeshed in their system and lack the assertiveness or autonomy to handle conflict constructively. In a flexible family, new ideas do not threaten the stability of the relationships, and members can learn from both outside and within the system.

Strategies for Constructive Conflict

Conflicts usually end in one of four ways: submission, compromise, standoff, and withdrawal. *Submission* involves one or more family members' going along with others. In *compromise,* family members find not always an ideal decision but one that the majority of individuals can accept. When family members can't agree, they reach a *standoff.* They recognize that in their particular conflict no one wins or loses. *Withdrawal* ends conflicts when one or more family members walk out or refuse to communicate. In an important study of conflicts, Vuchinich found that 36 percent of all conflicts ended early by family members' accepting corrections or ignoring the threat. However, if conflict starts, there is a 68 percent chance it will continue for up to five communication turns, when most conflicts subside. Most conflicts (61 percent) end in a standoff; submissions ended 21 percent; compromises ended 14.2 percent; and 3.8 percent ended in withdrawals (599). Although Chapter 14 describes specific methods of improving family communication, three of those constructive conflict behaviors will be briefly discussed here: listening, fair fighting, and managing the physical environment.

Listening. A cornerstone to constructive conflict may be found in good listening behavior. Listening is an important communication skill to use to defuse conflict and help clarify and focus on the issues being debated. Empathic listening requires that you listen without judging and try to hear the feelings behind the remarks. This means accurately hearing what the other is saying and responding to those feelings. Remarks like "You're really angry; I hear that" or "I am hearing you say that you have been misunderstood" indicate to a family member that you have listened yet not become trapped within your own emotions or thinking about "How can I best turn off this complaint?" Restating what you have heard a person say can be most helpful in slowing or stopping the escalation of conflict. "Bill, are you saying . . . ?" Asking Bill to repeat his contention is another helpful approach.

Some partners will go so far as to switch roles in a conflict and repeat the scene to check out the accusations. It gives the one partner a chance to try out the other's feelings. Parents may also have their children role-play their conflicts.

Gordon (1975), in his Parent Effectiveness Training program, has developed a "no lose" method for solving conflicts that depends on careful listening and involves compromise elements. This approach asks for partners to hear each other out, find the areas of agreement, and then zero in on the specific differences. Both sides seek some reward in the solution of the conflict. "If you let me do X, I'll do Y." The philosophy of caring and pleasing one another is basic to its success. Even on difficult family problems, the method can work because all parties recognize that no one can totally win or lose.

Fair Fighting.   Many bitter conflicts in families result from the use of unfair tactics by various members; such behavior can be changed with commitment to fair fighting. In a fair fight, equal time must be provided for all participants, and name calling or "below-the-belt" remarks are prohibited. In this system, family members agree upon how they will disagree. The procedures are agreed upon with time and topic limitations. They can be used only with the mutual consent of the parties involved and the assurance that each will listen to the other's messages.

"My mother always used a lot of verbal attacks to 'handle' conflict. Put-downs definitely intensify bad feelings. My mother knew the exact names to call me that really hurt. She used to call me chubby, fatso, and other similar words. These words only made me angrier and never settled any argument. My mother rarely used swear words when she was yelling, but if she called me those names, I would usually start swearing at her. When she went into treatment for drug abuse, the whole family got involved, and through counseling we learned to avoid the 'red flag' words that would set each other off."

In fair fighting, family members try to stay in the here and now. They specify what it is that they feel caused the conflict. Each family member takes responsibility for his or her part in the fight and doesn't blame the others. The following example illustrates these ideas.

Jim tells his wife, "I need to share a concern with you." "OK," Michaela replies, giving permission for Jim to release his feelings and do so without interruption. "I really felt angry this evening when you told Marissa she didn't have to go to the program with us. You let her run wild."

In this approach, Jim continues to release his anger during the time granted him by his wife. According to the rules of fair fighting, he can express his anger only verbally—no hitting or throwing things. Also, Michaela could have asked to postpone hearing the gripe until she had time to really listen. The idea of asking permission to be heard is essential, because it implies the obligation of the other party to listen.

Michaela can deny the charges Jim makes, which can lead to a careful recounting of what was said and with what intended meanings. This often helps clear the air. She can also ask for a break until later if she becomes angry and cannot listen. She can also admit her error in judgment, if one was made.

Sometimes flexibility and compromise will not solve conflicts. The consequences outweigh the advantages. An individual's self-worth may be more important than family expectations. Some families permit members to decide what is negotiable and nonnegotiable for them. Stating "This is not negotiable for me at this time" enables one to own his or her position and part of the problem. Being tentative and including the phrase "at this time" leaves the door open for future discussion. Other items may legitimately be nonnegotiable for you on a permanent basis.

"If I feel like Italian food, and Roger, my husband, has his heart set on Chinese food, Chinese it is. I have never thrived on conflict and will avoid it by settling for less than I would have liked, especially on 'little things.'

"In the case of a more serious conflict, I try to problem-solve. I believe that two people in conflict should never go to bed mad at each other. If the problem is big enough to cause conflict, it is worth the time and effort to solve it for the sake of the relationship."

Whatever rules or methods couples use in their fighting, the nonverbal aspects of conflict need special attention. Careful monitoring of nonverbal cues often reveals the true nature of conflict. Gestures of threat, harsh glares, and refusals to be touched or to look at others indicate the intensity of the conflict. In a study of marital communication, Beier and Sternberg (1977) found that the subtle nonverbal cues in a couple's messages determine the climate in which either conflict or peace reigns. By observing nonverbal cues, they discovered that couples who reported the least disagreement "sat closer together, looked at each other more frequently and for a longer period of time, touched each other more often, touched themselves less often and held their legs in a more open position than couples who reported the most disagreement" (96). This finding correlates directly with Gottman and colleagues' conclusion that "nonverbal behavior thus discriminates distressed from nondistressed couples better than verbal behavior" (469).

Sometimes nonverbal cues contradict verbal statements. A receiver of such mixed messages must decide "Do I believe what I hear or what I see?" On the other hand, supportive nonverbal cues can drastically reduce conflict. For example, a soothing touch or reassuring glance has great healing powers.

Managing the Physical Environment. Choice of space may dampen certain conflicts. Reducing the distance between adversaries may help reduce the noise level. Sitting directly across from someone makes for easy eye contact and less chance for missing important verbal or nonverbal messages. Choosing a quiet and appropriate space lessens distractions or related problems. Thus, conflicting family members need to be aware of all the factors that can escalate a fight.

"One thing I have learned about fighting with my teenage son is never to raise an argumentative issue when he is in his bedroom. Whenever we used to fight I would

go up to talk to him about school or about his jobs in the house; and five minutes after we started arguing, I would suddenly get so upset about the state of his messy room that we would fight about that each time also. By now I've learned to ask him to come out or to wait until he is in another part of the house to voice a complaint."

The rewards of better-managed family conflicts are numerous. Better use of positive communication practice stops the cumulative aspect of conflict. A series of minor conflicts left unsolved can escalate into separation, divorce, or emotionless relationships. Successful resolution of conflict that goes through the stages of our conflict model (Figure 9-2) leads to emotional reconciliation and affirmation of the participants. It also decreases fear and anxiety within the family. Future joint enterprises become possible for family members. Knowing how to manage conflicts leads to a greater appreciation for the talents of family members and enjoyment of each of them in the here and now of living together.

Yelsma's research emphasizes this conclusion. Couples who had high scores for managing conflict reported the highest degree of marital satisfaction. Also, too high a concern for one's own uniqueness appeared to lessen one's chances for happiness. However, reasonably high self-esteem and high task energy enhanced marital adjustments (60).

UNRESOLVED CONFLICT

What happens in the family if conflict cannot be solved? Usually, a loss occurs, which affects all members as psychological and/or physical estrangement creates and fosters separation among members. Young family members may remain in the home but withdraw from family activities until they go to school or establish a way to support themselves. If circumstances force a continued joint living arrangement, a wall of silence may become part of the family's lifestyle. Some members may be cut off from all contact with the family; they may be treated as nonexistent.

"When I married my husband, I was essentially making a choice between my parents and Joe. Joe is black, and my parents said they would never speak to me again if we married. Although I knew they were angry, I thought that they would come around when we had a baby. Melissa is two years old now and my parents have never seen her. My brother and sister have been to see me, but I am 'dead' as far as my parents are concerned."

Many unresolved marital conflicts result in divorce, clearly a rejection strategy. One or both members withdraw, seeing the ending of their formal relationship as the only logical solution. Yet, when children are involved, spouses are divorced from each other and not from the children; and not the children from one another. The system alters itself rather than ends. The original family system evolves into new forms, which may include new spouses and children. Legal action does not stop interaction of family members.

Some couples stop their conflicts short of divorce, because the cost of the final step may be too great; yet the rewards of living together are too few. For these people, destructive conflict characterizes much of their continued shared existence. Such unresolved conflict may add great tension to the entire family system, but not always. When an issue is unresolvable, it may be more functional for the family to avoid the issue and direct its communication to areas that bring cohesion (Fitzpatrick, Fallis, and Vance 1982).

CONCLUSION

Given the many stresses families face in today's world, conflict management becomes an ever more critical skill. Some families develop effective conflict styles through discussion and negotiation. One family realistically faced their problem when they sought outside help—a step that can reward a troubled family system.

"When I asked my wife what she wanted for our twenty-fifth anniversary, she said, 'Marriage counseling. The next twenty-five years have to be better than the first.' I knew we had many fights, but I never knew she was that unhappy. I agreed to the counseling, and we really worked on our differences and ways of resolving them. After a few months, were able to talk rationally about things we always fought over—money, my schedule, our youngest son. Next month we will celebrate our twenty-eighth anniversary, and I can say that the last three years were a lot better than the first twenty-five."

IN REVIEW

1. Take a position and discuss whether conflict is inevitable and necessary for the development of family relationships.
2. Describe how an individual's conflict style may vary with specific members of the family. Relate to the model of conflict style in Figure 9-1.
3. Using the stages of family conflict, describe a recurring conflict in a real or fictional family.
4. Create a position statement detailing your perception of how constructive conflict might function in families, and provide four or five reasons why this style of conflict may be difficult to achieve.
5. Interview three persons about their attitudes toward conflict that they learned in their families-of-origin and how they perceive they have learned to manage conflict today.

CHAPTER 10

Family Communication and Developmental Stress

Families evolve over time as each system and its members encounter developmental and unpredictable changes, each change generating some elements of stress. Any time there is either a natural change in the life of a family member or a catastrophic change, communication plays an important part in negotiating the transition from one stage to the next. No two family members move through these stages identically. One family life cycle evolves into another, like a great chain with connections from previous generations to the present. Many experts suggest that family patterns affect three or more generations (McGoldrick and Gerson 1985).

" 'Jesus, Mary, and Joseph, save my soul!' can be heard from the lips of my mother at least once a day. Mom thought three in diapers was bad but since has decided three teens are worse. Presently, we have three teens in driver's ed, three teens tying up the phone, three teens falling in and out of love. Mom threatens to run away once a day. Dad says we drive him crazy and should be locked up until we go away to college. We must be driving our parents nuts.''

Think about your own family. What has marked family changes? Some families emphasize marker events, or the transition stages in human development, more than others do. A child's first steps, a teenager's driver's license, or a wedding may serve to mark major changes. Other families emphasize unpredictable crises as significant symbols of change. A parent's cancer surgery or the death of a sibling may symbolize the greatest sense of change.

The ways individual members "organize their experience in their personal stimulus world . . . influence the shared perceptions the family develops of the social world in which they live" (Reiss and Oliveri 1983, 290). In other words, families view the world differently, thereby affecting their perceptions of stresses that enter their systems. If one family perceives the world as chaotic, disorganized, and frequently dangerous, any change may be upsetting. If another sees the world's operations as predictable, ordered, and greatly controllable, change may be perceived as manageable. How the family responds to stress depends upon its organizational structure prior to the stress (Lewis 1986). In a family systems approach, the organization needs flexibility to cope at the time of change. The family's first response to stress is to maintain the balance in the family system. If these homeostatic responses do not succeed, a series of changes begin that are reflected in communication patterns.

This chapter and the following chapter address family communication patterns in relationship to developmental and unpredictable stresses. This chapter first provides an overview of change by examining the sources of family stress and the adult and family developmental issues. It then looks at the stages of family development. Moving through these stages creates stress as family members separate from their families-of-origin, form their own systems, and live in those systems over a period of time. The next chapter will focus on those relatively unpredictable stresses that occur when families suffer losses such as illness, divorce, or death. Any time there is a change in the life of a family, either natural or catastrophic, communication plays an important part in negotiating the transitions and coping processes.

OVERVIEW OF FAMILY CHANGE

Sources of Family Stress: A Model

In their work on change in the family life cycle, Carter and McGoldrick (1988) present a model depicting stressors that reflect family anxiety and affect the family system (see Figure 10-1). Within the same family, individual members experience and react to stresses differently. Stress varies with the age of the family members and their position in their life cycle.

The vertical stressors include patterns of relating and functioning that are transmitted down generations. These patterns involve family attitudes, expectations, secrets, and rules. In other words, "these aspects of our lives are like the hand we are dealt: they are given" (8). Many of these communication-related stressors were discussed as the images, themes, myths, rules, boundaries, and expectations that come from one's families-of-origin.

The horizontal flow in the system includes the anxiety produced by the stresses on the family as it moves across time—both the predictable, or developmental stresses, and the unpredictable events that disrupt the life cycle. Pressures from these current life events interact with one another and with the vertical areas of stress to cause disruption in the family system. The greater the anxiety generated in the family at any transition point, the more difficult or dysfunctional the transition will be.

The past and present family stresses are affected further by all levels of the larger systems in which the family operates. The social, cultural, economic, and political context influences the levels of stress. One's community, extended and nuclear family, and personal resources also contribute to the process of moving through life. As you move through phases of your individual and family existence, these forces will positively or negatively influence the process. Thus, these three major factors—ver-

Figure 10–1 ―――――――――――――――――――――――――――
Sources of Family Stress

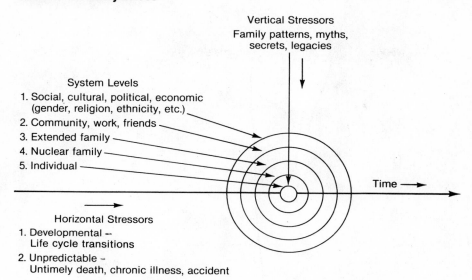

tical stressors, horizontal stressors, and system levels—taken together put the family life cycle into perspective.

General Adult Development Issues

Most researchers accept the position that individuals experience critical periods of change, or life stages, until death. All of the stages lead toward a sense of integrity, of having lived authentically and meaningfully, so that one can accept old age and death with dignity. The development of an individual life cycle perspective reflects the seminal work of Erikson (1968, 1950), Vaillant (1977), Levinson (1978), and Gilligan (1982). Hoffman (1980) describes developmental tasks that must be solved or completed in order to reach life satisfaction within a developmental period. For example, some representative tasks of adolescence include developing a sense of self, acquiring an appropriate sex role, and achieving autonomy. Sample tasks of middle age include adjusting to aging parents and assisting teenage children to become responsible, happy adults.

Levinson entitled his book *The Seasons of a Man's Life.* He explains the seasonal analogy in the following manner:

> To say that a season is relatively stable, however, does not mean that it is stationary or static. Change goes on within each, and a transition is required for the shift from one season to the next. Every season has its own time; it is important in its own right and needs to be understood in its own terms. . . . It

Like individuals, whole family systems also pass through various "seasons" of their lives.

is an organic part of the total cycle, linking past and future and containing both within itself. (7)

Just as individuals move through various seasons of their lives, whole family systems also pass through certain seasons, and such passages are reflected in their communication patterns.

Family Development Issues

Early thinking about family life cycles reflected the position that "normal" couples remained intact from youthful marriage through child rearing to death in later years. It was assumed that the communication components of these developmental stages would also be predictable. For example, communication differs throughout the developmental changes in family life as the courting relationship moves to marriage or cohabitation and decisions about becoming parents or remaining child-free, until eventually the cycle begins to repeat itself. The specific configuration of each family system means that it experiences stages of development somewhat differently than do other systems, yet each family passes through certain similar stages within the birth-death cycle. Although the majority of people begin life in two-parent biological families, as the years go by a large percentage of these families evolve into other forms. In contrast, other people are born into single families or into blended families where one or both parents have children from previous marriages. Some couples do not have children.

Most models of family stages apply to the middle-class intact American family life cycle. Historically, experiences such as untimely death or divorce removed families from stage considerations. Contemporary family theorists are beginning to call for a consideration of divorce as a normal stage, suggesting a "Y," or "fork in the road," model of development (Ahrons and Rodgers 1987). Others (Carter and McGoldrick) conceptualize divorce as an interruption or dislocation of the traditional family life cycle, which produces disequilibrium and a need to go through one or two more stages of the life cycle to restabilize and go forward developmentally at a more complex level.

No single model can reflect such complexities. The stages presented in this chapter reflect one perspective, variations of which will be addressed in the next chapter. What follows contains some perspectives on family development and change and draws some implications for family communication patterns.

FAMILY STAGES

Family researchers have attempted to apply the stage concept to whole families so that the entire system may be thought of as moving through particular stages. Other experts describe six (Carter and McGoldrick), seven (Glick 1989), eight (Duvall 1988), nine (Hill 1986), or twelve (Hohn 1987) stages. Such analysis has difficulties, because families consist of several individuals in different life stages, but it becomes more manageable than trying to account for each person. Such schemes provide simplicity but do not account effectively for families with numerous children or widely spaced children as they go through the middle stages of development. Nor do they focus on adult developmental stages or tasks unrelated to child rearing. More detailed perspectives exist, but their complexity limits their use. No matter which framework is adopted, communication emerges as a critical issue at each stage. The following stages are most appropriately applied to the intact middle-class American family life cycle. The following stages, detailed by Carter and McGoldrick, will be used for discussion: Table 10-1 describes the stages of the family life cycle.

1. Single young adults
2. The couple
3. Families with young children
4. Families with adolescents
5. Launching children and moving on
6. Families in later life

To further your understanding of the developmental process, imagine the cohesion-adaptability axis (see Figure 2-1) as an overlay for each family system's growth. For example, extremely cohesive families may resist certain changes, such as children leaving home, whereas low-cohesion families may splinter when children start to leave. The capacity for adaptability aids a family in moving through its stages of development. A rigid family may try to avoid necessary change, whereas highly

Table 10-1

The Stages of the Family Life Cycle

Family Life Cycle Stage	Emotional Process of Transition: Key Principles	Second-Order Changes in Family Status Required to Proceed Developmentally
1. Leaving home: Single young adults	Accepting emotional and financial responsibility for self	a. Differentiation of self in relation to family-of-origin b. Development of intimate peer relationships c. Establishment of self re work and financial independence
2. The joining of families through marriage: The new couple	Commitment to new system	a. Formation of marital system b. Realignment of relationships with extended families and friends to include spouse
3. Families with young children	Accepting new members into the system	a. Adjusting marital system to make space for child(ren) b. Joining in child rearing, financial, and household tasks c. Realignment of relationships with extended family to include parenting and grandparenting roles
4. Families with adolescents	Increasing flexibility of family boundaries to include children's independence and grandparents' frailties	a. Shifting of parent-child relationships to permit adolescent to move in and out of system b. Refocus on midlife marital and career issues c. Beginning shift toward joint caring for older generation
5. Launching children and moving on	Accepting a multitude of exits from and entries into the family system	a. Renegotiation of marital system as a dyad b. Refocus on midlife marital and career issues c. Realignment of relationships to include in-laws and grandchildren d. Dealing with disabilities and deaths of parents (grandparents)
6. Families in later life	Accepting the shifting of generational roles	a. Maintaining own and/or couple functioning and interests in face of physiological decline; exploration of new familial and social role options b. Support for a more central role of middle generation c. Making room in the system for the wisdom and experience of the elderly, supporting the older generation without overfunctioning for them d. Dealing with loss of spouse, siblings, and other peers and preparation for own death. Life review and integration

chaotic families may not place enough significance on life changes and rites of passage. Families characterized by low adaptation and high cohesion may fight the passage of time that carries them through developmental stages. Family themes, boundaries, images, and biosocial beliefs further complicate movement through the developmental stages.

The following treatment of stages discusses only highlights of a very complex subject. In order to understand the entire process more clearly, it is necessary to focus briefly on each developmental stage and its communication dimensions.

Leaving Home: Single Young Adults

Although this stage is not found in other life-cycle lists, McGoldrick and Carter include it as an essential stage that recognizes the young adult coming to terms with his or her family-of-origin and separating or leaving home to enter a new cycle. In short, this stage of the unattached young adult comprises that period of time when the individual has "physically, if not emotionally, left his or her family-of-origin, but has not yet established a family of procreation" (Aylmer 1988, 191). Until recently, this developmental task was not considered necessary for females, because it was assumed they would move from one attachment to another, defining themselves more as a supporter than as a self, thus reflecting attachment rather than autonomy.

Unless this task is successfully handled, communication problems can develop in the stages that follow. Young people need sufficient autonomy to separate and achieve their goals independently. If they remain enmeshed and overly dependent, this will affect their choices or options throughout their lives. The goal is healthy interdependence, with the parents' letting go and the young adult's establishing a career or completing school, finding close friends and establishing peer networks, defining the "self" as separate yet a part of the family-of-origin. An abrupt cutoff is not the answer. Bowen (1978) insists that an angry cutoff leaves the young adult emotionally bound to the old system. Cain (1990) indicates that young adults faced with their parents' divorce may experience severe life disruption. The ideal would be for the young adult to feel free to achieve his or her own goals and command the respect and encouragement of the parents, even if they might have hoped for other outcomes. From this viewpoint of the family system, successful resolution of this transition requires "(1) an ability to tolerate separation and independence while remaining connected; (2) a tolerance for differentness and ambiguity in career identity of adult children; and (3) the acceptance of a range of intense emotional attachments and lifestyles outside the immediate family" (Aylmer, 195). Young people and their parents need to find less hierarchical, or vertical, ways of communicating and to adopt more horizontal, or adult to adult, communication patterns.

"Ending college has been a period of great stress for me. My family always refers to me as the 'gazelle'—frightened by conflict. Yet I'm now battling with my parents to support my desire to go on a year-long mission for my church. They see this as inconceivable. I am struggling with my need for independence and the chance to move on my own."

Part of this process involves investing in intimate peer relationships, some of which may be romantic, and beginning the process of exploring deep interpersonal connections. Thus, young single adults must experience an individual orientation, or autonomy, in order to move toward future interdependence and attachment.

The Couple

You have heard the two classic explanations as to why people are attracted to each other—"opposites attract" and "birds of a feather flock together." Some people support the theory of complementary needs—that persons tend to select mates whose needs are complementary rather than similar to their own. Others hold out for similarity. However, research indicates that most people select a mate of similar socioeconomic background who shares similar values, interests, and ways of behaving. This reality of differential contact suggests that most persons find partners within a limited social network, or the persons with whom they regularly interact.

Proximity plays a large role in whom one encounters and eventually with whom one develops close relationships. People are more likely to date those who live nearby, attend the same school, or share their work and social backgrounds, which makes it likely that a large proportion of their attitudes and values will be in basic agreement from the start. Once a relationship becomes established, the couple's gradual discovery of just how much agreement exists becomes crucial in determining whether or not they decide to marry (Rubin 1979). Courtship may be viewed as a decision-making time because "the decision to marry is a prediction about how one person's life with another person will evolve in the future based on how it has evolved in the past" (Yerby, Buerkel-Rothfuss, and Bochner 1990, 98).

Lewis believes that all couples entering a relationship must resolve three developmental challenges in order to achieve satisfaction in later stages: commitment, power, and closeness (236). Commitment requires each to make the other his or her primary partner and lessen the ties to parents, siblings, and friends. Power refers to the ability to influence one family member to do what another wants. According to Lewis, power works most effectively when a couple shares it and when one partner does not dominate the other. Closeness relates to establishing a balance between separateness and attachment that is mutually satisfying for the couple. It is in this early stage that a couple develops distance regulation that enables them to find a mutually satisfactory degree of separateness and connectedness. The resulting cohesion comes from much trial and error. In this developmental stage, couples use verbal and nonverbal cues to negotiate what is an acceptable and nonacceptable distance.

"Sometimes I feel like a piece of Swiss cheese—full of holes. I grew up in a nontouching, often violent family. I realize I hunger for touch and affection. I can cuddle and hold my partner for long periods of time, but he gets uneasy after a while. We have to reach a point where both of us are comfortable."

The system formation period, usually the courtship/engagement, involves a couple's attempt to move to deeper levels of communication. Partners find out through permissions, granted verbally or nonverbally, that indicate the limits to their communication. Certain topics, feelings, or actions may frighten or offend the other. They create unwritten rules that will govern their communication when they encounter these issues.

Engagement involves a couple's attempt to move to deeper levels of communication.

The engagement communicates to outsiders the seriousness of courtship. Quite often, prior to the announcement, verbal and nonverbal signals from the couple indicate a deepening relationship. Significant jewelry may be exchanged; invitations to attend special family events such as weddings, bar mitzvahs, or reunions are extended.

> *"In my family, we always knew when relationships were serious when the annual family reunion time arrived. If you were serious about someone, you were expected to introduce this person to each member of the clan. However, you didn't go through this and take all the teasing that followed unless an engagement followed. Bringing a partner signaled an impending marriage."*

An engagement serves as a type of bonding, a statement to the world that the relationship is formalized and that a new familial unit will be established. The act of bonding, or institutionalizing the relationship, may change the nature of the relationship. Some parents may not be prepared for the separation issues involved; mothers especially may feel abandoned. Each family faces the question of realignment: How willing and able are we to accept a new member as an in-law?

The premarital period provides the time for self-disclosure and negotiation. The following issues may need discussion: time with friends, desires for children, sexual needs, career and educational planning, religious participation, money management, housing, in-laws, and acceptable conflict behaviors. The trend today is for shorter engagements; many couples are living together during this period.

Each person has to deal with the move from autonomy to attachment. This shift from self to mutuality with another requires time and examination. Yet, for many couples, the final part of the engagement period becomes hectic with rituals—wedding plans, bridal showers, and so forth—that may keep the focus off the separation issues until the ceremony is over. The vows may be repeated before a judge or minister, before three or three hundred beaming friends and relatives, as two individuals formally create a new family system. The actual ceremony is a communication event—a sign to the outside world that the ultimate formal bonding has occurred.

Marriages between young adults involve certain predictable tasks for most couples. It is a time of (1) separating further from the families-of-origin; (2) negotiating roles, rules, and relationships; and (3) investing in a new relationship. Some young people find it difficult to separate from their parents, establish an adult identity, and assume the role of spouse. Marriage at this time may continue unresolved conflicts with the parents. The new mate becomes the victim of angry projected feelings he or she did little to deserve. This is a period of unconscious negotiation between the couple and their families-of-origin regarding how the old and new systems will relate to each other.

"I had known my husband since childhood, and we dated since our junior year. Our parents knew each other and we attended the same church, yet we had some real difficulties in the first years of our marriage. I had difficulty in the following areas: (1) learning to live with my husband's habits, (2) trying to be a full-time employee and a housewife, (3) deciding at which family's house to celebrate holidays, (4) telling my husband when I was angry, and (5) dealing with the biggest problem—my husband's mother."

The initial stage of marriage is characterized by close monitoring of the relationship and more frequent and intense communication about the relationship than at any other stage (Sillars and Wilmot 1989). As spouses move through this period, many report that romance moves into reality. Most couples experience a shift in their social networks. Early marriage is accompanied usually by a decline in contact with friends. Much negotiation relates to the role of the "old friends" and autonomy. How much time will the spouses spend apart? How much togetherness will be demanded?

Equally important, but far more subtle, is the verbal and nonverbal negotiation related to cohesion and adaptability. Each person jockeys for the amount of togetherness he or she wishes as well as for the amount of flexibility that can be tolerated. Such moves are rarely dealt with openly, but the results have long-lasting effects on communication within the system.

As you may well imagine, the images, themes, boundaries, and biosocial beliefs experienced by each partner in his or her family-of-origin affect the new system's development. A woman whose biosocial beliefs create an image of a husband who is strong, unemotional, and powerful puts great pressure on her new husband to deal with such expectations. If one partner has experienced themes of open sharing and very loose boundaries and the other partner has experienced the opposite, much negotiation will be required.

Couple conflict patterns tend to establish themselves within the first two years of marriage and demonstrate great stability (Raush et al. 1974). In addition, a greater proportion of communication is devoted to the marital conflicts that gradually surface (Sillars and Wilmot). Usually, the balance of power between a couple is established early in the marriage and is based upon decision-making behaviors and role performance. Many couples set long-term patterns at this point.

In their study of couples over the first year of marriage, Huston, McHale, and Crouter (1986) found couples engaged in increasing conflict and decreasing intimacy. By the beginning of the second year, couples spent less time talking with each other about general topics and about their relationship. In an earlier study, Cutler and Dyer (1973) found gender differences in newlywed conversations. Husbands more than wives adopted a "wait and see" strategy; wives opted for greater sharing and discussion of problems. Many of the previous remarks reflect upon problems that can complicate communication in a new marriage. However, the research indicates that this is a happy stage, and differences are often not taken seriously or allowed to develop into crises.

A couple's ability to invest in their new relationship relates directly to the quality of their communication. This is a time of investing in the system, risking self-disclosure, building a pattern of sexual communication. Time, energy, and risk taking nourish the relationship and establish a range of acceptable intimacy for the system.

For some couples, this two-person system will be their permanent form. Partners may choose not to add children to their lives or may find it difficult to bear or adopt children. Yet, for most young couples, the two-person system eventually becomes a three-person one, with pregnancy heralding the transition to a new stage.

"The period before the children began to arrive was a critical point. If we had not established a really strong, trusting relationship in those first two years, we would have drifted totally apart in the next twenty-three years of child rearing. We lost all our time together. If I had it to do over, I would have waited five years before having children, to share who we really were before we tried to deal with who the four new people in our lives were."

Families with Young Children

As parents, adults move up a generation and become caretakers to the younger generation. One of the most important choices a couple makes concerns childbearing. Such a decision should, but does not always, involve intense communication—self-disclosure regarding the needs of the partners and how a child could fit into their lives. Input from all sources affects such a decision. The media, parents, friends, and other relatives often pressure the couple to fulfill parental roles and subtly suggest that they are being selfish if they do not. Men may perceive children as a way to prove themselves as mature and responsible. Children of divorce may be ambivalent toward parenting. For both spouses, producing a child is partially ego fulfilling, and they may desire to be the kind of parents they never had.

To examine the periods of child growth and outward movement, three phases will be discussed. Remember that each family will experience each phase differently, depending on its size and the ages of its members.

1. Family with first child
2. Family with preschool children (three to six years, possibly younger siblings)
3. Family with school-age children (oldest child six to twelve years, possibly younger siblings)

Family with First Child.   Parenthood is now coming later in life for most couples, because the age at marriage has steadily increased to twenty-four for women and twenty-six for men (Glick 1990). (On the other hand, 23 percent of children are born to unwed mothers, frequently teenagers.) For young couples, pregnancy occurs relatively close to the marriage. Because about one-fifth of all children born in the United States were conceived before marriage and many others are conceived during the first two years, many couples do not experience a lengthy period of intimacy before the child arrives. In contrast, some couples postpone having children for several years, so the first pregnancy forces choices and may cause far more interruptions in the woman's life than marriage did (Issod 1987). Many dual-career couples are having their first child in their early to mid-thirties. No matter when it occurs, the first pregnancy signals significant change in the couple's relationship. The intensity of the desire for a child by one spouse or both greatly influences the communication about the parenthood stage from the very beginning. When a couple desires a child and the pregnancy is uncomplicated, this can be a time with much intimate communication. There is still time to talk and to share without interruptions. Yet subtle communication changes occur as well as changes in conflict patterns. Contrary to popular myth, Raush and colleagues found no indication that wives become more emotional in dealing with conflict during pregnancy; but in the last stages of their wives' pregnancy, husbands do make greater efforts at nurturing and conflict avoidance.

Three factors influence couples during the transition to parenthood: their views on parental responsibilities and restrictions, the gratification child rearing holds for them as a couple, and their own marital intimacy and stability (Steffensmeier 1982). Middle-class mothers differ from lower-class mothers in their response to the stress of motherhood both during pregnancy and in the years following. Middle-class women take more time to adjust and feel fewer pressures than lower-class women, who must worry more about support and work roles (Reilly, Entwisle, and Doering 1987).

As the wife's body dramatizes the life changes, some couples begin to feel pregnancy has trapped them into a loss of independence. This is a time when the spouses need mutual confirmation as individuals and as a couple evolving into parenthood. Women may need extra reassurance as to their continued physical desirability.

Naming the child becomes a communication event. Names may serve to link family generations; often they reflect attitudes or dreams of a parent. Additional important communication may center around the role of the father in the birth process. Decisions concerning this issue require careful examination, because years later, one may feel left out or abandoned by the other at this crucial moment.

> "I have never felt closer to my wife than at the moment of Ryan's birth. I helped her breathe, wiped her forehead, and rubbed her back between contractions. I actually felt a part of the birth process. When Ryan was finally delivered, Christie and I cried and laughed and cried again because of the power of the drama we had created. It's indescribable—to share in the birth of your own child."

If you have ever lived with a newborn baby, you are well aware how one extremely small person can change an entire household. Sillars and Wilmot compare the adjustment following childbirth to the adjustment following marriage, saying, "There is a gradual decline from the emotional high experienced initially to a state more tempered by negative as well as positive feelings" (233). The initial question is, To what extent is there space in the environment for a child? According to Bradt (1988), children can be born into an environment that has space for them, has no space for them, or has a vacuum the child is expected to fill. The answer to this question influences directly the development of the new family.

At the point when the dyad becomes a triad, alliances or subsystems emerge. All family members cannot receive undivided attention at the same time. Simply put, all three people cannot experience eye contact or direct speech from each other simultaneously. One person is temporarily "out." Such triangling has the potential to evolve into powerful alliances.

Within this stage, the couple must deal with the following communication-related issues: (1) renegotiating roles, (2) transmitting culture and establishing a community of experiences, and (3) developing the child's communication competence. Moderately flexible families are likely to weather this period more easily than are relatively rigid systems.

Parental roles may become so powerful that the spouses may lose sight of each other for a period of time. New parents may feel inept caring for their child. Because mothers traditionally have taken the major responsibility for childcare, until recently few fathers have been exposed to much modeling regarding how to share the caregiving role. Currently, family life education is increasingly supporting equal roles for male and female, and young men are presented with a wider range of models of male family life (Hey and Neubeck 1990).

When fathers do become involved in childcare, some evidence demonstrates that they are just as sensitive and responsive to infant needs as are mothers. In fact, fathers of newborns are as competent as mothers in providing attention, stimulation, and necessary care (Sawin and Parke 1979). Due to cultural and economic changes, many more families are experiencing shared parenting responsibilities. Although men's roles are changing slowly, there are indications that men, especially those with working wives, are accepting more family responsibility, particularly if the system is adaptable (Patterson and McCubbin 1984).

Women may have to deal with the demands of motherhood and with the loss of a job or profession that held high interest or economic value. If they return to work, they must deal with separation from their child. Husband, wife, and infant must communicate to work out their relationships within the context of their roles. Intimacy between the couple certainly changes with the birth of a child. Privacy is almost impossible when the baby needs attention (Kelly 1988). Although research points to increasingly positive involvement of the father in parenthood, the birth of a first child tends to have a "traditionalizing influence in marriage, prompting greater role specialization, male dominated decision making and a shift toward traditional ideology" (Sillars and Wilmot, 234).

The first child represents a link to posterity and continuation of the family name and heritage—a potentially heavy burden. Thus, parents become involved in transmission of culture and the creation of a community of experiences for their new family. When you think about your own children or of your future children, what parts of your background do you wish to pass on to them? Do you wish they could experience the same type of Passover Seders you did as a child? Do you want them to have a strong African, Italian, or Norwegian identity? Are there family traditions, picnics, celebrations you want to continue? What type of sexual identity or religious belief should your child develop? Such are the issues of transmission of culture.

"The birth of our first child revived many issues that we had fought about in our courtship period and that we finally agreed to disagree about. Sean and I were from very different backgrounds, religiously, culturally, and even economically. As a couple, we were able to ignore many of the differences, but once Wendy was born, we each seemed to want certain things for her that we had experienced growing up. And our families got into the act also. We've dealt with almost everything except religion, and we are due for a showdown on that soon, because Wendy is now five and should begin some religious training soon."

For many people, a child represents a link to the past and the future, a sense of life's flow, and a sense of immortality. Hence, children often serve as receptacles for what we consider our best parts, our strengths, and our expectations for the family. Once a couple becomes a triad, certain dormant issues may arise—particularly unresolved ones. A father's unfulfilled dreams may be transferred to his son. The couple's difference in values, religious beliefs, traditions, or ethnic background may be highlighted by the small member of the next generation. Thus, spousal conflicts may arise over what is to be "passed down." The transmission of both the cultural heritage and the family's own heritage is a demanding, frightening, and exciting task that depends on marital intimacy. Simultaneously, three people are forming a community of experiences, a process begun by the couple but deepened and intensified by the arrival of their offspring. As additional children arrive, the process will be repeated and extended.

> *"It was amazing for me to watch my sister and her husband with their first child. After almost twenty-five years, my sister could remember so many of the songs that our mother sang to us as little ones. She and Lee took great pleasure in creating new words and expressions from things that Jonathan did. They set certain patterns for birthday parties, established Friday night as 'family night,' and began to take Jonathan to museums, children's theater, and library storybook programs together. They created their own world, which now incorporated a little boy."*

Through communication, new patterns of life are formed and maintained that reflect the uniqueness of the three-person system. In-jokes, camping trips, long walks, or Sunday pizza dinners may all contribute to one family's community of experiences. Young married couples who have not had extensive contact with their parents may suddenly feel a need to connect their child to grandparents and other relatives. In most families, contact with the extended family increases after the birth of a child. However, the amount of support and quality of help from a couple's parents depends more on their relationships prior to the birth of grandchildren. Other couples may find themselves resisting overeager relatives who wish to envelop the child. Appropriate boundaries usually require careful consideration and negotiation.

Finally, parents are deeply involved in providing their children with a means to deal with interpersonal relationships. Their relationship serves as the first model for the child's development of communication skills. From the earliest weeks of existence, a child learns how much connectedness or separateness is acceptable within the family system and how to attain that level through verbal and nonverbal means.

The moment of birth exposes the child to the world of interpersonal contacts, as a powerful parent-child bonding process begins through physical contact, facial/eye contact, and reciprocal vocal stimulation. In his classic work, *Touching*, Montagu (1978) stresses the importance of body contact with the mother. The child makes its first contact with the world through touch, and this becomes an essential source of comfort, security, and warmth. According to Worobey (1989), maternal holding as a soothing strategy is employed over 80 percent of the time; newborns recognize and prefer their mother's voice over other sounds. He concludes that "watching and smiling behaviors that characterize adult forms of sound communication, contribute greatly to the success of early mother-infant interactions"; he suggests that such encounters facilitate later interactions (16).

The first few months mark the critical beginning of a child's interpersonal learning. A child's personality is being formed in the earliest interchanges with nurturing parents. Children begin to respond to words at six to seven months; by nine or ten months, they can understand five or six words and will begin to use language soon thereafter. Parents set the stage for positive interpersonal development by verbally and nonverbally giving a child the feeling of being recognized and loved.

As couples experience parenthood, their lives undergo massive changes. Most couples experience a decline in marital satisfaction with the birth of the first child. This is followed by increases in satisfaction later in life when children leave home (Sillars and Wilmot; Spanier and Lewis 1980). Because infants cause the couple to feel fatigued, frustrated, and tied down with little time for self or spouse, there is a corresponding decrease in marital satisfaction (Ventura 1987). The baby's fussy behavior is stressful to both parents, but less to the father. Men avoid spouses whom they perceive to be unfriendly and distance themselves until the wife adapts to the mother role.

As more children arrive, variations of this process occur. Nevertheless, later births do not cause as many major changes as the first one (Terkelsen 1980). Increasingly, with the declining birth rate, many parents raise only one or two children. Today the average child has only one sibling, creating greater rivalry and intensity in sibling communication (Gudykunst, Yoon, and Nishida 1986). After the first years of great dependency, children develop a sense of self and mastery of skills that allow them to become more independent persons. Such growing independence has a direct bearing on family interaction.

Family with Preschool Children. The preschool family (child three to six years) experiences less pressure than in the previous period. Parents have learned to cope with a growing child. Barring physical or psychological complications, the former baby now walks, talks, goes to the bathroom alone, and can feed and entertain himself or herself for longer periods of time.

Watching a three- or four-year-old, you may be amazed at this or her language skills. A four-year-old may produce well over 2000 different words and probably understands many more (Wood 1981). Children at this age begin to develop more sophisticated strategies for gaining such ends as later bedtimes or favorite foods. They are likely to express their gender roles nonverbally. As children become more independent, parents may directly influence their language acquisition skills through enrichment activities such as reading, role playing, story telling. The parents' own communication behavior in this stage serves as an important model for the child.

As noted in the discussion of roles, communication with children will differ depending on whether the family is position-oriented or person-oriented. Whereas a child in a position-oriented family is required to rely on accepted roles as communication guides the child in a person-oriented family is more likely to use a range of communicative behaviors and to understand their effectiveness in relation to the specific listener. The difference is essentially one of the degree to which the child is provided with verbalized reasons for performing or not performing certain communicative functions at certain times with certain individuals. Persons growing up in a household where things are done "because I am the father and you are the child" do not gain training in adapting to the unique personal relationships of the individuals involved. Children growing up in a person-oriented family are more likely to receive explanations for performing communication behaviors: "Apologize to your mother because name calling hurts her feelings" or "I need your cooperation because I don't feel well today."

Children must learn not only to relate to parents or other adults, but they may have to incorporate new siblings into their world. During this period, many couples have more children, increasing the complexity of the family's relationship network. The arrival of second and third children moves the triad to a four- or five-person system and places greater demands on the parents. Each additional child limits the amount of time and contact each child has with the parents and the parents with each other.

Additional children trigger a birth-order effect, which combines with sex roles to affect parent-child interaction. You may have heard characteristics attributed to various people because "She is the middle child" or "He is the baby of the family." There appear to be differences in parent-child communication based on sex and position. Boys may be allowed to ask for more comforting and receive more comforting and praise, particularly if they are firstborn. Mothers tend to become intensely involved with their firstborn children and appear more anxious about their performance in other settings. Whereas mothers are more likely to praise firstborn boys and second-born girls more often, they will generally correct firstborn girls and second-born boys. Finally, mothers are more likely to control their daughters than their sons (Toman 1976). Hoopes and Harper (1987) in a study of birth order, characterized firstborns as self-assured and responsible high achievers; second-born children question their place and have some difficulty with expectations, feelings, and expressing wishes in their communication; third-born offspring develop trust slowly, but once committed to a relationship remain connected and find it difficult to end relationships; fourth-born siblings are quite personable, adventurous, and less ambitious. They are often caregivers, and family members may want more from them than they can give. Fifth-born children tend to repeat the patterns of those firstborn; sixth of those second-born, and so forth. In short, triangles and subsystems multiply. "Each time a new person is added, the limited time and other resources of the family have to be divided into smaller portions but the mother and father still have only two arms and two ears" (Satir 1972, 153).

"Angie was three when Gwen was born, and it was a very hard period for her and, therefore, for us. Angie changed from being a self-sufficient, happy child to a whining clinger who sucked her thumb and started to wet her pants again. Jimmy and I had to work very hard to spend 'special' time with her, to praise her, and to let her 'help' with the baby when she wanted to. Luckily, Gwen was an easy baby, so we could make the time to interact with Angie the way she needed us to."

Parents need direct communication with an older child or children before the next baby's birth or adoption and during the months to come. This may include hospital phone calls or visits and time alone after everyone is home. Siblings three or more years older are more likely to treat the baby with affection and interest, because they are more oriented to children their own age and less threatened by the new arrival. A sibling close in age may engage in aggressive and selfish acts toward the baby.

How parents relate to children affects sibling cooperation. In keeping with the system of mutual causality, Bradt suggests that parents should hold all children in a particular conflict situation accountable for working things out, rather than judging one child as "the cause." He also suggests that children may help each other understand relationship issues.

In the three- to six-year stage, children begin to communicate on their own with the outside world. Some attend nursery school; and at five years, most enter kindergarten. Some parents experience difficulty in letting their children go even at this early stage and develop patterns of possessiveness. From their young peers, children learn about friendship and establish relationships outside the family. Children's interactions with one another vary in response to each other's gender and social characteristics such as dominance or shyness (Haslett and Perlmutter-Bowen 1989). These researchers suggest life-long implications of improving children's social skills, saying, "New social skills and experiences may occur as a result of improving a child's communication abilities, and some negative consequences, e.g., relative isolation, social rejection from peers, and benevolent neglect by adults might be avoided" (50).

As children grow and become less helpless, parents gain more control over their own lives, but time alone for the couple remains a problem. Even after they have adjusted to any possible income losses because of the new members, husbands and wives are likely to fight over the absence of joint recreation.

Family with School-Age Children. The school-age family experiences new strains on its communication as children begin to link further with outside influences. The family system now overlaps on a regular and continuous basis with other systems—educational, religious, and community. Families with very strong boundaries are forced to deal with new influences. Schools provide an introduction to a wider world of ideas and values. New beliefs may be encountered; old beliefs may be challenged.

School-age children may spend many hours away from the home environment and influence. In addition to the school experience, religious organizations provide educational and recreational events. Community organizations such as the Scouts, sports leagues, or 4-H clubs compete for family members' time. Parents establish rules that set boundaries in space, time, and energy that their children can expend in these new activities. During this period of growth, children come under the influence of peer pressures, which may conflict with parents' views. Often, conflict develops, because children feel compelled to please friends rather than parents.

As children continue their emotional and physical growth, their communication skills change. Negotiation and priority setting become important aspects of child-parent communication as extrafamilial demands conflict with family time. Family role orientation continues to influence behavior. For example, Bearison and Cassel (1975) found that first-grade children from person-oriented families are more able to accommodate their communication to the perspectives of listeners than are children of the same age who come from position-oriented families. The authors attribute the differences to the more differentiated role systems of the children from person-oriented families.

Children at this age prefer peer communication with the same sex, often declaring dislike for the opposite sex. Knowing that this normally characterizes interactions of children between ages 8–12 helps parents understand the messages they receive from their children.

During the school years, the identity of the family as a unit reaches its strongest form. The family can enjoy all kinds of joint activities, which bring a richness to the intimacy of the family relationship. Due to the intense activity level, some partners neglect their own relationship or use the children as an excuse to avoid dealing with marital problems.

This period may be very comfortable for highly cohesive families because joint activities can be enjoyed, and children still remain an active part of everyday family life. The more parents know about child development in this stage, the more skill they have in creating a supportive environment. In fact, the more parents are aware of the importance of providing play material and interacting with their children in fun and learning activities, the better will be the language development of their children in these important early stages (Stevens 1984).

Families with Adolescents

A family system may be transformed as members attempt to manage the adolescent stage. Although a number of investigations suggest that the extent of adolescent and parental turmoil during this period has frequently been exaggerated, there is general agreement that adolescence, and particularly early adolescence, has traditionally been a challenging and sometimes trying time for both the young and their parents (Amato 1986; Richardson 1986). Research has consistently shown that marital satisfaction is at its lowest when children are of school age and later when the oldest child becomes an adolescent (Silverberg and Steinberg 1987).

According to Offer and Sabshin (1984), a wide range of adolescent experience can be identified. A minority experience a tumultuous adolescence; a larger percentage move through the period in spurts, emotionally and mentally demonstrating less introspection than other groups; a third group appear to exhibit high levels of confidence. Very few of this final group reported anxiety and depression, but they did report receiving affection and encouragement for independence from their parents. The switching of moods in adolescents, varying from helplessness and dependence to defiance and independence two hours later, can be explained in terms of the struggle for individuation, the development of a sense of self. The life-cycle task is the mutual weaning of parents and children (Herz 1980, 228).

Teenagers experience internal struggles in coping with changes and individuation particularly in areas of sexuality, identity, and autonomy (Garcia-Preto 1988). These struggles affect the entire family system at a time when parents may be facing predictable midlife issues. Prior interest in same-sex relationships switches to a growing interest in the opposite sex. "All he does is chase after girls now instead of fly balls." "Keep Out" signs appear on doors; phone calls become private. The upsurge in sexual thoughts and feelings serves as an undercurrent to many interactions that may make parents uneasy because they are forced to consider their child as a sexual being. Young people begin to set their own physical and psychological boundaries, which may limit communication with some or all persons approaching adulthood.

Adolescent self-esteem is related to family relationships. Through communication interactions, adolescents gain a sense of their own identity. Parental support, involvement with their children, and willingness to grant autonomy and freedom for decisions lead to high self-esteem (Gecas and Schwalbe 1986). Self-esteem for boys is more closely related to good family relations than it is for girls. Perhaps boys express their self-esteem needs in ways that encourage Mom and Dad to respond with support, control, and communication behaviors, whereas girls use fewer overt nonverbal and verbal cues that initiate the same responses from parents (Demo, Small, and Savin-Williams 1987, 713). The need for privacy often accompanies the search for identity.

"I grew up in a home where doors were always open, and people knew each other's business. I remember going through a terrible period starting at the end of junior high when I hated sharing a room with my sister. I would spend hours alone sitting on my bed listening to music with the door shut, and if anyone came in, I would have a fit. I even locked my sister out a number of times."

A major task of adolescence is to loosen family bonds while establishing friendship bonds with peers. According to Erikson, the identity work that a child goes through within the family needs to be similarly repeated within society. Blos (1979) concurs that all youths reach puberty with intrapsychic tensions that require reworking in adolescence if full adulthood is to follow.

Adolescents are engaged in a process of forging a "workable, acceptable identity" (Douvan 1983, 63), a process dependent on communication experiences with peers. Such companions serve as relatively noncritical confidants, supporters, and listeners. Therefore, the adolescent begins to develop the communication skills necessary to develop voluntary relationships.

Concurrent with this move, a young person becomes more other centered and begins to develop a true sense of empathy and the ability to take another's perspective (Ritter 1979). Such capacities eventually allow the late adolescent to interact with his or her friends and parents on an increasingly adult level.

Personal decision making provides a sense of autonomy for teenagers. The changes between ages 13–19 coincide with the individuation that occurs when a young person becomes self-reliant and insists upon making up his or her own mind. This leads to independence and confidence in decision making. By asserting his or her developing talents to speak out, work, or perform tasks without constant help and supervision, the adolescent signals to parents that past communication directives no longer fit the situation. Recent work addressing gender issues in adolescent development highlights females' relational concerns and their communication components (Gilligan, Lyons, and Hammer 1989). Future work in identity and autonomy will reflect these issues.

In a revealing study of middle-class families, parents related quite differently to their adolescents. Girls reported better relationships with their mothers than did boys. Daughters not only spent more time with mothers but felt mothers were less strict. The closeness in age between children also influenced their communication with parents. The wider the spacing in years, the more likely the adolescents perceived the discipline from their fathers as fair. Spacing did not affect mothers in this way (Richardson et al.).

The adolescent's struggles to work through developmental tasks of sexuality, identity, and autonomy send reverberations throughout the family system. The sexual awakening of their children has a powerful effect on many parents. Opposite-sex parents and children may find a gulf between them as a response to the power of the incest taboo in society. Unfortunately, in many families this results in the end of nonverbal affection, as the next example illustrates.

> *"I will never forget being hurt as a teenager when my father totally changed the way he acted toward me. We used to have a real 'buddy' relationship. We would spend lots of time together; we would wrestle, fool around, and I adored him. Suddenly, he became really distant, and I could not understand whether I had done something. But I did not feel I could talk about it either. Now that I am older, I can see the same pattern happening with my two sisters. Obviously, within his head there is a rule that when your daughter starts to develop breasts, you have to back off; and for him, that means having almost no relationship at all. Now I can understand that it hurts him as much as it hurts us."*

Same-sex parents and children may face internal conflicts if they perceive a major contrast between their children's budding sexuality and their own sexual identity. Such conflicts are tied to the parents' stages of development and negative self-evaluations. Because facing this issue would be uncomfortable, such perceptions may result in conflict over more "acceptable" issues, such as friends, money, independence, or responsibility. Adolescents are more likely to accept parental guidelines when they have clear, open lines of communication and feel that their parents respect their values (Conger 1977, 207). A cross-generational coalition was found to exist when young people described themselves as emotionally closer to one parent than the other. This affected their later development of satisfying intimate relationships in early adulthood. If the parents had problems with intimacy, it was more likely their offspring would experience the same (West, Zarski, and Harvil 1988, 173–174).

In his study of adolescent communication, Rawlins (1989) reports that adolescents viewed parents as more likely than their friends to criticize them, yet they felt their parents cared for them more than their friends did. The criticisms reflected genuine concern. Parents were seen as viewing adolescent concerns through the historical lens of "having been through it." Parent-adolescent conversations reflected a choice of topic, anticipated response, and perceived degree of caring. Yet maintaining a caring and supportive relationship with parents aids the development of an adolescent autonomy (Youniss and Smollar 1985).

The exploring adolescent often challenges family themes, boundaries, and biosocial beliefs. He or she is forever introducing the family system to people or modes of behavior that may threaten the family's identity. The adolescent's new input forecasts the eventual departure of the exploring child and forces the family to reevaluate itself (Ackerman 1980). A relatively flexible family may encounter less difficulty with an acting-out adolescent than a family with rigid rules. For example, Kantor and Lehr (1976) noticed that stress during the adolescent stage causes the system, particularly a closed one, to change form by developing open strategies. This change produces "a curious hybrid such as a family with closed-system goals and open-system means of attaining these goals" (157).

Some parents of adolescents report increased marital conflict because, as Troll (1975) states, "They don't report fighting over their children until the children are old enough to get into deliberate trouble [in adolescence]" (90). During this stage, parents often become aware of such issues as lack of companionship, sexual difficulties, or dominance in their relationship. At this point, the father's self-esteem relates highly to the quality of communication he has with adolescent children, and the mother's relates to the degree of stress she has experienced in parenting teenagers (Demo, Small, and Savin-Williams).

Some adolescents get caught in perverse triangles, finding themselves an emotional support to one parent, thus establishing a cross-generational coalition. This affects their later development of satisfying intimate relationships in early adulthood. If the parents have problems with intimacy, it is more likely that their offspring will experience the same (West, Zarski, and Harvil).

Adolescents are more likely to accept parental guidelines when they have clear, open lines of communication and feel that their parents respect their values. Communication that supports gradual separation, rather than pushes persons away from one another or holds them rigidly close, eases the transition. Failure to negotiate the adolescent stage successfully, as reflected by an increase in suicides, has caused concern among family experts. In 1985, the National Center for Health Statistics reported a suicide rate of 12.4 per 100,000 adolescents, double the rate of ten years earlier.

Launching Children and Moving On

The departure from home of the oldest child signals one more major stage and necessitates major family reorganization. At this stage, it is very difficult to generalize about specific predictable events, because so many different things may be occurring. Most theories propose some variation of one of the following scenarios: (1) the "empty nest" model, which suggests that at least one of the parents is having difficulty letting the children go, and (2) the curvilinear model, which concentrates on the increased freedom and independence of the parents (McCullough 1980). The transitions and tasks related to this stage include (1) the development of parent-child adult-to-adult relationships, (2) changes in function of marriage, (3) family expansion to include in-laws and grandchildren, and (4) opportunities to resolve relationships with aging parents (McCullough and Rutenberg 1988).

This is the period when parents move from being responsible for children to a sense of mutual responsibility between caring adults. When young people start living on their own, especially if they totally support themselves, they more readily take on the responsibilities of adulthood and caring for themselves, and begin the process of becoming emotionally comfortable living apart from their families-of-origin. It is a time of vacating the bedrooms, sending along the extra coffee pot, and letting go of the predictable daily interactions at breakfast or bedtime that tied parents and siblings into a close, interactive system.

If the separation takes place without conflict or parental strings attached, communication usually remains open and flexible. Frequent contact with parents and siblings via phone calls, letters, or visits maintains family links and strengthens the bonds. At this time, communication issues may involve handling money, negotiating living space, making career decisions, and keeping regular hours.

"Since I've been in college, I call home about once a week, and sometimes I sense that my mother is upset about something. If I ask about it, she will say something like, 'Oh, don't you worry about it. It's not your problem; you don't live here anymore.' That upsets me, because I still feel I am part of the family."

Some parents force a separation before their children may feel ready for the break. This often results in hard feelings, conflict, and resentment. Yet many children resist being "on their own." In some communities or cultures, it is expected; in others, children may remain home indefinitely. For example, many Hispanic, Italian, and Polish families prefer, and sometimes insist, that daughters remain with them until marriage. In many cultures getting an apartment would be quickly vetoed for a 21-year-old working woman.

The high cost of living today makes leaving home difficult. In fact, some leave home and later return because they miss the comforts of their parents' homes and don't earn enough to live on their own. In fact, most young adults are now living with their parents; in 1988, 55 percent of 20–24-year-olds did just that (Glick 1990). Another trend is married children divorcing and returning "home" as single parents because of financial difficulties. A countertrend has been young people leaving home to live independently prior to marriage, with some of them entering cohabiting relationships (Santi 1987). Women, more than men, who moved away from home married later than those who stayed with a parent (Waite 1987).

Conflicts may occur when young people remain home during their early twenties, because established family rules and regulations tend to be challenged. "You don't need to wait up for me—I'm not seventeen!" "Pay room and board? I can't afford it and make car payments" may typify certain interactions when new adult-adult roles are not negotiated. If young adults remain longer than expected, some families develop adverse effects (Harkins 1975). If parent-child conflicts created problems in earlier years, this pattern is likely to continue (Suitor and Pillemer 1987). Some aging parents want time alone as a couple, and if the children delay leaving, this may create frustrations and negative communication patterns. Rather than separate from the family, a young person may remain connected, enjoying the advantages of home and family comforts without working to function as an independent adult.

Major changes occur in the husband-wife relationship after children leave as opportunities for increased intimacy present themselves. Troll comments, "Mothers in the launching stage, whose children are getting ready to leave home, are seldom enthusiastic and often bitter about the loss of their husband's affection and companionship. It is only after the children are gone that the second honeymoon occurs—if it is going to" (Lewis, Freneau, and Roberts 1979, 517). It is impossible to state which parent is more affected by the shift. Some men have psychologically invested more in the parenting relationship than in their spousal relationship. Fathers with fewer children report greater unhappiness over their leaving than do fathers with several children. Also, older fathers react more strongly than younger fathers. This finding further relates to family communication: the most unhappy fathers reported they felt most neglected by their wives, received the least amount of understanding, sensed loneliness most, were least enthusiastic about wives' companionship, and believed their wives least empathic. Ironically, Bart's (1975) research with women revealed many of the same complaints about men and the same communication barriers. It is interesting to note that Silverberg and Steinberg (1987) found that husbands' marital satisfaction was closely related to the quality of their relationship with firstborn sons, and wives' happiness was related to firstborn daughters.

In many families, the postparental period presents few crises and becomes a part of the sequence and rhythms of the life cycle. The effects of the empty nest largely disappear two years after the departure of the last child. In a fascinating study of roles throughout the life cycle, Schaefer and Keith (1981) found that equity in the tasks of cooking, homemaking, and providing grows across the stages, with the greatest growth in the launching stage and middle years after the children leave home. A recent study confirmed again that older couples with no children in the home are happier than those with children (Pittman and Lloyd 1988).

In the middle years, communication in the family mainly involves the original dyad. As opposed to earlier days when families were larger and life expectancy was shorter, the empty nest transition now occurs in middle age rather than old age. A century ago a typical couple lived together for thirty-one years before losing a spouse; today the figure is forty-four years (Glick 1989). Many contradictory reports about this period appear in family literature. "Second honeymoons" are counterbalanced by a high divorce rate. Images of decreasing sexuality are matched by reports of this as a period of sexual revitalization. Such factors as health, economics, and social class tend to interact with the couple's development and satisfaction at this stage. Wives' adjustments to midlife concerns, more than husbands', affect marital satisfaction. Women undergo a reappraisal and achieve more autonomy and power as they let go of child-raising responsibilities.

Spouses who have allowed their children to become their main focus for so many years may find themselves back at the lower stages of relationship development. Partners may sense a distance between them and feel unable, or unwilling, to try to reconnect. For many couples, the readjustment to a viable two-person system requires hard work. Divorces occur frequently in this midlife transmission period.

"When the children left, I discovered myself living with essentially a mute man. We hadn't realized that for years we had talked little to one another—that most of our communication was with the children or about them. Because we both worked, always took vacations with the kids, and kept busy chasing after kids' activities, we never had time for ourselves. Now I've got time to talk, and I have to compete with TV—that's the 'other woman' in my house."

Much adult parent-child interaction appears to be carried out through the female networks rather than through male ones, resulting in a potential distancing of the adult child's father (Troll et al. 1979, 103). Mothers tend to remain in even more constant contact with adult daughters, especially those who have children. The presence of grandchildren contributes significantly to changes in family communication.

Grandparenthood. The experience of being a grandparent or grandchild is becoming increasingly common, given increased longevity. Currently, a child has a 50 percent chance of having two living grandparents (Cryer-Downs 1989). Children in blended families may experience up to eight grandparent figures! Given the reality of a mobile society, some grandparents and grandchildren experience limited and formal or distant contacts. Yet grandparents are being called on to take a more participative role in modern families, particularly in situations of divorce and dual-career marriages.

In a society where "grandparents range in age from 30 to 110 and grandchildren range from newborns to retirees" (Hagestad 1985, 36), styles of grandparenting vary. In their classic study, Neugarten and Weinstein classified five grandparent styles as (1) formal, (2) fun seeker, (3) second parent, (4) family sage, and (5) distant figure. Such roles may vary across ages; for example, one study found that children ages 4–5 liked indulgent grandparents, at ages 8–9 preferred fun-loving ones, and at ages 11–12 began to distance themselves (Barranti-Ramirez 1985).

Assuming the role of grandparents opens the door for unique communication experiences. Grandparents and grandchildren who interact frequently express feelings of closeness; some grandparents experience continuity, and grandchildren develop added self-identity through the narration of oral history.

Grandparenthood provides an opportunity for new roles and meaningful interaction, because it usually does not entail the responsibilities, obligations, and conflicts of parenthood. Also, grandparents and grandchildren may have a "common enemy" in the parents (Walsh 1982, 204). Conflicts can result if grandparents are drawn into parental conflicts; on occasion, grandparents act as a refuge for children in a strife-torn family.

In certain cultural groups, grandparents are expected to assume a major role in child rearing; but in other cultures, if grandparents are coerced into childcare, they are likely to resent it (Kahana and Kahana 1970; Lopata 1973). Such cross-generational contact provides opportunities for extended transmission of culture and for development of a sense of family history. Grandparents serve as one source of a child's sense of identity; children gain access to their roots and have the opportunity to see the functioning of the two families-of-origin that influenced their parents, and hence, themselves.

In contrast to grandparenting, the middle, or parental, generation has to deal with changing relationships with their parents and their retirement, disability, dependency, or death.

In spite of the decisions about major changes in midlife, this period can be a happy one for families. Financial worries lessen if money has been managed well over the years. The period between the time the children leave home and the retirement of the parents is when family income is at its highest level. Husbands earn most between 55 and 64 years of age (Glick 1989). Children become less of an everyday concern, and a couple or single parent may have the opportunity to focus on old or new relationships and experiences.

Many families have to negotiate the relationship between parents and grown children who may now be entering parenthood. Highly cohesive families may attempt to keep inappropriate ties. For example, if a child or grandchild is constantly more important than a spouse, the partners are not dealing with their own development.

Families in Later Life

Family relationships continue to be significant throughout later life. According to Walsh (1989), 70 percent of older adults live with spouses or other relatives, including children, siblings, or aged parents. Eighty percent of those who do live alone tend to be elderly widows, yet "most of those with children report that a child could be there within minutes if needed and tend to maintain at least weekly contact" (311). The myth of the isolated elderly is not reality for the majority of older Americans. Total isolation is very rare.

Older family members face issues of self-identity related to retirement, health concerns, interpersonal needs (especially if they lose a spouse), and facing their own death. Some couples experience "reentry" problems when one or both return to the home and remain there twenty-four hours of most days. The increased contact may lead to a deepening of the relationship or result in friction from the forced closeness. The retired persons may undergo severe role adjustments and the loss of certain functions (e.g., providing) that served as self-definition. The loss of a large social communication network places increased pressure for intimacy on the couple. Yet this may be a time of rejuvenation. The couple now has time to enjoy one another. A study of couples married over fifty years shows the aging stage as one of the happiest, with more time together for travel and activities, which they previously could not manage (Sporakowski and Hughston 1978). When postretirement activates previously developed needs and hobbies, couples remain happy (McCubbin and Dahl 1985).

A second issue that affects all communication is related to the health and declining strength of the couple. Ill health creates a need for nurturing communication and taps the couple's physical, mental, and financial resources. Aging predictably involves some sensory loss, such as changes in visual or auditory acuity as well as taste, smell, and tactility, which affects interpersonal communication (Benjamin 1988). Such health concerns compound the problem of maintaining relationships. Frustration and low self-esteem may make individuals reluctant to initiate contact, while listeners may decline because of their impatience with the older person's infirmities.

Interpersonal communication becomes increasingly important at this stage. "Satisfaction with an intimate relationship is related to life satisfaction and psychological well-being, especially for elderly women" (Thompson and Nussbaum 1988,

95). Many older family members engage in the "elder function," or the sharing of the accumulated wisdom of their lives with younger people, usually family members. There is a need to feel of use to the coming generation; and, for many older persons, such feelings come from revealing information or spinning stories designed to guide the younger listener. The focus of reminiscence is usually the family. It can be used as a coping mechanism, to defend self-esteem, to feel loved, to gain self-awareness, and to see oneself in a larger historical context. This oral history can enrich a family, especially its members' sense of their family-of-origin. It gives the elderly a chance to communicate to those they love, helped raise, or even harmed by their actions their need to "set the record straight" or to correct, and express sorrow for, mistakes.

"I'm glad my Dad lived past seventy-five. Only then did we come to terms with one another. Long after he retired, he mellowed and became approachable. He talked about the depression, the war years, and the struggle to pay for the farm. Then I sensed what had made him so tough and noncommunicative."

Elderly individuals who remain interested and have opportunities for keeping abreast of world and national events enjoy life more and disengage themselves less from the family (Nussbaum 1983, 317).

Two basic functions seem to be served by the elderly parent-adult child relationship: affect and mutual aid. Positive affect provided to the elderly by their children significantly increases their feelings of well-being (Thompson and Nussbaum). Although older Americans see their children with some regularity, many older persons are prevented from maintaining the interpersonal contacts they desire due to concerns of economics, safety, and health. Rising costs of living restrict the travel and entertainment aspects of older persons' budgets, and many urban senior citizens do not feel safe attending evening meetings or social activities.

Older couples who reach their retirement together may turn inward toward each other and share intensely their remaining years. Loss becomes a part of aging, and this increases when close friends and relatives die. In order to prevent their becoming "the last one out," older couples often move beyond their age range and establish friendships through communicating with younger adults. This may be difficult if infirmities prevent mobility.

The developmental stages of both middle and older years are important periods for introspection. Intrapersonal communication about the meaning of one's life allows an individual to see his or her life in perspective. Turning to oneself for insights can be painful and lead to despair, because some aging adults sense their faults and shortcomings and recognize that too little has been accomplished and too little time and energy is left to change. This affects their self-concept and interpersonal communication with other family members. The intrapersonal communication has systemic effects, because how the aging individual comes to terms with his or her own sense of wholeness affects other members' sense of identity.

After the death of one spouse, the other must face the adjustment inherent in becoming a widow or widower. Working through the grief period, an older family member may make great demands on younger members who may be resentful of, or unprepared for, such pressures. This is coupled with the younger members' personal grief at the loss of a parent. The surviving spouse has to renegotiate roles and boundaries as he or she attempts to create or maintain interpersonal contacts. It is important that older family members have a say in their care and be a part of all communication that concerns them as long as possible.

Much to the surprise of their adult children, many widows or widowers begin to date. The importance of dating among older persons is growing, not necessarily as prelude to marriage. Interpersonal motives for dating include meeting possible mates, meeting other possible dates, exchanging intimacies, remaining socially active, interacting with the opposite sex, engaging in sex, and maintaining a stable identity (Thompson and Nussbaum).

Eventually, an elderly person must confront his or her own death (Thompson 1989). Many families resist addressing the issue directly with the elderly member, yet relationships that allow discussion of death and that provide direct emotional support are more helpful. Family members—particularly adult children—may face their own crises as they try to (1) deal with the loss of the generation that separates them from death, (2) make sense of the experience, (3) anticipate shifts in the family formation, and (4) deal with their own feelings. Often these concerns get in the way of saying farewell in a direct and meaningful manner.

Transitions Between Stages

It is important not to underestimate the effects of transitions between each of these developmental stages. Haley, Bowen, and other therapists observed that dysfunctional families have members who fail to make these transitions at the appropriate times in their lives. These members cause imbalance in their family systems by remaining "stuck" at one developmental stage and not moving on. In these troubled families, they have observed a piling-up effect, with one or more members stuck at the same stage. Some of these same family members express external stresses (illness, separation, divorce) simultaneously with developmental changes and become unable to cope. However, functional families take these stages in stride and experience the transitions with temporary, but not permanent, stress.

This does not mean that marital satisfaction does not suffer during the family life cycle, with consequent effects upon family communication. In a large study, which followed couples from the childless stage through the years of childbearing, adolescence, and stages beyond, Olson and McCubbin (1983) found a steady decline in satisfaction that did not level off until the children began to individuate and separate from their parents. Then, satisfaction increased in the postparental period when the children left and established their own families. Regarding cohesion and adaptability over the stages, they found wives believed their families more cohesive and adaptable than did their husbands. Adolescents consistently reported lower levels of cohesion and adaptability than did either of their parents. In fact, cohesion and adaptability declined in the first five stages to the lowest points in the adolescent and launching stages and increased in the last two stages. Not only does this show differences in perceptions by family members but differences between stages that affect communication. It is interesting to note that families coped with these stresses by using the communication strategy of reframing their difficulties in ways they could manage. This required the communication skills of negotiation, problem solving, and decision making.

Nock (1981) found that functional families experienced transitions as challenging and, at times, unpleasant events, but not as long-lasting negative influences. Transitions into marriage or birth of a child, for example, affected family functioning, but the family progressed through them at a normal maturation process. Transitions out of marriage, such as divorce, desertion, or death, had negative effects and caused higher stress over longer periods of time. Steffensmeier studied the transition into parenthood and concluded that whether couples experienced difficulty with the stage depended on their views on parental responsibilities; the amount of gratification they received from the role was related to the quality of their intimacy and stability prior to and during the developmental stage. Thus, transitions are like hurdles set before a functional family. Normally, they are easily taken in stride, but if other factors intervene, the family has more difficulty. Communication is affected accordingly.

As they struggle with changes and transitions, most persons experience life in its moments and often ignore the larger process. In short, the movement across the life span becomes lost in the moments. Carter and McGoldrick's (1988) comments serve to summarize this experience:

> Families characteristically lack time perspective when they are having problems. They tend generally to magnify the present moment, overwhelmed and immobilized by their immediate feelings; or they become fixed on a moment in the future that they dread or long for. They lose the awareness that life means continual motion from the past and into the future with a continual transformation of familial relationships. (10)

CONCLUSION

This chapter provided an overview of the effects of developmental stresses on communication within families. After presenting the mode of stress and indicating the movement of individuals through a life cycle, the chapter focused on a stage model for intact American families. The stages included were (1) single young adults, (2) the couple, (3) families with young children, (4) families with adolescents, (5) launching children and moving on, and (6) families in later life. As families move through the years, each generation faces predictable developmental issues as couples marry, beget children, and live through stages of child development superimposed upon individual adult developmental changes. As children leave home to form new systems, the original couple faces the middle years and adjustment issues. The cohesion-adaptability axis overlay influences each system's personal growth, and themes, images, and biosocial beliefs may be challenged as the years pass.

The entire family developmental process is extremely complex and challenging. Achieving the developmental tasks in each stage represents accomplishment and psychological growth for each family member. Some stresses get expressed in the interpersonal communication that follows as the family member struggles for balance between self needs and family system needs.

IN REVIEW

1. Reflecting upon your own family or one you know well, which stage of development seemed to have the greatest number of communication problems? Describe sample problems and hypothesize why this stage was so problematic.
2. Using your own family or a family you know well, give examples of verbal or nonverbal communication patterns that seemed commonplace at different developmental stages in the family life cycle.
3. Referring to your own family or a family you have observed, describe how a couple has dealt with the communication tasks of incorporating a child into their system and dealing with the following communication-related issues: (1) renegotiating roles, (2) transmitting culture, (3) establishing a community of experiences, and (4) developing the child's communication competence.
4. What appears to characterize communication in families during the period when there are one or more adolescents living within the system?
5. How is communication affected by the moving out of young adults in the launching stage in two-parent systems?
6. Compare and contrast communication patterns you have observed in the interactions between middle-aged and older family members. To what extent were reminiscing, reflection, and sorting out important to members at these stages?

CHAPTER 11

Family Communication and Unpredictable Stress

What are your chances of becoming an overnight multimillionaire? of experiencing a plane crash? of watching a younger sibling die? Most people imagine that life will continue in a relatively predictable pattern. You do not really believe you will win the lottery. You do not expect to parent a handicapped child. You think your family members will live together to a ripe old age. Sometimes your expectations are correct; often your expectations are wrong. Each person, each family encounters different types of stresses. In addition to the developmental, or more predictable, stresses faced by family systems, you must also face unpredictable, or external stresses. Unpredictable stresses are brought about by events or circumstances that disrupt life patterns but cannot be foreseen from a developmental perspective. Such stresses may be positive, although more frequently they are perceived as negative. These are the "slings and arrows of outrageous fortune," shocks to the system. Such stresses conjure up images of loss such as that involved in untimely death, divorce, economic reversal, or serious injury. Some positive events, such as a large inheritance, a job promotion and transfer, or the rediscovery of long-lost relatives, are also stresses for the system.

Although we are dealing with unpredictable stresses as distinct from the more predictable developmental changes, there may be certain overlaps. Becoming pregnant or having a child may be considered a developmental event, but an unwanted pregnancy or the birth of a severely handicapped child may also be classified as an unpredictable stress. Death is a developmental experience for all persons, but the untimely death of a family member is a severe crisis for the system. Whether the entire family or only certain members are initially affected by the event, the family system will eventually reflect the tension of such stresses in its communication behavior.

Crises occur when a family lacks the resources to cope with one or more stressful events. All families undergo some degree of strain or stress. Strain can be defined as tension or difficulty sensed by family members which indicates that change is needed. Stressor events discussed in this chapter are characterized by their unexpectedness, their greater intensity and chronicity, and their undesirability and serious effects (Lavee, McCubbin, and Olson 1987, 859).

"There were nine children in our family, and three had muscular dystrophy. I remember how hard it was for Mom to accept their illness. She wouldn't talk about it within the family. Her rule was that it was better not discussed, yet I would find her alone in her room crying. We all learned from Marilyn, Dan, and Virginia. Communication reached a tense stage when Marilyn was the first to die. We knew the fear and panic in Dan and Virginia. It took time to get them to talk about these fears. Finally, near their own deaths, they would joke about who was going next. All of this was strictly with two sisters and myself. Mom, Dad, and the rest couldn't handle any humor on the subject. I feel Dan and Virginia would like to have shared these feelings with all of us, but some of the living in our family put great distance between themselves and those who were dying."

The previous chapter contains a model of family stressors (Figure 10-1) and a description of the developmental stresses a family faces. This chapter concentrates on the second type of horizontal stressors—the external, unpredictable stressors. It examines (1) the patterns of coping with unpredictable stress (including the stressors), a model for coping, and the stages of family crisis, and (2) communication patterns for coping with stresses such as untimely death, illness/disability, and separation/divorce.

UNPREDICTABLE STRESS AND FAMILY COPING PATTERNS

Stress involves a physiological response to stressors, events, or situations that are viewed as powerful negative or positive forces. Individuals or families under stress reflect these physiological changes through their anxiety and attempts to cope.

Systems under stress tend to fall into predictable patterns—some functional, some dysfunctional—as the members try to handle the anxiety. As you might imagine, what is a major stressor to one family may be a minor concern to another; what one family does to reduce tension differs greatly from another family's strategies. In order to appreciate the process and the coping, you need to examine family stressors, models of coping, and stages of crisis.

Stressors

Family researchers have examined stresses and crises for over forty years. In his early work, Hill (1949) identified family disruptions that cause crises. These include (1) the coming apart of the family due to the death of a member; (2) the addition of new or returning family members; (3) the sense of disgrace that may result from infidelity, alcoholism, nonsupport; and (4) a combination of the above, which could include suicide, imprisonment, homicide, or mental illness. In their classic work on life stressors, Holmes and Rahe (1967) identified forty-three events that cause stress. The top twelve reflected strong family connections, such as death of a spouse, divorce, marriage, retirement, change in a family member's health, or pregnancy. In 1967, remarriage or stepparenting did not make the top twelve, even though today it might. Addiction to drugs or alcohol might also. Bain (1978) provided important insights into a family's capacity to cope with stress. He found that a family's coping capacity was tied to four major factors: (1) the number of previous stressors the members had faced, (2) the degree of role change involved in the coping, (3) the social support available to members, and (4) the institutional support available to members.

As you might imagine, the severe illness of a child is likely to be very difficult for a family that has recently dealt with major financial or marital problems. It may cause greater strain if a parent has to change roles, such as give up a career, to tend the child. A family with the social support of friends and relatives and the institutional support of doctors, teachers, and religious leaders is likely to cope better than a family left to its own stressed resources. Yet, often a family has to ask for the support and not assume that people will know what is needed or know how to respond.

"As a teacher, I watch a few students' families undergo divorce each year. The ones who seem to cope reasonably well with the pain are those who have some strengths or resources to bring to the process. Usually this is the family that has strong extended family or neighborhood friends and the family that tells the school or church what is going on. In short, this family lets people in on the pain and asks for some help."

More recent research on family stress has examined concerns such as ongoing environmental stress; for example, refugees or those living in dangerous inner city areas (McCubbin et al. 1983; Hines 1988).

Throughout the family stress literature, writers emphasize the possible productive outcomes of dealing with stress as well as the difficulties inherent in such a process. In a new move, McCubbin and McCubbin (1988) attempt to identify typologies of resilient families, taking into account factors of social class and ethnicity. They suggest the following:

Resilient families appear to cultivate a commitment to ensuring stability by creating a sense of rhythm to family life through its rituals and routines . . . [and] by a family emphasis on developing a sense of centeredness . . . [and] confidence in its own ability to manage change. (253)

These authors suggest that resilient low- to low–middle-income families have internal strengths complemented by community support, service, religious programs, and a sense of belonging to the community. In order to understand the coping process more fully, you need to examine the process described in a well-known model.

A Model for Coping

Each family exhibits unique coping behaviors. Coping implies "the central mechanism through which family stressors, demands, and strains are eliminated, managed, or adapted to" (McCubbin et al. 1983, 3). The primary models currently used to understand family crisis have evolved from Hill's original model, which proposed that:

> A [the stressor event], interacting with B [the family's crisis-meeting resources], interacting with C [the family's definition of the event] produces X [the crisis] (McCubbin and Patterson 1983, 6).

An explanation is in order. The stressor, *a*, represents a life event or transition that has the potential to change a family's social system. Such events as the loss of job, untimely death, serious illness, or good luck in the lottery may fall into this category. The *b* factor represents the resources a family can use to keep an event or change from creating a crisis, such as money, friends, time and space, or problem-solving skills. This factor ties into a family's levels of cohesion and adaptability in terms of how it has learned to deal with various crises over time.

The *c* factor represents the importance a family attaches to the stressor (*a*). For example, in one family a diagnosis of a member's juvenile diabetes might overwhelm the entire system, whereas another family might cope well with that news, perceiving the diabetes as a manageable disease, one not likely to alter their lives drastically. The definitions of both the family and families-of-origin may come to bear on the perception of crises. For example, a three-generation family that has never experienced a divorce may define a young granddaughter's marital separation as a severe crisis. A multigenerational system with a history of divorce may not see the separation as a crisis. Together, *a*, *b*, and *c* contribute to the experience of stress that is unique to each family, depending on its background, resources, and interpretation of the event.

The *x* factor represents the amount of disruptiveness that occurs to the system. It is characterized by "the family's inability to restore stability and by the continuous pressure to make changes in the family structure and patterns of interaction" (McCubbin and Patterson, 10). In short, it is the experienced anxiety and demands.

Other family researchers have developed a Double ABCX model based on Hill's original work but incorporating postcrisis variables (Figure 11-1) or the next stages of coping. Whereas Hill's *abcx* model focused on precrisis areas, the Double ABCX model incorporates the family's efforts to recover over time. In this model, the *aA* factor includes not only the immediate stressor (e.g., death) but also the demands or changes that may emerge from individual systems' members, a system as a whole, and the extended system. McCubbin and Patterson suggest that the *aA* factor includes (1) the initial stressor or developmental stage issues, (2) normative transitions, (3) prior strains, (4) the consequences of the system's coping attempts, and (5) ambiguity.

Imagine, for example, the death of a man, age 36, in a family with a wife and three daughters, ages 6, 10, and 12. If a young father dies, the system must deal with

Figure 11–1
The Double ABCX Model

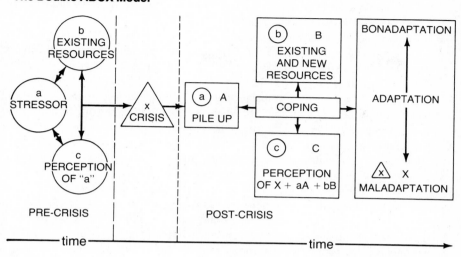

the immediate loss as well as economic uncertainty and changes in the mother's role. In addition, the developmental stage of some children may soon require the family to cope with an adolescent's need for independence. This is compounded by any prior strains, such as in-law problems or mother-daughter conflicts. A consequence of the family's attempts to cope might be the mother's new job, which keeps her from meeting the children's needs for active parenting. Finally, ambiguity might be caused by the confusion of new roles now that the father has left the system. Boundaries shift. Mother might consider remarriage. Changes become expected. Thus, aA is larger than the original conception of a.

The bB factor represents the family's ability to meet its needs. This factor includes family resources from an individual, system, and community point of view. A family may use existing and expanded resources. Existing resources are part of a family's background. In the case of death, these may include the ways in which a family coped in the past when Father was gone on business. The expanded family resources emerge from the crisis itself. A widow may create such resources by studying accounting, which leads to increased income, or by sharing in a widows' self-help group. The emerging social systems are a critical element in the bB factor.

The cC factor is the way in which a family interprets a crisis, including the meaning the family gives to the stressor event and to the added stressors caused by the original crisis, plus its perception of how to bring the family into balance. When a young father dies, a family must cope with that event and its meaning. If the widow comes to believe she has lost her only chance at happiness in life, her perceptions will strongly influence her attempts at recovery and those of her children. The members must also interpret the changes in finances, changes in the mother's role, and how the entire family is affected. Families who cope well can manage the situation through flexible changes in responsibilities and through support of one another. Families who have difficulty coping cannot see a sense of challenge and find themselves overwhelmed, with little sense of hope or opportunity for growth.

The xX factor is the effect of the family's adaptation on the individual system, and community levels. Family adaptation is achieved "through reciprocal relationships where the demands of one of these units are met by the capabilities of another so as to achieve a 'balance' of interaction" (McCubbin and Patterson, 19). If members' demands are too great for the family's capabilities, there will be an imbalance. There will also be imbalance if the family demands more than the community is capable of providing. For example, the family and work community may create an imbalance by demanding too much of one parent. The positive end of the continuum of outcomes of a crisis, called *bonadaptation,* is characterized by balance between (1) member and family and (2) family and community. The negative end, or *maladaptation,* reflects imbalance, or severe losses for the family. In some families, drastic changes allow members to renegotiate their relationships in positive ways. Thus, disruptions may have positive or negative effects on the family system.

In keeping with this orientation toward family coping, Bain supports the importance of (1) the amount and type of recent stress a family has faced, (2) the type of support from institutions, (3) the support from a family's social network, and (4) the magnitude of the role changes involved. The ways in which a family has established patterns of cohesion and adaptability have great bearing on its ability to cope with external stress. A family with a high capacity for adaptation and above average cohesion is likely to weather stressor events more easily than families who are rigid and fragmented. More adaptable families have the capacity to find alternative ways of relating and can adjust their communication behavior to encompass an event. As shown in the example at the beginning of the chapter, a family that has a rule against discussing debilitating illness has little ability to cope openly with and communicate about the impending death of a member. During a crisis, family members often wish to rely on each other for comfort and support, a behavior that cannot suddenly occur if the family has a history of separateness.

Such issues also interrelate with family functions related to boundaries, themes, images, and biosocial issues. Families with rigid boundaries may be unable to cope adequately when severe external stresses occur. By greatly limiting communication with such institutions as hospitals, courts, and schools, members deprive themselves of necessary information and possible emotional support. Additionally, boundaries that prevent a social network (friends or extended family) from knowing what is happening within the family eliminate potential sources of strength and comfort that might help "carry" a family through a critical period.

"My mother, Aunt Maria, and Aunt Elena kept each other going through some terrible times. If the men were out of work at the steel mill, the women still had to find ways of putting food on the table, help to keep the children feeling secure, and deal with their husbands who were depressed. Somehow I see these women as people who managed—sharing house, food, and clothes with each other, or simply talking about their troubles."

Families with themes of total self-sufficiency or images of rocklike members may find support from strong members of the family. Members may find that such themes and images prevent them from turning outward when the pain becomes too great for the family to handle functionally, resulting in severe conflict or separation. The number and magnitude of stresses may determine how functional these themes and images can be.

Finally, families with inflexible beliefs related to such biosocial issues as sex roles or authority may find that such beliefs aid them through a crisis or may interfere with its resolution. For example, in a family that sets very distinct male-female roles, the father's loss of a good position may leave the family emotionally and financially devastated because this belief causes the man to feel inadequate and prevents the woman from working to support the family.

Seemingly positive events can create great stress. Newspapers contain accounts of the pressure put on lottery winners by the expectations of family and friends and the loss of a settled way of life. A long-wished-for promotion may be accompanied by the loss of a familiar co-worker, pressure to succeed at a new level of responsibility, and the possibility of a stressful family move to a new city or neighborhood. Family members may find it painful to cope with the marriage or the departure for college of a much-loved child. Great joys may be accompanied by great losses.

Because communication affects and is affected by all these behaviors, it plays a central role in the experiencing and eventual resolution of such stresses and contributes specifically to the family's movement through stages of stress reaction. In some families, members use direct verbal messages to explore options, negotiate needs, express feelings, and reduce tension. In other families, the members' stress may be apparent through the nonverbal messages that indicate their anxiety and other feelings. Members constantly interpret others' verbal and nonverbal messages as part of the coping pattern.

Stages of Family Crisis

In any serious crisis situation, a family goes through a definite process in handling the grief or chaos that results. Depending upon the event, the stages may last from a few days to several months or years. These stages may be more pronounced in the case of a death, divorce, or news of an incurable illness, but in any crisis, family members experience a progression of feelings from denial to acceptance. Yet, because no two families accept a crisis in the same way, and because family systems are characterized by equifinality (see p. 13), they will reach the final stages of the process in a variety of ways. The following stages approximate the general process of dealing with severe stress. Although the stages usually follow one another, they may overlap, and some may be repeated a number of times.

1. Shock, resulting in numbness or disbelief, denial
2. Recoil stage, resulting in anger, confusion, blaming, guilt, and bargaining
3. Depression

4. Reorganization, resulting in acceptance and recovery (Kübler-Ross 1970; Dunlop 1978; Parkes 1972; Feifel 1977; Mederer and Hill 1983)

The process of going through such stages after a serious life event usually results in transformation of the system. Persons may find themselves more separated from, or connected to, different members and may find a shift in adaptability patterns. Communication behavior reflects and aids progress through the stages. Understanding the process allows one to analyze others' progress through the stages or to be more understanding of one's own behavior and personal progress.

At the *shock stage,* family members tend to deny the event or its seriousness. Denying comments such as "It can't be true," "It's a mistake," or "It's temporary" are accompanied by nonverbal behavior, such as setting a dead person's place at the table, misplacing attempts at smiles and encouragement with a terminally ill person, or spending money lavishly when the paycheck has been cut off.

Most persons quickly move from this stage and exhibit behaviors that indicate a recognition of reality. Principal family members acknowledge their grief and feel the pain of the loss. Crying or sullen quietness for those who find it hard to cry characterizes communication. The truth of the crisis news begins to take on fuller meanings, such as "Mom will never get well" or "She has left and will never return." This kind of reasoning sends messages to the self that confirm the reality.

Denial is transformed into an intense desire to recapture what has been lost, especially in the case of a family death, desertion, or severe injury. This may lead to attempts to recapture memories; for example, "I keep expecting to see her in the kitchen."

After the initial blow, the family may move into the *recoil stage* of blaming, anger, and bargaining. Blaming often takes place as the grieving family members seek reasons for what has happened. This may include blaming the self ("I was too trusting; I should have watched closer" or "I never should have let her go") or blaming others ("It's his own fault" or "The doctors never told us the truth soon enough"). Such behavior may be interspersed with feelings of "It's not fair," "Why did this happen to us?" and "We don't deserve this." Anger may be directed at the event or person most directly involved or may be displaced onto others, such as family members, friends, or co-workers. Attempts at real or imagined bargains may occur. "If I take a cut in pay, they could hire me back." "If you come back I'll stop gambling forever."

Thoughts of the unfairness of the world, that God has been cruel to let this happen, that potentials of the members involved had never been realized and now never will be, fill the minds of family members and then are released to one another. Again, the pain of the loss comes out through strong feelings.

Usually, family members need to talk about what has happened. In fact, they often retell the crisis news over and over, a normal and healthy response for the family as they feel the intensity of the loss. This is especially necessary for families that will experience a long period of suffering because of death, incurable illness, permanent injuries, a long jail sentence, or mental breakdown. People outside the family often fail to understand the communication that goes on within and may attempt to avoid the people or the subject, not recognizing that support may only be possible from those not as directly affected. Families may allow their boundaries to become more flexible in order to gain this support. Often, family confusion and disorganization may be so great that outsiders tend to take over and guide decision making.

The release of hurt feelings leads into the third stage—depression. At the depths of depression, a family realizes their old status quo or balance will never return. The death, divorce, or injury cannot be undone, and turning back the clock is unrealistic. The loss of a good job, especially one that has been held for many years, may not entail the same emotions as death or divorce, but the adjustments forced upon a family to cut back its standard of living, for example, can also lead to depression. Some people in this stage speak of having a sinking feeling—a sense of helplessness in not knowing or even caring about what to do. Verbally and nonverbally they communicate an overwhelming sadness usually accompanied by a tiredness and slowness of response.

"I have never felt so much sorrow and stress as when my wife left with the children and I was without the daily company of my kids. Among other things, life became totally unpredictable, and I felt I lost my identity. For months I functioned in a total fog. I can compare the anger and despair to some of my experiences as a medic in Vietnam."

Grief-stricken people normally pass through this stage to what they describe as a "turning point." Usually, a decision on their part marks the event. It may be a decision to take a trip, to sell a failing business, to get rid of mementos that serve as daily reminders, to register with a placement bureau, or to join Alcoholics Anonymous. Nonverbally, this decision signals that the individual has moved into the fourth crisis stage—the *acceptance* and *reorganization* of events in his or her life to effect a recovery. This stage is characterized by family members' taking charge of their lives and making the necessary changes forced upon them by the crisis. They may not like the changes required, but they communicate an ability to cope in spite of the loss. Reorganization may require all sorts of adjustments, and the time required varies greatly with the type of crisis and the individuals involved. It may take six weeks for one family to recover from a job loss; it may take another family suffering a death or divorce a year to eighteen months to achieve a semblance of balance in the systems.

If emotions in crises could be diagrammed, the line would descend to the lowest point with depression. The descent begins with the impact of the news and continues the downward spiral with some rises in the recoil stages to descend again as reality returns (see Figure 11-2).

Throughout this process, communication links members in sharing their reactions and links one or more to outside sources of institutional or social support, which can provide acceptance of the emotions that need to be expressed. If a family or member is cut off from support, the process may be incomplete; the family may remain stuck at some point, unable to complete the process and reach acceptance. The next section will consider some common types of family crises and the communication issues involved with each.

Figure 11–2
Linear Scale of Emotions During Crises

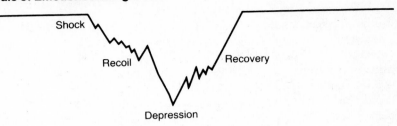

COMMUNICATION AND SPECIFIC FAMILY CRISES

Communication patterns and networks shift dramatically when members face major life crises. Interaction becomes unpredictable as individuals withdraw into silence, explode into anger, or move into constant talking as a way to handle the stress or grief. Although this action focuses on three major crises, remember that less dramatic events, such as moving, losing a job, or receiving a promotion or large inheritance, also disrupt the family system.

Untimely Death

The finality of death closes off relationship options, making it an emotionally overwhelming crisis for most families. Although the death of any family member carries with it a sense of grief, the death of an elderly person who has lived a full life usually does not contain the anger aroused by untimely death, nor does it carry the potential for major role changes among young or middle-aged family members. Hence, untimely death serves as a major unpredictable crisis for all families.

Untimely death may be expected or unexpected. Sudden death throws a family into severe shock, allowing no chance for farewells or the resolution of relationship issues (Herz-Brown 1988). Prolonged death, even when untimely, provides the family with the opportunity to mourn, say farewells, and resolve relationship issues, if members can use the time in this manner.

Communication within families dealing with death ranges from the highly intense and emotional to the very superficial and denial oriented. Persons who are dying and their family members often resort to silence, new rules, and verbal games to maintain a two-sided pretense that "Everything is going to be all right." Family members in their own grief may go into a denial of the information of a terminal illness. They shield the dying from such knowledge and begin a series of new communication rules around the dying person. Bowen (1976) calls death our chief taboo subject, saying, "A high percentage of people die alone, locked into their own thoughts which they cannot communicate to others. People cannot communicate the thoughts they have lest they upset the family or others" (336). Triangles may form as two people draw in a third to relieve tension, or subgroups may collude to avoid any discussion of the impending death. This lack of communication about death is common even between marriage partners (Thompson 1989). For men whose lives reflect a traditional sex role orientation that includes restrained emotionality and control, communicating about death can be particularly difficult (Silverberg 1985). Such silent attempts to fool the patient can create tremendous stress for a rational, articulate human who has the capacity to cope with news of his or her own death, because the pretense frequently becomes apparent. Often, the dying member knows and then has to play the game of "not knowing" to protect the rest of the family. Such rules block dealing with all the interpersonal feelings, caring, and relationships, as well as with some of the immediate fears and loneliness.

"I will never forget my uncle's complaining bitterly two days before he died about his family treating him like a helpless child and insisting he would recover whenever he started to talk about dying or his fear of never leaving the hospital. I was only fourteen and did not fully understand what he was trying to tell me at the time, but I never forgot his pain or anger as he tried to explain the feeling of dying without emotional support."

Dunlop declares that "the dying person has his own grieving to do. We should remember too, that the dying person is not just losing himself (which is a considerable loss that other grievers are not having to deal with), but the dying person is also about to lose everything which is important and everyone who is significant to him and whom he loves" (2). Kübler-Ross suggests that death should be regarded as an "intrinsic part of life," and it should be discussed openly like other events in family life, especially since almost all terminally ill patients are aware of their grave situation. The question should change from "Do I tell?" to "How do I share the information?" If a family confronts the issue openly, they can go through preparatory grief together, which facilitates the later bereavement process. According to Herz-Brown, "there is a greater likelihood of emotional and/or physical symptom development when family members are unable to deal openly with one another about death" (473).

Reasons vary for not telling a family member that he or she has a terminal illness. Dunlop states, "Perhaps it is done out of the belief that if the dying person were told he was dying, he would become depressed and despondent; however, in time he will be both, and must be both if his dying is to have some psychological comfort to it" (5). In determining whether to tell a patient, Verwoerdt (1967) lists these criteria: (1) the dying member's emotional and intellectual resources to handle the news, (2) what the dying member already knows or has guessed, (3) the personal meaning the disease has for the dying based on his or her knowledge of others who had the same terminal illness, and (4) the degree to which the dying member wants to know his or her fate (10). The answer to the question of whether to tell the dying person requires considerable skill in assessing verbal and nonverbal communication from that person.

Even those persons who choose their own death through suicide find that many of their preparatory messages are denied or ignored. In many cases, their attempts to communicate suicide plans go unrecognized until after the event. Parents of young people are advised to watch for such behaviors as talking of suicide, giving away possessions, acting abnormally cheerful after depression, and losing appetite. Those who deal with the elderly are advised to look for depression, withdrawal, isolation, changes in sleep patterns, lower self-image, and bereavement (Wass and Myers 1982, 133). However, many refuse to see such signs for what they are.

Kübler-Ross's classic five stages present one model for the process of dying: (1) denial, (2) anger, (3) bargaining, (4) depression, and (5) acceptance (36). The sequence of stages may vary, but eventually the dying person will progress through all of them if he or she lives long enough and does not become stuck at a particular point. The length of time one stays in a stage varies according to the individual, and persons may move back and forth through the stages, reworking certain issues.

Persons preparing for death need to express their denials—to articulate why such cannot be the case, to explore other remedies. They need to vent their anger at themselves, those they love, and possibly at God, science, medicine, or other institutions. Bargains must be struck or attempted—silently and openly. Finally, the loneliness, fears, and practical concerns must be unloaded, ranging from "What is really on the Other Side" to "How will they run the house without me?" Crying, praying, philosophizing, swearing, touching, worrying, and some joking contribute to the conversations.

Regardless of the phase, dying persons need an empathic listener who does not insist they will be better if they think about something else. Most dying people welcome an opportunity to talk about their deaths (Parkes, 131). Bowen, who has counseled dying patients for over thirty years, declares, "I have never seen a terminally ill person who was not strengthened by such a talk. This contradicts former beliefs about the ego being too fragile for this in certain situations" (337). Kübler-Ross agrees, "Dying persons will welcome someone who is willing to talk with them about their dying but will allow them to keep their defenses as long as they need them" (37). She further states that those patients who die comfortably have had a chance to rid themselves of guilt and were "encouraged to express their rage, to cry in preparatory grief, and to express their fears and fantasies to someone who can sit quietly and listen" (119). For family members, this means giving a dying person free expression to sort out his or her feelings, even though the other members may be in pain. Family members can create a sense of oneness that facilitates open expression of fears of dying—fears unlike any previously encountered. Although watching a person die can be devastating to the family members, "terminal illness of a family member (unlike sudden death) does allow the family, if the system remains open, to resolve relationship issues, reality issues, and to say the final goodbye before death" (Herz 1980, 228).

From their study of caregiver communication with the dying, Miller and Knapp (1986) identified a number of commonly used communication strategies. The strategy labeled "being reflexive" was noted as the most appropriate at all time periods and across all emotional states. They describe this strategy as follows:

Be Reflexive. The caregiver's presence is the primary force behind this strategy—not the initiation of specific words or behaviors. Here the caregiver allows the dying person to set the conversational agenda and adapts accordingly. Listening, "being there," and acting as a communicative reflector are the key elements of this strategy. Topics such as personal faith, current events, or love and affection are appropriate as the dying person initiates them. (727)

Whereas losing a family member through early or untimely death used to be a pervasive aspect of life even in the early 1900s, now it is a rare event. Hence, the untimely death of a member isolates a family and often forces it to cope without extensive community support. After the death of a family member, the other members go through a bereavement process—from numbness, to pining and depression, to recovery (Parkes; Thompson). An unexpected death, either by accident or illness, forces a family into an initial state of shock. Eventually, the shock wears off and the bereavement process begins. The event traumatizes the family, even in cases where members know of an impending death. The survivors experience anger and depression. There may be many regrets about unspoken issues: "If only I had told him how much I loved him." "If I had only taken time to listen to her." Survivors, too, need supportive listeners.

The death of an anticipated family member may have similar results. In recent years, studies of the devastating effect of experiencing stillbirth or newborn death indicate that many parents experience tremendous loss and many couples report high levels of marital stress (Callan and Murray 1989). Friends and family members often are unaware of the impact of this loss.

It is important to recognize the process nature of grief and realize that people will be upset and irrational and communicate differently. If the death has been caused by a long terminal illness or injury, the bereaved may have been so occupied with the care of the individual and with maintaining a semblance of order in the family system that only the death frees them to get in touch with their feelings. Many bereaved persons report the sense of a continuing relationship with the deceased and a sense of being unfinished with the relationship because they wanted to do or say additional things (Thompson).

Much also depends upon the place that the deceased had filled in the family system. The death of a parent of young children leaves many child-rearing jobs and family role responsibilities to the remaining parent. "The loss of a husband, for instance, may or may not mean the loss of a sexual partner, companion, accountant, gardener, baby-minder, audience, bed warmer, and so on depending upon the particular roles normally performed by this husband" (Parkes, 7). The surviving spouse has additional burdens because he or she must learn new role functions and do so without the aid of the principal person who had been depended upon. If the household contains young children, the remaining person has to help them through the crisis without allowing his or her own emotions to create distance from the child.

The death of a child carries with it parental images and hopes for the future, creating extreme family pain. From her summary of the literature on childhood death, Herz-Brown suggests that family disruption is a common aftereffect, with divorce or

Death and disability are unpredictable stresses that families must first cope with and then come to terms with.

separation occurring in a large number of the cases (467). Siblings may experience great stress and pressure (Bank and Kahn 1987).

Many families experience a return of sadness or distancing communication on anniversaries of deaths of family members. Such dates serve as markers of loss, forcing memories to surface with great force. Thus, the death of a family member alters the entire family system, requiring the other members to go through a grieving process with as open communication as possible, in order to reintegrate the smaller system at a later point.

Family-of-origin plays a significant role in how a family deals with death (Herz-Brown). Black families, Irish families, and Italian families believe in a "good" send-off. White Anglo-Saxon Protestant families limit the emotions expressed. Puerto Rican families, especially the female members, suffer publicly. Jewish families, reflecting a tradition of shared suffering, tend to deal openly and directly with death. Chinese families believe a "good death" includes relatives surrounding the dying person. Rituals at the funeral service, including the burning of paper money and clothes, ensure a happy next life. Cultures that have rituals for dealing with death, a strong sense of community, and tolerance of verbal expressions provide members with support.

Illness/Disability

A family with a permanently disabled or seriously ill member goes through an important coping process before coming to terms with the problem. Coping with a child's birth defects or the effects of a debilitating disease or accident requires major adjustments involving physical and emotional energy. The immediate disruption to the family in no way equals the long-term drain on family resources and energies required to help the injured family member deal with what may be a lifelong situation.

The mourning process that parents of impaired children undergo parallels the stages of coping with death. Fortier and Wanlass (1984) propose a stage model describing the family process that follows the diagnosis of a handicapped child. Each of these stages has a communication component. The stages include impact, denial, grief, focusing outward, and closure.

At the *impact* stage, the family learns, immediately or gradually, of the child's disability, for example, muscular dystrophy. Anxiety and tension characterize this period. Usually, the family responds in a frantic and disorganized manner. Information given to the family about the disability reassures rather than informs or educates. The family can absorb very little information and has very limited responses. Usually, the *denial* state follows the initial impact, carrying with it a sense of disbelief and distorted expectations. Parents may reject the diagnosis, fictionally explain the child's failure to perform normally, and find themselves unable to hear what others are saying about the problem. It is a period of fear and isolation.

Anger and sadness characterize the *grief*. Parents question why this happened to them or to their child. They may blame each other for the disability, isolate themselves from interacting with usual friends and extended family, and prevent open and supportive communication. These parents experience great sadness. Often, sharing in support groups of parents with similarly affected children provides a sense of comfort.

Eventually, parents move toward the *focusing outward* stage, beginning a process of seeking information, discussing options, asking for help, and expressing feelings. Signs of relief are evident at this point as the family moves toward dealing with the issues. The *closure* stage represents a reconciliation with reality and a sense of adaptation to the child's needs. The family pulls together and adjusts in ways that allow the members of the altered system to move forward and to communicate directly about their concerns.

A family working through the process experiences each of these stages. Some families may experience one stage very briefly and find themselves stuck in another for a long period of time. Some families block this mourning process by preventing the necessary communication at each stage. This is most likely to occur when individuals or systems operate according to such rules as "Keep a stiff upper lip" or "Solve your own problems." The family must support open communication if the system is to move through the necessary stages. Parents do not dream of giving birth to a child with a disability. The family must grieve the loss of a limb, loss of health, or whatever before they can become fully attached to this child (Bristor 1984, 2). In addition to the emotional stresses associated with handicapped family members, the financial demands can send a family into economic difficulty.

An older injured patient may also experience similar stages when faced with his or her own disability. The person who loses a limb or a vital capacity mourns the lost leg, eyesight, or strength by responding with denial strategies, expressions of anger, attempts at bargaining, depression, and eventually, if the process is not arrested, acceptance. Communication must be kept open and the injured or ill member given free rein to express his or her feelings.

A serious disability or disease affects the overall family system (Zeitlin, Williamson, and Rosenblatt 1987, 443). As might be predicted following the onset of a chronic disease, it is typical for a patient to assume a central position in the family. This shift in focus, if continued over a longer period of time, affects marital and parent-child relationships. In some families, adolescents may use illness to cross generational boundaries and regulate marital distance or parental conflict (Frey 1984, 253). Parents who are forced to focus on a demanding child have little time or energy to deal with each other. McCubbin and colleagues (1983) suggest that communication breakdowns occur between family members and between the family and relatives or neighbors due to a lack of leisure time and less energy for the relationships. In a study of the coping patterns of parents with a child with cystic fibrosis, these same authors have found that both parents contribute to the coping process, but the mother's coping behavior focuses more on the interpersonal dimensions of family life—family cohesiveness and expressiveness (367).

"A year and one-half ago, my brother Steve suffered a paralyzing head injury when he swerved his motorcycle to miss a dog. He dreams of driving his Chevy pickup again but knows he might live the rest of his life in a nursing home. When asked when he expects to get out, his eyes go blank. 'Never,' he says. My father discourages such talk. 'Now if you work real hard you might get your legs going again, right?' he says. Steve's eyes grow red. 'OK,' he replies and stares at the wall."

Recent research on sibling response to a disabled child indicates that siblings may have a surprising lack of information about the disability. This lack of information may confuse siblings in the following ways:

1. They may feel responsible for a particular condition.
2. They may wonder whether it can be transmitted or "caught" and whether they are susceptible to the same disorder.
3. They are confused about how they should communicate to family and friends about the handicap.
4. They wonder what implications a brother's or sister's handicap has for their future.
5. They may feel perplexed and overwhelmed by such discomforting feelings as anger, hurt, and guilt (Seligman 1988, 168).

Disability puts stress on the marriage, usually in negative ways. For some couples, it limits their ability to have a family. Couples with families have reported their inability to go to certain places or do certain things together. In addition, role function burdens placed on the spouse who is not disabled add to the family's stress. A severe illness or handicap stresses a family system over a period of time. As in the Double ABCX model described earlier, the family marshals its current resources at the outset of the crisis and then attempts to develop new resources to carry them through the crisis. The ability of family members to communicate in a direct and supportive manner directly influences the coping process.

Separation/Divorce

Divorce is a major disruption of the family life cycle and is characterized by loss, change, and complexity. According to Peck and Manocherian (1988), the normal life cycle tasks "interrupted and altered by the divorce process, continue with greater complexity due to the concomitant phase of the divorcing process" (335). Unlike death, which forces a family to adjust to a smaller number of members, the family in a divorce must adapt to an altered state. In most cases, except total desertion, each parent remains somewhat involved with the children, thus continuing the parenting aspects of the original system.

Although divorce alters a family system, it does not end it, except in cases of total desertion or total distancing of partners without children. Even in these situations, the extended family may maintain significant ties. When children are involved, a couple becomes divorced *to* each other rather than *from* each other. Family members remain linked around the children and must find ways to function as an ongoing altered system.

A systemic view of divorce acknowledges that both partners contribute to the dissolution of a marriage. When you think about the issues of mutual influence and punctuation, it is fruitless to assign blame, because the immediate split may have been preceded by months or even years of dysfunctional communication. At some time in their relationship, a painful new pattern evolved.

The separation and divorce processes essentially follow the mourning pattern described earlier in this chapter. At some point, the spouses mourn the loss of the relationship, although one or the other may have mourned the "death" of the marriage years before the divorce became a reality. Initially, spouses may deny that anything is really wrong and communicate to children or others that "Our problems aren't all that serious" or "Daddy will be back soon so don't tell anyone he's gone." As the reality takes hold, anger, bargaining, and depression intermingle. There may be attempts at reconciliation: "We had a great thing going once; we can have it again." Failed attempts may be met with such messages as "How can you leave after all I've done for you" and "What kind of a mother would move out on her children?" Painful accusations and negative conflict are often heightened by the adversarial positions required in legal divorce proceedings. Finally, depression reflects the sense of loss and/or rejection often accompanied by great loneliness.

In terms of communication, the couple may experience a descent through the stages of development in the "social penetration model" described in Chapter 5. Thus, they move from whatever stage they had reached, for example, affective exchange, back down toward the lower stages. As their relationship falls apart, partners gradually withdraw affect and intimate contact, and are likely to deal with one another to a lesser extent. In other words, as a relationship deteriorates, the high self-disclosure, predictability, uniqueness, openness, and spontaneity that characterize the higher levels of a relationship disintegrate. Little effort is invested in the relationship; risk taking declines.

Eventually, communication moves down the continuum toward orientation level behavior. Personal issues are avoided; nonverbal behaviors are restrained; little uniqueness and spontaneity remain. Many former spouses relate to each as casual acquaintances or almost strangers, except perhaps around highly charged issues such as money and children.

According to Knapp (1984), a relationship that is "coming apart" reflects (1) a recognition of differences, (2) an experience of constricted interaction, (3) a sense of stagnation or marking time, (4) a pattern of avoidance, and (5) the immediate or protracted experience of termination. Partners at these stages create messages that communicate an increasing physical and psychological distance and an increasing disassociation from the other person. Levels of cohesion drop to reflect the distancing; little connectedness remains.

The amount of stress in the childhood of the parents influences the effect of separation and divorce. If the adults experienced losses in earlier periods of their lives, letting go of present relationships, starting a new single life, and assuming the single-parenting role may be particularly difficult (Chiriboga, Catron, and Weiler 1987). These pressures are intensified by the predictable and problematic withdrawal of social supports. Divorce is the only major crisis in which social supports fall away (Wallerstein and Blakeslee 1989). Others are afraid to "take sides," or they act as if they believe divorce might be contagious.

Studies have shown adverse effects of divorce on children (Wallerstein and Kelly, 1980; Peterson and Zill 1986, Glenn and Kramer 1987; Wallerstein and Blakeslee). Some have especially indicated problems in the predivorce, transition, and early postdivorce periods, with children acting out their frustrations and rage. Some adolescents experience accelerated parent-child separation, which promotes earlier individuation, ego maturity, and courtship activity. Some students from divorced homes rate their parents, especially fathers, less favorably than do students from intact families. In fact, some make angry emotional cutoffs from the parent they least like (Lopez 1987). Many children witness intense verbal and physical anger acted out by parents in the acute stage of divorce. Over time the system recalibrates itself to deal with its altered form and its new communication dynamics. The presence of siblings makes the transition easier to manage for young people (Combrinck-Graham 1988; Cain 1990), because they may protect each other from parents' attempts to hook them into the struggle, may share the "care" of a distraught parent, or may support each other.

Most children experience a sense of confusion and chaos when parents divorce.

"When parents divorce, although it may be a relief from the fighting and constant tension, children experience a sense of loss and acquire many new fears about themselves and their future. Death elicits many of these same feelings, but death gives its survivors an adjustment period. Children are expected to be greatly affected by a death and are encouraged to express their feelings about it. But children who experience divorce are expected to 'bounce back.' Children are just expected to adapt, which most of us do, but usually without being given a grieving period. As a result, we repress these feelings and fears, and since they are never really addressed, they often resurface years later to haunt us."

Although there is limited information on communication during the divorce process, current research indicates most couples do not discuss this decision in lengthy detail with all members. As a result of their longitudinal study of divorcing families, Wallerstein and Kelly expressed surprise at the limited communication between parents and children about the divorce, suggesting that the "telling is not a pronouncement but should initiate a gradual process" (40). In many cases, children are informed about the divorce but not encouraged to discuss their concerns. Four-fifths of the youngest children in this study were not provided with either an adequate explanation or assurance of continued care (39). Because parents are so anxious about the discussion, many make it impossible for the children to express their feelings. Children may be told "You'll see more of Daddy now" or "You'll be able to get a dog," comments intended to make the child feel positive but which deny the child's distress. In their study of the long-range effects of divorce, Wallerstein and Blakeslee suggest "nearly 50 percent of the families that we counsel waited until the day of the separation or afterward to tell their children that their familiar world is coming apart" (302). The abruptness of communication about the divorce often contributes to the children's inability to explore the issues and to release their feelings directly. Whereas loss through death involves a socially expected mourning period, there is no socially sanctioned mourning period for the loss of the "family that was," a situation that may prevent the use of resources available to a child. Just as there must be support systems available to the child at the time of divorce, there must also be resources available during the postcrisis period.

Usually, communication between former spouses becomes less conflictual in the years following a divorce. Hetherington, Cox, and Cox (1976) found that two months after the divorce, 66 percent of the exchanges between partners involved conflicts over finances, support, visitation, child rearing, and relating to others in the system (423). This same study followed families over a two-year period and noted that conflicts and contact with fathers diminished over time. This statement from the study certainly reflects the changing nature of communication in divorced families:

> The divorced father wants his contacts with his children to be as happy as possible. He begins by initially being extremely permissive, indulgent, and becoming increasingly restrictive over the two-year period, although he is never as restrictive as fathers in intact homes.

Other researchers believe this study makes an important contribution to understanding postdivorce interaction patterns. It describes the cycle of negative parent-child interaction that occurs in many families as the acceptable levels of anger are increased (Levitin 1979). The bad effects of divorce are fewer if the child lives with a same-sex parent following the divorce or maintains a good relationship with either parent or both. If parents remarry again or repeatedly, the effects are more likely to be negative (Peterson and Zill, 295). Mediation or counseling can often help parents to work out their differences and lessen the stress on children (Grebe 1986, 379). Many partners experience ambivalent feelings of love and hate in the divorce process. Children sense this, and talking about this conflict helps to sort out the entangled feelings. Children also can blame one parent or the other and take sides unfairly.

Although it is impossible in a divorce to remove all the negative aspects of stress upon children and their communication, parents can certainly reduce the stress. If neither parent uses the child as a go-between or encourages "tattletale" behavior, opportunities for conflict are reduced. If each supports the other's discipline, the child cannot play one against the other. For all involved, divorce involves a sense of loss, especially for those who have lost their support systems as well as their current sense of family.

Support and Communication

Throughout any of these crises—death, illness, disability, or divorce—the family's capacity for open communication, reflective of its levels of cohesion and adaptation and its images, themes, boundaries, and biosocial beliefs, determines how the system will weather the strain. A family with low cohesion may fragment under pressure unless such pressure can connect the unconnected members. A family with limited resources for adaptation faces a painful time, because such crises force change upon the system, which must respond with internal changes of its own. A family whose images and themes allow outside involvement in family affairs may use its flexible boundaries to find institutional and social support. A family with rigid biosocial beliefs faces difficult challenges if key family figures are lost or injured and others are not permitted to assume some of the role responsibilities. Throughout this process, communication among family members either facilitates or hinders the revising of the system to meet the demands of the crisis.

Every family undergoes periods of unpredictable stress. Many of these stresses are not as immediately critical as death, illness, or divorce, but they do eat away at members' resources. Negative stresses, such as alcoholism, drug abuse, child abuse, economic reversals, and job transfers, take their toll on a family's resources. Each of these issues has strong family systems implications (Lewis 1986; Kugler and Hansson 1988). A stress, such as divorce, reduces the family's support systems at the same time that the family's pain is increasing. The result can be extreme crisis. Without a strong communication network, the individuals—forced to rely on themselves—may become alienated or severely depressed. Even such seemingly positive experiences as having a gifted child, getting a high-powered position, adopting a child, or receiving large sums of money can stress the system. In order to understand a family's coping capacity, a family's immediate and postcrisis resources must be understood. Only then can one judge the long-term effects of the crisis as either destructive or growth enhancing for the members involved.

Families that are willing to maintain flexible boundaries and communicate with and accept support from institutional sources and social networks (friends and extended family) are more likely to work through their crises and return to functional communication than are those who block outside support.

In recent years, self-help support groups have become increasingly large and visible. In a society characterized by mobility and smaller families, persons are finding interpersonal support from others who share similar experiences and pain. Chapters of groups such as Alcoholics Anonymous, Parents Without Partners, Candlelighters, Overeaters Anonymous, and so forth, are found in most communities. The twelve-step program developed by AA has been adopted by related groups such as Al-Anon and Alateen and by groups created to support persons dealing with other addictions or losses. In all cases, the self-help groups rely on members' communication and support as a healing process.

CONCLUSION

This chapter examined communication and unpredictable life stresses. Specifically, it focused on (1) the process of dealing with unpredictable stresses and (2) communication during certain major stressful life events, such as death, illness/disability, and divorce. Over the years, every family system encounters external stress from crisis situations as well as stress from developmental change. The system's ability to cope effectively with stress depends on a number of factors such as the number of recent stresses, the role changes, and the social and institutional support. The Double ABCX model provides an effective explanation of family coping, because it focuses on precrisis and postcrisis variables. Death, illness, and divorce necessarily alter family systems over long periods of time. Communication may facilitate or restrict a family's coping procedures. In most families, sharing of information and feelings can lower the stress level. The family with flexible boundaries has the capacity to accept support and the potential for surviving crises more effectively than families who close themselves off from others. Many family members find support through membership in self-help organizations.

IN REVIEW

1. Using a real or fictional family, analyze the effects on the family of a severe stress that impacted one member (e.g., drug problem, serious car accident, or severe illness).
2. Using the same example of family stress, compare and contrast an analysis of the problem according to the ABCX model and the more recent Double ABCX model.
3. Describe how a "happy event" has brought high levels of stress to a family with whom you are familiar.
4. How do different cultural and/or religious attitudes toward death aid or restrict the mourning process for surviving family members?
5. What guidelines for communication would you recommend to spouses who have children and are about to separate?

CHAPTER 12

Communication Within Various Family Forms

Imagine your family in the year 2025. Will you have had a dual-career partnership for all those years? Might you be a cohabiting grandparent, a stepgrandparent? Will your parents have divorced and one remarried? A generation ago you may have been more certain of your answers.

As you listen to everyday conversation, read the newspapers, or watch television, you are confronted with discussions of "the breakdown of the American family." Such terminology is misleading and potentially destructive. Our culture appears to have an idealized view of the family, vividly depicted in holiday television advertising, that involves a middle-class, blood-related family with smiling parents and grandparents. In reality, this system represents only one family form, and only a small percentage of today's American families.

The American family does not exist. Harevan (1982) suggests that American families have always represented great diversity and that our nostalgia is for a lost family tradition that never really existed. Historically, the American family has fulfilled its members' extensive economic, socialization, education, and emotional needs. Harevan expresses her concern with the idealized two-parent middle-class family, claiming, "American society has contained within it great diversities in family types and family behavior that were associated with the recurring entrance of new immigrant groups into American society. Ethnic, racial, cultural, and class differences have also resulted in diversity in family behavior" (461). Family descriptors shifted from ethnic terms, to social class terms, to the current focus on marital status, new family forms, or sexual preference (Sporakowski 1988). Diversity is acknowledged in a more forthright manner.

This chapter will explore some of the specific communication issues and behaviors related to various family forms. The following pages will focus specifically on communication within (1) single-parent systems, (2) stepfamily systems, (3) homosexual partners and gay and lesbian parents, and (4) other variations.

COMMUNICATION WITHIN SINGLE-PARENT SYSTEMS

A single-parent family consists of one parent and one or more children. This formation may include an unmarried woman or man and her or his offspring; men or women who lost spouses through death, divorce, or desertion and their children; single parents with adopted or foster children. Today nearly one-fourth of all families with children are single-parent families; most are formed through divorce, yet one-quarter are systems where the parent never married. Among black families with young children, one-third are maintained by a never-married mother (Glick 1989a; 1989b). In a recent analysis of American youth, Otto (1988) concludes that "the normal experience of today's youth is for a child to live with only one parent sometime before reaching age 18" (385). Thus, the single-parent system usually results from the loss of a parent figure but may result from the addition of a child through birth or adoption. Most single-parent households are headed by a working mother. For many children, the experience in a single-parent system is temporary until the parent remarries. Given the current divorce and remarriage rates, a large percentage of the American population will spend some time as a member of a single-parent system.

Single-parent families face task overload and emotional overload, most evident in the life cycle of single mothers with young children. Social isolation, increased anxiety, depression, loneliness, and economic worries affect the single parent. Single parents frequently find themselves emotionally cut off from extended family relationships and social networks (Beal 1980). Divorced persons find themselves separated from their spouse's extended family as the boundaries are tightened against them. Friends frequently withdraw social support from both parties during and after a divorce (Wallerstein and Blakeslee 1989).

Pressured single parents function more effectively when they experience consistent social support systems. Friends may support an individual going through a loss as he or she attempts to change self-perceptions, experiment with new behaviors, and move into a broader social world (Eggert 1987). Unmarried women with children may find more support within their extended families, particularly in matriarchal systems. Because they do not have a partner with whom to share their problems and joys or discuss decisions, single parents need to function as part of strong communication networks. They need other adults to talk with about their own pressures and specific parenting issues. Such network support keeps single parents from relying too heavily on one child for emotional support.

> *"My sister and I rely on each other for so many big and little things. If I'm having a bad day, I call her. If she has a fight with her boyfriend, she calls me. We share childcare responsibilities and often travel together with the kids. I turned down a new job because it meant moving too far away from her."*

A one-parent system creates special issues related to power and roles. The two-against-one model of the two-parent home may force children to abide by parental wishes; when one parent leaves the system, some power may be removed from the parental image. Any troubled parent-child relationship cannot be adequately balanced by the other parent. When one parent leaves the system, the other may attempt to place a child in the vacated role to provide emotional support or perform household duties. The child may become the confidant or may be expected to share decision making. "You're the man of the house now" typifies this lowering of boundaries between parental and child subsystems and often results in communication breakdowns. This new role may place great pressure on the child, alienate the child from other siblings, and eventually interfere with the normal process of separating from the family at the appropriate developmental point. Gender-related role expectations may be created in mother-son systems which never had a functioning father figure. In a description of his adolescent life in a single-parent home, Goldberg (1983) remembers his worries about support checks, the parental date who might appear at breakfast, and the younger siblings who could not remember a two-parent household. He indicates the difficulty of trying to give advice on dating, give support on childcare, and stay in the middle between warring parents. Such experiences are not rare as parents rely on children as their support systems.

Most single-parent systems face economic pressures. The economic status of women is likely to decline 30 percent during the first year after a divorce (Glick 1989). Single-parent families generally experience a lower standard of living than two-parent systems. Economic concerns in the single-parent family have direct bearing on communication patterns. When a single mother's income is low and the father fails to pay for child support, many children become pawns in the battle. Over one-quarter of mothers receive no support; many others get limited support. Communication with the children's father may be restricted, or the children may become part of a chain network relaying requests for, and responses about, the money. In either situation, the children experience great stress. In their landmark study, Wallerstein and Blakeslee found that one in four children experienced a severe and lasting drop in their standard of living and observed a major discrepancy between their mother's and father's homes. "They grew up with their noses pressed against the glass, looking at a way of life that by all rights should have been theirs" (298). This economic pressure escalates the stress within the single-parent system and may be played out in excessive conflict or depression.

"Although I try not to put my kids in the middle I resent their father's lifestyle. We worry about buying school clothes, and he's paying $700 for a dog! The kids live like royalty six days a month—and then there's 'life with Mom.' I know they hear me bad-mouth Dwayne, but I just can't help it."

Numerous researchers have debated the problems of the single-parent family, especially as they relate to children. These studies have importance because they relate to family communication. In measuring self-concept, which also includes assessment of social and personal adjustment, Raschke and Raschke (1979) found that children were "not adversely affected by living in single-parent families but that family conflict and/or parental unhappiness can be detrimental" (373). After comparing intact families with single-parent families, they discovered that in both types there was a high correlation between perceived happiness and children's healthy self-concepts. Herzog and Sudia examined research on the effects of children living in fatherless homes and concluded that there was little evidence to support the assumption that households headed by women had a detrimental effect upon children (Raschke and Raschke, 368). Beal stresses the importance of distinguishing between life in conflict-laden intact families and life in well-functioning single-parent homes, concluding that the latter leads to better adjustment (257).

In her summary of research findings on single-parent homes, Gongla (1982) indicates the following major points: (1) children can develop normally in warm and not conflict-ridden families; (2) children gain in responsibility and power by performing some of the volume of tasks that cannot be performed by one parent; (3) initially, the mother may be restrictive and the children may be aggressive, but this changes over time if supports exist; and (4) interdependence of family members grows (11). The role of the father in the family after divorce, separation, or out-of-marriage birth is important. Researchers suggest that maintaining supportive contact on important child-related matters has beneficial consequences for the mother and children (Gongla, 20). Children who are not forced to choose between parents suffer less stress than those who are discouraged, directly or indirectly, from such contact. Gongla concludes her summary by calling for more research that concentrates on the single parent *as a family*, from a systems perspective.

Recent work questions some of these assumptions. After studying long term effects of divorce on children, Wallerstein and Blakeslee report that, whereas divorced parents may have found their second chances, many of the children found conditions in the postdivorce family more stressful and less supportive than conditions in the failing marriage. Some of the children in their study "literally brought themselves up, while others were responsible for the welfare of a troubled parent as well" (299). Although the research on divorce indicates an initial decline in the capacity to parent in a surprising number of families, the diminished parenting continues, permanently disrupting the child-rearing functions of the family (302). In contrast to earlier work, they suggest that parental happiness does not necessarily result in more effective parenting. Another recent study reports that when other adults live in the home, children are described more positively by their parents (Risman and Park 1988). This finding may indicate a lessening of emotional and/or financial pressure on the single parent. The recent rise in families headed by unmarried mothers remains under-researched. Only over time will the effects of living in such a system become clear.

The type of communication possible within single-parent homes created through loss such as death or divorce reflects the ability of the family to adjust to the new systemic arrangement, whether through the permanent or partial loss of a member. As conflicts diminish, increased cohesion may develop among members. Families with high adaptability can create new and functional communication networks. In almost all cases, boundaries are adjusted to reflect the system's need or desire for outside influence. Themes, images, and biosocial beliefs may also experience adjustment. No matter what, a family with low adaptability will face a more painful time than a family with high adaptability, as evidenced by the following family's inability to adapt to a new identity as a single-parent system.

> "The issue of boundaries is one of the main functions that I have to negotiate with my own two children at this time. We all lived with my parents after my divorce. While living with my parents, my children started to view and treat me as a friend or older sibling. Now in our own home, I am trying desperately to find an even medium in which I am respected as an authority, but more of a teacher or guide than a threatening policewoman. I would like our rules to be made and agreed upon by all of us together."

Any single-parent family, whether formed through the loss of a parent or addition of a child, needs support from its community of extended family and friends. The family may also need economic or counseling support, depending on its specific needs. Functional stability must exist or all the family energy will be devoted to issues of basic life necessities, a concern that often evokes conflict.

Eventually, many single parents marry and form stepfamilies. At that time, they must alter the single-parent system to create a stepfamily, which includes children from one or both parents. This transition brings new stresses and communication concerns.

COMMUNICATION WITHIN STEPFAMILY SYSTEMS

The stepfamily has been compared to a challenging and complex chess game, to a delicate and intricate spider's web, and to a chaotic and confusing toddler's birthday party (Einstein 1982). No matter what the analogy, the stepfamily is a complex, growing, and little-understood segment of American family life. At the start of the 1980s, 35 million adults were stepparents. Currently, one-eighth of children living with two parents are stepchildren (Glick). Probably a third of all children growing up today will be part of a stepfamily before they reach adulthood (Furstenberg 1987). Many other adult children will see their parents divorce after twenty to fifty years of marriage. Demographers estimate that over one-half of today's young persons may be stepchildren by the turn of the century.

The term *stepfamily* refers to many types of family forms that can be created as two adults and the children of one or both come together. These systems, although similar to other two-parent forms, have eight characteristics:

1. A history of loss emerges for those who were previously in a two-parent system.
2. Some or all members bring past family history from a relationship that has changed or ended.
3. The couple does not begin as a dyad but rather, the parent-child relationship predates the spousal bond.
4. One or two biological parents (living or dead) influence the stepfamily.
5. Children may function as members of two households.
6. The family has a complex extended family network.

7. Strong triangles exist, which involve biological parents/former spouses, that influence the stepfamily.
8. No legal relationship exists between the stepparent and the stepchildren. (Visher and Visher 1982; Mills 1984; Pasley and Ihninger-Tallman 1987)

As was noted in Chapter 1, a stepfamily reflects ties to former systems. Death or divorce represents the end of a marital relationship, but not the termination of a parental relationship. When children are involved, the death or divorce alters, rather than ends, the family system. After a death, the remaining family members are faced with the necessity of restructuring themselves into a smaller system. The hole must be closed; the family cannot continue limping indefinitely due to the "missing" member. After a divorce, the members may exist for a long period of time in an altered system of the same size, which still functions around issues of the children or monetary considerations. Eventually, altered systems may expand into stepfamilies.

These stepfamilies continue to be influenced by the original marital system. In their discussion of forming a remarried family, McGoldrick and Carter (1980) suggest that the emotions connected with the breakup of the first marriage can be visualized as a "roller coaster" graph with peaks of intensity at the following points:

1. Decision to separate
2. Actual separation
3. Legal divorce
4. Remarriage of either spouse
5. Death of either ex-spouse
6. Life-cycle transitions of children (graduations, marriage, illness, etc.) (271)

In a divorce that includes children, each of these points causes disruption for original system members and must be handled carefully in order to keep a remarriage stabilized. Many counselors consider that a couple is divorced *to* each other rather than *from* each other, especially when children are involved. Thus, a fully reconstituted system is formed. For example, a family system may expand to include a woman, two children, her current husband, and her former husband who has remarried and has a stepson. The following diagram (Figure 12-1) will demonstrate how the original marital system of Peggy and Seth has grown and altered. Although Seth does not live with his children and former wife, there are emotional, economic, and practical ties that bind all these people to each other. If Mary Anne has difficulty in school, her mother, natural father, and stepparents may all be affected by the problem.

Stepfamily Development

How often have you heard comments such as "I wish Dad would leave Sally home during my wedding" or "My mother's husband thinks he can tell me what to do." The stepfamily represents a family form frequently created on the basis of some involuntary, conflictual relationships between the stepparent and stepchildren as well as the voluntary positive relationship between the spouses. As you remember from Chapter 5, literature on relationship development emphasizes the voluntary,

Figure 12–1
Reconstituted Family System

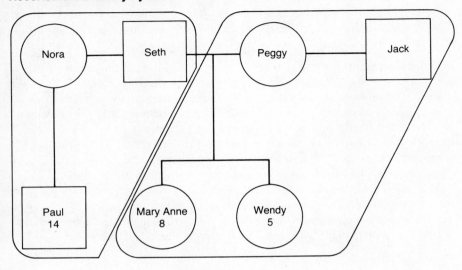

romantic involvements. Parent-child communication literature presumes biological or voluntary connections between these persons, which date from the birth of the child. In contrast, many individuals involved in stepfamily relationships, specifically as a stepparent or as a stepchild, enter involuntarily into a so-called familial relationship with implied parent-child status and the intense involvement of a third party, the biological parent. In short, many stepfamilies are formed from a conflictual and complicated beginning.

Many stepparent-stepchild relationships fall outside the realm of the relationship development model described in Chapter 5. This is true for these reasons:

1. One or both parties may resist the relationship.
2. A third party, the biological parent, serves as the catalyst and, in some cases, the only reason for this relationship.
3. Society provides expectations for how people should relate within a "family."
4. The instant family may force immediacy of shared time and space.
5. The stepfamily relationships are built from a history of loss, at least for one "side" of the family.

To date, few scholars have addressed stepfamily development (Papernow 1984; Mills; Ahrons and Rodgers 1987), but those that do call for models distinct from the biological family model. In order to understand the complexity of stepfamily life, particularly in its first years, it is helpful to examine a model of a stepfamily that describes the stages most families experience as they try to blend two systems, at least one of which reflects a previous parent-child relationship. In this model (Table 12-1), Papernow describes seven stages of stepparent development and places these within a developmental framework for stepfamilies, which includes early, middle, and later stages.

Within the early stages, the stepfamily remains divided primarily along previous system lines of emotional support, agreement of rules or rituals, and general alliances among people. During this early period, stepparents fantasize about what can be created. They may imagine that they will rescue stepchildren from inadequate situations and that they will create a loving, nurturing, devoted new family characterized by emotional sharing. Most new stepparents report a high level of fantasies and hopes for family life, as well as high expectations for gratitude from the stepchildren (Turnbull and Turnbull 1983). On the other hand, the children are more likely to fantasize the departure of the stepparents and the reunion of their biological family, unless one of the biological parents is dead or has deserted the family.

At the assimilation stage, members become acutely aware of their different rhythms, rules, relational currencies, and everyday behaviors, and recognize the difficulty in blending them. Stepchildren experience tremendous clashes of loyalty as they try to sort out how to deal with a stepparent without being disloyal to the same-sex biological parent. Often, this confusion is exhibited through anger or indifference. The biological parent, pleased to have an adult partner, is frightened by that partner's inability to establish satisfactory relationships with his or her children. Most stepfamilies encounter a persisting inequality of the biological parent-child relationship; therefore, truly shared parenting functions seldom become reality (Mills). It becomes clear that something is not working, but due to fear of repeated failure, it is too frightening to address the issue directly.

The confusion of this early stage affects the entire larger system of grandparents, aunts, uncles, and cousins who have to negotiate their relationship with this new family. This extended family might include four sets of grandparents as well as large numbers of relatives who have experienced close connections to certain members of the reconstituted system. These extended members provide feedback to the family on how they are seen, either by emphasizing the differences (giving expensive toys to biological grandchildren and token gifts to a stepgrandchild) or by reinforcing the newly formed system by treating all children equally. During these early stages it is hard for the adults involved to share what is going on within them and to really hear what their spouse is saying. Their dreams and fantasies are hard to forego. Reality implies pain and conflict. Therefore, for newly formed stepfamilies, boundaries may be biologically, legally, and spatially unclear. Members may be confused about family membership and norms for behavior (Pasley 1987, 210).

Table 12–1
Stages in Stepfamily Development

Early Stages:	1. Fantasy
	2. Assimilation
	3. Awareness
Middle Stages:	4. Mobilization
	5. Action
Later Stages:	6. Contact
	7. Resolution

As the early stages conclude, awareness of the situation emerges, and family members start to make sense out of what is happening to them. According to Papernow, "While the pain doesn't go away, the picture of where it comes from and why it hurts so much gets clearer" (358). The biological parent may be feeling great stress as a central figure trying to protect the children and mollify the spouse, finding little gratification in either.

Although some families remain stuck in the early stages for many years, most systems move on to the middle stages and begin the process of mobilizing their resources and airing differences. During this period, spouses are more likely to address their differences directly, expressing feelings, needs, and perceptions about life in the stepfamily. Such directness leads to important conflicts. At the time, some of the issues may appear trivial, but the conflicts represent the underlying issues of the family's structure. Such comments as "You're too tired to go to the grocery store, but when Jill calls, you are awake enough to pick her up from work!" addresses the alliances and strengths of certain boundaries within the system. A stepfather may claim that he needs time alone with his wife, thereby upsetting his children but strengthening the marital boundary. A stepchild may express concern at the interrogation that follows every visit with her natural mother; she may demand privacy in that part of her life. All members may indicate their distress with the expectations of family "quasi kin," or extended family members of the stepparent.

"I think our family's divorce ended up on the longer end of the recovery spectrum because the divorce initially created such upheaval. The house was sold, I went off to college, my brother Seth changed schools, and my father got a new wife—all in the period of about two months. Because these drastic changes were extremely sudden, I think the wounds have taken longer to heal. Seth's reactions were typical for a 6-year-old. His insecurity and fears exposed themselves through his sudden hyperactivity and inability to concentrate. He became quite the bully and a well-practiced fibber. Even now, two years later, he causes chaos at my father's house, constantly forcing my father to choose between him and Dad's wife. I hate being there with Seth."

As the middle stages continue, the family moves into an action mode that marks the beginning of truly working together. This involves sharing the former dreams and expectations while remaining connected enough to engage in active problem solving around past and current issues. Some solutions may reflect former ways of doing things for certain members, while others involve creative attempts to represent the desires of the blended group, a creation of "middle ground" (Papernow 1987). For example, a family may decide to adopt certain holiday rituals that one part of the system experienced before, while creating new ones reflecting the new system. Although the time when a stepfamily identity is being built is a perfect time to establish new traditions (Einstein), many families never discuss expectations; all members assume that old ways will be carried on. Such silence only deepens the pain as members feel misunderstood or disconfirmed.

Because part-time stepparenting can be very stressful for the family and visiting children, family members may agree to change the way they function when noncustodial stepchildren spend time at their house. They may move to low-key sharing of time rather than a frantic period of "entertainment." In other circumstances, spouses may decide to limit a child's access to his biological mother's charge card because it creates inequality among all the children. Most families at these stages renegotiate rules for everyday events and discuss acceptable ways of handling anger and affection within the system. They may begin to create an identity for themselves in a positive light, instead of working from a sense of deficiency. This action period reflects a sense of "we-ness" for stepfamilies who believe they are taking charge of their destinies.

This sense of "we-ness" comes very gradually. For example, in the first two years of a remarriage, stepfathers reported themselves low on "felt" or "expressed" affection for stepchildren. Compared with biological fathers, stepfathers express less positive affection and fewer negative or critical responses (Hetherington, 1987). This cautiousness reflects the tentative nature of building new, and sometimes unwanted, relationships.

As families enter the later stages, members experience greater intimacy and authenticity. In this stage "the couple relationship, previously polarized by step issues, is now more often felt as an intimate sanctuary in which to share these issues, including painful or difficult feelings" (Papernow 1984, 360). The triangles that had consumed the couple's attention and energy have diminished, allowing them to function more adequately in all areas of family life.

Eventually, the question as to how biological parents and stepparents are to be integrated into the children's lives is resolved. Papernow (1984) ascribes the quality of the stepparent role in this way:

(a) The role does not usurp or compete with the biological parent of the same sex; (b) The role includes an intergenerational boundary between stepparent and child; (c) The role is sanctioned by the rest of the stepfamily, particularly the spouse; (d) The role incorporates the special qualities this stepparent brings to this family. (361)

Family members experience a sense of clarity and security, which is even reflected in their language. Confusion about how to refer to family members has passed; discussion of the stepfamily is comfortable. Levels of openness once considered impossible may now exist. The original fantasies have been explored in the light of reality.

The step-relationships at the resolution stage not only provide a sense of satisfaction but also feel reliable. Family members have developed dyadic relationships characterized by personal interaction, not just by marital merger. Wallerstein and Blakeslee suggest that an "independent relationship between a stepparent and stepchild is made of countless transactions and responses through which the child learns, hey, this person cares about me. I have a claim separate from my mom. When a stepparent brings this feeling about, it is a magical moment created by sweat and tears" (252).

A stepfamily is one family form that requires extensive initial adaptation.

Present situations move into the foreground, whereas past struggles and issues become part of the background. This does not imply permanent resolution of all issues, because certain concerns reappear indefinitely—the later phases of the "roller coaster" graph described earlier. Clearly, well-functioning stepfamilies don't just "happen."

Communication in Stepfamilies

The complexity of stepfamily formation is reflected in members' communication concerns and patterns. As a remarried system forms, partners bring communication patterns from (1) families-of-origin, (2) the first marriage, and (3) the period between marriages. Children bring patterns from the second and third situations. Forming such a system requires extensive initial adaptation if functional cohesion and adaptability levels are to be established. Family members are cast instantly into multiple roles. A single man may become husband and stepfather. A woman may become wife, stepmother, or even stepgrandmother with a simple "I do." The results of research on stepparent and stepchildren relationships indicate areas where problems in communication can develop.

A stepfamily's initial communication may reflect the directness or indirectness of communication surrounding the divorce. If children were not prepared for the divorce and assured that all major changes would be discussed with them, then the same pattern may influence remarriage. Many children learn about their stepfamily status through comments such as "I'm getting married next week. You'll like Sue when you get to know her" or "Guess what we did last weekend!" More aware adults give children plenty of time and opportunities to discuss how the new family will be created and work. Future stepsiblings are given opportunities to meet; they are encouraged to identify similarities; and the possible rewards of such a relationship are made as clear as possible.

If they are to be able to communicate openly with both parents, children need to understand that they did not cause the divorce. Each parent needs to assure children that it's acceptable to love the other parent and that parent-child love in no way diminishes because of divorce. Nothing positive in communication can be gained by bad-mouthing the ex-spouse. Often, one spouse says little, but children sense the nonverbal disdain when the other's name is mentioned. Divorced parents need to remember that as children grieve, they may act out their own feelings of loss and alternately blame one parent for the divorce, or they may take out their anger on a stepparent (Luepnitz 1979).

Each member of a remarried system must participate in the creation of new family themes, images, boundaries, and biosocial beliefs. Disparate backgrounds and negative feelings about the remarriage will result in intense periods of conflict, reflected verbally and nonverbally, as family members jockey for position and power. The former oldest child may fight against the role of middle daughter. A child used to great freedom and autonomy may rebel against themes that push for strong cohesion and similarity among family members. Each new system must negotiate such boundaries issues as the following:

1. Membership (Who are the "real" members of the family?)
2. Space (What is mine? Where do I really belong?)
3. Authority (Who is really in charge? Of discipline? Of money? Of decisions? etc.)
4. Time (Who gets how much of my time, and how much do I get of theirs?) (McGoldrick and Carter, B. 1988, 406–407)

The issue of membership and boundaries is resolved more easily "when members interact on a regular basis (physical presence) and come to see one another as belonging to the existing family unit (psychological presence)" (Pasley, 210). Discussions need to be held addressing who is "in" the family. This may be less evident than it first appears. In a study of stepfamily membership, 15 percent of stepparents did not list stepchildren who lived in their households. Thirty-one percent of stepchildren excluded a residential stepparent, and 41 percent of children excluded a residential stepsibling (Furstenberg, 50). Wallerstein and Blakeslee found that half the children whose mother remarried did not feel welcome in the new family (239). For many stepchildren, a physical space indicated acceptance and a "place" in the family. In addition, participation in family tasks may strengthen a feeling of being a member rather than being a visitor. New authority patterns emerge in stepfamilies. Both sons and daughters in divorced families are allowed more responsibility, independence, and power in decisions than are children in nondivorced families (Hetherington, 194). This freedom affects life in remarried families. Stepfathers initially tend to allow the mother to exert most of the authority; in fact, stepfathers make significantly fewer control attempts and are less successful in gaining control with both sons and daughters than are biological fathers. Over time, their control of stepsons is better. Stepdaughters tend to be more resistant. Mothers and stepmothers both tend to exert authority. The biological parent may be caught between discipline beliefs of a spouse and ex-spouse.

Time is a highly valued currency in stepfamilies, particularly for dyads such as spouses or biological parent and child. Such pressure often leaves a stepchild or stepparent feeling "left out" and a biological parent feeling "pulled between two worlds." Sometimes the time is frustrating because "visiting" appears awkward and creates depression in the noncustodial fathers because the father is removed from the daily flow of routines.

Communication networks must expand to encompass new members and possibly to maintain ties with first marriage members, as children and former spouses and extended family members attempt to maintain necessary contacts. Negative remarks or overt conflict between members of former systems creates pressures. Children may feel "pulled to one side." Each group may establish communication rules to keep information from the other. "Don't tell your mother about my trip to Mexico" or "Don't mention that I'm dating someone." Children may be filled with secrets and resentments, which they cannot divulge. A difficult situation arises as former spouses criticize each other in front of the children. An area of great stress for adolescents was experiencing one natural parent's talking negatively about the other natural parent (Lutz 1983).

If members of the extended family take sides, the children suffer additional pressures. A spouse may unwisely permit relatives or friends to make derogatory remarks about the other spouse in the children's presence. A grandparent may remind the children of the "no-good" qualities of their father and, when the children become boisterous, argue, or get into fights, may declare, "You're just like your father."

Reconstituted systems are becoming a common part of the American way of life, but the issues of living in such a system remain varied and complex. To date, society's vocabulary has not even developed words to deal with the roles and relationships involved. For example, a child has no names for her stepgrandparents, no way to communicate easily about her relationship to the son of her father's second former wife, no name for the first stepfather who is now divorced from her mother. Such difficulties make contact with outsiders and institutions more difficult and sometimes more painful. As society becomes more comfortable with these new family forms, more effective ways of communicating about them will develop.

"The power of language in the family is amazing. Over the past eight years my stepdaughter and I have struggled mightily to create a working relationship. We have come a long way. Yet it's always been clear that I am 'Jean, my stepmother' and her mother is 'Mom.' That's been okay. Now that her mother is about to remarry, I hear my stepdaughter referring to 'my other father,' and it really hurts. The first time I heard that it felt like a knife went into my stomach because I have never been 'my other mother.' "

There is still much to be learned about communication within a stepfamily, a form that usually involves nonvoluntary relationships. This growing segment of family life presents challenges that have yet to be appreciated fully from a communication perspective.

COMMUNICATION AND HOMOSEXUAL PARTNERS AND PARENTS

Alternative family forms are becoming more commonly recognized, including same-sex couples and families headed by homosexuals (Macklin 1980). In describing the recognition of various family forms, Harevan suggests that an alternative, such as same-sex couples, is not necessarily a new family form but rather a form that is becoming more visible. Although census figures on gay male couples and lesbian couples are not available and little hard data exist on homosexual parents, there is growing interest in these family forms. According to DeVito (1979), depending on the data used and the definition of "gay" or "lesbian," statistics range from 4 to 25 percent. Golanty and Harris (1982) estimate that 5 to 10 percent of the population maintains sexual and emotional involvements exclusively with members of the same sex.

This text is concerned with homosexual persons who have formed couple attachments in which they consider each other as family or with those who are functioning as parents. The study *American Couples* included same-sex couples as a significant part of their population. Blumstein and Schwartz (1983) found that 71 percent of their sample of gay men between ages 36 and 45 were living with a partner. In the 1970s, Bell and Weinberg (1978) found strong support among lesbians for being in a permanent relationship (45). Blumstein and Schwartz suggest that until the 1970s, gay men and lesbians were a real but fairly invisible part of the American population. Yet the authors suggest that "couplehood," either as a reality or as an aspiration, is as strong among homosexuals as it is among heterosexuals (44). In their work on homosexual relationships, Bell and Weinberg identified what they called the "close couple," or the homosexual relationship most similar to heterosexual marriage. In this relationship, partners are sexually exclusive and rely on each other for interpersonal satisfaction. Other studies in the 1970s and 1980s point toward the desire for couple relationships within the gay and lesbian community (McWhirter and Mattison, 1984; Majors 1983; Johnson 1984; Zacks, Green, and Marrow 1988). The AIDS crisis of the 1980s created a climate that supports more monogamous long-term relationships.

Although many similarities exist between heterosexual and homosexual couples, important differences also exist. Some of the differences occur in areas of relationship development, sources of recognition/support, and ways of dealing with money, sex, and power (Majors; Blumstein and Schwartz; DeVito). In describing gay male relationships, Majors maintains, "Sound research has indicated that significant differences between male/male couples and male/female couples do indeed exist and drastically alter the nature of all aspects of relationship formation and development"

(1). In most cases, young homosexuals are denied role models and positive images of long-term same-sex relationships. Such a lack of role models forces a more pressured trial-and-error discovery in relationship development and maintenance. This is particularly difficult for males, because men in general are "less likely to develop the interpersonal skills that make for easy and comfortable dealing with feelings, sharing of inner concerns, empathy and listening skills" (Majors, 6). The lack of role models exacerbates the situation.

The lack of interpersonal and institutional support creates great pressure for homosexual partners and parents. Many individuals cannot tell even their own families about their lifestyle. Others feel comfortable sharing their relationship with only very few friends or family members. In certain urban areas, the large recognized gay community has provided support for couples or families, but in other areas, persons live in secretive isolation.

Even when partners are recognized as a couple, the interpersonal support remains different. Current language does not support such relationships. For example, there is no appropriate descriptive term for two men who have been together for ten or thirty years. "In gay parlance they are 'lovers' but as popularly used and understood the term is too general and does not include the years of commitment, the permanency of the relationship, and a host of other dimensions that are included in both the denotative and connotative meanings of the term marriage" (DeVito, 8). Some homosexual couples live together openly after going through a marriage ceremony similar to heterosexual rites, but such community celebrations are rare (Stinnett, Walters, and Kay 1984). Most couples are forced to rely more on each other to meet interpersonal needs than are their heterosexual counterparts.

"One of the most difficult parts of our lifestyle is the intense dependence we have to have on each other because we cannot discuss our relationship or certain other serious aspects of our lives with many other people. We experience an isolation as we function among friends who live a heterosexual lifestyle and can be more open about the good and the bad parts of their lives. I value the closeness of our relationship, but I recognize the strains caused by the need to depend so totally on each other."

In addition to limited social support, homosexual partners and parents receive almost no societal support. Whereas spouses in heterosexual partnerships become immediately eligible for health insurance, tuition rebates, or organizational benefits, long-term homosexual unions entitle a partner to nothing. The child of a partner cannot receive tuition rebates or other medical benefits. Most religious or educational institutions give little or no support to homosexual partners or parents. These few examples highlight the kinds of pressures placed on long-term same-sex relationships that heterosexual couples do not experience.

In their study of couples from the perspectives of money, work, and sex, Blumstein and Schwartz uncovered many differences between heterosexual couples and same-sex couples and also between gay male and lesbian couples. Money establishes the balance of power in most relationships, except among lesbians.

Whereas in heterosexual couples the greater the amount of money the wife earns the freer she is to spend the money as she sees fit, in lesbian couples the balance of power appears unrelated to income. "They make a conscious effort to keep their relationships free of any form of domination, especially if it derives from something as impersonal as money" (55). In gay male couples, income is an extremely important force in determining which partner is dominant. When partners are disappointed with the amount of money the couple has, they find their entire relationship less satisfying, except among lesbians. Schrag (1984) reports that money and property seem to be the issue of how to keep the relationship together in the face of career demands. This contrasts with the heterosexual concern of who has the right to work. The majority of same-sex couples believe that both should work, although lesbians are more likely to feel obligated to support a partner than are gay males.

Same-sex couples, due to a lack of traditional marital role models, tend to negotiate each conflict rather than rely on societal expectations or previous gender role models for their answers. In dealing with the issue of "work versus the relationship," same-sex couples tended to be relationship oriented. Lesbians of all ages cannot seem to find enough time to share together. A recent study of cohesion and adaptability in lesbian relationships confirms previous findings of high cohesion in female couples, a reality that may help them function more successfully in a primarily heterosexual world (Zacks, Green, and Marrow 1988, 471). This is consistent with Day and Morse's (1981) conclusion that lesbian pairs appear to be equalitarian in style.

Gay men appear more satisfied with the time they have available to them. Blumstein and Schwartz speculate that one reason same-sex couples are so relationship centered may be their capacity to spend their leisure time together, having been socialized to enjoy many of the same activities and interests.

"There's a comfort just being in the same room together. We can sit and be quiet and feel very comfortable for hours. We often find ourselves doing the same things, buying the same cards, planning the same meals, starting to say the same things. We are very much alike and share the same interests. We can leave a great deal unsaid and still understand each other."

The pressure of high cohesion and limited social support creates serious stress and violence in some relationships. Recent studies have explored abuse in same-sex couples. Like heterosexual couples, gay male and lesbian couples may use physically aggressive or, occasionally, violent tactics to resolve relationship conflicts (Kelly and Warshafsky 1987). Hart (1986) explains lesbian battering as a pattern of violence or coercive behaviors "whereby a lesbian seeks to control the thoughts, beliefs, or conduct of her intimate partner or to punish the intimate for resisting the perpetrator's control" (173). Although the patterns of conflict may be similar between heterosexual and same-sex couples, the stigmatization of such couples may affect their willingness to seek help and the responses of those called on to help (Renzetti 1989). Thus, conflict and abuse plague same-sex as well as heterosexual couples.

Blumstein and Schwartz report that sexual frequency varies among the couple types. Gay men have sex more often in the early part of their relationship than any other type of couple. But after ten years, they have sex together far less frequently than do married couples. Lesbians have sex less frequently than any other type of couple. The quality of sexuality is important to all couples. In same-sex couples, it is the more emotionally expressive partner who initiates sex most frequently. As a distinction between same-sex couples types, gay men value physical attractiveness of a partner more highly than do lesbians.

Parenting serves as a joy and a concern for a small number of same-sex couples. There is very little research on gay male or lesbian parents, yet it seems reasonable to assume that communication around this issue would be difficult. Discussing one's own homosexuality with a child creates enormous concerns. In one of the few studies in this area, Miller (1979) found that gay men feared it would lessen the children's respect and affection for their fathers. Of the men who had told their children, all found the children more positive than had been anticipated (548). The children reported that their father's honesty had relieved some family tension and helped to strengthen the parent-child relationship. Children who showed the greatest acceptance of their fathers were those who were gradually introduced to the subject of homosexuality through printed material, discussion, and meeting gay family friends before the full parental disclosure.

Same-sex couples with children face many issues similar to those of heterosexual couples. For example, in her study of lesbian partner abuse, Renzetti found that thirty-five couples lived with children, and in one-third of the cases these children were abused by the violent partner as well.

Although same-sex couples represent a small percentage of American families, they are included as a family form because of the growing societal recognition of the existence of long-term committed relationships within the gay community.

COMMUNICATION AND OTHER VARIATIONS OF FAMILY FORMS

Although there are many other family forms that could be considered, we will highlight two: cohabitation and joint physical custody. These forms are becoming increasingly common in our society.

Cohabitation

If you live with a boyfriend or girlfriend for three weeks, are you a cohabitor? If you keep two apartments but sleep together in one or the other, are you a cohabitor? Although definitions of cohabitation abound, cohabiting generally refers to the lifestyle created by two unrelated and unmarried adults of the opposite sex living together, with or without children, over a period of time. Cohabiting implies an indefinite agreement to share living quarters, not a convenient response to a college schedule or apartment shortage. A commitment to each other and recognition of each other as a "family" are also implied. This definition limits the number of couples or families to be considered.

Estimating the population of cohabitors with any accuracy is difficult. Unmarried couples living together totaled 2.6 million in 1988. Putting these figures in perspective means that 5 percent of all couples, or one couple in twenty, are unmarried. Whereas some cohabitors have never been married, others have experienced one or more marriages. Wallerstein and Blakeslee found that 10 percent of the divorcing parents eventually moved to long-term cohabitation arrangements (277). They report that usually one of the partners in long-term cohabitation does not want marriage, leaving the other powerless to force the issue.

"We are as married as any of our 'legal' friends but, having been through a terrible divorce, I cannot see marrying again. The children on both sides treat us as a couple, and since we don't plan to add to that population, I see no need to marry. In fact, I think we do so well because we don't take each other for granted."

Communication differs in some respects between cohabiting and married couples. Without the legal ties and ceremonial rituals that publicly announce the relationship as a long-term commitment, partners may have difficulty communicating to friends and relatives that their living together, especially in the beginning, represents love more than sexual needs.

Statistical estimates of the number of couples who cohabit and eventually marry vary from one in four to one in eight; thus, the partners themselves may fear that their relationship will not last. This can influence patterns of conflict and decision making. In his study of communication of married and cohabiting couples of various ages, Yelsma (1986) found that older couples were less likely to discuss sexual interests, disagreements, and personal problems than were younger couples.

Cohabiting does not predict future marital satisfaction. One study of cohabiting couples who married reports that in the year after the marriage, wives perceived a significantly lower quality of communication, and both spouses reported significantly lower marital satisfaction (DeMaris and Leslie 1984, 77). In another study, couples who had not cohabited had higher marital adjustment scores one year after marriage than did those who had cohabited (Watson 1983). The results of these and similar studies contradict earlier studies, which indicated that cohabitation effectively screened out incompatible couples, served as a training/adjustment period for couples, and improved mate selection and the chances of avoiding divorce (Ridley, Peterman, and Avery 1978; Trost 1975; Watson). The differences in these studies may be in the ages of the couples or the definition of cohabiting used, or it may be that cohabiting couples who marry expect more from marriage and adapt less readily to role expectations of conventional marriage (DeMaris and Leslie, 83).

As you remember from Chapter 6, role performance may differ greatly from original expectations. Being a wife or husband may bring with it a set of pressures from the spouse or other forces that cause the role to be played out differently than expected. In his classic book, *Becoming Partners*, Carl Rogers (1972) records poignant statements about this process from two young people who married after living together for a lengthy period of time:

Dick: "When Gail and I were living together we were sort of equal partners in making the living, and if we were broke, nobody really took the blame for it; but when we moved back and came into such close proximity with our respective in-laws, all of a sudden it became *my* fault when we weren't making any money, and *I* was the bum who wasn't going out and looking for work."

Gail: "I sort of had expectations like he did, you fall into a role even if you don't want to . . . of a husband is supposed to be this way and a wife is supposed to be this way. . . . So it put me into a big conflict because I'm thinking, 'Well, I've *got* to be like this, I'm married and I'm supposed to do this . . . ' " (43).

In this case, both personal expectations and family pressure forced individuals to view their roles differently than they expected. The lack of clear definition of cohabiting roles may increase the partners' sense of individual freedom. Blumstein and Schwartz found that cohabiting couples regard money, sex, and work differently than do other couples. These varying perceptions influence the ways cohabiting couples negotiate differences and establish patterns and rules affecting their interaction. Cohabiting couples reported a stronger sense than married couples of each partner's contributing his or her share. More time may be spent communicating about this topic.

Cohabiting women view money as a way to achieve equality in their relationships. Thus, cohabiting women seek independence and want to avoid economic dependence or dominance by the man in their household. The cohabiting men expect this behavior more than do married men. The cohabiting partner with the greater income determines more of the couple's recreational activities, including vacations. Cohabiting couples usually maintain separate checking accounts, and when they do, they fight less about finances than do married couples (53–109).

These same researchers found that cohabitors believe that both partners should work and expect sharing of housework. Yet women do more of this work than men. Male cohabitors, more than married men, rank the relationship as more important than their job. However, male cohabitors are more competitive with their partners, but the partners' success or lack of it has less effect on the relationship. Cohabitors more frequently spend time on their own, including going places alone or with friends, than either married, gay male, or lesbian couples.

Sexual communication also differs, because cohabitors report having sex more frequently than married couples. Cohabiting women more readily express an interest in sex by initiating it, but in a long-standing relationship, the male cohabitor usually resents it. In a summary of cohabiting couples' experiences, Pearson (1989) concludes that (1) cohabiting couples appear to be more egalitarian, (2) more independent of each other, and (3) more loving toward each other than married couples (106–107).

Many parents of cohabiting children have difficulty accepting their children's wishes to live together in a trial marriage. Family communication can be difficult at holidays or other times when parents are confronted with visiting cohabitors' requests to share a bedroom, especially when other relatives plan to stay in the same household. Frequently, communication in the family network becomes quite complicated, with certain members or subsystems knowing the "secret" and others kept uninformed. Cohabitation represents a small but growing type of family form with certain unique communication concerns.

Joint Physical Custody

At the end of the 1980s, at least thirty-three states made joint custody a preference or at least an option. This family form involves an approach to shared parenting after divorce. Whereas legal joint custody refers to shared parental responsibility or decision making, the new family form involves joint physical custody. Joint physical custody, or shared custody, occurs when divorced parents share parenting in separate homes, as children move between residences spending substantial amounts of time with the mother and the father. Some ex-spouses work out weekend or every-other-night arrangements, or three or four nights with one parent and then an equal number with the other. Instead of separating the child, more or less permanently, via divorce from one parent, this arrangement enables the child to know and share time with each (Galper 1978). Joint custody is an attempt to soften the child's loss of one parent, usually the father, and to maintain fathers in crucial child-rearing roles (Wallerstein and Blakeslee, 257). Some children readily adapt to the two-home situation and, after a short time, prefer it. The following account describes such a working arrangement.

"In the year following the divorce, we continued to fight constantly over raising Mike. At school, Mike was constantly in trouble. As a father, I wasn't satisfied with an overnight visit on the weekend, and I kept running over to the house to see Mike before his mother returned from work. We worked out an every-other-night agreement, but this seemed to be too much moving back and forth for Mike. We switched to changing every three days, and this suited everyone fine. Mike has his own room, clothes, and toys at each home, including a dog at mine and a cat at his mother's. Now Mike does well in school; when we settled down, he did too."

Joint custody has practical benefits. One study revealed that parents who share custody return to court less than half as often as couples in which one partner receives complete custody (Clausen et al. 1983, 44). Joint custody especially appeals to fathers who want to remain in close contact with their children and have more decision-making rights about their children's lives. Joint custody works best when parents accept their past differences and decide that "the best interest of the children" is a goal worth cooperating to achieve (Scheiner, Musetto, and Cordier 1982, 105).

Co-parenting requires cooperation and commitment to the idea and very regular communication. It necessitates both parents' living close to one another, although some couples who have moved to different cities alternate school years. Both parents experience the joy and share the tribulations of child raising (Nehls and Morgenbesser 1980, 117). Both parents assume active responsibility for the children. Joint custody arrangements, by their nature, require much flexibility on the part of the children involved. They may need to adapt to major differences in communication rules, gender expectations, boundaries, and relational currencies. In a recent study, all parents involved in joint physical custody agree that children encounter real problems on "changeover day," the day of moving from one household to another (Wallerstein and Blakeslee, 261). Children experience anxiety, but find comfort in sameness and routines at each home.

Voluntary joint custody requires a special skill in communicating between the parents, plus in some cases, their new partners. They have to separate their history of marital troubles from their parental roles for it to work. If the former spouse's communication remains conflictual, a child will be constantly in the middle of war. In short, successful co-parenting, or joint custody, requires the parents to work out an interactive "divorced relationship." Communication must be frequent, constructive, and mutually supportive, especially if small children are involved. Some partners fear that this continued involvement will perpetuate old arguments or patterns of dominance. In remarried systems, stepparents become part of the process with significant power to support or sabotage the custody arrangements. Clearly, this involves effort and patience, but for many adults, it represents the best alternative for their children and, therefore, is worth the effort.

The long-term effects of joint custody on children remain to be seen. Wallerstein and Blakeslee report that, for their small sample, the results were surprising. "Two years after divorce, children raised in joint custody households are no better adjusted than children raised in sole custody homes," yet "fathers in joint custody families are more committed to their children" (271). They conclude that different custody models are suitable for different families.

Because of the more limited range of role models for some of the family forms discussed in this chapter, the successful development of an operating family system requires extensive effort and mutual understanding on the part of the members involved. Without the ability to share information and feelings and to negotiate constructively, the stresses may lead to dissolution. Maintenance of the system depends heavily on the communication between and among the system members.

CONCLUSION

This chapter develops a position stated earlier in this text—there is no one right way to be a family—and its corollary, there is no one right way to communicate in a family. Single-parent systems, an increasingly common form, may experience destructive pressure if they lack appropriate economic, emotional, and social supports. Single parents fare better when strong communication networks are in place for them. Creating stepfamilies, the process of blending two systems, and the communication tasks inherent in this process reflect a highly complex type of family formation. A system created out of loss, with voluntary and involuntary relationships, presents a host of communication challenges. Same-sex partners, who may also function as parents, function with limited support systems both interpersonally and legally. The AIDS crisis, encouraging more gay men and lesbians into monogamous relationships, is predicted to increase this type of system. Finally, family systems formed through cohabitation and joint physical custody reflect changing lifestyles and carry with them unique communication demands. Each of these family forms requires the conscious effort of members to communicate their needs and feelings during the development and maintenance of the family. In short, it takes effort to create a family, of any form, that works.

IN REVIEW

1. What language changes have you encountered that support the emerging and growing family forms?
2. What do you see as some communication-related differences between a single-parent system with three children and a two-parent system with three children?
3. Apply Papernow's model of stepfamily development to a real or fictional stepfamily, indicating (1) experiences similar to or different from the model and (2) communication patterns indicative of certain stages.
4. Take a position and discuss: When children are involved, ex-spouses are divorced "to" each other rather than "from" each other.
5. In what ways might unrelated persons communicate to outsiders that they consider each other to be a family?

CHAPTER 13

Family Context: Environmental Dimensions of Communication

All family interaction takes place within an environmental context of space and time. Just as it is important to understand the individual within the family context, so too the family must be understood within its environmental context. Decontexted individuals do not exist; decontexted families do not exist. Therefore, to understand familial interaction fully, one needs to explore family relationships through the dual lenses of space and time within the context of "home."

"I have always been part of a strong extended family and have lived with my parents since my divorce four years ago. Although my children are eight and five, we have, until now, been connected with the overall family, so we adapted to that household and acted as they did. This week we moved into our own apartment and realized that a lot had changed. We looked at each other around the small kitchen table, which seemed so incomplete with just the three of us. Here we were, alone, in our own space, and a little scared. We sat in uneasy silence for a while before we began the tentative discussion about how we would live in this new world."

The following questions may stimulate your initial thinking about family relationships as they are affected by environmental context:

1. What was the best place and time to talk to a parent about personal problems when you were younger?
2. When having dinner, did all family members eat at the same time while sitting in specific places, or did you eat when you felt like it, anywhere you chose? Were there certain rituals connected with particular meals?
3. Could family members shut the door to rooms to be alone? If doors were closed, did you knock first, or did you just open them and walk in? Did family members have special spaces that were theirs?

4. How were holidays celebrated in your home? Who was included? How did the house or the community reflect the event?
5. As a small child, what were the safety boundaries surrounding your home that you could not cross? A neighbor's yard? The apartment hallway? A main street? How did this change as you grew older?
6. How did the cultural, regional, or religious nature of your community affect your family's interaction? Did your family reflect the community or differ from the community?

These are some of the issues that will be explored further as you view family interactions through spatial and temporal lenses, investigating the interaction between environmental factors and the interpersonal relationships within a family.

Advances in environmental psychology have led architects, designers, and social scientists to focus more directly on the environment as a context for, as well as a type of, communication. Professionals involved in social service have developed ecological approaches to understanding human behavior by examining interaction between people and their environment (deHoyos 1989). The environmental context creates a system of communication that is learned, socially understood, and structured like language (DeLong 1974). Persons learn to react appropriately within particular dimensions of space and time because the messages received from the environment provide cues about appropriate behavior. In addition, the environment contains cultural expectations for interaction that become routine for persons familiar with it.

Psychologist Albert Scheflen (1971) suggests that hierarchical levels of social relationships, including parent/child and family relationships, provide and demand certain traditional patterns of task performance, spacing, speech, and body language; and each of these traditions dictates how we are to think and feel about every kind of situation. He maintains that these systems of behavior are organized spatially and temporally (429–430). Reiss (1981) refers to space and time as two fundamental resources a family requires for conducting its day-to-day life. He proposes that families are "strikingly different in their management of these two resources" and that these differences are crucial to how a family defines itself (233).

Environmental issues of space and time provide part of the boundaries that limit and define a family's experience and, hence, communication. If you analyze the structures within which you relate to people, you will begin to understand how the structural design, arrangement of furniture and objects within the structure, and time of day or year within the structure can influence (1) who interacts with whom, (2) where, (3) when, (4) for how long, and (5) the style or tone of the interaction and the kinds of things about which you can communicate. In more concrete terms, certain family members are more likely to have greater interactions because they share a room, play basketball in the backyard, or sit up together for an evening cup of coffee. Whereas basketball games do not foster intense, deep conversations but provide shared experiences, talking in your room or at the kitchen table with one other person may lead to special and deep conversations and greater cohesion; it may encourage the airing of strong conflicts that result in greater distance or, possibly, greater closeness. Patterns of behavior, which may include roles and past experiences in the same space, influence the tone or style of interaction.

A way of life and its context are interdependent. Failure to respect this intrinsic wholeness may result in overlooking the interrelations that support the stability of the entire system (Duncan 1964; deHoyos). Communication occurs within a culture-bound context, which influences the kinds of interaction that can and will occur. Places, as well as people, form the context for communication events; and, although physical home or time patterns do not *determine* the kinds of family interactions that take place, they do *influence* interactions that occur both within and outside the home. Thus, a family ecology viewpoint recognizes that the total environment has a strong impact on family development.

FACTORS OF FAMILY CONTEXT

The environment and people in it combine to form a communication system. This section will examine the environmental factors of space and time and then will demonstrate how these interrelate with each other and may affect communication within family systems across cultures.

Space

Proxemics. The study of distances as a function of communication, or proxemics, is based on an understanding of how people use space. Anthropologist Edward Hall (1966) conceptualized the ways humans use space, such as fixed feature space, semifixed feature space, and informal space (103–112). *Fixed feature space* refers to that physical space organized by unmoving boundaries, such as walls in a room or the invisible line dividing space that is recognized by those who use it. The latter may be called a nonphysical or psychological boundary. Each type serves as a "real" boundary to which inhabitants must adapt. The actual wall between the kitchen and the dining room may keep the cook out of the conversation. Such boundaries are obvious. Yet, if you shared a room with a brother or sister, you may remember the times that your side of the room and his or her side became separate territories, and you did not cross the line or drop things on the other bed.

Semifixed feature space refers to flexible space created by the arrangement of furniture and/or other movable objects over which the inhabitants have control. You probably remember rearranging your room according to your moods or having to help rearrange the living room when one of your parents decided to encourage conversation at a party.

Informal space refers to the way people position their bodies as they relate to others. Hall has divided into four major levels the distances at which a person relates: intimate space, ranging from zero to eighteen inches; personal space, ranging from eighteen inches to four feet; social space, ranging from four to twelve feet; and public space, which encompasses interaction at distances over twelve feet.

Whereas "intimate space" encourages the nonverbal expression of such emotions and behaviors as hugging, kissing, tickling, lovemaking, wrestling, hitting, and whispering, "personal space" supports interpersonal discussions, decision making, and the sharing of emotions with some physical contact. Within "social space," small groups may engage in social or business conversations. "Public space" encourages short discussions or waves and greetings from a distance. Touch is not possible, but unique communication signs, such as a wink or a disapproving look, may travel between persons who know each other well.

Extensions of Hall's work in proxemics has found practical applications in areas such as family therapy. Famous therapists such as Jay Haley and Salvador Minuchin have written about observing family seating patterns for clues to a family's hierarchy and affiliation patterns (Haley 1976; Minuchin 1974). In addition, the area of proxemics has yielded some interesting and consistent variations across age, gender, and culture (Lomrantz 1976; McGoldrick, Pearce, and Giordano 1982; McGoldrick, Anderson, and Walsh 1989). Yet the consistency within gender, age, or cultural groups supports the need to examine such patterns.

Territory/Privacy. *Territoriality*, a basic concept in the study of animal behavior, involves behavior by which an animal lays claim to an area and defends it against members of its own species. Territoriality is concerned with places for "doing" things: places to learn, places to play, safe places to hide. Hall relates territory to the concepts of fixed feature space when he suggests, "The boundaries of the territories remain reasonably constant, the territory is in every sense of the word an extension of the organism which is marked by visual, vocal, and olfactory signs and, therefore, it is relatively 'fixed' " (9). Family territory may be understood as an area that a member of a close-knit group in joint tenancy claims and will "defend." Individual family members may claim territory within the system. In other words, a family or a person stakes out real or imagined space and lays personal claim to it.

Those who own a territory or others who recognize the territory behave in particular ways as they approach the boundary, even if it is not marked by fences, walls, or other barriers. Scheflen suggests that small territories may be marked by postural behavior, such as an arm that defends a space, or by the placement of possessions. People defend their territory through verbal and nonverbal communication strategies, such as aggression or dominance.

Territory in a home may be as real as "my parents' room," or as nonphysical as "Mike's part of the yard." Places may be recognized as belonging to someone by decrees ("This is my chair"), by tenure ("I always sat there"), by markers ("We left our books here because we were coming back"), or by agreement ("After I've had the hammock for fifteen minutes, it's your turn"). If you think about your own home, you should be able to identify numerous territorial behaviors by which members declare their spatial demands. Some of these behaviors may also indicate a desire for privacy within certain space. Yet, without mutual agreement among those who believe the territory is "theirs" and other potential users, the concept of limited use may eventually disappear or conflicts about the use will arise.

Privacy may be viewed as the "claims of individuals, groups, or institutions to determine for themselves when, how, and to what extent information about them is communicated to others" (Westin 1967, 10). Privacy maintains an individual's need for personal autonomy through which he or she can control the environment, including the ability to be alone or to have private communication with another.

Choice is essential to the concept of privacy, a point supported by Marshall (1972) when she says "It is not enough simply to be alone, for example; one must be alone when one chooses to be" (93).

"In our family, there seems to be a careful balance between allowing someone to have total personal control of space and allowing everyone to go wherever they please. A rule is that when a door is shut, a person wants to be left alone, and nobody should enter the room without knocking and getting permission first. Friends frequently enter our home at various hours and often unannounced, without disruption or question. The only exceptions to this rule occur when family members have set aside time to be home alone together, and such visits seem to be intrusions. Then we try to cut the visit short so we can enjoy our time alone with each other."

Some homes encourage such privacy, whereas others cannot or do not. If you share a home with seven others and a bedroom with two others, privacy may be a luxury attained only outside the home. Yet, in certain households with ample physical space, privacy is restricted by family rules or one's own perceptions (Marshall). Privacy and territory interrelate to provide the means of protective communication, such as the sharing of confidences, problems, and affection.

As with spatial distance, territory and privacy are relative within and between cultures. In certain types of homes, personal places and possessions are held in high regard, whereas in others, total sharing is the norm. One gains privacy in some cultures by isolation, whereas in other cultures, psychological withdrawal permits privacy within a group. In his study of urban families, Scheflen asked women, "What do you do when you want to be alone?" and discovered that one-half of the Puerto Rican wives "did not comprehend the implication of the question in American middle-class terms. They said they never wanted to be alone . . . the other half said they went home to see family" (437). The concept did not have the same meaning as it does to persons of other cultures.

Time

The way in which a family lives in time interacts with how it lives in space. Kantor and Lehr (1976) discuss families' use of time as *orientation, clocking,* and *synchronization.* Families or individuals may experience an *orientation* toward the past or future that supersedes life in the present. Each person orients himself or herself toward the past, present, or future. You have met people who live in the "good old days" and whose communication reflects a respect for, or delight in, yesterday. A recent orientation reflects a concern for the here and now. Current relationships are valued, and current joys and sorrows take top priority. In a present-oriented family, less time is spent reminiscing or planning than is spent on daily issues. A future orientation emphasizes what is to come. Planning, dreaming, and scheming characterize such a mind-set and have typified many

American families on their way to "the good life." Such orientations may be reflected in household furnishings, contacts with kin, patterns of friendship, attitudes toward money, and career planning (Reiss et al.). Time is a commodity, the use of which indicates much about a family's view of the world.

Whereas orienting refers to an overall temporal perspective, *clocking* refers to the daily use of time. It regulates the order, frequency, length, and pace of immediate events. Certain family rules, such as who talks first in certain situations or who gets the last word, may be part of a subtle sequencing pattern. On a more obvious level, some families must establish functional rituals for moving into a day.

"In our attempt to maintain a two-career family with two small children, we have become very organized. We have very specific morning patterns so we can get out of the house on time and in a good frame of mind. I get up and start to make breakfast. My wife then gets out of bed, dresses, and starts to wake our daughters. When they come into the kitchen, I dress while Helen fixes the rest of breakfast. During the week, no one eats breakfast until he or she is dressed and ready to go. This way we can have a semipeaceful morning, talk a little, and minimize the conflict."

Families clock how often and for how long things may be done. Growing up, you may have experienced limits on how often you saw certain friends or how long you were allowed to argue with them before someone yelled, "That's enough." All families need some built-in repetition and guidelines to keep their lives functional. Clocking also refers to the speed with which a day is lived. Do you do fifty-two things and call it a "good day," or do you like to take things easy and maintain a slower pace? Pacing varies with age, health, and mental state. Large variations in pacing patterns often lead to conflict among family members.

An additional aspect of time involves *synchronization,* or the process of maintaining a program for regulating the overall and day-to-day life of a family. Often, this is done through discussing how things are going and setting or reaffirming plans and priorities. Family members integrate individual schedules to create an overall approach to spending time. A spouse may turn down a position that requires a great deal of travel because it would keep him or her away from the family. A couple may agree to a long-term separation because a commuter marriage would set the groundwork for a desirable lifestyle in five years. Family discontent may lead to a reorganization of original priorities. Some families may establish respect for individual "clocks," whereas others may dictate a "family clock" to which everyone must adhere. Just as other factors are culture bound, the use of time varies according to culture. For example, American families may stress punctuality, whereas Latin-American families may not recognize this as a value.

"Time is very regular in our family. Mealtimes are precise and never to be missed. Even on weekends the kids want lunch at a specified time at home. Dinner is sacred. This is non-negotiable. You are always at dinner and on time to help set

---

up, and always stay to help clean up. Church is a regular Sunday event. This is also usually the day that chores around the house are to be done by the kids and the parents. Missing a meal or missing church is a major event."

Space and time are synchronized to some degree in families as members go about the patterned routines of their lives. There may be appropriate times for being alone and times when togetherness is important. Children may be allowed to play in adult spaces until an adult indicates that the space is taken. Holidays may require the presence of all family members in a particular space for a specified time, particularly if their themes and images stress togetherness. Biosocial beliefs interact with how time may be spent "legitimately" by males or females. The degree of synchronization may distinguish well-functioning families from those experiencing conflict and/or change. For example, collective activities cannot be planned because of disagreement about the priorities or commitment to the outcome.

Listen to how people talk about time and to the metaphors they use. Do they see time in economic terms, as something to save, buy, or spend, or do they see it as a gift to be enjoyed, made the most of, or shared? Underlying beliefs about time are played out in family discussions and in the messages members receive about "using" time. Thus, space and time are important dimensions of a family's communication context. In order fully to understand the interrelationships of these factors, you need to examine the family dwelling as a specific communication context.

THE HOME WORLD: OUTSIDE AND INSIDE

Sometimes the terms *home* and *house* (or apartment) are used synonymously, although the words may carry different meanings. Not all houses or apartments qualify as "homes." Many environment scholars believe that a "person's concept of home is better understood as a *relationship* to such an environment, rather than the environment itself" (Horwitz and Tognoli 1982, 335). Saegert maintains that a house has strong psychological and social meaning, suggesting that "it is part of the experience of dwelling—something we do, a way of weaving up a life in particular geographical spaces" (1985, 287). The physical dwelling is an important factor in the development of a sense of home, which must be examined in conjunction with related environmental factors such as time and territory. Thus, we will examine the home environment to understand how it influences the family.

The house influences the interactions that occur within it, because its structure and design affect the development of relationships with oneself and between family members, friends, and strangers (Lawrence 1987; Werner 1987). In his work on environment and interaction, psychologist Osmond (1970) distinguished between sociofugal and sociopetal space. *Sociofugal space* discourages human interaction; *sociopetal space* supports it. "Sociopetality is that quality which encourages, fosters, and even enforces the development of stable interpersonal relationships and which may be found in small face-to-face groups, in home or circular wards" (576). Both the exterior and interior of a house contributes to the creation of relational experiences for the family members. In addition, the design and use of home interiors and their external appearance reflect cultural and social values (Lawrence).

Exterior Arrangement

A dwelling's exterior may affect the interactions of family members with the community at large and specifically with neighbors. Some studies of homogeneous populations indicate that housing planned for easy social interaction (such as doors opening on a common court or homes built around a cul-de-sac) promotes neighborliness (Chilman 1978, 108). Housing style may carry symbolic meaning to observers. In a study of the perception of house styles, Nasar (1989) found that farm-style homes were perceived as most friendly, whereas colonial-style homes were seen as unfriendly. The exterior of a dwelling may be understood by examining its placement, the surrounding community, and the management of boundaries.

Housing Placement. Housing placement influences with whom you interact and therefore, to some extent, with whom you develop friendships. In a famous study, researchers Festinger, Schachter, and Beck (1950) examined the development of friendships in a new housing project for married students. This development consisted of apartment structures arranged in U-shaped courts with the two end structures facing the street. They were able to demonstrate that the distance between apartments and the direction in which an apartment faced affected friendships. Friendships developed more frequently between next-door neighbors and less frequently between persons who lived in apartments separated by more than four or five other apartments. In addition, those who lived near the mailboxes, stairways, entrances, and exits tended to make more friends because they encountered other residents regularly. Such findings remain current even today (Crime . . . 1983). If your front or back door leads into a heavily trafficked area, you have a greater chance of developing neighborhood relationships and becoming a central part of the communication network than if you live off the beaten track.

The Neighborhood. The surrounding territory may partially dictate a family's way of relating to the outside world. A planned community may expect certain social responses from its individual households; those who choose to live another lifestyle may find themselves ostracized. Particular communities may set expectations for attendance at coffee klatches or participation in the local Fourth of July parade—activities that require space and time commitments. As families move from one home to another, a new community can partially influence their interactions.

Planned communities continue to expand, ranging from such highly structured communities as Reston, Virginia, to more informal communities developed by an individual builder. Even some high-rise buildings attempt to foster a sense of community through the integration of stores, athletic facilities, and movie theaters into their overall construction plans. The current aging of the U.S. population points toward continued growth of retirement communities, such as Sun City (Baker 1984).

In contrast, certain communities may prevent attempts at socialization or communication because the territory is "unsafe." Scheflen conducted a classic study of 1,200 primarily black, Puerto Rican, and Eastern European families living in the East Tremont urban ghetto in upper Manhattan. He reported:

> [Within this area] a black teenager can often go out for the evening. But the Puerto Rican child may not even be allowed to go out of the apartment let alone the street or to a neighbor's house. The mother may consider any area outside the apartment to be dangerous, and often she is right. (437)

In St. Louis, Missouri, urban high-rise buildings in the Pruitt Igoe housing project were razed because of the dangerous conditions created by this type of housing. Life in "unsafe" territory is accompanied by many rules about whom not to talk to. Yet, even if you get to the street in such a territory, you may find that surrounding territories, a gang "turf," or a different ethnic ghetto can limit movement.

Certain territories encourage or permit particular behaviors. For example, a single family home may not encourage romantic behavior in teenagers due to the presence of other family members, but the car or a secluded hallway may provide the environment for such behavior.

"I observed a difference in the socialization process in my housing complex and the project building. My peers in the project stayed out much later and had more freedom to go places than those in the housing complex. They began to have sexual intercourse and children at an earlier age. I observed intimate behavior when I visited my friends, while on the elevator, or walking up the stairs. The parents knew what their kids were doing and acknowledged the fact by trying to get them to use some type of birth control. They had boyfriends before my friends from the housing complex and I did, and they began kissing early in grammar school."

In some cases, communities are slow to support members who represent differences. For example, African American families in suburbia often find themselves rejected and isolated by their new neighbors. They also feel estranged from the friends, relations, and associates they left behind in the city (Billingsley 1988, 421).

An increasing architectural concern is the development of appropriate housing for the aged. A growing awareness exists of the need for elder housing that (1) encourages interaction and (2) stimulates participation in new activities (Jordan 1984; Crime . . .). Thus, buildings designed for senior citizens may have carefully designed eating or recreation areas, and programs ranging from drama and exercise classes to intergenerational day-care experiences. Many communities are developing day-care centers for elderly citizens in order to expand their network of regular contacts.

Families form boundaries through which they find safety.

Boundary Management

One purpose of home design is to distinguish between public and private domains (Lawrence). Each family engages in managing its boundaries to regulate physical traffic across its borders. Kantor and Lehr call this process *bounding*. Through bounding, a family sets a perimeter and defends its territory. It says, "This is ours, we are safe here" (68). It may defend these territorial borders through the use of devices to regulate entrance to the home. Buzzers, shades, peepholes, bushes, and double locks all provide some privacy and control. Children may experience a designated territory, which is permitted for safe exploration. In housing projects, there may be no safety beyond the front door, so the boundary may be synonymous with the apartment. In other areas, a neighbor's yard or the road in front may be the limits. A family can create boundaries by turning off the phone, establishing rules or hours for visiting, and appearing not to have the time for interaction. Lack of availability sends a temporal message about the desire for limited interaction.

A family with flexible boundaries in a safe territory may indicate a desire for interaction by using the openings of a house to invite in the outside world. Neighborhood children may run through unlocked doors, or friends may shout through the window. In some urban communities, an apartment may overflow to a porch, steps, or the street below where folding chairs extend the living room to the sidewalk. A less-scheduled, flexible family can make time for these distractions more easily than a family that runs on a tight clock.

Interior Arrangement

Home interiors are organized spatially and temporally. The fixed and semifixed feature spaces stand as supports for, or as barriers to, interpersonal communication. The interior design influences how much privacy can be attained and how easily members can come together, whereas the furnishings and decor contain messages about how to relate. Each of these factors reflects cultural values.

Rooms and Floor Plan. One way to view a house spatially is to start with the floor plan and determine the possible relationships that may or may not occur based on how space is arranged. Interpersonal communication and general living activities may be seen in relation to the public and private zones of a home (Kennedy 1953; Werner 1987). The more public zones provide great possibilities for social interaction, whereas the more private zones exclude persons from some or all interpersonal contact. Different areas of the home may be associated with specific family functions and hence, to the system and subsystem boundaries. Various levels and types of interactions are acceptable in different spaces, reflected in the range of highly interpersonal to highly private spaces. As you move through a home, the spaces may become more highly private to members, whereas persons outside the system or subsystem may be excluded from certain spaces. In many homes, there are spaces for interpersonal interactions with guests, close friends, and other family members. For example, in one family, visitors may have access to living, dining, and kitchen areas but may not enter the bedrooms under usual circumstances. In another family, there may be a formal living room for socializing with guests and a family room for relaxing and talking with family members. Some families establish clear spatial boundaries for nonmembers; others do not.

> *"If I have friends I'm close with over, we don't go into the dining room. We sit in the kitchen, smoke, talk, and drink coffee. If it's someone I don't know well, we go into the living room."*

Member boundaries may vary. Some families set rigid standards for privacy. In such cases, bathrooms and bedrooms are locked, and special possessions are concealed (Reiss et al.). On the other hand, you may come from a family where one person may be showering, the next brushing his teeth, and another urinating in the same small bathroom. Such variables as age, sex, culture, and family size all interact with the spatial dimension.

The actual floor plan can dictate which persons will have the greatest contact and, potentially, the greatest communication. If you share adjoining territories with your sister, you are more likely to communicate with her than with some other family members. If your mother spends more time in a central place, such as the kitchen, she is more likely to serve as a network hub.

> *"When my mother remarried, she married a widower with eight children, which meant that our family suddenly had twelve children, ten of whom lived at home.*

This led Mom and Grant to remodel the attic, where they created bedrooms on the second floor. This really determined the way relationships developed in the family. I didn't see much of the boys who stayed upstairs or who were out playing sports. Because we were on the same floor and always were in and out of each other's rooms, all the girls became really close, and some of us would sit up until 2:00 A.M. talking about people and things."

The size of a dwelling affects the distances between the people in it. Small apartments force greater contact than do larger houses. Yet, even when space is held constant, families differ in their use of informal space. In his study of distance between interacting family members, Steinglass (1979) found average distance ranging from four to nine feet. Crane and colleagues (1987) report that spatial distance may be seen as an indicator of conflicted marital relationships, because distressed couples tended to converse at greater distances than did nondistressed couples.

Space, in some houses, may discourage communication among family members. Although in previous generations children shared beds and rooms, many children today have separate rooms equipped for autonomous living. This may lead to limited experience in certain interpersonal encounters. If each child has a room and even a television set and stereo, there may be little reason to learn sharing and problem-solving skills. Thus, two children do not have to decide together, for example, which television show to watch; rather, "You watch your show, I'll watch mine." Similarly, if the child and parent are at odds, the child can easily say, "I'm going to my room." That room then becomes an escape hatch when personal relationships falter (Kahn in Eshbach 1976, 3). In certain large homes, no one may know if the others are home or what they are doing.

"Although each member feels free to use any space in the house to do what he or she would like without fear of retribution, some limits on this do exist. For example, it's okay for Aaron to build his science project on the kitchen table, but after a few nights of eating supper on the couch, one of my parents usually asks Aaron to find a new spot to house his volcano."

Yet, in many cases, small, cramped quarters result in difficulties or pressure. For example, a study of two hundred families suggests that there is a marked difference in stress levels between families with one bathroom and families with a small half-bath in addition to the bathroom (Guenther 1984). A new set of stresses befall a divorced parent when children visit, and the space adequate for one or two adults does not comfortably hold four or five. Families experiencing the "refilling nest" syndrome report stress as adult children return to live at home. Many of today's families are attempting to integrate home and occupational spheres. Just as multiple simultaneous roles have been thought to be stress producing for farm wives (Berkowitz and Perkivs 1984), the new rise of cottage industries and part-time work at home adds stress to family interaction.

Countless immigrant and poor families experience stress due to crowding. Many Asian immigrants choose to sacrifice short-term needs for adequate shelter in hopes of providing professional career education for their children. Yet the self-sacrifices can be great. The loss of familiar environmental and social support networks makes the family's functioning more difficult (Shon and Davis 1983). Large families in Scheflen's East Tremont study lived in small apartments, and most of the time everyone functioned in the living room. In the Puerto Rican families, all members remained in the living room either bundled together or divided between the TV area and conversational area. Few secrets or personal conversations occurred within these systems. Black women attempted to keep the living room as a parlor, although children usually had to be allowed access to it. If company arrived, the children were likely to be sent to play in a bedroom. Conversations were more likely to be separated for "appropriate ears." Often, an overlapping of space occurred in these cramped quarters so that space was scheduled to be used according to the time of day. As Scheflen states:

> In one Puerto Rican family, breakfast occurred at a fixed time every day. Then Father went to work, the children settled down to watch television, and Mother began a highly regular schedule of chores. In the afternoon, a single visitor came, sat in a particular chair and talked with the mother. At noon each day, the older children were allowed to go out for an hour. (These observations were made in the summer when school was not in session.) Then at a fixed time, the mother cooked dinner, and the children ate in the living room. An hour later the father came home from work, sat at a small table in an alcove and had his supper served to him. Then Mother cleaned up and the family settled down for an evening in the living room before the television set. In this case the same sites were used by the same people each day, according to a regular schedule of household activities. (444)

In many homes, individuals or subsystems may have to plan for time and space to be alone. Sometimes it may be very structured, or sometimes it seems to occur naturally, as noted in the following contrasting situations:

"Growing up, there was a rule in our house that no one bothered our parents before 11:00 A.M. on Saturday. Their bedroom door was locked, and it was understood they were not to be disturbed."

"My parents still manage to have some privacy, although I don't know how, because their bedroom door has always been open to us day and night, and many times their bedroom serves as a place to go if you cannot sleep."

In each family, rules evolve for locking doors, opening drawers, reading mail, or using another's things. Frequently repeated statements such as "always knock before opening a closed door" or "never listen to another's phone call or open another's mail" evolve into operating rules. Sometimes status or liking can be understood by watching the access patterns within a household. Parents may have the right to invade privacy; babies may have access to places that are off-limits to teenagers, or vice versa; or a favorite sibling may be able to use special space. Furniture arrangement may encourage or discourage particular types of interaction. Themes, images, and biosocial beliefs interact with spatial and temporal environments.

For many families, mealtime has specific rituals and is a communication event that takes place in a very specific spatial and temporal setting. A study of dinnertime in middle-class families with small children revealed that dinner occurred in a dining room, dining area, or kitchen at a dinner table that was almost always rectangular. The formal eating territories were distinct.

> Within families, the members sat in the same places at the table every evening. Among families, the only invariable positioning of family members at the dinner table was that the father occupied one side (the head of the table by himself). Mother's position could be either opposite him, or on his right or left. In about half of the families observed, the mother and father sat opposite each other at the table. . . . In over two-thirds of our families the mother sat next to the youngest child in the family. (Dreyer and Dreyer 1984, 294–295)

Yet, in a different social/economic setting, things are done differently. Scheflen found that the average ghetto kitchen measured nine by twelve feet and held cabinets, closets, sink, stove, and refrigerator. If a table existed, it was small, with two or three chairs pushed against the wall. Because there were no dining rooms, all the members of large families could not physically eat together, resulting in two major adapting patterns. Some members carried their plates to the living room and ate off their laps; some of the children were fed from a small children's table in the kitchen. In the middle-class family, mothers welcomed others into their domain; but in cramped quarters, a mother usually staked out the kitchen as her territory and would not welcome "intruders."

Kantor and Lehr capture the regulation of distance within a house with their concept of "linking." For example, a large dining room table may encourage people to come together and may set up some interaction networks. Or because an apartment is so small that everyone needs to eat and interact in the living room, members may retreat to their rooms to study or to "regain a sunny disposition." At a family party, teenagers may be sent to the yard and basement while adults converse. Everyone may interact together, or a variety of patterns may develop. Through the linking process, family members regulate their contact within the home environment.

Furnishings and Decor. A home's furniture and decorations carry strong messages about how persons should communicate within that space. Some homes contain arrangements of chairs or couches in the family room that are conducive to relaxed conversations. Perhaps you and your best friend are allowed the privacy and time to talk for hours in your bedroom. On the other hand, you have probably seen a cavernous living room with plastic furniture covers and realized this was not the place for relaxed conversation. In his study of interpersonal discussions in living rooms, Scott (1984) found that "both the topic and the indicated relationship of the person in the other chair were significantly related to distance between chosen chairs" (35). Thus, distance may not determine, but it does affect, communication.

Additionally, the quality of communication in a home may be enhanced by a decor that either stimulates conversation or represents an integral part of the family; the decor allows you to understand the inhabitants and talk about appropriate topics. Past memories, present experiences, and future dreams of each person are linked to the objects in the environment (Csikszentmihalyi and Rochberg-Halton 1981). Intriguing pieces of art, rock collections, matchbooks, family pictures, hunting rifles, or plants may provide the stimulus for good interaction. Certain items may lead you to the "core" of the family. Symbols of religion, ethnic heritage, hobbies, and family life may indicate what is important. In their study of the meaning of things to people, Csikszentmihalyi and Rochberg-Halton found that objects such as furniture, visual art, and photographs carried special meaning, reflecting ties to past events, family members, and other people (61). Eighty-two percent of the respondents cherished at least one object because it reminded them of a close relation. For example, photographs were valued as the prime vehicle for preserving the memory of family members. The lack of significant objects may also make a statement. One home designer indicates, "People have begun to reexamine the role of possessions in their lives—the energies they take to maintain, the ways they may restrict one's freedom—and out of this there's been a certain paring down, rather than a building up" (Murphy 1984, 98D).

The esthetic design of a room, along with lighting and acoustics, plays its part in influencing communication. In the often-replicated beautiful-ugly room study by Maslow and Mintz, the ugly room was variously described as producing "monotony, fatigue, headaches, discomfort, sleep, irritability, and hostility." In contrast, the beautiful room produced feelings of "pleasure, comfort, enjoyment, importance, energy and desire to continue activity" (Knapp 1972, 31). This correlates with Mehrabian's finding (1971) that people tend to be more pleasant in pleasant settings than in unpleasant settings (75–76). This does not mean to imply that you must grow up in beautiful and expensive surroundings in order to have good communication within the family. Pleasant surroundings can enhance relationships if they help people become comfortable and relaxed, but so many other factors intervene that environment cannot be seen as the single influencing factor. Some researchers go so far as to say that the quality of relationships is not really affected by the quality of habitat, except in extremely adverse conditions, but that "high satisfaction with home and community may ameliorate high dissatisfaction with mate or parent-child relationships" (Chilman, 106).

Every family engages in "centering" behavior, or regulating space according to its values and beliefs. Thus, space reflects the family's view of itself and supports the values held by its members. There are family rules for how space is used (when one may go outside, who may be allowed in). There also may be specific ways of using things to keep the family in touch with each other. Blackboards, memo boards, and notes can keep a family in touch. Objects that remind a family of its identity and values, such as crucifixes, travel posters, or trophies, serve a centering function. Highly cohesive families may have stronger rules about family togetherness and how to achieve it within the home than families characterized by low cohesion.

Family Fit and Environment

An ecological approach to group interaction focuses on the way human beings and their environment accommodate each other. "Goodness of fit" is reflected in mutual interaction, negotiation, and compromise (deHoyos). The concept of "fit" has been applied to people and their home environments. Lennard and Lennard (1977) describe the "fit" between the style of family interaction and the home environment as the isomorphic fit, complementary fit, and nonfit (58).

Isomorphic fit implies congruence between the family and its environment. It occurs when aspects of the environment are clear expressions of the family's identity, of the way the members relate, and of the way they see the outside world. Let us use the Cameron family as an example. The Camerons could be characterized as a generally cohesive and highly adaptable family with few intrafamily boundaries, who live by such themes as "We work hard and play hard" and "We stick together in hard times." The Camerons (mother, father, four boys, and one girl) bought a large, old farmhouse and have torn out some of the walls on the first floor to create more open space. The Camerons engage in outdoor activities together and exhibit a rough-and-tumble style of interpersonal interaction. The farmhouse contains a large "mudroom" for skis and assorted sporting equipment. The large kitchen provides a place where the family can congregate when someone is cooking, or a number of people can be involved in a cooking operation at once. The family room is a place that invites informality and occasional wrestling matches. The house does not have a formal living room. The bedrooms are small, but because no one seems to spend time alone, it does not matter. The Camerons and their home are well matched.

A *complementary fit* implies a balance of opposites among two or more aspects of a family's interaction and home environment. This kind of fit can reflect the contrasting elements that exist within the family, or it can be consciously selected by a family in order to balance or counteract a special feature of family life. For example, the Muellers are a blended family with four teenagers (two from each former system) who tried their best to avoid one another when they first began their new life together. At that point in their development, interaction was difficult. The family was characterized by low cohesion and limited adaptability. Themes at this period reflected the lack of connectedness, such as "We don't get involved." In the former family homes, each child had a large, well-equipped room to which he or she retreated whenever any discomfort arose. When the families merged, the parents purposefully invested in a townhouse with fewer, smaller bedrooms. This forced the two boys to room together and all four young people to spend time in common areas, such as the attractively furnished family room. The parents consciously selected a home style that was complementary to the lifestyle that had evolved in their former homes.

The *nonfit* category includes those homes that are unsuited to the family's interaction pattern. Obviously, most lower-income housing falls into this category, because many families are trying to fit large numbers of people into a few tiny rooms that cannot hold them comfortably. Yet this style need not apply solely to families economically unable to afford larger housing. When the Morrises married, they decided not to have children. During their early thirties, they built their "dream house," a wood and glass structure with such features as cathedral ceilings, open walkways and staircases, and a small kitchen with a breakfast bar for all their meals. Their life was characterized by a belief that "We are complete as a couple"; their energies were directed toward cultural and educational pursuits. As they approached age 40, they rethought their decision, and at age 39, Sharon Morris brought a baby girl home to the "dream house." During the next few years, the Morris family and the house entered a nonfit stage. The unrailed walkway across the living room became a dangerous bridge, and their daughter could never be left alone on the second floor. She fell off the stairs many times. The lack of a regular dining area became a problem. Eventually, the dream house included gates, railings, Plexiglass panels, and other odd additions.

The concept of fit also applies to how families use time. An isomorphic fit characterizes a family that functions according to a particular orientation and clocking pattern that reflects the family's values. The Breznehan family consists of a father and three school-age children. Their world involves, among other things, swimming, baseball, and soccer, along with orthodontist visits and newspaper routes. This is a present- and future-oriented group of people who can adapt to tight schedules and fast pacing. Gus Breznehan's schedule is flexible, and he can adjust it relatively easily. Because family priorities include getting ahead and self-improvement, this lifestyle is consistent with group goals.

Grant and Jean Foster are a couple whose jobs take them to exciting places and whose pace of life never slows down. They place great priority on their marriage and value a connected interpersonal relationship, believing that "Together we can cope with whatever life deals us." Yet they became afraid that this hectic, work-oriented lifestyle could destroy their relationship unless they created a retreat for being together. Scorning a fashionable high-rise condominium, they bought a large, old farmhouse in a growing suburban area and dedicated themselves to redoing the home in precise historic fashion and to cultivating large flower and vegetable gardens. Except when Jean travels, they spend most of their personal time at a slower pace and in a past-orientation to consciously counteract the hectic, present-oriented pace of their daily lives. They have created a complementary style of living with time for their personal needs.

A small baby has thrown the McConnell family into a temporary nonfit situation. As a two-career, sociable couple with good positions, they had planned a lifestyle in which each person would take equal responsibility for the baby, whom they expected to take to many social functions. Five months into parenthood, they became totally frustrated trying to share responsibilities, because Tim's job requires that he stay late for meetings, and Myra's real estate position requires her to drop everything and run when a potential buyer wants to talk. Although Melissa is a healthy baby, she gets fussy and seldom sleeps through the night. She cannot be taken easily into adult situations. Thus, each parent needs more ability to live in the present and according to the baby's schedule. Each also needs time to do more around the house.

Although the examples of spatial fit and temporal fit have been developed separately, you can see the need for an integration of the spatial and temporal needs of a family. Some people can integrate these with their levels of cohesion and adaptability for a comfortable fit, whereas others have real difficulty. A past-oriented family may take great pleasure in remodeling a large, old home. Some people may enjoy investing this time and effort in order to live in a home that represents a previous era. Yet, if the family members would rather read historical fiction or travel to historical sites, the demands of furnishing and maintaining such a home cause problems. Another family who loves to participate in sports may choose an apartment that does not require much maintenance or care, thus freeing the family to engage in their activities.

At other times, people have to make significant changes in order to overcome their spatial and temporal situations. A big new house may lessen but not solve all a family's conflictual problems unless new negotiating behaviors also accompany the move to larger quarters. Slowing down the pace by eliminating activities may have a limited effect on relationships unless the new lifestyle includes positive interpersonal messages and activities for people to share within the more or less frantic world. Large families in small apartments have the capacity to develop strong nurturing relationships, just as a co-parenting situation does not mean that the quality of a mother-daughter relationship needs to be cut in half. Unlimited time together has the potential to enhance a relationship, but the quality of the interactions will finally determine the nature of the relationship. For example, in his study of geographically separated premarital partners, Stephen (1986) found such couples could overcome the separation and the restricted verbal/vocal means of communication via the telephone. Members of these couples worked to overcome the handicap—perhaps by focusing their talk on topics significant to the relationship or by deemphasizing the importance of talk. Thus, Lennard and Lennard explain this issue as one of choice and control: "To the extent that the interrelationships between a family and the environment are made explicit, the family's area of freedom and control is enlarged" (49–50).

Finally, a family's living experience is tied to culture. Csikszentmihalyi and Rochberg-Halton capture this point, stating: "Although we live in physical environments we create cultural environments within them. Persons continually personalize and humanize the given environment as a way of both adapting to it and creating order and significance. Thus, the importance that the home has . . . also depends on values" (122). Awareness of these factors can help you begin to alter or modify your spatial/temporal environment to enhance your relationships. Spatial and temporal factors can only create an atmosphere conducive to nurturing family communication. It is up to the people involved to follow through.

CONCLUSION

This chapter examined the family environment as a context for communication. Each family's use of space and time affects who interacts with whom, where, when, for how long, about what, and in what way. A consideration of family environment indicated that a relationship exists between family members' communication and the spatial/temporal world in which the family functions.

To understand the family context, you must examine the issue of time and the issue of space, including spatial distance, territory and privacy. A family's physical dwelling must be considered within the context of its exterior arrangements, including its community and the actual physical surroundings as well as its interior arrangements. The room arrangements, plus furnishings and decor, play a role in establishing a communication conflict. Finally the fit between the family and the dimensions of time and space was explored. This chapter is based on the assumption that a way of life and its context are interdependent; environmental patterns do not determine but they do influence family interaction.

IN REVIEW

1. Take a position and discuss: How significantly does the physical environment affect family interaction patterns?
2. Describe how the cultural dimensions of space and/or time have affected the communication patterns in a real or fictional family.
3. Using the floor plan of a home found in a magazine or newspaper ad, predict how this floor plan might affect the interaction patterns of a family who lived there.
4. Using a real or fictional family, describe the spatial and temporal fit between the family and its environment. If possible, cite implications for the family's communication patterns.
5. Take a position and discuss: To what extent should communities support the development of restrictive housing, that is, housing excluding children or housing designed for senior citizens only? What are the communication implications of such decisions?

CHAPTER 14

Improving Family Communication

How do members of healthy families live, grow, and relate to each other year after year? How do they cope with problems and change? To what extent can family members create new communication patterns, develop different ways of loving, fighting, or making decisions? Up to this point, you have encountered a primarily descriptive view of family interaction, indicating the role of communication in the development of family relationships. This chapter will focus on functional families and how people make choices to reach or keep satisfying family relationships.

Many people believe that life happens *to* them, giving them no sense of control or ability to improve on human relationships. Thus, these people become reactors, taking no responsibility for personal change or for change in relationships. Other persons serve as actors, believing they can make personal changes and can be part of constructive changes within relationships. They are able to recognize when things are not working well and identify ways of trying to create a change.

" 'That's the way I am. Take me or leave me' was the common comment of my first husband. He believed that if you had to work on a relationship there was something wrong with it. Needless to say, after a few years we dissolved the marriage. Now I am engaged to a man who wants to talk and think about how to keep a relationship growing over a lifetime. We have even had some premarital counseling to explore important issues before the marriage. Life is very different when both people are open to change."

As human systems, families have the potential to grow and change in chosen directions, although such growth may require great risk, effort, and pain. The systems perspective implies that whenever change is attempted by some members, it may be resisted by the other members who wish to keep their system in balance no matter how dysfunctional that balance is. It is difficult, although not impossible, for an individual to initiate change in the system. Change is more easily accomplished when most or all members are committed to an alternative way of relating.

There is no "one right way" for all families to behave; the members of each family have to discover what works well for their system. A family's unique membership, ethnic heritage, and developmental stage influence this process. Communication may be considered the cornerstone for changing family systems. It is hoped that families develop flexible communication patterns that support the growth of the system and its members. The communication behaviors learned within a family-of-origin will influence greatly a person's future relationships. These communication patterns tend to pass from generation to generation unless they are consciously changed. Family members have the potential to learn from these historical patterns and improve their interaction patterns.

This book has focused on healthy, or functional, families, rather than severely troubled, or dysfunctional, ones, recognizing that every functional family has periods of ease and periods of stress. Yet separating functional/dysfunctional or healthy/unhealthy in an either-or manner does not reflect reality. Families must be considered on a continuum ranging from severely dysfunctional to optimally functional.

Troubled	Functional	Optimal

◄──►

As you might imagine, few families remain at the optimal extreme indefinitely because of tension caused by developmental or unpredictable stress; yet many do function within the functional to optional range over long periods of time. The question is, How do they do it? This chapter will attempt to answer that question by exploring (1) factors that characterize functional to optimally functional families, with an emphasis on communication, and (2) approaches for creating and maintaining effective communication within families. These will include personal, educational, and therapeutic approaches.

"I have been fortunate enough to spend much of my life in two reasonably healthy family systems. I grew up as the oldest of seven in a farm family, and, although I did a great deal of caring for the little ones, we had a strong sense of family. I watched my parents struggle to make ends meet, but they struggled together. Unlike my friends, I did not marry until I was thirty-four, and I married a widower with grown children. We have chosen not to start another family of small children, but I have been accepted by his children and I love being a grandmother to their kids. Martin and I have a full life with each other, and we work at staying in touch with each other's needs."

As you have participated in and observed families over the years, you must have found some that appeared to work well. People in them seemed to "have it all together." Yet each of these functional families probably reflected differences as well as similarities in the ways members related to each other. Each family shares the systems characteristic of equifinality or many ways to achieve the same end. Therefore, highly functional families exhibit both similarities and differences in all areas of living, including communication.

VIEWS OF THE HIGH-FUNCTIONING FAMILY

In recent years, much attention has been given to family strengths and well-family functioning, both in professional circles and through the popular media. The following sections highlight representative views of academic or therapeutic experts and of popular investigations.

Expert Views

Just as there is no one right way to be a family, there is no one family expert who has all the answers. Each expert reflects his or her own professional and personal orientation to family life, as evidenced by the emphasis given to different areas of concern. In some of the earliest work on family functioning, Henry (1973) studied five dysfunctional families intensively and identified certain characteristics of family psychopathology. These include the following: (1) interactions are highly complex; (2) there is more cruelty and less compassion; (3) one person, usually a child, is viewed as an "enemy" and treated as a scapegoat; (4) members do not know how to restrain their reactions appropriately; (5) means of satisfaction are distorted, so boundaries may be blurred; (6) life is taken too seriously; and (7) misperceptions govern interactions as sick members are treated as if well, or young members treated as if old (Bochner and Eisenberg 1987).

In contrast, one may reverse Henry's findings and hypothesize that functional families may exhibit the following characteristics: (1) some or all of the interactions are patterned and meaningful; (2) there is more compassion and less cruelty; (3) persons are not scapegoated because problems are identified with the appropriate persons; (4) family members exhibit appropriate self-restraint; (5) boundaries are clear; (6) life includes joy and humor; (7) misperceptions are minimal.

Virginia Satir, a family therapist well known for her writings on healthy families, maintains that untroubled and nurturing families demonstrate the following patterns: "Self-worth is high; communication is direct, clear, specific, and honest; rules are flexible, human, appropriate, and subject to change; and the linking to society is open and hopeful" (1988, 4). In other words, she sees that untroubled families contain people who feel good about themselves, level with each other, function within a flexible system of rules, and whose boundaries are flexible enough to permit extensive contact with new people and ideas. In addition to understanding Satir's values, including leveling, or direct, open communication, it is important to recall the discussion of the curvilinear self-disclosure model (Figure 5-3, p. 93), which suggests that totally honest communication can be handled in the unique cases where mutual, high self-esteem, risk, commitment, and confirmation exist. Such communication may not be possible or desirable for every family.

In his description of functional versus dysfunctional families, another therapist, Stachowiak (1975), identified four factors of family effectiveness: (1) family productivity or efficiency, (2) leadership patterns, (3) expression of conflict, and (4) clarity of communication (70). By watching families solve problems, he found that adaptive families reached many more group decisions in the allotted time period than did maladaptive families. Members of adaptive families tended to carry on active discussions, whereas members of maladaptive families tended to carry on monologues. Negotiation was more difficult in the latter group. Painful conflict patterns characterized maladaptive families, whereas functional families tended to have the resources to resolve issues. Finally, Stachowiak found that maladaptive family members were likely to avoid direct communication (turning away or avoiding eye contact) and to give more "general speeches" (conversation not directed at any family member). Thus, the patterns described by Satir appear reinforced by this indication that functional families are more likely to be characterized by flexibility and clarity of communication.

"My grandmother has always sworn that my sister looked just like her daughter Lorraine, who died at sixteen. She has tried to replace her daughter with her first granddaughter in the hopes of reviving a communication pattern that once existed but now is gone. Yet my sister Lori has had to fight this distorted perception all her life, and her communication with Grandma is very confused."

One way of interpreting successful family functioning is to understand its position on the circumplex model, which assesses the family's cohesion and adaptability (see Figure 2-1, p. 20). Researchers have indicated that families at different stages of development seem to function better in different areas of the model (Olson and McCubbin 1983). For example, young couples without babies function best in either the upper right- or lower left-hand quadrants. Families and adolescents function best in the central, or balanced, areas; older couples relate best in the lower right-hand quadrant. Childless young couples are frequently found at the high end of the cohesion/adaptability scale or in the lower opposite side with lower cohesion and adaptability. It may seem contradictory, but young couples seem to be either highly cohesive and enmeshed or rather disengaged and low in cohesion and adaptability, with possible numerous ties to their old friends and families-of-origin at this point in their new marriages. Adolescents function best when they have average cohesion, being neither enmeshed with parents nor disengaged, and when their adaptability is midway between rigidity and chaos. Obviously, these results indicate adolescents' needs for a family system without threats or rigid rules. Older couples function best when cohesion is high but adaptability is low. Older family members need the closeness of family ties and therefore give up their adaptability, accepting and adopting greater predictability in their life patterns. Although results may differ for families from particular backgrounds or ethnic origins, these findings demonstrate the variability in well-family functioning.

In his early research on family competence, Beavers (1976) views families on a continuum of functioning, ranging from severely disturbed, to midrange, to healthy. He details each of these continuum locations in terms of five major areas: power structure, degree of individuation, acceptance of separation and loss, perception of reality, and affect. His data suggest that families with adaptive, well-functioning offspring have a structure of shared power, great appreciation and encouragement of individuation, and ability to accept separation and loss realistically. Additionally, they have a "family mythology consistent with the reality as seen by outside observers, a strong sense of the passage of time and the inevitability of change, and a warm and expressive feeling tone" (80). Beavers describes healthy families as "skillful interpersonally," whose members who can (1) participate in and enjoy negotiation, (2) respect the views of others, (3) share openly about themselves, (4) see anger as symptomatic of necessary changes, (5) view sexual interest as positive, and (6) establish meaningful encounters outside the family system. He found that the most effective families use humor, tenderness, warmth, and hopefulness to relate. Family members make negative feelings known but do so with a keen awareness of whom or what they dislike. Also, they are supportive while doing so. Effective families more readily recognize their conflicts, deal with them promptly, and find solutions quickly.

In his later work, Beavers (1982) holds that well-functioning families consciously operate from a systems orientation characterized by a flexible position on human behavior. In short, family members intuitively adopt a systems perspective. This does not mean that the family members know technical systems terminology and apply it to their everyday lives. It means that the family members maintain a flexible position on human behavior.

Beavers describes the four basic assumptions of families that take a systems orientation as follows:

1. An individual needs a group, a human system, for identity and satisfaction.
2. Causes and effects are interchangeable.
3. Any human behavior is the result of many variables rather than one "cause"; therefore, simplistic solutions are questioned.
4. Human beings are limited and finite. No one is absolutely helpless or absolutely powerful in a relationship. (45)

When a family holds the first assumption, its members presume that people do not exist in vacuums but that human needs are met through relationships. Even after children from these families are grown, they seek a sense of human community in new family systems or social networks. Holding the second assumption reflects an understanding of mutual influence. Family members see actions as responses and stimuli to other actions. For example, anger in one person promotes withdrawal in another, and that withdrawal promotes anger.

Persons holding the third assumption recognize that human behavior reflects many influences. Beavers describes this clearly by listing some possible explanations for a three-year-old's spilled milk. Possible explanations include (1) accident—no motive, (2) interpersonal meaning—child is upset with mother, (3) child is tired, (4) glass is too heavy or large for child's hand (145). Whereas a dysfunctional family may always attribute spilled milk to one explanation, an optimally functioning family's responses vary according to each situation. Holding the final assumption implies an awareness that humans are fallible and that self-esteem comes from relative competence. Therefore, total control over one's own life or the lives of others is impossible. Striving for goals in a realistic way is desirable.

> "My stepfather represents the kind of parent I would like to become. He seems to operate from a basic belief of optimism and faith in people. He usually can see both sides of an issue, can see both parties' points of view, and tries to create solutions without dumping blame on one person. He says, 'You do your best and go on.'"

In their recent summary of work on family process, Bochner and Eisenberg summarize the following features as characteristic of optimal family functioning: (1) Strong sense of trust. Members rarely take oppositional attitudes and avoid blaming each other. (2) Enjoyment. Optimal families are spontaneous, witty, and humorous. (3) Lack of preoccupation with themselves. Family members do not overanalyze their problems looking for hidden motives; life is not taken too seriously. (4) Maintenance of conventional boundaries reflecting a strong parental coalition and clear sense of hierarchy (559).

Many other experts address high-functioning families but reflect similar positions (Barnhill 1979; Gantman 1980; Ammons and Stinnett 1980). Almost all experts, such as those cited above, speak to the centrality of effective communication in well-functioning family systems. Fitzpatrick (1987) suggests that the strong correlations between marital satisfaction and self-reports of communication behavior may constitute evidence for strongly held beliefs about the role of communication in marriage; that is, the happily married believe that they have remarkably good communication with their spouses. The same beliefs may be held by those in well-functioning family systems.

Popular Advice

Just enter any bookstore or video store in any shopping mall and you will be surrounded by books, magazines, audio- and videotapes, all addressing the issues of "How to Have a Healthy Marriage" or "How to Create a Happy Family." Most of the popular advice literature, based on expert opinion and research, supports the positions of academic experts but couches the ideas in readable and prescriptive language. Some popular material directly reflects particular religious or moral positions, or reflects the life-changing experience of the author.

In a survey of professionals in family-related areas, Curran (1983) found "the ability to communicate and listen" selected most frequently as an indicator of family health. She lists these hallmarks of a family who communicates well:

1. Parents demonstrate a close relationship.
2. Parents have control over TV.
3. All family members can listen and respond.
4. Family members recognize and value nonverbal messages.
5. Family members respect individual feelings and independent thinking.

6. Family members avoid turnoff and put-down phrases.
7. Family members interrupt, but equally.
8. Family members process disputes into reconciliations. (55)

After studying more than three thousand families, Stinnett and DeFrain (1985) listed six crucial traits of strong families:

1. Family members are committed to each other. Family unity is valued.
2. Family members spend a good deal of time—quality time—together.
3. Family members show appreciation for each other.
4. Family members have good communication skills and spend a lot of time talking to each other.
5. Family members view crises and stresses as opportunities for growth.
6. Family members reflect spiritual wellness, a sense of a greater power that gives them strength or purpose.

In her book *Families*, journalist Howard (1978) presents another conception of well-functioning families. The author has traveled across the country, interviewing the members of various types of family systems (two-parent biological, blended, single-parent, and extended, including social, racial, and sexual variations) in an attempt to understand what makes them work well. In her conclusion, she lists the general characteristics of what she calls "good" families (241–245):

1. Good families have a chief, heroine, or founder—someone around whom others cluster. Such a person may appear in different generations, but somehow this figure sets an achievement level that inspires others.

"I grew up in an extended family with my grandparents and great-grandparents. Although there was no one living in the base household while I was growing up, many of the family members had lived with the dominant figures at one time or another. My great-grandmother was very special. Everyone in the family loved and respected her, and we would sit for hours listening to how she and our great-grandfather started their lives together with nothing in a strange city. She has always been someone I looked up to."

---

2. Good families have a switchboard operator—someone who keeps track of what the others are up to. This person also may be the archivist who keeps scrapbooks or albums that document the family's continuity.

3. Good families are much to all of their members but everything to none. Links to the outside are strong, and boundaries are not so tight that people cannot become passionately involved in nonfamily activities.

4. Good families are hospitable. There are surrounding rings of relatives and friends who are cared about and supported, just as they serve as the family's support system and as extended family members in many cases.

5. Good families deal directly with problems. Problems and pains are not avoided in hopes they will disappear. Communication is open. Countless rules do not exist to restrict touchy or painful topics of conversation; people level with each other directly.

6. Good families prize their rituals. These may be the formal traditions of Passover, Christmas, birthdays, funerals, or the informal ones unique to the individual family or clan, such as the annual Fourth of July picnic or St. Patrick's Day party that becomes a unifying ritual to the people involved.

7. Good families are affectionate and willing to demonstrate and share that affection with other family members. Children learn this pattern of affection from their first moments.

8. Good families have a sense of place—a sense of belonging that may be tied to a specific geographic location or to the mementos that make a house a home for specific individuals, such as the old dining room table, the Precious Moments figurines, or the photographs that declare "This is home." You may find comfort in being a Bostonian or Iowan, or you may carry with you important pieces of your life that symbolize roots and family connectedness.

9. Good families find a way to connect to posterity. For many, this involves having children; for others, it means becoming involved in a sense of the generation—connecting to the children in some way.

10. Good families honor their elders. The wider the age range, the stronger the clan. This may involve biological or "adopted" grandparents and vice versa, but strong families have a sense of generations. (241–245)

"I have come to realize the importance of traditions and rituals in families. When my father married my stepmother, she spent a great deal of time and energy creating ways to celebrate holidays. We had celebrations for Valentine's Day, Halloween, as well as the usual big ones. At first it seemed rather silly, but over the years I have come to look forward to seeing the decorations and participating in the preparations because these events seem to bind us together. They are part of our identity as a family and give me a sense of place and belonging."

In a more specifically directed work, *Second Marriage*, Stuart and Jacobson (1985) discuss issues common to remarriage and suggest beliefs and attitudes that characterize a workable second marriage:

1. Realistic expectations that every marriage has good and bad times.
2. The willingness to examine your role in every positive and negative exchange in the relationship.
3. The willingness to consider everything negotiable, with no demands that your partner accept your way of doing things without fair consideration of alternatives.
4. The willingness to learn to understand your partner's point of view.
5. A commitment to try different ways of doing things long enough to see if the new way works.
6. The maturity to forgive your partner for mistakes made in good faith efforts to make your marriage better.

As the members of stepfamilies increase exponentially, popular advice to such families does the same (Berman 1986; Einstein 1982; Visher and Visher 1988;

Bernstein 1989; Einstein and Albert 1986). Each of these contain suggestions that might apply to any family form plus special issues unique to stepfamilies, such as these ideas for a stepparent:

1. Encourage the child's relationship with the biological parent. Do not undermine it.
2. Accept grief and loss as part of the reality, and encourage the expression of these feelings.
3. Plan time alone with stepchildren. Invite them to do things with you.
4. Allow children to talk about their time with the other parent.
5. Develop ways of neutralizing the transitions of visitation. (Einstein and Albert).

You can find thousands of pages of prose detailing how happy or functional families live, or how they should live. As you read these descriptive and prescriptive views on well-family functioning, what is your personal reaction? Are these views too idealistic or too culture specific? What characteristics would you defend as critical to well-family functioning?

Author Views

Your authors hold strong beliefs about the healthy family that are based on our concern for communication within such a system. These beliefs reflect many of the issues introduced in earlier chapters.

A healthy family recognizes the interdependence of all members of the system and attempts to provide for growth of the system as a whole, as well as of the individual members involved. Such families develop a capacity for adaptation and cohesion that avoids the extremes of the continuum but changes over time, reflecting the course of external and developmental life events.

We have been influenced by the experience of counseling families. We repeatedly see families who lack the necessary communication skills to negotiate their difficulties. Recurring themes, boundaries, and rules from couples' families-of-origin interfere with their present relationships. Often, our task involves helping family members sort out both the values and weaknesses of past experiences and learn how they can use these in combination with the resources in their own family.

Family systems need constant and consistent nurturing. In most families, day-to-day routines overwhelm members' lives, resulting in primarily functional rather then nurturing communication patterns. Families can profit from taking time to ask "How are we doing as a family?" and "How could we improve our communication?" "How can we reach our goals while remaining committed to each other?" Healthy families are able to engage in metacommunication; they are able to talk about how members relate to each other and how, if necessary, the current communication patterns could be strengthened.

Strong families have learned the values of communication, commitment, caring, and change. The following section will describe some specific strategies couples and families have used to strengthen their relationships.

Family members often participate in a structured program to talk about their difficulties.

APPROACHES FOR IMPROVING FAMILY COMMUNICATION

If you believed that communication in your family could be improved, what would you do about it? Would you be willing to talk about the difficulties with other family members or to participate in a structured improvement program? As you saw in the last two chapters, a family goes through predictable developmental stresses and unpredictable external stresses, which affect the system's well-being; but often, members do not know how to help themselves deal with the difficulties.

Approaches to family change may be viewed on a continuum ranging from personal through instructional to therapeutic approaches.

| Personal | Instructional | Therapeutic |

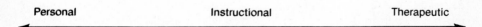

Most of the personal and instructional approaches are designed for functional couples or families who wish to change some aspect of their relationship or wish to find ways to deal with a particular stressful situation. Some instructional and most therapeutic approaches are designed to aid a couple or family cope with a particular problem or repair a troubled relationship.

Personal Approaches

Personal approaches include (1) seeking personal education, such as that found through books or the media, (2) engaging in personal negotiation with partners or family members, (3) creating ongoing programs or meetings for the family members, and (4) relying on friends or members of a support network.

Do you believe that a couple or family can deal with their communication problems on their own? Many individuals have consciously set out to change their communication with other family members. Many couples or whole family systems have tried to change old, dysfunctional communication patterns. Many of these endeavors reflect a personal approach in which system members embark on the process without significant active outside support.

Personal Education. Concern for family issues appears widespread in all areas of society, resulting in the growth of preventive approaches designed to aid family members before things really fall apart. A walk through a local bookstore or video store reveals many books and magazine articles and ideas on improving your marital or family life. There are checklists, rules, and prescriptions for family meetings, intimate vacations, and constructive conflict. Most of these prescriptions contain some directives about improving communication among family members.

The use of books or media sources to gain personal growth has increased significantly. The field of family-related self-help resources continues to expand with materials developed for every type of family form. Often readers or viewers find relief in discovering that their "problems" are "normal" for a family or couple in a particular situation. For example, bibliotherapy has become a common tool to educate new stepfamily members and normalize their intense emotional experiences (Cooper 1989).

Personal Negotiation. Often, couples and family members create ways to enhance their communication that are based on information, instruction, or therapy. In some homes, husbands and wives attempt to identify recurring, potentially upsetting "trouble spots" in their relationship and to plan how to avoid them. They may learn to recognize times when intimacy or conflict is too threatening; this knowledge helps move them into a negotiation mode.

Other couples practice their own rules for fair fighting, perhaps constructed through an agreement never to devastate the other in an argument. They may agree to avoid gunnysacking and physical abuse. They may struggle to restate the other's position or to find areas of compromise. Parents may force themselves to develop new vocabulary when dealing with children that is reflected in the use of "I" statements rather than blaming "you" messages, or to share their feelings when objective analysis would be more comfortable but less effective. Children may agree to limit name-calling.

"In my own marriage, my wife and I have been using two mechanisms to serve as a kind of checkup on our marital relations. First, we have learned to commu-

nicate both the negative and the positive feelings we have. Periodically, we sit down together with no outside distractions and, while maintaining eye contact, express our innermost feelings or our current concerns. We each try very hard to listen to rather than judge the other. This ritual is a special part of our relationship."

In-laws may restrain themselves from asking questions that could be considered meddling, whereas children may refrain from "answering back," even though the temptation is very great. Family members may create quality time together to eat, sing, ride bikes, or just talk. A couple may attempt a second honeymoon. Father and son may find a mutual hobby or discussion area of joint interest.

The "checkup" stands as an important concept in a personal approach to improving marital or family communication. In their classic work, *Mirages of Marriage*, Lederer and Jackson (1968) called for marital checkups, saying, "It seems to us that marriages deserve the same care and attention given our bodies, or our automobiles" (358–359). Couples or families may call for a conversation on the question "How are we doing?"—the equivalent of the preventive medical annual physical.

You may wonder, "How do these conversations actually start?" In some systems, one or more members have nagging feelings that things could be different. They may compare themselves to other families and see something lacking. They may encounter new ideas or models for relationships through the media, friends, or religious and educational figures. Then they take the risk of trying out new behaviors and evaluating their effectiveness. Such approaches take mutual cooperation. If only one member attempts to make the efforts, changes will occur more slowly and may be met with strong resistance.

Ongoing Meetings. In addition to personal negotiation, long-range approaches exist for couples or whole families, the most common of which is "couple time" or the "family council." Growing up, you may have participated in some variation of this approach. Couple time or a family council occurs when persons come together regularly to solve problems that affect one or more members.

"Sunday morning breakfasts are our sacred family time to check in and see how everyone is doing. Sometimes we eat in, and other times we head for a local coffee shop, but all times we talk about family concerns. We may check practical things, like members' schedules, or we may air gripes, fears, or joys. Without these breakfasts, our family conflicts might have been much greater."

Many couples find that their fast-paced life provides few obvious interludes for personal exploration and discussion unless that time is built into their weekly schedules. Therefore, couples at all stages of family development and representing varied types of family forms are carving out predictable times to be together and to "really talk." Some couples find that their topics emerge easily and directly; others prefer to use a guidebook that prescribes topics or provides questions or evaluation material. For example, in their work *Time for a Better Marriage*, Dinkmeyer and

Carlson (1984a) prescribe couple time commitments including daily dialogue, encouragement meetings, and marriage meetings.

Family meetings or family councils provide opportunities for all family members to address mutual concerns. Rudolf Dreikurs (1964), a founder of the family council movement, recommends that councils be established formally as an ongoing part of family life. A definite hour on a definite day of the week should be set aside for this purpose; it should become part of family routine. Every member is expected to be present. According to Dreikurs, should one member not wish to come, that person must still abide by the decision of the group. Therefore, it pays for him or her to be present to voice an opinion. The principles of family councils include the following:

> Each member has the right to bring up a problem. Each one has the right to be heard. Together, all seek for a solution to the problem, and the majority opinion is upheld. In the Family Council, the parents' voices are no higher or stronger than that of each child. The decision made at a given meeting holds for a week. (301)

Such experiences provide children with practice in discussion and decision making, which may prove extremely valuable in later family life. Obviously, many families attempt to join together for more than solving problems.

The Mormons' Family Home Evening is probably the most well-known family meeting program. Established in the late 1950s, the program requests Mormons to set aside an evening each week for family group meetings or activities centered around the annual guidebook *Family Home Evening,* which contains weekly lessons.

Although its emphasis is on religious instruction, *Family Home Evening* materials often contain ideas appropriate for improving interpersonal communication. Discussion of such topics as "learning to love each other" and "organizing yourself" requires self-disclosure, risk taking, and sharing. Listening skills are frequently taught. Many of the ideas suggested for sharing require the family to use positive modes of communication. Other churches and community groups operate similar programs.

Support Networks. In an era when the extended family is increasingly inaccessible, individuals, couples, and families are creating informal or formal support systems to help them face family problems.

> *"For eight months I have participated in a divorce recovery group through our church, and it has helped me with parenting my three sons and with coping with my ex-husband's remarriage. This group has saved my sanity more than once, and I have reached some important insights about loss and change."*

Informal support networks, such as friends and neighbors, provide adequate support for some persons. Having an objective ear, a good friend may put things into perspective or just serve as a point of emotional release. In other cases, a more structured support system has advantages. This may take the form of an ongoing couples group in which problems are discussed and solutions shared within a context of privacy and confirmation.

Occasionally, whole families form a support network. One such approach is known as the Family Cluster, best described as a "group of four or five complete family units which contract to meet together periodically over an extended period of time for shared educational experiences related to being in relationship with their families" (Sawin 1979, 27). Through Family Cluster, families gain mutual support and help in developing skills that enhance family relationships. The designer suggests, "When starting a new family cluster, it is usually helpful to begin with a unit of communication. . . . Communication is a vital force for group building, as well as a crucial element in the family system" (47).

> *"As a single person, I have found it very rewarding to belong to a Family Cluster because it provides me with a support system of caring people, and it allows me to be of service to some of them in return. I truly enjoy interacting with the children in our Cluster, and I'm known as the 'game lady' because I usually spend part of my time playing games with the children. I enjoy interacting with young people, and their parents are pleased."*

Some structured programs for family support stress the importance of parents' educating their children to seek peace and justice both in the political and personal arenas. They suggest that parents develop a consistent set of humanistic values and then struggle to live by them and teach them to their children. They present goals and values for families to achieve and ways for parents to communicate these to their children and communities (McGinnis and McGinnis 1981; True 1982). Such programs emphasize conflict management, listening, problem solving, and building self-esteem. Other approaches, such as "Toughlove," attempt to help families cope with current crises, often through shared storytelling and interpersonal support (Hollihan and Riley 1987).

The previously discussed approaches are only a few of the many ways of involving individuals, families, and groups of families in enriching their relationships. Would you be willing to make the effort required to participate fully in a structured Family Council meeting or a support network? In addition to personal approaches, couples or individuals may attempt to improve family communication through direct instruction.

Instructional Approaches

> *"My husband and I are team leaders for the Jewish Marriage Encounter, and we keep trying to tell our friends that every marriage should have an 'annual checkup.' People spend thousands of dollars on 'preventive maintenance' for their cars, teeth, bodies, and homes, but how much do we spend either in dollars, effort, or time to have a marital examination? Too often in attempting to get couples to attend an Encounter weekend, I am told, 'Our marriage is OK' or 'We don't*

need to go on any weekend, as we have no problems.' I am both angry and sad at such blindness, stupidity, and fear. There is not a marriage existing that does not have some problems, and if they are not attended to, they will get bigger.''

If a member of your family suggested that you all go on a communication enrichment weekend, how would you react? Would you be willing to attend some classes on improving parent-child communication? The past three decades have witnessed a tremendous growth in marital and family enrichment programs designed to instruct individuals, couples, and whole family systems. Generally, their purposes are educational, not therapeutic; they are oriented toward enrichment, not counseling.

Most persons who attend enrichment programs are self-referred and self-screened. Potential participants receive the message "If your marriage or family life is in serious trouble, our program is not for you. We are designed to help good relationships become better." If identified before the program, couples contemplating divorce or families experiencing chaos are referred to therapeutic means of dealing with their problems or to enrichment programs that use trained counselor-facilitators (Hof and Miller 1983).

Marital Enrichment Programs. At least twenty-five national organizations offer marriage enrichment programs (Mace 1987). These programs are designed to enhance couple growth. Family growth may result in an extension of change in the marital pair. Most programs insist that the couple attend together in order to affect the system.

Communication skills appear as the core of most of these marital enrichment programs. According to Wackman (1978), the communication emphasis may be attributed to three factors. First, research on marriage has shown a consistent, though modest, relationship between "good" communication by members of a married couple and marital satisfaction and happiness; research with "healthy" families indicates the same moderately positive correlation between "good" communication and satisfaction of family members. Second, theoretical developments in thinking about the family system have focused on the crucial role of communication in both marriage and the family. Third, communication training seems to be an easy, safe, and nonthreatening way to bring about enrichment, because communication skills and principles can be taught fairly readily.

Although there are numerous systems-oriented marital and family enrichment programs that stress communication, only a few representative ones will be noted. The most well known and frequently attended marital enrichment programs include the religion-based Marriage Enrichment, Marriage Encounter, and Marriage Communication Lab programs, and the privately developed Couples Communication program, Training in Marriage Enrichment program (T.I.M.E.), and Relationship Enhancement (Otto 1975; Hof and Miller; Guerney 1977; Garland 1983; Dinkmeyer and Carlson 1984a,b). Each places a heavy emphasis on communication. As you read the following brief descriptions, remember that there may be some variations depending on sponsoring groups and specific leaders.

One of the Marriage Enrichment programs sponsored by the Methodist church is a small-group experience conducted by a leader or leader-couple who works with four other couples through a structured weekend. After having been prepared by leader modeling, reflecting, and role playing, each couple engages in a series of interactions within the small-group framework. Couples prepare for this through guided rehearsal sessions with nonspouses. Group members also give feedback to each couple. Some of the weekend experiences include sharing the qualities one admires in his or her spouse and discussing wished-for behaviors from the spouse. Thus, intimacy receives great focus. The actual sharing and discussion behavior is constantly monitored and corrected by the team leader, who is trying to teach communication skills. The small group functions as a powerful support system for trying new behaviors.

Marriage Encounter is a weekend program conducted by three couples and a religious leader. The format follows a simple pattern. Each husband and wife "give" each other the Encounter, with the team members merely providing the information and modeling to facilitate each couple's private dialogue. Through a series of nine talks, team members reveal personal and intimate information to encourage participants to do the same when alone. After the talks, each husband and wife separate and write individual responses to the issues raised in each talk. Specific questions to be considered may be provided, or the individual may write his or her feeling about the topic. The couple then comes together for private dialogue, using each other's written responses as a starting point. The Marriage Encounter process involves exposition, reflection, encounter, and mutual understanding. Dialogue topics include understanding of the self; relationship with the partner; and the couple's relationship with God, their children, and the world. Although the program began within the Catholic church, the past years have witnessed the growth of Jewish and Protestant Marriage Encounters.

The Couples Communication program involves a small group experience with five to seven couples meeting with an instructor one night a week for four consecutive weeks. The "couples" may be spouses, friends, or work teams. This program serves as an educational experience in which couples identify, practice, and experiment with communication skills around topics of their choice. Each couple receives feedback on their skills from the leader and other couples. No attempt is made to deal with the content of an interaction; the focus remains solely on skills accomplishment. Practice sessions are held with nonpartners, but the final demonstration of skills occurs with one's partner. The approach in Couples Communication is to have the couple do exercises so they can experience new ideas and approaches to relating to one another, not just learn about them (Garland, 21).

Finally, the PREPARE/ENRICH materials and programs should be noted because they serve as a bridge between instructional and therapeutic approaches. Developed by Olson and colleagues, the PREPARE/ENRICH program is grounded in the circumplex model of family functioning and consists of three inventories and guidelines for counselor/leader training. PREPARE and PREPARE-MC (Married with Children) are designed for couples entering marriage either as two adults or adults with children. ENRICH is designed for use in marriage enrichment programs or marriage counseling. After couples complete the inventories and receive their computerized results, they may discuss the findings with a religious leader as part of a premarital program, within a marriage enrichment program, or with a therapist. Recent research supports the predictive validity of these instruments, which are being used widely by professionals in religious and academic circles (Larsen and Olson, 1989).

Sometimes, variations of weekend programs are offered over eight to fifteen weeks in two- to four-hour sessions. The advantages include spaced learning and the opportunity to do homework and practice new skills, but such disadvantages as fights, irregular attendance, and the routines of daily life weaken the communication focus (Hof and Miller).

As you read the descriptions of these major marital enrichment programs, it becomes clear that communication assumes a central place within each. Desirable interpersonal behavior may be taught differently through modeling, role playing, lecture, guided feedback, and readings, but it is incorporated into each program. The unique feature of such programs is the learning context; you learn and practice communications skills with people with whom you have a relationship. In her summary of the communication instruction contained within these three marital enrichment programs, Galvin (1978) concludes:

> All programs give attention to the five skills of empathic communication, recognizing and owning feelings, descriptiveness, self-disclosure, and behavioral flexibility, with descriptiveness receiving the least attention except in Marriage Enrichment. The skills of self-disclosure and recognizing and owning feelings command extensive attention as each program devotes a large proportion of its time to the area of feelings. Marriage Enrichment provides the most predictable structure and uses the most direct approach to teach these skills. Marriage Encounter relies heavily on modeling and direction to teach communication skills. (26–27)

In a similar summary of communication training within overall marital enrichment programs, Cleaver (1987) reports that the following three aspects receive major focus: (1) listening skills, (2) speaking skills, and (3) negotiating or problem-solving skills. Almost every national program has a communication component. Many churches and private organizations run unique marital communication programs for their own congregations or specific constituents such as remarried couples, engaged couples, or senior couples.

Appraisal of Marital Enrichment Programs. Although these programs may sound very exciting, we need to note some cautions in considering their effectiveness. There may be difficulties in attempting to teach communication principles and skills without a shared desire on the part of both partners. If such mutual commitment does not exist, the results may be contrary to the expected outcomes. Additionally, the skills must be combined with a desire or spirit of goodwill to motivate partners to use them appropriately (Miller, Corrales, and Wackman 1975; Davis et al. 1982; Stevens 1984).

The research on these programs does not attribute undisputed success to their efforts. Gurman and Kniskern (1977) summarized twenty-nine studies that purported to examine the impact of marriage enrichment programs. Although positive results were found in a majority of the measures, most studies used self-report measures in which the questionnaires or interviews were administered immediately after the program. Thus, few changes in behavior or long-range effects could be documented. Although the programs are designed to help couples with satisfactory marriages, Powell and Wampler (1982) found that this was not always the case. Many couples entered such workshops because they felt a need for help. Powell and Wampler suggested more stringent controls and measures to determine each partner's commitment to the enrichment experience and also examinations of the makeup of the control groups. Witteman and Fitzpatrick (1986) examined marital enrichment programs and compared them unfavorably to therapy, particularly because of the lack of skills orientation.

In their admittedly critical appraisal of the Marriage Encounter program, Doherty, McCabe, and Ryder (1978) suggest that the program can create illusions through emotional "highs," deny the importance of differences between people, lead to a kind of ritual dependency and guilt if the couple does not engage in the follow-up, and other possible difficulties. A content analysis of interview and essay data from couples who attended Marriage Encounter revealed that those who were highly positive or highly negative about the experience were likely to report experiencing serious marital distress prior to the weekend (Doherty, Lester, and Leigh 1986). The authors suggest that distressed couples who attend are likely to suffer greater marital deterioration. This observation leads the authors to recommend more careful screening of the potential participants, changes in the program structure to encourage more leader-participant interactions, and specific crisis training for leaders.

Couples Communication is the most extensively documented instructional program ever developed. Since 1971, thirty-one studies have been published in professional journals or as doctoral dissertations. More are in progress. Most of the research has been conducted at major universities throughout the United States in cooperation with CC instructors in a variety of community contexts. The findings indicate (1) an extremely positive impact on behavior immediately after the program with most studies finding partial decline at follow-up; (2) increases in relationship satisfaction, with some decline at follow-up; (3) no documented negative effects (Thirty-one . . . 1989).

Even the structure of the program may affect the outcome. In a study comparing psychological changes in couples who attended a weekend program with couples who were involved in a five-week program, the latter group gained more improvement in their marital adjustment scores. In both groups, wives changed in more positive ways than did their husbands (Davis et al. 89).

A key consideration in evaluating enrichment programs lies in the extent of skill training provided. Witteman and Fitzpatrick maintain that behavior changes in marital communication are tied to some type of skills training and not the discussion of communication, an approach frequently found in church-related enrichment programs. Information without skills does not provide enough bases for change.

Most research on marital enrichment examines outcome criteria of marital satisfaction, relationship skill development, and individual personality variables. In their summary of such, Dinkmeyer and Carlson (1986) report that positive change is usually demonstrated on approximately 60 percent of the criterion tests in these general categories following completion of the enrichment experience. Yet this research is based primarily on self-report measures. Giblin, Sprenkle, and Sheehan (1985) report generally positive gains for couples involved in marital enrichment, especially for those in Relationship Enhancement programs for couples, followed by those in the Couples Communication program and Marriage Encounter.

Isolated studies of other programs exist. In her follow-up study of Marriage Enrichment couples, Ellis (1982) reported that participants talk more freely about their feelings to spouses and to other persons than they had before their involvement. Former participants are able to express negative feelings more constructively. Yet some participants reported that, although they were emotionally expressive during the weekend, they could not sustain this later. Additional critiques of programs note positive and negative effects (L'Abate 1981; Wampler and Sprenkle 1980; Witteman and Fitzpatrick).

"As a minister I used to suggest to all couples I worked with that they become involved in a marriage enrichment program. It seemed like a cure-all for my congregational members because of the emphasis on communication skills. Yet, over time, I've learned more about the program and am more discriminating in my recommendations, because I no longer see it as a panacea but as a valuable resource for many couples. I no longer refer severely troubled couples to this resource, because the time is too limited and they do not have a high enough trust level to practice the communication skills effectively."

Research on the long-term effectiveness of marital enrichment programs is too limited to draw secure conclusions. More information is needed in order to answer Wackman's important questions about the impact of such programs:

1. Do the programs result in changes in communication that last for a reasonable period of time? And if so, do the changes in communication skills result in positive changes in the relationships so the marriages are truly enriched?
2. Do the marriage programs result in changes that generalize to other relationships, particularly with children, thereby enriching family life?
3. What are the major factors in these programs that create the impacts that occur: the specific skills taught? the format (group vs. individual couple)? the degree of structure? (6–7)

In recent years, new approaches to marital enrichment have been developed to reflect recent research and to include a research component, thus ensuring a more systematic approach to evaluation (Worthington, Buston, and Hammonds 1989; Cleaver; L'Abate 1984).

Family Enrichment Programs. Although programs for families have developed more slowly, many marital programs have fostered familial counterparts, encouraging entire families to examine and improve their relationships. The Marriage Encounter program now offers the Family Weekend Experience. As in Marriage Encounter, the family members "give" each other the weekend. Parents and their children of school age spend their waking weekend hours in a local facility engaging in activities, listening to short talks, seeing films, and holding family discussions. Families are encouraged to examine their everyday lives and to discuss nine "blocks" to a family relationship—such as fighting, criticism, or indifference—and the means to overcoming such blocks, including listening, acceptance, and respect. Family members experience personal reconciliation with each other and plan ways to maintain the feelings of closeness they have achieved.

One of the most widely accepted family-oriented programs has been PET, Parent Effectiveness Training (Gordon 1975), through which parents spend eight evenings attempting to learn more effective parenting skills, relying heavily on communication strategies. This program encourages parents to examine their own self-concepts, to reevaluate their verbal and nonverbal messages, and to find new approaches to deal with old problems, primarily through the communication skill "active listening."

Relationship Enhancement (RE) (Guerney) includes a skills approach that may be taught to all family members. In describing her experience with this model, Kirk (1989) declares that RE is based on a family systems perspective, focusing on the improvement of interpersonal communication and problem-solving skills. The skills are implemented through a set of specific techniques such as the expresser mode, empathic responder mode, problem/conflict resolution mode, and the generalization/maintenance mode. Kirk describes the results of her teaching as follows:

> The family learned the skills and were able to both share their feelings and also resolve their conflicts. The parents had originally felt uncomfortable when they disciplined their stepchildren, and the children felt resentful when they adhered to their stepparents. Their communication climate eventually became one of silence and hostility until they were able to communicate in a skilled manner. (20–21)

The Understanding Us program relies on the circumplex model of family systems as its conceptual base (Carnes 1981). Referring to the model as a "family map," the program attempts to help family members understand themselves from a systems perspective during a four-session course. After examining themselves in light of the topics (1) adapting, (2) caring, (3) growing, and (4) changing, family members are expected to achieve a deeper understanding of their system and options for change. In recent years, specialized programs for stepfamilies have emerged aimed at normalizing the stepfamily experience and developing communication skills of stepfamily members (Einstein and Albert 1986).

Many self-help groups are oriented toward specific topics that also provide formal or informal instruction in family communication for their members. Such groups include Alcoholics Anonymous, Al-Anon, Parents Anonymous, Families

Anonymous, Parents Without Partners, Parents of Gays, Families Who Have Adopted Children of Every Skin, Compassionate Friends, and Candlelighters.

Therapeutic Approaches

The next section introduces the therapeutic approaches to improving family communication. Because this text is concerned with communication issues of functional families, therapeutic approaches are presented only in order to extend the continuum of options for improving relationships. There is a vast body of literature that explores these approaches in detail, so this section highlights only some relevant issues.

For those families who live with dysfunctional communication or experience temporary crises, therapeutic interventions may be warranted. In contrast to previous eras when the "identified patient" or "problem person" was shipped off to be "fixed" by a counselor, many family-related problems are addressed through family therapy or systems therapy. Individual therapy has long been an established approach to dealing with personal problems or illnesses. This counselor-client situation remains one valid therapeutic approach for certain issues.

"Two years ago, my family went into therapy because my younger brother was flunking school and shoplifting, and his treatment center required the entire family to become involved in the treatment program. Over about a year we were able to understand the patterns of family interaction that "fed" Chris's problem. The therapist kept stressing that Chris's acting out was a family problem, not just Chris's problem. The therapy forced my mother and stepfather to deal with some problems in their marriage that they had been ignoring and allowed us to make enough changes so that Chris could return to high school and control the shoplifting."

The family therapy movement's roots are found in the research and clinical developments of the 1950s, including hospital psychiatry, group dynamics, interpersonal psychiatry, the child guidance movement, research in communication and schizophrenia, and marriage counseling. Persons such as John Bell, Don Jackson, Nathan Ackerman, Murray Bowen, Jay Haley, Virginia Satir, Carl Whitaker, Lyman Wynne, Ivan Boszormenyinagy, James Framo, Gerald Zuk, Christian Midelfort, and Salvador Minuchin were significant pioneers of family treatment.

Communication issues emerged as a key feature of the family therapy movement, because many of these pioneers, most notably Satir, focused explicit attention on communication patterns. In his description of the roots of the family therapy movement, Nichols (1984) notes how communication was an integral part of early methods.

Family therapy as a treatment method began when clinicians first brought families together for observation. Doing so forced a shift in focus from intrapsychic content to interpersonal process. Instead of trying to understand what is going on inside people, family therapists began to manipulate what goes on between them. Clarifying communication, and issuing tasks and directives were the first methods used to outwit resistance and to help families change. Even in the early days of family therapy, however, different practitioners developed alternate strategies and tactics of change. (118)

The family therapy approach is rooted in a systems perspective, reflecting assumptions about change and context reflecting systems theory. Napier and Whitaker (1978) describe the initial signals that forced therapists to consider systems approaches.

Some therapists discovered the family system by being bruised by it . . . working with an individual and being totally defeated by the family's power over the patient; or seeing the client "recover," only to witness all the progress undermined by the family; or treating the scapegoat child "successfully," only to find another child in the family dragged into the role; or working with an individual patient and feeling the fury of the family's sudden explosion just as the patient improved. (52–53)

In many cases, once therapists examined a whole family system, they realized that the "problem" member, or symptom bearer, reflected the rest of the system's dynamics. Thus, events in families must be examined in the context in which they happen and attention given to how communication among family members affects connections and relationships (Papp 1983, 7).

From a systems perspective, marital issues need to be addressed through couples counseling rather than individual counseling. In making this argument, many scholars cite Hurvitz's (1967) list of problems that arise when only one spouse (in this case, the wife) is seen in therapy. These include the following:

1. Problems come to be regarded as less amenable to couples' own efforts to work them out.
2. Therapy offers a permissive setting within which she disparages her husband with impunity and reinforces negative attitudes toward him.
3. Wife's gains make husband feel inadequate.
4. Husband may resist wife's effort to impose new interaction patterns upon relationship. (Hurvitz, cited in Gurman and Kniskern 1978, 7)

Family therapy looks at the family unit as the client to be treated; the focus shifts from the individuals to the entire unit and the relationships among people. Ackerman (1966) describes family therapy as "the therapy of a natural living unit; the sphere of the therapeutic intervention is not a single individual but the whole family unit" (209). Attempts are made to change the system, not just the "problem" person, because this person's "acting out" may be thought of as symptomatic of the system's problems (Satir 1967; Gurman and Kniskern 1981; Nichols 1984).

The primary goal of family therapy is to effect changes in the interpersonal relationships among members of the family system, but there are many schools of thought regarding the most effective ways to alter family systems. Therapeutic approaches may be classified in numerous ways. Kaslow (1987) identifies the major recognized theories of family therapy in her classification system, which includes the (1) psychoanalytic, (2) Bowenian, (3) contextual-relational, (4) experiential, (5) problem-solving, (6) communicational-interactional, (7) structural, (8) strategic-systemic, (9) behavioral, and (10) integrative, dialectic, or multimodal. She suggests that each theory offers a different view of the "reality" of the family.

Many therapists borrow freely across the approaches. In a recent survey of family therapists, Rait (1988) found that 34 percent of therapists reported they used eclectic family-oriented approaches, 18 percent classified their approach as structural, and 12 percent saw themselves as systemic/strategic. The rest reflected diverse general approaches. Family therapists may work with individuals, couples, families, or entire social networks—a therapeutic range that necessitates flexibility. Whereas one therapist may value an examination of family history to uncover family of origin or transgenerational patterns, another may focus exclusively on the here-and-now interaction patterns. Family therapy has influenced approaches to treatment for drug and alcohol abuse, eating disorders, major illness, sexual abuse and related areas.

"Over the sixteen years of our marriage, we have experienced marital or family therapy two times, each a very different experience. Early in our marriage, we had trouble separating from my original family, so we worked a lot on couple identity and family-of-origin issues using genograms. During our daughter's lengthy hospitalization for kidney disease, the other four of us went into therapy to keep us functioning and to release our feelings. Now I would be comfortable going again if an issue arose that we could not handle."

Currently, American family therapists are grappling with critical issues of culture and gender as they affect the treatment process. The growing number of families, representing varied cultures, who need the services of family therapists has led to extensive interest in cross-cultural family norms and treatment approaches and a move away from ethnocentric approaches (McGoldrick, Pearce, and Giordano 1982; Boynton 1987). Recent accusations of gender blindness by major architects in the field have led to consideration of gender as a fundamental organizing principle of families and a significant area for future concern (Walsh and Scheinkman 1989).

The past two decades witnessed an increase in research addressing the overall effectiveness of family therapy and specific issues of unique approaches (Gurman and Kniskern 1978 and 1981; Wells and Denzen 1978; Barton et al. 1988; Beach and O'Leary 1985; Johnson and Greenberg 1988; Kaslow). The effectiveness of family therapy has been investigated primarily through an analysis of family improvement through treatment, treatment results compared to no treatment, and comparison of family treatment to other forms. Traditional research in family therapy indicates that 65 to 75 percent of the families seen in family therapy improve (Kniskern 1983).

The complexity of family dynamics and the relative infancy of the field is reflected in debates as to the methods of studying the field. In a published debate on research methods, Kniskern argues that traditional research methods have been effective and have yielded data "supporting the conclusion that family therapies are valid and effective methods of intervening in family and individual problems" (38). An opponent, Tomm (1983), argues against studies using experimental design due to their linear approach, calling instead for more holistic approaches. Even as researchers uncover some answers to key questions, there is more to be examined because, according to Nichols, "There are many studies that verify the overall effectiveness of family therapy, but too few that deal with specific questions about which methods work with which patients and in what circumstances" (119).

For many families, the systemic orientation of family therapy has provided the basis for their eventual change. The emphasis on patterns, rather than individual blame, has permitted all members to accept some responsibility for their family's current state and has given them keys to future change.

As you change the current communication patterns within your family system, many options are open to you, ranging from individual efforts on the part of family members, to participation in organized programs, to seeking counseling for the system. The most exciting aspect is the possibility of change. Communication can be improved; families can grow through effort, time, and struggle. Relationships take work to maintain, and communication stands at the core of that process.

CONCLUSION

This chapter attempts to explore (1) factors that characterize functional to optimally functional families, with an emphasis on communication, and (2) approaches for creating and maintaining effective communication within families. Historically, academic and therapeutic experts have emphasized effective communication as a central factor in well-family functioning. Although there is no absolute agreement on definitions and terminology, one may hypothesize that functional families may exhibit the following characteristics. Some or all of the (1) interactions are patterned and meaningful; (2) there is more compassion and less cruelty; (3) persons are not scapegoated as problems are identified with the appropriate persons; (4) family members exhibit appropriate self-restraint; (5) boundaries are clear; (6) life includes joy and humor; (7) misperceptions are minimal. Popular literature espouses similar ideas in a prescriptive mode.

Approaches to improving marital and family communication include personal actions, instructional programs, and therapeutic interventions. Such approaches can be helpful because they require a level of commitment and openness to change. By forcing the participants to move beyond the daily maintenance issues, they provide a chance to reflect on family experience. These opportunities provide a chance for individual and system self-examination. Each approach reflects a communication component.

A FINAL WORD

As authors, we have grown from the process of writing this book and hope that you have developed new insights about families in general, and your family in particular. We close with our belief, shared with Beavers (1976), that a healthy family may be viewed as a "phoenix." It grows in an atmosphere of flexibility and intimacy. It accepts conflicts, change, and loss. It declines—to rise again in another healthy generation, which, in turn, produces healthy family members.

IN REVIEW

1. How would you describe communication in a well-functioning family? Answer within a context of specific developmental stage, culture, and family form.
2. Analyze the prescriptions for marital or parent-child communication found in a popular book or magazine article, and evaluate their effectiveness based on your understanding of family systems and communication patterns.
3. What goals and criteria would you establish for a successful marriage or family enrichment program with a communication focus?
4. Take a position: To what extent should couples be required by religious or civic institutions to engage in marital workshops or therapy?
5. In what ways would you predict that family therapy would differ from individual therapy?

Bibliography

Abelman, A. (1975). *The relationship between family self-disclosure, adolescent adjustment, family satisfaction, and family congruence.* Unpublished dissertation. Northwestern University, Evanston, IL.

Ackerman, N. J. (1966). Family therapy. In S. Arieti (Ed.), *American handbook of psychiatry.* New York: Basic Books.

Ackerman, N. J. (1980). The family with adolescents. In E. Carter and M. McGoldrick (Eds.), *The family life cycle: A framework for family therapy.* New York: Gardner Press.

Acock, A. C., & Yang, W. S. (1984). Parental power and adolescents' parental identification. *Journal of Marriage and the Family, 46,* 487–494.

Adelman, M. (1988, November). *Sustaining passion: Eroticism and safe sex talk.* Paper presented at the Speech Communication Association Convention, New Orleans.

Ahrons, O., & Rodgers, R. (1987). *Divorced families.* New York: W. W. Norton.

Alberts, J. (1988). Analysis of couples' conversational complaints. *Communication Monographs, 55,* 184–197.

Allen, C. M., & Straus, M. A. (1979). Resources, power, and husband-wife violence. In M. A. Straus & G. T. Hotaling (Eds.), *The social causes of husband-wife violence.* Minneapolis: University of Minnesota Press.

Altman, I., & Taylor, D. (1973). *Social penetration.* New York: Holt, Rinehart & Winston.

Amato, P. (1986). Marital conflict, the parent-child relationship and child self-esteem. *Family Relations, 35,* 403–409.

Ambert, A. M. (1986). Being a stepparent: Live-in and visiting stepchildren. *Journal of Marriage and the Family, 48,* 795–805.

Ammons, P., & Stimett, N. (1980). The vital marriage: A closer look. *Family Relations, 30,* 37–42.

Anderson, C. (1982). The community connection: The impact of social networks on family and individual functioning. In F. Walsh (Ed.), *Normal family processes* (pp. 425–621). New York: Guilford Press.

Anderson, S., & Nuttall, P. (1987). Parent communications training across three stages of childrearing. *Family Relations, 36,* 40–44.

Argyle, M., Henderson, M., & Furnham, A. (1985). The roles of social relationships. *British Journal of Social Psychology, 24,* 125–139.

Arntson, P., & Turner, L. (1989). Sex role socialization: Children's enactment of their parents' behaviors in a regulative and interpersonal context. *Western Journal of Speech Communication, 51,* 304–315.

Avery, C. (1989, May). How do you build intimacy in an age of divorce? *Psychology Today,* pp. 27–31.

Aylmer, R. (1988). The launching of the single young adult. In B. Carter & M. McGoldrick (Eds.), *The changing family life cycle: A framework for family therapy* (2nd ed., pp. 191–208). New York: Gardner Press.

Bach, G. R., & Wyden, P. (1966). *The intimate enemy.* New York: William Morrow & Co.

Bain, A. (1978). The capacity of families to cope with transitions: A theoretical essay. *Human Relations 31,* 675–688.

Baker, M. (1984). Arizona retirement communities and the changing needs of an aging population. *Arizona Review,* pp. 14–22.

Ball, R., & Robbins, L. (1986a). Black husbands' satisfaction with their family life. *Journal of Marriage and the Family, 48,* 849–855.

Ball, R., & Robbins, L. (1986b). Marital status and life satisfaction among black Americans. *Journal of Marriage and the Family, 48,* 349–394.

Balswick, J., & Averett, C. (1977). Differences in expressiveness: Gender, interpersonal orientation, and perceived parental expressiveness as contributing factors. *Journal of Marriage and the Family, 39,* 121–127.

Bank, S. P., & Kahn, M. D. (1987). Formulations of self and family systems. *Family Process, 26,* 185–202.

Barbour, A., & Goldberg, A. (1974). *Interpersonal communication: Teaching strategies and resources.* ERIC/RCS. Speech Communication Association.

Barge, K. (1984, April). *A power primer: A review and critique of conceptions of power.* Paper presented at Central States Speech Association Convention, Chicago.

Barnhill, L. R. (1979). Healthy family systems. *The Family Coordinator, 28,* 94–100.

Barranti-Ramirez, C. (1985, July). The grandparent/grandchildren relationship: Family resource in an era of voluntary bonds. *Family Relations, 34,* 343–355.

Bart, P. (1975). The loneliness of the long distance mother. In J. Freeman (Ed.), *Woman: A feminist perspective* (pp. 156–170). Palo Alto, CA: Mayfield Publishing.

Barton, C., Alexander, J., Waldron, H., Turner, C., & Warburton, J. (1988). Generalizing treatment effects of functional family therapy: Three applications. *American Journal of Family Therapy, 13,* 16–26.

Bavelas, J., & Segal, L. (1982). Family systems theory: Background and implications. *Journal of Communication, 32,* 99–107.

Beach, S., & O'Leary, D. (1985). Current status of outcome research in marital therapy. In L. L'Abate (Ed.), *Handbook of family psychology and therapy* (Vol. 2). Homewood, IL: Dorsey Press.

Beal, E. W. (1980). Separation, divorce, and single-parent families. In E. A. Carter & M. McGoldrick (Eds.), *The family life cycle: A framework for family therapy* (pp. 241–264). New York: Gardner Press.

Bearison, D. J., & Cassel, T. Z. (1975). Cognitive decentration and social codes: Communication effectiveness in young children from differing family contexts. *Developmental Psychology,* pp. 29–36.

Beavers, R. W. (1976). A theoretical basis for family evaluation. In J.M. Lewis, W.R. Beavers, J.T. Gossett & V.A. Phillips (Eds.), *No single thread: Psychological health in family systems* (pp. 46–82). New York: Brunner/Mazel.

Beavers, R. W. (1982). Healthy midrange, and severely dysfunctional families. In F. Walsh (Ed.), *Normal family processes* (pp. 45–66). New York: Guilford Press.

Beier, E. G., & Sternberg, D. P. (1977). Marital communication: Subtle cues between newlyweds. *Journal of Communication, 27,* 92–103.

Bell, A. P., & Weinberg, M. S. (1978). *Homosexualities: A study of diversity among men and women.* New York: Simon & Schuster.

Bell, R. (1987). Did you bring the yarmulke for the cabbage patch kid?: The idiomatic communication of young lovers. *Human Communication Research, 14,* 47–67.

Benjamin, B. (1988). Aging and normal changes in speech-language-hearing. In C. W. Carmichael, C. H. Botan & R. Hawkins (Eds.), *Human communication and the aging process* (pp. 45–56). Prospect Heights, IL: Waveland Press.

Berardo, D., Shehan, C., & Leslie, G. (1987). The residue of tradition: Jobs, careers, and spouses' time in housework. *Journal of Marriage and the Family, 49,* 381–390.

Berger, C. R. (1980). Power and the family. In M. Roloff & G. Miller (Eds.), *Persuasion: New direction in theory and research* (pp. 174–224). Beverly Hills: Sage.

Berger, C. R., & Bradac, J. J. (1982). *Language and social knowledge.* London: Edward Arnold.

Berkowitz, A., & Perkivs, H. W. (1984). Stress among farm women: Work and family as interacting systems. *Journal of Marriage and the Family, 46,* 161–166.

Berman, C. (1986). *Making it as a stepparent: New roles/new rules* (2nd ed.). New York: Harper & Row.

Bernstein, A. (1989). *Yours, mine, and ours.* New York: Charles Scribner's Sons.

Bernstein, B. (1970). A sociolinguistic approach to socialization: With some reference to educability. In F. Williams (Ed.), *Language and poverty* (pp. 25–61). Chicago: Markham.

Beutler, I., Burr, W., Bahr, K., & Herrin, D. (1989). The family realm: Theoretical contributions for understanding its uniqueness. *Journal of Marriage and the Family, 51,* 805–815.

Billingsley, A. (1988). The impact of technology on Afro-American families. *Family Relations, 37,* 420–425.

Blood, T. O., & Wolfe, D. M. (1960). *Husbands and wives: The dynamics of married living.* New York: The Free Press.

Blumstein, P., & Schwartz, P. (1983). *American couples.* New York: William Morrow.

Bochner, A., & Eisenberg, E. (1987). Family process: System perspectives. In C. Berger & S. Chaffee (Eds.), *Handbook of communication science,* (pp. 540–563). Beverly Hills: Sage.

Bowen, M. (1976). Family reaction to death. In P. H. Guerin (Ed.), *Family therapy: Theory and practice* (pp. 335–349). New York: Halsted Press.

Bowen, M. (1978). *Family therapy in clinical practice.* New York: Jason Aronson.

Bowen, S., & Michal-Johnson, P. (1989). The crisis of communicating in relationships: Confronting the threat of AIDS. *AIDS and Public Policy Journal, 4,* 10–19.

Boyd, L., & Roach, A. (1977). Interpersonal communication skills differentiating more satisfying from less satisfying marital relationships. *Journal of Counseling Psychology 24,* 540–542.

Boynton, G. (1987). Cross-cultural family therapy: An escape model. *American Journal of Family Therapy*, 15, 123–130.

Bradt, J. O. (1980). The family with young children. In B. Carter & M. McGoldrick (Eds.), *The family life cycle: A framework for family therapy* (pp. 121–146). New York: Gardner Press.

Bradt, J. (1988). Becoming parents: Families with young children. In B. Carter & M. McGoldrick (Eds.), *The changing family life cycle: A framework for family therapy* (2nd ed., pp. 237–253). New York: Gardner Press.

Breines, W., & Gordon, L. (1983). The new scholarship on family violence. *Signs*, 8, 490–531.

Brighton-Cleghorn, J. (1987). Formulations of self and family systems. *Family Process*, 26, 198–201.

Bristor, M. (1984). The birth of a handicapped child: A wholistic model for grieving. *Family Relations*, 33, 25–32.

Broderick, C. (1975). Power in the governance of families. In R. E. Cromwell & D. H. Olson (Eds.), *Power in families*. (pp. 117–128). New York: Halsted Press.

Broman, C. (1988). Household work and family life satisfaction of blacks. *Journal of Marriage and the Family*, 50, 743–748.

Burgess, E. W., Locke, H. J., & Thomas, M. M. (1963). *The family: From institution to companionship*. New York: American Book Company.

Burgess, R. L., & Conger, R. D. (1979). Family interaction in abusive, neglectful, and normal families. *Journal of Youth and Adolescence*, 8, 1163–1178.

Burgoon, M., Dillard, J., & Doran, N. (1984). Friendly or unfriendly persuasion: The effects of violations of expectancy by males and females. *Human Communication Research*, 10, 283–294.

Burke, R. Weir, T., & Harrison, D. (1976). Disclosure of problems and tensions experienced by marital partners. *Psychological Reports*, 38, 531–542.

Burnett, E., & Daniels, J. (1985). The impact of family-of-origin and stress on interpersonal conflict resolution skills in young men. *American Mental Health Counselors Association Journal*, pp. 162–171.

Cahn, D. (1987, November). *Male/female communication and relationship development: Communication characteristics of mateship stages*. Paper presented at the Speech Communication Association Convention, Boston.

Cain, B. (1990, February 18). Older children and divorce. *New York Times Magazine*, pp. 26, 50, 54–55.

Callan, V. J., & Murray, J. (1989). The role of therapists in helping couples cope with stillbirth and newborn death. *Family Relations*, 38, 248–253.

Camerer, C. (1988). Gifts as economic signals and social symbols. *American Journal of Sociology*, 94, S180–S214.

Carlson, J. (1976a). The recreational role. In F. I. Nye (Ed.), *Role structure and analysis of the family* (pp. 131–148). Beverly Hills: Sage.

Carlson, J. (1976b). The sexual role. In F. I. Nye (Ed.), *Role structure and analysis of the family* (pp. 149–162). Beverly Hills: Sage Publications.

Carmichael, C., Botan, C., & Hawkins, R. (1988) *Human communication and the aging process*. Prospect Heights, IL: Waveland Press.

Carnes, P. J. (1981). *Family development I: Understanding us*. Minneapolis: Interpersonal Communication Program.

Carter, B., & McGoldrick, M. (1988). Overview, the changing family life cycle: A framework for family therapy. In B. Carter & M. McGoldrick (Eds.), *The changing family life cycle* (2nd ed., pp. 3–28). New York: Gardner Press.

Chilman, C. (1978). Habitat and American families: A social-psychological overview. *The Family Coordinator*, 27, 105–111.

Chiriboga, D., Catron, L., & Weiler, P. (1987). Childhood stress and adult functioning during marital separation. *Family Relations*, 36, 163–166.

Clausen, P. (1983, January 10). Divorce American style. *Newsweek*, C11–103, 42–48.

Cleaver, G. (1987). Marriage enrichment by means of a structured communication program. *Family Relations*, 36, 49–54.

Cline, K. (1989). The politics of intimacy: Costs and benefits determining disclosure intimacy in male-female dyads. *Journal of Social and Personal Relationships*, 6, 5–20.

Clinebell, H., & Clinebell, C. (1970). *The intimate marriage*. New York: Harper & Row.

Coleman, L., Antonucci, T., Adelmann, P., & Crohan, S. (1987). Social roles in the lives of middle-aged and older black women. *Journal of Marriage and the Family*, 49, 761–771.

Combrinck-Graham, L. (1988). When parents separate or divorce: The sibling system. In M. Kahn & K. Lewis (Eds.), *Siblings in therapy* (pp. 190–208). New York: W. W. Norton.

Conger, J. J. (1977). *Adolescence and youth* (2nd ed.). New York: Harper & Row.

Constantine, L. (1986). *Family paradigms: The practice of theory in family therapy*. New York: Guilford Press.

Cooke, B., Rossmann, M. M., McCubbin, H. I., & Patterson, J. M. (1988). Social support. *Family Relations, 37*, 211–216.

Cooper, P. (1987). Sex role stereotypes of stepparents in children's literature. In L. Stewart & S. Ting-Toomey (Eds.), *Communication, gender and sex roles in diverse interaction contexts* (pp. 61–82). Norwood, NJ: Ablex Publishing.

Cooper, P. (1989). *A bibliotherapy approach to teaching students-at-risk.* Paper presented at the Central States Communication Association Convention, Kansas City, MO.

Corrales, R. G. (1975). Power and satisfaction in early marriage. In R. E. Cromwell & D. H. Olson (Eds.), *Power in families* (pp. 197–216). New York: John Wiley & Sons.

Coser, L. A. (1967). *Continuities in the study of social conflict.* New York: The Free Press.

Courtright, J. A., Millar, F. E., & Rogers-Millar, L. E. (1979). Domineeringness and dominance: Replication and expansion. *Communication Monographs, 46*, 179–192.

Crane, D. R., Dollahite, D., Griffin, W., & Taylor K. (1987). Diagnosing relationships with spatial distance: An empirical test of a clinical principle. *Journal of Marital and Family Therapy, 13*, 307–310.

Crime prevention through environmental design. (1983). *Habitat, 26*, 2–7.

Cromwell, R. E., & Olson, D. H. (Eds.). (1975). *Power in families.* New York: Halsted Press.

Cronen, V., Pearce, W. B., & Harris, L. (1979). The logic of the coordinated management of meaning: A rules-based approach to the first course in inter-personal communication. *Communication Education, 23*, 22–38.

Cryer-Downs, V. (1989). The grandparent-grandchild relationship. In J. Nussbaum (Ed.), *Life-span communication: Normative processes* (pp. 257–281). Hillsdale, NJ: Laurence Erlbaum.

Csikszentmihalyi, M., & Rochberg-Halton E. (1981). *The meaning of things: Domestic symbols and the self.* Cambridge UK: Cambridge University Press.

Curran, D. (1983). *Traits of a healthy family.* Minneapolis: Winston Press.

Cushman, D. P., & Craig, R. T. (1976). Communication systems, interpersonal implications. In G. R. Miller (Ed.), *Explorations in interpersonal communications.* Beverly Hills: Sage.

Cutler, B. R., & Dyer, W. G. (1973). Initial adjustment processes in young married couples. In M. E. Lasswell and T. E. Lasswell (Eds.), *Love, marriage, family: A developmental approach* (pp. 290–296). Glenview, IL: Scott, Foresman.

Dadds, M. (1987). Families and the origins of child behavior problems. *Family Process, 26*, 341–357.

Davis, E. C., Hovestadt, A. H., Piercy, F. P., & Cochran, S. W. (1982). Effects of weekend and weekly marriage enrichment program formats. *Family Relations, 31*, 85–90.

Day, C. L., & Morse, B. W. (1981). Communication patterns in established lesbian relationships. In J. W. Chesebro (Ed.), *Gayspeak: Gay male and lesbian communication.* New York: Pilgrim Press.

DeFrain, J. (1979). Androgynous parents tell who they are and what they need. *Family Coordinator, 28*, 237–43.

DeFrain, J., & Stinnett, N. (1985). *Secrets of strong families.* Boston: Little, Brown.

deHoyos, G. (1989). Person in environment: A tri-level practice model. *Social Casework, 70*(3), 131–138.

Dell, P. F. (1982). Beyond homeostasis: Toward a concept of coherence. *Family Process, 21*, 21–42.

Dell, P. F. (1989). Violence and the systemic view: The problem of power. *Family Process, 28*, 1–14.

DeLong, A. (1974). Environments for the elderly. *Journal of Communication, 24*(4), 101–112.

DeMaris, A., & Leslie, G. R. (1984). Cohabitation with future spouse: Its influence upon marital satisfaction and communication. *Journal of Marriage and the Family, 46*, 77–84.

Demo, D., Small, S., & Savin-Williams, R. (1987). Family relations and the self-esteem of adolescents and their parents. *Journal of Marriage and the Family, 49*, 705–715.

deTurck, M. (1985). A transactional analysis of compliance gaining behavior: Effects of noncompliance relational context and actor's gender. *Human Communication Research, 12*, 54–78.

deTurck, M., & Miller, G. (1983). Adolescent perceptions of parental persuasive message strategies. *Journal of Marriage and the Family, 45*, 543–552.

deTurck, M., & Miller, G. (1986). The effects of husbands' and wives' social cognition on their marital adjustment, conjugal power, and self-esteem. *Journal of Marriage and the Family, 48*, 714–724.

DeVito, J. (1979). *Education responsibilities to the gay and lesbian student.* Paper presented at the Speech Communication Association Convention, San Antonio, TX.

deYoung, A. J. (1979). Marriage encounter: A critical examination. *Journal of Marital and Family Therapy, 5*, 27–41.

Dickson, P. (1988). *Family words.* Reading MA: Addison-Wesley.

Dilworth-Anderson, P., & McAdoo, H. P. (1988). The study of ethnic minority families: Implementations for practitioners and policy-makers. *Family Relations, 37*, 265–267.

Dinkmeyer, D., & Carlson, J. (1984a). *Time for a better marriage.* Circle Pines, MN: American Guidance Service.

Dinkmeyer, D., & Carlson, J. (1984b). *Training in marriage enrichment.* Circle Pines, MN: American Guidance Service.

Dinkmeyer, D., & Carlson, J. (1986). A systematic approach to marital enrichment. *American Journal of Family Therapy, 14,* 139–144.

Doherty, W. J. (1981). Locus of control differences and marital dissatisfaction. *Journal of Marriage and the Family, 43,* 369–377.

Doherty, W. J. (1987). Have yourself a merry little Christmas . . . or else. *Family Networker, 11*(6), 53–56.

Doherty, W. J., Lester, M., & Leigh, G. (1986). Marriage encounter weekends: Couples who win and couples who lose. *Journal of Marital and Family Therapy, 12,* 49–62.

Doherty, W. J., McCabe, P., & Ryder, R.G. (1978). Marriage encounter: A critical appraisal. *Journal of Marriage and Family Counseling, 4,* 99–106.

Douglas, S. R., & Wind, Y. (1978). Examining family role and authority patterns: Two methodological issues. *Journal of Marriage and the Family, 40,* 35–47.

Douvan, E. (1983). Commentary: Theoretical perspectives on peer association. In J.L. Epstein & N. Karweit (Eds.), *Friends in school: Patterns of selection and influence in secondary schools* (pp. 63–69). New York: Academic Press.

Dreikurs, R. (1964). *Children: The challenge.* New York: Hawthorn Books.

Dreyer, C., & Dreyer, A. (1984). Family dinner time as unique behavior habitat. *Family Process, 12,* 291–302.

Duck, S. (Ed.). (1984). *Personal relationships: Repairing personal relationships.* New York: Academic Press.

Duck, S., Miell, D., & Miell, D. (1984). Relationship growth and decline. In H. Sypher & J. Applegate (Eds.), *Communication by children and adults* (pp. 292–312). Beverly Hills: Sage.

Duncan, O. D. (1964). Social organization and the ecosystem. In R. Farris and L. Farris (Eds.), *Handbook of modern sociology* (pp. 36–82). Chicago: Rand McNally.

Dunlop, R. S. (1978). *Helping the bereaved.* Bowie, MD: Charles Press.

Duvall, E. (1988). Family development's first forty years. *Family Relations, 37,* 127–134.

Eggert, L. (1987). Support in family ties: Stress, coping and adaptation. In T. Albrecht & M. Adelman (Eds.), *Communicating social support* (pp. 80–104). Newbury Park, CA: Sage.

Einstein, E. (1982). Stepfamily: Chaotic, complex, challenging. *Stepfamily Bulletin, 1*(1), 1–2.

Einstein, E., & Albert, L. (1986). *Strengthening your stepfamily.* Circle Pines, MN: American Guidance Service.

Ellis, T. (1982). *The marriage enrichment weekend: A qualitative study of a particular weekend experience.* Unpublished dissertation, Northwestern University, Evanston, IL.

Elman, M. R., & Gilbert, L. A. (1984). Coping strategies for role conflict in married professional women with children. *Family Relations, 33,* 317–327.

Epstein, N. B., Bishop, D. S., & Baldwin, L. M. (1982). McMaster model of family functioning. In F. Walsh (Ed.), *Normal family processes* (pp. 115–141). New York: Guilford Press.

Erikson, E. H. (1950). *Childhood and society.* New York: Norton.

Erikson, E. H. (1968). *Identity, youth, and crisis.* New York: W.W. Norton.

Eshbach, E. (1976, May 16). Your dream house could give a family nightmares. *Chicago Tribune,* Sec. 5, 3.

Evans, N. (1987). A framework for assisting student affairs staff in fostering moral development. *Journal of Counseling and Development, 60,* 191–193.

Falicov, C., & Karrer, B. (1980). Cultural variations in the family life cycle: The Mexican-American family. In E. A. Carter & M. McGoldrick (Eds.), *The family life cycle: A framework for family therapy* (pp. 383–425). New York: Gardner Press.

Family Home Evening: Love makes our house a home. (1974). Salt Lake City: The Church of Jesus Christ Of Latter-day Press.

Family Home Evening resource book. (1983). Salt Lake City: The Church of Jesus Christ of Latter-day Saints Press.

Feifel, H. (1977). *New meaning of death.* New York: McGraw-Hill.

Feldman, L. B. (1979). Marital conflict and marital intimacy: An integrative psychodynamic-behavioral systemic model. *Family Process, 18,* 69–78.

Feldman, L. B. (1982). Sex roles and family dynamics. In F. Walsh (Ed.), *Normal family process* (pp. 345–382). New York: Guilford Press.

Festinger, L., Schachter, S., & Beck, K. (1950). *Social pressure in informal groups: A study of human factors in housing.* New York: Harper & Row.

Filley, A. C. (1975). *Interpersonal conflict resolution.* Glenview, IL: Scott, Foresman.

Fitzpatrick, M. A. (1977a, December). *Dyadic adjustment in traditional, independent, and separate relationship: A validation study.* Paper presented at the Speech Communication Association Convention, New York City.

Fitzpatrick, M. A. (1977b). A typological approach to communication in relationships. In B. Rubin (Ed.), *Communication yearbook I* (pp. 263–275). New Brunswick, NJ: Transaction Press.

Fitzpatrick, M. A. (1987). Marital interaction. In C. Berger & S. Chaffee (Eds.), *Handbook of communication science* (pp. 564–618). Newbury Park, CA: Sage.

Fitzpatrick, M. A. (1988). *Between husbands and wives.* Beverly Hills: Sage.

Fitzpatrick, M. A., & Badzinski, D. M. (1985). All in the family: Interpersonal communication in kin relationships. In M. L. Knapp & G. R. Miller (Eds.), *Handbook of interpersonal communication* (pp. 687–736). Beverly Hills, CA: Sage.

Fitzpatrick, M. A., & Best, P. (1979). Dyadic adjustment in relational types: Consensus, cohesion, affectional expression, and satisfaction in enduring relationships. *Communication Monographs, 46,* 165–178.

Fitzpatrick, M. A., Fallis, S., & Vance, L. (1982). Multifunctional coding of conflict resolution strategies in marital dyads. *Family Relations, 31,* 61–70.

Floyd, F. (1988). Couples' cognitive/affective reactions to communication behaviors. *Journal of Marriage and the Family, 50,* 523–532.

Ford, D. A. (1983). Wife battery and criminal justice: A study of victim decision making. *Family Relations, 32,* 463–476.

Forehand, R., McCombs, A., Long, N., Brady, G., & Fauber, R. (1988). Early adolescent adjustment to recent parental divorce: The role of interparental conflict and adolescent sex as mediating variables. *Journal of Consulting and Clinical Psychology, 56,* 624–627.

Forgatch, M. (1989). Patterns and outcomes in family problem solving: The disrupting effect of negative emotion. *Journal of Marriage and the Family, 51,* 115–124.

Fortier, L., & Wanlass, R. (1984). Family crisis following the diagnosis of a handicapped child. *Family Relations, 33,* 13–24.

Framo, J. L. (1976). Family of origin as a therapeutic resource for adults in marital and family therapy: You can and should go home again. *Family Process, 15,* 193–209.

French, J. R. P., Jr., & Raven B. H. (1962). The bases of social power. In D. Cartwright & A. Zander (Eds.), *Group dynamics* (pp. 607–623). Evanston, IL: Row Peterson.

Frey, J. (1984). A family/system approach to illness-maintaining behaviors in chronically ill adolescents. *Family Process, 23,* 251–260.

Furstenberg, F. (1987). The new extended family: The experience of parents and children after remarriage. In K. Pasley & M. Ihninger-Tallman (Eds.), *Remarriage and stepparenting: Current research* (pp. 42–61). New York: Guilford Press.

Gagnon, J. (1977). *Human sexuality.* Glenview, IL: Scott, Foresman.

Galper, M. (1978). *Co-parenting: A sourcebook for the separated or divorced family.* Philadelphia: Running Press.

Galvin, K. M. (1978 November). *An analysis of communication instruction in current marital interaction programs.* Paper presented at the Speech Communication Association Convention, Minneapolis.

Galvin, K. M. (1982 November). *Pishogues and paddywhackery: Transmission of communication patterns and values through three generations of an extended Irish-American family.* Paper presented at the Speech Communication Association Convention, Louisville.

Galvin, K. M. (1985). *Family communication workshops.* Annandale, VA: SCA/ERIC.

Galvin, K., & Cooper, P. (1990, June). *Development of involuntary relationships: The stepparent/stepchild relationship.* Paper presented at the International Communication Association Conference, Dublin, Ireland.

Gantman, C. (1980). A closer look at families that work well. *International Journal of Family Therapy, 2,* 106–119.

Garcia-Preto, N. (1988). Transformation of the family system in adolescence. In B. Carter & M. McGoldrick (Eds.), *The changing family life cycle: A framework for family therapy* (2nd ed., pp. 255–283). New York: Gardner Press.

Garland, D. S. (1983). *Working with couples for marriage enrichment.* San Francisco: Jossey-Bass.

Gecas, V., & Schwalbe, M. (1986). Parental behavior and adolescent self esteem. *Journal of Marriage and the Family, 48,* 37–46.

Giblin, P., Sprenkle, D., & Sheehan, R. (1985). Enrichment of outcome research: A meta-analysis of premarital, marital and family interventions. *Journal of Marital and Family Therapy, 11,* 257–271.

Gilbert, L. A., Hanson, G. R., & Davis, B. (1982). Perceptions of parental role responsibilities: Differences between mothers and fathers. *Family Relations, 31,* 261–270.

Gilbert, S. (1976a). Self-disclosure, intimacy, and communication in families. *Family Coordinator, 25,* 221–229.

Gilbert, S. (1976b). Empirical and theoretical extensions of self-disclosure. In G. Miller (Ed.), *Exploration in interpersonal communication* (pp. 197–215). Beverly Hills: Sage.

Giles, H., & Wiemann, J. (1987). Language, social comparison, and power. In C. Berger & S. Chaffee (Eds.), *Handbook of communication science*. Beverly Hills: Sage Publications.

Gilligan, C. (1982). *In a different voice*. Cambridge, MA: Harvard University Press.

Gilligan, C., Lyons, P., & Hammer, T. (Eds.). (1989). *Making conversations: Interpreting the interpersonal world of adolescent girls at Emma Willard School*. Troy, NY: Emma Willard School.

Giordano, J. (1988). Parents of the baby boomers: A new generation of young-old. *Family Relations, 37,* 411–414.

Glenn, N., & Kramer, K. (1987). The marriages and divorces of the children of divorce. *Journal of Marriage and the Family, 49,* 811–826.

Glick, P. (1989, February). *American families: As they are and were (realities in fact)*. Paper presented at the Florida Conference on Family Development, Jacksonville.

Glick, P. (1989). The family life cycle and social change. *Family Relations, 38,* 123–129.

Glick, P. (1990). Marriage and family trends. In D. Olson & M. K. Hanson (Eds.), *2001: Preparing families for the future* (pp. 2–3). Minneapolis: National Council on Family Relations.

Golanty, E., & Harris, B. B. (1982). *Marriage and family life*. Boston: Houghton Mifflin.

Goldberg, L. (1983, March). They stole our childhood. *Newsweek on Campus,* p. 32.

Goldner, V. (1989). Generation and gender: Normative and covert hierarchies. In M. McGoldrick, C. Anderson & F. Walsh (Eds.), *Women in families* (pp. 42–60). New York: W. W. Norton.

Gongla, P. (1982). Single parent families: A look at families of mothers and children. *Marriage and Family Review* (Vol. 6, pp. 5–27). New York: Hayworth Press.

Gordon, T. (1975). *Parent effectiveness training*. New York: New American Library.

Gottman, J. M., Markham, H., & Notarius, C. (1977). The topography of marital conflict: A sequential analysis of verbal and nonverbal behavior. *Journal of Marriage and the Family, 39,* 461–477.

Gottman, J. M. (1979). *Marital interaction: Experimental investigations*. New York: Academic Press.

Gottman, J. M. (1982a). Emotional responsiveness in marital conversations. *Journal of Communication, 32,* 103–120.

Gottman, J. M. (1982b). Temporal form: Toward a new language for describing relationships. *Journal of Marriage and the Family, 44,* 942–962.

Grebe, S. (1986). Mediation in separation and divorce. *Journal of Counseling and Development, 64,* 379–382.

Greene, B. (1970). *A clinical approach to marital problems*. Springfield, IL: Charles C Thomas.

Gudykunst, W., Yoon, Y. C., & Nishida, T. (1986). The developmental tasks of siblingship over the life cycle. *Journal of Marriage and the Family, 48,* 703–714.

Guenther, R. (1984, April 11). Real estate column. *The Wall Street Journal,* p. 1.

Guerney, B. G. (1977). *Relationship enhancement: Skill training programs for therapy, problem prevention, and enrichment*. San Francisco: Jossey-Bass.

Gurman, A., & Kniskern, D. (1977). Enriching research on marital enrichment programs. *Journal of Marriage and Family Counseling, 3,* 3–10.

Gurman, A., & Kniskern, D. (1978). Research on marital and family therapy: Progress, perspective and prospect. In S. Garfield & A. Bergin (Eds.), *Handbook of psychotherapy and behavior change,* (2nd ed.). New York: John Wiley & Sons.

Gurman, A., & Kniskern, D. (1981). *Handbook of family therapy*. New York: Brunner/Mazel.

Gwartney-Gibbs, P. (1986). The institutionalization of premarital cohabitation: Estimates from marriage license applications. *Journal of Marriage and the Family, 48,* 423–434.

Gwartney-Gibbs, P., Stockard, J., & Bohmer, S. (1986). Learning courtship aggression: The influence of parents, peers and personal experiences. *Family Relations, 48,* 276–282.

Hagestad, G. (1985). Continuity and connectedness. In V. Bengtson & J. Robertson (Eds.), *Grandparenthood* (pp. 31–48). Beverly Hills: Sage.

Hagestad, G. (1988). Demographic change and the life course: Some emerging trends in the family realm. *Family Relations, 37,* 405–410.

Haley, J. (1974). Establishment of an interpersonal relationship. In B. R. Patton & K. Griffin (Eds.), *Interpersonal communication: Basic text and readings* (pp. 368–373). New York: Harper & Row.

Haley, J. (1976). *Problem-solving psychotherapy*. San Francisco: Jossey-Bass.

Hall, E. T. (1966). *The hidden dimension*. Garden City, NY: Doubleday.

Hare-Mustin, R. (1987). The problem of gender in family therapy. *Family Process, 26,* 15–27.

Hare-Mustin, R. (1988). Family change and gender differences: Implications for theory and practice. *Family Relations, 37,* 36–41.

Hare-Mustin, R. (1989). The problem of gender in family therapy theory. In M. McGoldrick, C. Anderson & F. Walsh, (Eds.), *Women in families*. New York: W. W. Norton.

Harevan, T. (1982). American families in transition: Historical perspective on change. In F. Walsh (Ed.), *Normal family processes* (pp. 446–465). New York: Guilford Press.

Harkins, E. B. (1975). Effects of empty nest transition on self-report of psychological and physical well being. *Gerontologist, 15,* 43.

Hart, B. (1986). Lesbian battering: An examination. In K. Lobel (Ed.), *Naming the violence* (pp. 173–189). Seattle: Seal Press.

Haslett, B., & Perlmutter-Bowen, S. (1989). Children's strategies in initiating interaction with peers. In J. Nussbaum (Ed.), *Life-span communication: Normative processes* (pp. 27–52). Hillsdale, NJ: Lawrence Erlbaum.

Heiss, J. (1968). An introduction to the elements of role theory. In J. Heiss (Ed.), *Family roles and interaction* (pp. 3–27). Chicago: Rand McNally.

Henry, J. (1973). *Pathways to Madness.* New York: Vintage Books

Herz, F. (1980). The impact of death and serious illness on the family life cycle. In E. A. Carter & M. McGoldrick (Eds.), *The family life cycle: A framework for family therapy* (pp. 223–240). New York: Gardner Press.

Herz, F., & Rosen, E. (1982). Jewish families. In M. McGoldrick, J. Pearce & J. Giordano (Eds.), *Ethnicity and family therapy.* New York: Guilford.

Herz-Brown, H. (1988). The post divorce family. In B. Carter & M. McGoldrick (Eds.), *The changing family life cycle: A framework for family therapy* (2nd ed., pp. 371–398). New York: Gardner Press.

Hess, R., & Handel, G. (1959). *Family worlds.* Chicago: University of Chicago Press.

Hetherington, E. M. (1987). Family relations six years after divorce. In K. Pasley & M. Ihninger-Tallman (Eds.), *Remarriage and stepparenting: Current research* (pp. 185–205). New York: Guilford Press.

Hetherington, E. M., Cox, M., & Cox, R. (1976). Divorced fathers. *Family Coordinator, 25,* 417–428.

Hey, R., & Neubeck, G. (1990). Family life education. In D. Olson & M. K. Hanson (Eds.), *2001: Preparing families for the future* (pp. 7–25). Hillsdale, NJ: Lawrence Erlbaum.

Hill, M. (1988). Class, kinship density, and conjugal role segregation. *Journal of Marriage and the Family, 50,* 731–741.

Hill, R. (1949). *Families under stress.* New York: Harper & Brothers.

Hill, R. (1986). Life cycle stages for types of single parent families: Of family development theory. *Family Relations, 35,* 19–29.

Hill, W., & Scanzoni, J. (1982). An approach for assessing marital decision-making processes. *Journal of Marriage and the Family, 44,* 927–940.

Hines, P.M. (1988). The family life cycle of poor black families. In B. Carter & M. McGoldrick (Eds.), *The changing family life cycle: A framework for family therapy* (2nd ed., pp. 513–544). New York: Gardner Press.

Hobart, C. (1988). The family system in remarriage: An exploratory study. *Journal of Marriage and the Family, 50,* 649–661.

Hocker, J., & Wilmot, W. (1985). *Interpersonal conflict,* (2nd Ed.). Dubuque: William C. Brown.

Hof, L., & Miller, W. R. (1983). *Marriage enrichment.* Bowie, MD: Brady/Prentice-Hall.

Hoffman, L. (1980). The family life cycle and discontinuous change. In E. A. Carter & M. McGoldrick (Eds.), *The family life cycle: A framework for family therapy* (pp. 53–68). New York: Gardner Press.

Hohn, C. (1987). The family life cycle: Needed extension of the concept. In T. K. Burch & K. W. Wachter (Eds.), *Family demography: Methods and their application* (pp. 156–180). New York: Oxford University Press.

Hollihan, T., & Riley, P. (1987). The rhetorical power of a compelling story: A critique of a "Toughlove" parental support group. *Communication Quarterly, 35,* 13–25.

Holmes, T. H., & Rahe, R. H. (1967). The social readjustment rating scale. *Journal of Psychosomatic Research, 2,* 213–218.

Hood, J. (1986). The provider role: Its meaning and measurement. *Journal of Marriage and the Family, 48,* 349–359.

Hoopes, M. (1987). Multigenerational systems: Basic assumptions. *American Journal of Family Therapy, 15,* 195–205.

Hoopes, M. M., & Harper, J. M. (1987). *Birth order roles and sibling patterns in individual and family therapy.* Rockville, MD: Aspen Publishers.

Hopper, R., Knapp, M. L., & Scott, L. (1981). Couples' personal idioms: Exploring intimate talk. *Journal of Communication, 31*(1), 23–33.

Horwitz, J., & Tognoli, J. (1982). Role of home in adult development: Women and men living alone describe their residential histories. *Family Relations, 31,* 335–341.

Howard, J. (1978). *Families.* New York: Simon & Schuster.

Hurvitz, N., & Komarovsky, M. (1977). Husbands and wives: Middle class and working class. In C. Greenblatt et al. (Eds.), *The marriage game* (2nd ed.). New York: Random House.

Huston, T. L., McHale, S. M., & Crouter, A. C. (1986). When the honeymoon's over: Changes in the marriage relationship over the first year. In R. Gilmore & S. Duck (Eds.), *The emerging field of personal relationships* (pp. 109–132). Hillsdale, NJ: Lawrence Erlbaum.

Ihninger-Tallman, M., & Pasley, K. (1987). Divorce and remarriage in the American family: A historical review. In K. Pasley & M. Ihninger-Tallman (Eds.), *Remarriage and stepparenting: Current research* (pp. 3–18). New York: Guilford Press.

Indvik, J., & Fitzpatrick, M. A. (1982). If you could read my mind love. . . . Understanding and misunderstanding in the marital dyads. *Family Relations, 31,* 43–52.

Issod, J. (1987). A comparison of "on-time" and "delayed" parenthood. *American Mental Health Counselors Association Journal, 9,* 92.

Jackson, D. D. (1957). The question of family homeostasis. *Psychiatric Quarterly, 31,* 79–90.

Jaramillo, P., & Zapata, J. (1987). Roles and alliances within Mexican-American and Anglo families. *Journal of Marriage and the Family, 49,* 727–735.

Johnson F. (1978). *Communication with children: Toward a healthy construction of communicative roles.* Paper presented at the Central States Speech Association Convention, Chicago, IL.

Johnson, R. (1984). *Conflict management in established gay male dyads: A qualitative study.* Paper presented at the Speech Communication Association Convention, Chicago, IL.

Johnson, S., & Greenberg, L. (1988). Relating process to outcome in marital therapy. *Journal of Marital and Family Therapy, 14,* 175–183.

Jones, E., & Gallois, C. (1989). Spouses' impressions of rules for communication in public and private marital conflicts. *Journal of Marriage and the Family, 51,* 957–967.

Jones, T. (1982, November). *Analysis of family metaphor: Methodological and theoretical implications.* Paper presented at the Speech Communication Association Convention, Louisville.

Jordon, J. (1983–1984). The challenge: Designing buildings for older Americans. *Aging, 342,* 18–21.

Jourard, S. (1971). *The transparent self.* New York: Van Nostrand Reinhold.

Jourard, S. (1974). Some lethal aspects of the male role. In J. Pleck & J. Sawyer (Eds.), *Men and Masculinity.* (pp. 21–29). Englewood Cliffs, NJ: Prentice-Hall.

Kahana, R., & Kahana, B. (1970). *The theoretical and research perspectives on grandparenthood.* Paper presented at the American Psychological Association Meeting.

Kalmuss, D. S. (1984). The intergenerational transmission of marital aggression. *Journal of Marriage and the Family, 46,* 11–19.

Kantor, D., & Lehr, W. (1976). *Inside the family.* San Francisco: Jossey-Bass.

Kaslow, F. (1987). Marital and family therapy. In M. B. Sussman & S. K. Steinmetz (Eds.), *Handbook of marriage and the family* (pp. 835–860). New York: Plenum Press.

Kelly, D. (1988). Privacy in marital relationships. *The Southern Speech Communication Journal, 53,* 441–456.

Kelly, D., & Warshafsky, L. (1987). *Partner abuse in gay male and lesbian couples.* Paper presented at the Third National Conference for Family Violence Researchers, Durham, NC.

Kennedy, R. W. (1953). *The house and the art of its design.* New York: Reinhold.

Kerr, M. (1981). Family systems theory and therapy. In A. Gurman & D. Kniskern (Eds.), *Handbook of Family Therapy.* New York: Harcourt Brace Jovanovich.

Kidder, T. (1985). *House.* Boston: Houghton Mifflin.

Killmann, R., & Thomas, K. (1975). Interpersonal conflict handling behavior as reflections of Jungian personality dimensions. *Psychological Reports, 37,* 971–980.

Kirk, L. (1989). *Contemporary family scripts and intergenerational communication.* Paper delivered at the Speech Communication Association Convention, San Francisco.

Knapp, M. L. (1972). *Nonverbal communication in human interaction.* New York: Holt, Rinehart & Winston.

Knapp, M. L. (1984). *Interpersonal communication and human relationships.* Boston: Allyn & Bacon.

Knapp, M. L., Miller, G., & Berger, C. (1987). The issues at issue: A discussion. *Communication Education, 36,* 387–401.

Kniskern, D. (1983). The new wave is all wet. . . *Family Therapy Networker, 7,* 39–41.

Kohlberg, L. (1964). Development of moral character and moral ideology. In M. L. Hoffman & L. W. Hoffman (Eds.), *Review of child development research 1* (pp. 383–431). New York: Russell Sage Foundation.

Kohlberg, L. (1969). Stage and sequence: The cognitive developmental approach to socialization. In D. Goshen (Ed.), *Handbook of socialization theory and research* (pp. 347–480). Chicago: Rand McNally.

Kohlberg, L. (1973). Continuities in childhood and adult moral development revisited. In P. Baltes & K. W. Schaie (Eds.), *Life-span developmental psychology: Personality and socialization* (pp. 179–204). New York: Academic Press.

Kolb, T. M., & Straus, M. A. (1974). Marital power and marital happiness in relation to problem solving ability. *Journal of Marriage and the Family, 36,* 756–766.

Kramer, C. H. (1980). *Becoming a family therapist.* New York: Human Sciences Press.

Kramer, J. (1985). *Family interfaces: Transgenerational patterns.* New York: Brunner/Mazel.

Krueger, D. L. (1983). Pragmatics of dyadic decision making: A sequential analysis of communication patterns. *Western Journal of Speech Communication, 47,* 99–117.

Kübler-Ross, E. (1970). *On death and dying.* New York: Macmillan.

Kurdick, L. (1989). Relationship quality in gay and lesbian cohabiting couples: A 1-year follow-up study. *Journal of Social and Personal Relationships, 6,* 39–60.

L'Abate, L. (1981). Skill training programs for couples and families. In A. Gurman & D. Kniskern (Eds.), *Handbook of family therapy* (pp. 631–661). New York: Brunner/Mazel.

L'Abate, L. (1984). Structured enrichment (SE) with couples and families. *Family Relations, 34,* 169–175.

Laing, R. D. (1972). *The politics of the family.* New York: Vintage Books.

Larsen, A., & Olson, D. (1989). Predicting marital satisfaction using PREPARE: A replication study. *Journal of Marital and Family Therapy, 15,* 311–322.

Lavee, Y., McCubbin, H., & Olson, D. (1987). The effect of stressful life events and transitions on family functioning and well-being. *Journal of Marriage and the Family, 49*(4), 857–873.

Lawrence, R. (1987). What makes a house a home? *Environment and Behavior, 19*(2), 154–158.

Lederer, W., & Jackson, D. D. (1968). *The mirages of marriage.* New York: W. W. Norton and Co.

Lee, C. (1988a). Meta-commentary: On synthesis and fractionation in family theory and research. *Family Process, 27,* 93–97.

Lee, C. (1988b). Theories of family adaptability: Toward a synthesis of Olson's circumplex and the Beavers systems models. *Family Process, 27,* 73–84.

Lee, G. (1988). Marital satisfaction in later life: The effects of nonmarital roles. *Journal of Marriage and the Family, 50,* 775–783.

Lennard, S., & Lennard, H. (1977). Architecture: Effect of territory, boundary, and orientation on family functioning. *Family Process, 16,* 49–66.

Leonard, L. (1982). *The wounded woman.* Boston: Shambala Publishers.

Lerner, H. (1989). *The dance of intimacy.* New York: Harper & Row.

Levinger, G., & Senn, D. J. (1967). Disclosure of feelings in marriage. *Merrill Palmer Quarterly, 13,* 237–249.

Levinson, D. (1978). *The seasons of a man's life.* New York: Knopf.

Levitin, T. E. (1979). Children of divorce: An introduction. *Journal of Social Issues, 35,* 1–23.

Lewis, J. (1986). Family structure and stress. *Family Process, 25,* 235–247.

Lewis, J. M., Beavers, W. R., Gossett, J. T., & Phillips, V. A. (1976). *No single thread: Psychological health in family systems.* New York: Brunner/Mazel.

Lewis, R. (1973). A longitudinal test of a developmental framework for premarital dyadic formation. *Journal of Marriage and the Family, 1,* 16–25.

Lewis, R. A. (1978). Emotional intimacy among men. *Journal of Social Issues, 34,* 108–121.

Lewis, R. A., & Pleck, J. H. (1979). Men's rols in the family. *The Family Coordinator, 29,* 108–121.

Littlejohn, S. (1989). *Theories of human communication* (3rd ed.). Belmont, CA: Wadsworth Publishing.

Lomrantz, J. (1976). Cultural variations in personal space. *Journal of Social Psychology, 99,* 21–77.

Lopata, H. Z. (1973). *Widowhood in an American city.* Cambridge, MA: Schenkman.

Lopez, F. (1987). The impact of parental divorce on college student development. *Journal of Counseling and Development, 65,* 484–486.

Luepnitz, D. A. (1979). Which aspects of divorce affect children? *Family Coordinator, 28,* 79–85.

Lutz, P. L. (1983). The stepfamily: An adolescent perspective. *Family Relations, 32,* 367–376.

Lyson, T. (1985). Husband and wife work roles and the organization and operation of family farms. *Journal of Marriage and the Family, 47,* 759–764.

Mace, D. (1987). Three ways of helping married couples. *Journal of Marital and Family Therapy, 13,* 179–185.

Macklin, E. (1980). Nontraditional family forms: A decade of research. *Journal of Marriage and the Family, 42,* 905–922.

Maddock, J. (1989). Healthy family sexuality: Positive principles for educators and clinicians. *Family Relations, 38,* 130–136.

Majors, R. (1983, November). *A comparison of phase models in gay male primary relationship development.* Paper presented at the Speech Communication Association Convention, Washington D.C.

Malone, T., & Malone, P. (1987). *The art of intimacy.* New York: Prentice-Hall.

Manz, C. C., & Gioia, D. (1983). The interrelationship of power and control. *Human Relations, 36,* 459–476.

Marshall, L., & Rose, P. (1988). Family-of-origin violence and courtship abuse. *Journal of Counseling and Development*, 66, 414–418.

Marshall, N. (1972). Privacy and environment. *Human Ecology*, 1, 93–111.

Maxwell, C., & Weider-Hatfield, D. (1987, November). *Level of marital satisfaction as it relates to verbal and paralinguistic cues in discussion of conflict topics.* Paper presented at the Speech Communication Association Convention, Boston.

McAdams, D., & Power, P. (1985). *Power, intimacy, and the life story.* Homewood, IL: Dorsey Press.

McClelland, R., & Caroll, S. (1984). Applying social epidemiology to child abuse. *Social Casework*, 65, 214–218.

McCubbin, H. I., & Dahl, B. (1985). *Marriage and family: Individuals and life cycles.* New York: John Wiley & Sons.

McCubbin, H. I., & McCubbin, M. A. (1988). Typologies of resilient families: Emerging roles of social class and ethnicity. *Family Relations*, 37, 247–254.

McCubbin, H. I., & Patterson, J. M. (1983). Family transitions: adaptation to stress. In H. I. McCubbin & C. R. Figley (Eds.), *Coping with normative transitions* (Vol. 1, pp. 5–25). New York: Brunner/Mazel.

McCubbin, H. I., Patterson, J.M., Cauble, A.E., Wilson, W.R., & Warwick, W. (1983). CHIP-coping health inventory for parents: An assessment of parental coping patterns in the case of the chronically ill. *Journal of Marriage and the Family*, 45, 359–370.

McCullough, P. (1980). Launching children and moving on. In E. A. Carter & M. McGoldrick (Eds.), *The family life cycle: A framework for family therapy.* New York: Gardner Press.

McCullough, P. G., & Rutenberg, S. K. (1988). Launching children and moving on. In B. Carter & M. McGoldrick (Eds.), *The changing family life cycle* (2nd ed., pp. 285–309). New York: Gardner Press.

McDonald, G. W. (1980a). Family power: The assessment of a decade of theory and research, 1970–1979. *Journal of Marriage and the Family*, 42, 841–852.

McDonald, G. W. (1980b). Parental power and adolescents' parental identification: A reexamination. *Journal of Marriage and the Family*, 42, 289–296.

McDonald, G. W. (1981). Structural exchange and marital interaction. *Journal of Marriage and the Family*, 43, 825–840.

McGinnis, K., & McGinnis, J. (1981). *Parenting for peace and justice.* Maryknoll: Orbis Books.

McGoldrick, M. (1982a). Normal families: An ethnic perspective. In F. Walsh (Ed.), *Normal family processes* (pp. 399–424). New York: Guilford Press.

McGoldrick, M. (1982b). Irish families. In M. McGoldrick, J. Pearce & J. Giordano (Eds.), *Ethnicity and family therapy.* New York: Guilford Press.

McGoldrick, M., Anderson, C., & Walsh, F. (Eds). (1989). *Women in families: A framework for family therapy.* New York: W. W. Norton.

McGoldrick, M., & Carter, B. (1988). Forming a remarried family. In B. Carter & M. McGoldrick (Eds.), *The changing family life cycle: A framework for family therapy* (2nd ed., pp. 399–429). New York: Gardner Press.

McGoldrick, M., & Carter, E. A. (1980). Forming a remarried family. In E. A. Carter & M. McGoldrick (Eds.), *The family life cycle: A framework for family therapy* (pp. 265–329). New York: Gardner Press.

McGoldrick, M., Garcia-Preto, N., Hines, P. M., & Lee, E. (1989b). Ethnicity and women. In M. McGoldrick, C. Anderson & F. Walsh (Eds.), *Women in families* (pp. 169–199). New York: W. W. Norton.

McGoldrick, M., & Gerson, R. (1985). *Genograms in family assessment.* New York: W. W. Norton.

McGoldrick, M., Hines, P., Lee, E., & Preto, N. (1986). Mourning rituals. *Family Therapy Networker*, 10, 30–36.

McGoldrick, M., Pearce, J., & Giordano, J. (Eds.). (1982). *Ethnicity and family therapy.* New York: Guilford Press.

McLanahan, S., & Bumpass, L. (1988). Intergenerational consequences of family disruption. *American Journal of Sociology*, 94(1), 130–152.

McWhirter, D. P., & Mattison, A. M. (1984). *The male couple.* Englewood Cliffs, NJ: Prentice-Hall.

Mederer, H., & Hill, R. (1983). Cultural transitions over the family span: Theory and research. In H. McCubbin, M. B. Sussman & J. M. Patterson (Eds.), *Social stress and the family* (pp. 39–60). New York: Hayworth Press.

Mehrabian, A. (1971). *Silent messages.* Belmont, CA: Wadsworth.

Michal-Johnson, P., & Bowen, S. (1989). AIDS and communication: Matter of influence. *AIDS and Public Policy Journal*, 4, 1–3.

Midelfort, C. F., & Midelfort, H. C. (1982). Norwegian families. In M. McGoldrick, J. Pearce & J. Giordano, (Eds.), *Ethnicity and family therapy* (pp. 438–456). New York: Guilford Press.

Millar, F., Rogers-Millar, L. E., & Villard, K. (1978, April). *A proposed model of relational communication and family functioning.* Paper presented at the Central States Speech Association Convention, Chicago.

Miller, B. (1979). Gay fathers and their children. *Family Coordinator, 28,* 544–552.

Miller, S., Corrales, R., & Wackman, D. B. (1975). Recent progress in understanding and facilitating marital communication. *The Family Coordinator, 24,* 143–151.

Miller, V., & Knapp, M. (1986). The *post nuntio* dilemma: Approaches to communicating with the dying. In M. McLaughlin (Ed.), *Communication Yearbook* (Vol. 9, pp. 723–738). Beverly Hills: Sage.

Mills, D. (1984). A model for stepfamily development. *Family Relations, 33,* 365–372.

Minuchin, S. (1974). *Families and family therapy.* Cambridge, MA: Harvard University Press.

Minuchin, S. (1984). *Family kaleidoscope.* Cambridge, MA: Harvard University Press.

Minuchin, S., Montalu, B., Rosman, B. L., & Schumer, R. (1967). *Families of the slums.* New York: Basic Books.

Mirowsky, J., & Ross, C. (1987). Belief in innate sex roles: Sex stratification versus interpersonal influence in marriage. *Journal of Marriage and the Family, 49,* 527–540.

Moen, P., & Dempster-McClain, D. (1987). Employed parents: Role strain, work time, and preferences for working less. *Journal of Marriage and the Family, 49,* 579–590.

Montagu, A. (1978). *Touching: The human significance of skin.* New York: Harper & Row.

Montgomery, B. M. (1981). The form and function of quality communication in marriage. *Family Relations, 30,* 21–30.

Mooney, L., & Brabant, S. (1988). Birthday cards, love, and communication. *Social Science Research, 72,* 106–109.

Murphy, W. (1984). Albert Hadley—The search for right clues. *Architectural Digest, 41,* 98–98J.

Napier, A., & Whitaker, C. (1978). *The family crucible.* New York: Harper & Row.

Nasar, J. (1989). Symbolic meanings of styles. *Environment and Behavior, 21,* 235–257.

Nash, J. (1973). The father in contemporary culture and current psychological literature. In M. E. Lasswell & T. E. Lasswell (Eds.), *Love, marriage, family: A developmental approach* (pp. 352–364). Glenview, IL: Scott, Foresman.

Nehls, N., & Morgenbesser, S. (1980). Joint custody: An exploration of issues. *Family Process, 19,* 117–124.

Neugarten, B. L. (1975). The future of the young-old. *The Gerontologist, 15,* 4–9.

Neugarten, B., & Weinstein, K.K. (1964). The changing American grandparent. *Journal of Marriage and the Family, 26,* 119–204.

Nichols, M. (1984). *Family therapy: Concepts and methods.* New York: Gardner Press.

Noller, P. (1987). Nonverbal communication in marriage. In D. Perlman & S. Duck (Eds.), *Intimate relationships: Development, dynamics and deterioration* (pp. 149–176). Newbury Park, CA: Sage.

Noone, R. (1989). Systems thinking and differentiation of self. *Center for Family Communication Consultation Review, 1*(1).

Norton, A., & Moorman, J. (1987). Current trends in marriage and divorce among American women. *Journal of Marriage and the Family, 49,* 3–14.

Norton, C. S. (1989). *Life metaphors.* Carbondale: Southern Illinois University Press.

Nussbaum, J. F. (1983). Relational closeness of elderly interaction: Implications for life satisfaction. *Western Journal of Speech Communication, 47,* 229–243.

Offer, D., & Sabshin, M. (1966). *Normality and the life cycle.* New York: Basic Books.

Olson, D., Fournier, D., & Druckman, J. (1987). Counselor's manual for PREPARE/ENRICH (rev. ed.). Minneapolis: PREPARE/ENRICH.

Olson, D. H., & McCubbin, H.I. & Associates. (1983). *Families: What makes them work.* Beverly Hills: Sage.

Olson, D., Sprenkle, D., & Russell, C. (1979). Circumplex model of marital and family systems: Cohesion and adaptability dimensions, family types, and clinical applications. *Family Process, 18,* 3–28.

O'Neill, N., & O'Neill, G. (1972). *Open marriage.* New York: Avon Books.

Osmond, H. (1970). Function as the basis of psychiatric ward design. In H. Proshansky, W. Ittleson & L. Rivlin (Eds.), *Environmental psychology* (pp. 560–568). New York: Holt, Rinehart & Winston.

Otto, H. (1975). Marriage and family enrichment programs in North America: Report and analysis. *Family Coordinator, 24,* 137–142.

Otto, L. B. (1988). America's youth: A changing profile. *Family Relations, 37,* 385–391.

Papernow, P. (1984). The stepfamily cycle: An experiential model of stepfamily development. *Family Relations, 33,* 335–363.

Papernow, P. (1987). Thickening the middle ground: Dilemma and vulnerabilities of remarried couples. *Psychotherapy, 24,* 630–639.

Papp, P. (1983). *The process of change.* New York: Guilford Press.

Parkes, C. M. (1972). *Bereavement.* New York: International Universities Press.

Pasley, K. (1987). Family boundary ambiguity: Perceptions of adult stepfamily members. In K. Pasley & M. Ihninger-Tallman(Eds.), *Remarriage and stepparenting: Current research* (pp. 206–224). New York: Guilford Press.

Pasley, K., & Gecas, V. (1984). Stresses and satisfactions of the parental role. *Personnel and Guidance Journal, 62,* 400–404.

Pasley, K., & Ihninger-Tallman, M. (Eds.). (1987). *Remarriage and stepparenting: Current research.* New York: Guilford Press.

Patterson, J. M., & McCubbin, H. I. (1984). Gender roles and coping. *Journal of Marriage and the Family, 46,* 95–104.

Pearce, W. B., & Sharp, S. M. (1973). Self-disclosing communication. *Journal of Communication, 23,* 409–425.

Pearson, J. (1989). *Communication in the family.* New York: Harper & Row.

Peck, J., & Manocherian, J. (1988). Divorce in the changing family life cycle. In B. Carter & M. McGoldrick (Eds.), *The changing family life cycle* (2nd. ed., pp. 335–369). New York: Gardner Press.

Perlmutter, M. (1988). Enchantment of siblings: Effects of birth order on family myth. In M. Kahn & K. Lewis (Eds.), *Siblings in therapy* (pp. 25–45). New York: W. W. Norton.

Peterson, J., & Zill, N. (1986). Marital disruption, parent-child relationships and behavior problems in children. *Journal of Marriage and the Family, 48,* 295–318.

[The] Philip Morris Family Survey. (1987). New York: Philip Morris Companies.

[The] Philip Morris Family Survey II: Child care. (1989). New York: Philip Morris Companies.

Pilkington, C., & Richardson, D. (1988). Perceptions of risk in intimacy. *Journal of Social and Personal Relationships, 5,* 503–508.

Pittman, J., & Lloyd, S. (1988). Quality of family life, social support, and stress. *Journal of Marriage and the Family, 50,* 53–67.

Pleck, J. (1985). *Working wives, working husbands.* Beverly Hills: Sage.

Powell, G. S., & Wampler, K. S. (1982). Marriage enrichment participants: Levels of marital satisfaction. *Family Relations, 31,* 389–394.

Rait, D. (1988). Seeing results. *Family Therapy Networker, 12,* 52–56.

Raschke, H. J., & Raschke, V. J. (1979). Family conflict and children's self-concepts: A comparison of intact and single-parent families. *Journal of Marriage and the Family, 41,* 367–374.

Raush, H. L., Barry, W. A., Hertel, R. K., & Swain, M. A. (1974). *Communication conflict and marriage.* San Francisco: Jossey-Bass.

Raven, B., Centers, C., & Rodriges, A. (1975). The bases of conjugal power. In R. E. Cromwell & D. H. Olson (Eds.), *Power in families* (pp. 217–234). New York: John Wiley & Sons.

Rawlins, W. K. (1989). Rehearsing the margins of adulthood: The communication management of adolescent friendships. In J. Nussbaum (Ed.), *Life-span communication: Normative processes* (pp. 137–154). Hillsdale, NJ: Lawrence Erlbaum.

Reilly, T., Entwisle, D., & Doering, S. (1987). Socialization into parenthood: A longitudinal study of the development of self-evaluation. *Journal of Marriage and the Family, 49,* 295–309.

Reiss, D. (1981). *The family's construction of reality.* Cambridge, MA: Harvard University Press.

Reiss, D., & Oliveri, M. E. (1980). Family paradigm and family coping: A proposal for linking the family's intrinsic adaptive capacities to its responses to stress. *Family Relations, 29,* 431–444.

Remer, R. (1984). The effects of interpersonal confrontation on males. *American Mental Health Counselors Association Journal, 6,* 81–90.

Renzetti, C. (1989). Building a second closet: Third party responses to victims of lesbian partner abuse. *Family Relations, 38,* 157–163.

Rexcoat, C., & Shehan, C. (1987). The family life cycle and spouses' time in housework. *Journal of Marriage and the Family, 49,* 737–750.

Richardson, R., Abramowitz, R., Asp, C., & Petersen, A. (1986). Parent-child relationships in early adolescence: Effects of family structure. *Journal of Marriage and the Family, 48,* 805–811.

Ridley, C. A., Peterman, D. J., & Avery, A. W. (1978). Cohabitation: Does it make for a better marriage? *Family Coordinator, 27,* 129–136.

Risman, B., & Park, K. (1988). Just the two of us: Parent-child relationships in single-parent homes. *Journal of Marriage and the Family, 50,* 1049–1062.

Ritter, E. (1979). Social perspective-taking ability, cognitive complexity and listener-adopted communication in early and late adolescence. *Communication Monographs, 46,* 42–50.

Rodgers, R. (1987). Postmarital reorganization of family relationships. In D. Perlman & S. Duck (Eds.), *Intimate relationships: Development, dynamics and deterioration* (pp. 239–268). Newbury Park, CA: Sage.

Rogers, C. R. (1972). *Becoming partners: Marriage and its alternatives.* New York: Delta Books.

Rogers, E. (1984, September). *Potentials in family communication research.* Paper presented at the SCA/Northwestern University Research Conference on Family Communication.

Rogers-Millar, L. E., & Miller, F. E. (1979). Domineeringness and dominance: A transactional view. *Human Communication Research, 5,* 238–246.

Rogler, S., & Procidano, M. (1986). The effect of social networks on marital roles: A test of a Bott hypothesis in an intergenerational context. *Journal of Marriage and the Family, 48,* 714–724.

Rollins, B., & Bahr, S.J. (1976). A theory of power relationships in marriage. *Journal of Marriage and the Family, 38,* 619–627.

Roloff, M. (1987). Communication conflict. In C. Berger & S. Chaffee (Eds.), *Handbook of communication science* (pp. 484–534). Beverly Hills: Sage.

Rosenberg, E. (1988). Stepsiblings in therapy. In M. Kahn & K. Lewis (Eds.), *Siblings in therapy* (pp. 209–227). New York: W. W. Norton.

Rosenblatt, P. C., Titus, S. L., & Cunningham, M. R. (1979). Disrespect, tension, and togetherness-apartness in marriage. *Journal of Marital and Family Therapy, 5,* 47–54.

Rosenfeld, R. (1986). U.S. farm women: Their participation in farm work and decision making. *Work and Occupations, 13,* 179–202.

Rotunno, M., & McGoldrick, M. (1982). Italian families. In M. McGoldrick, J. Giordano & J. Pearce (Eds.), *Ethnicity and family therapy* (pp. 340–363). New York: Guilford Press.

Rubin, J. Z., & Brown, B. R. (1975). *The social psychology of bargaining and negotiation.* New York: Academic Press.

Rubin, L. (1979). *Women of a certain age: The midlife search for self.* New York: Harper & Row.

Russell, C. S. (1979). Circumplex model of marital and family systems: III. Empirical evaluation with families. *Family Process, 18,* 29–45.

Ryan, K., & Ryan, M. (1982). *Making a marriage.* New York: St. Martin's Press.

Saegert, S. (1985). The role of housing in the experience of dwelling. In I. Altman & C. Werner (Eds.), *Home environments: Human behavior and environment* (Vol. 8, pp. 287–309). New York: Plenum Press.

Safilios-Rothschild, C. (1970). The study of family power structure: 1960–1969. *Journal of Marriage and the Family, 32,* 539–552.

Santi, L. (1987). Change in the structure and size of American households: 1970–1985. *Journal of Marriage and the Family, 49,* 833–837.

Satir, V. (1967). *Conjoint family therapy.* Palo Alto, CA: Science & Behavior Books.

Satir, V. (1972). *Peoplemaking.* Palo Alto, CA: Science & Behavior Books.

Satir, V. (1988). *The new peoplemaking.* Mountain View CA: Science and Behavior Books.

Sawin, D. B., & Parke, R. D. (1979). Fathers' affectionate stimulation and caregiving behaviors with newborn infants. *Family Coordinator, 28,* 509–519.

Sawin, M. (1979). *Family enrichment with family clusters.* Valley Forge, PA: Judson Press.

Scanzoni, J. (1972). *Sexual bargaining.* Englewood Cliffs, NJ: Prentice-Hall.

Scanzoni, J., & Polonko, K. (1980). A conceptual approach to explicit marital negotiation. *Journal of Marriage and the Family, 42,* 31–44.

Scanzoni, J., & Szinovacz, M. (1980). *Family decision making: A developmental sex role model.* Beverly Hills: Sage.

Schaap, C., Buunke, B., & Kenkstra, A. (1987). Marital conflict resolution. In P. Noller & M. A. Fitzpatrick (Eds.), *Perspectives on marital interaction* (pp. 203–244). Philadelphia: Multilingual Matters.

Schaefer, R. B., & Keith, P. M. (1981). Equity in marital roles across the family life cycle. *Journal of Marriage and the Family, 43,* 359–367.

Schaeffer, N. C. (1989). The frequency and intensity of parental conflict: Choosing response dimensions. *Journal of Marriage and the Family, 51,* 759–766.

Scheflen, A. (1971). Living space in an urban ghetto. *Family Process, 10,* 429–449.

Scheiner, L. C., Musetto, A. P., & Cordier, D. M. (1982). Custody and visitation counseling: A report of an innovative program. *Family Relations, 31,* 99–108.

Schrag, K. (1984). Relationship therapy with same-gender couples. *Family Relations, 33,* 283–291.

Schumm, W., Barnes, H., Bollman, S., Jurick, A., & Bugaighis, M. (1987). Self-disclosure and marital satisfaction revisited. *Family Relations, 34,* 241–247.

Schwartzman, J. (1985). Macrosystemic approaches to family therapy: An overview. In J. Schwartzman (Ed.), *Families and other systems* (pp. 1–26). New York: Guilford Press.

Scoresby, A. L. (1977). *The marriage dialogue.* Reading, MA: Addison-Wesley.

Scott, J. (1984). Comfort and seating distance in living rooms: The relationship of interactants and topic of conversation. *Environment and Behavior, 16,* 35–54.

Seccombe, K. (1986). The effects of occupational conditions upon the division of household labor: In application of Kohn's theory. *Journal of Marriage and the Family, 48,* 839–848.

Seligman, M. (1988). Psychotherapy with siblings of disabled children. In M. Kahn & L. Lewis (Eds.), *Siblings in therapy: Life span and clinical issues* (pp. 167–189). New York: W. W. Norton.

Shamir, B. (1986). Unemployment and household division of labor. *Journal of Marriage and the Family*, 48, 195–206.

Sheehan, N., & Nuttall, P. (1988). Conflict, emotion, and personal strain among family caregivers. *Family Relations*, 37, 92–98.

Shepard, W. (1980). Mothers and fathers, sons and daughters: Perceptions of young adults. *Sex Roles*, 6, 421–433.

Shimanoff, S. B. (1980). *Communication rules: Theory and research*, Newbury Park, CA: Sage.

Shimanoff, S. B. (1983). The role of gender in linguistic references to emotive states. *Communication Quarterly*, 30, 174–177.

Shon, S., & Davis, J. (1983). Asian families. In M. McGoldrick, J. Giordano & J. Pearce (Eds.), *Ethnicity and family therapy* (pp. 208–228). New York: Guilford Press.

Sieburg, E. (1973). *Interpersonal confirmation: A paradigm for conceptualization and measurement.* Paper presented at International Communication Association, Montreal, Quebec. ERIC document No. ED 098 634 1975.

Sillars, A. L., Pike, G., Jones, T., & Redmon, K. (1983). Communication and conflict in marriage. In R. Bostrom (Ed.), *Communication yearbook* (Vol. 7, pp. 414–429). Beverly Hills: Sage.

Sillars, A., Weisberg, J., Burggraf, C., & Wilson, E. (1987). Content themes in marital conversations. *Human Communication Research*, 13, 495–528.

Sillars, A., & Wilmot, W. (1989). Marital communication across the life span. In J. Nussbaum (Ed.), *Life-span communication: Narrative processes* (pp. 225–254). Hillsdale, NJ: Lawrence Erlbaum.

Silverberg, R. A. (1985). Men confronting death: Management versus self-determination. *Clinical Social Work Journal*, 13, 157–169.

Silverberg, S., & Steinberg, L. (1987). Adolescent autonomy, parent-adolescent conflict and parental well-being. *Journal of Youth and Adolescence*, 16, 293–312.

Simon, R. (1982). Reflections on the one-way mirror: An interview with Jay Haley, Part II. *Family Therapy Networker*, 6(6), 32–36.

Slevin, K. F., & Balswick, J. (1980). Children's perceptions of parental expressiveness. *Sex Roles*, 6, 293–299.

Spanier, G. B., & Lewis, R. A. (1980). Marital quality: A review of the seventies. *Journal of Marriage and the Family*, 42, 825–839.

Spitzack, C., & Carter, K. (1987). Women in communication studies: A typology for revision. *Quarterly Journal of Speech*, 73(4), 401–423.

Spitze, G. (1988). Women's employment and family relations. *Journal of Marriage and the Family*, 50, 595–618.

Spooner, S. (1982). Intimacy in adults: A developmental model for counselors and helpers. *Personnel and Guidance Journal*, 60, 168–170.

Sporakowski, M. (1988). A therapist's views on the consequences of change for the contemporary family. *Family Relations*, 37, 373–378.

Sporakowski, M. J., & Hughston, G. (1978). Prescriptions for happy marriage: Adjustments and satisfactions of couples married 50 or more years. *The Family Coordinator*, 27, 321–328.

Stachowiak, J. (1975). Functional and dysfunctional families. In V. Satir, J. Stachowiak & H. A. Taschman (Eds.), *Helping families to change*. New York: Jason Aronson.

Steffensmeier, R. H. (1982). A role model of the transition to parenthood. *Journal of Marriage and the Family*, 44, 319–334.

Steinberg, L., & Silverberg, S. (1987). Influences on marital satisfaction during the middle stages of the family life cycle. *Journal of Marriage and the Family*, 49, 751–761.

Steinglass, P. (1979). The home observation assessment method (HOAM): Real-time naturalistic observation of families in their homes. *Family Process*, 18, 337–354.

Steinmetz, S. K. (1977). The use of force for resolving family conflict: The training ground for abuse. *Family Coordinator*, 26, 19–26.

Steinor, C. (1978, March). Problems of power. Lecture delivered at the National Group Leaders Conference, Chicago.

Stephen, T. (1984). A symbolic exchange framework for the development of intimate relationships. *Human Relations*, 37, 393–408.

Stephen, T. (1986). Communication and interdependence in geographically separated relationships. *Human Communication Research*, 13, 191–210.

Stephen, T., & Enholm, D. (1987). On linguistic and social forms: Correspondences between metaphoric and intimate relationships. *Western Journal of Speech Communication*, 51, 329–344.

Stevens, J. H., Jr. (1984). Child development knowledge and parenting skills. *Family Relations*, 33, 237–244.

Stinnett, N., & DeFrain. (1985). *Secrets of strong families*. Boston: Little, Brown.

Stinnett, N., Walters, J., & Kay, E. (1984). *Relationships in marriage and the family* (2nd ed.). New York: Macmillan.

Straus, M. A. (1974). Leveling, civility, and violence in the family. *Journal of Marriage and the Family, 36*, 13–29.

Straus, M. A. (1979). Measuring intrafamily conflict and violence: The conflict tactics (C. T.) scales. *Journal of Marriage and the Family, 41*, 75–88.

Stuart, R., & Jacobson, B. (1985). *Second marriage.* New York: W. W. Norton.

Suitor, J., & Pillemer, K. (1985, November). The presence of adult children: A source of stress for elderly couples' marriages? *Journal of Marriage and the Family, 49*, 717–725.

Tardy, C., Hosman, L., & Bradac, J. (1981). Disclosing self to friends and family: A re-examining of initial questions. *Communication Quarterly, 29*, 263–268.

Terkelsen, K. G. (1980). Toward a theory of the family life cycle. In E. Carter and M. McGoldrick (Eds.), *The family life cycle: A framework for family therapy,* (pp. 21–52). New York: Gardner Press.

Thirty-one studies published on couple communication. (March, 1989). *Relationship Building, 3*(1), 1–5.

Thomas, J. (1977). *Marital communication and decision making: Analysis, assessment, and change.* New York: The Free Press.

Thompson, T. (1989). Communication and dying: The end of the life-span. In J. Nussbaum (Ed.), *Life-span communication: Normative processes* (pp. 339–359). Hillsdale, NJ: Lawrence Erlbaum.

Thompson, T., & Nussbaum, J. (1988). Interpersonal Communication: Intimate relationships and aging. In C. W. Carmichael, C. H. Botan & R. Hawkins (Eds.), *Human communication and the aging process* (pp. 95–110). Prospect Heights, IL: Waveland Press.

Toffler, A. (1971). *Future shock.* New York: Bantam Books.

Toman, W. T. (1976). *Family constellations* (3rd ed.). New York: Springer.

Toman, W. T. (1988). Basics of family structure and sibling position. In M. Kahn & K. Lewis (Eds.), *Siblings in therapy: Life span and clinical issues* (pp. 46–66). New York: W. W. Norton.

Tomm, K. (1983). The old hat doesn't fit. *Family Therapy Networker, 7*, 39–41.

Troll, L. E. (1975). *Early and middle adulthood.* Monterey, CA: Brooks-Cole.

Troll, L. E., Miller, S., & Atchley, R. (1979). *Families in later life.* Belmont, CA: Wadsworth.

Trotter, R. (1987). Project day care. *Psychology Today,* pp. 32–38.

True, M. (1982). *Homemade social justice: Teaching peace and justice in the house.* Mystic, CT: Twenty-Third Publications.

Tschann. J. (1988). Self-disclosure in adult friendship: Gender and marital status differences. *Journal of Social and Personal Relationships, 5*, 65–81.

Turk, J. L., & Bell, N. W. (1972). Measuring power in families. *Journal of Marriage and the Family, 34*, 215–222.

Turnbull, S. K., & Turnbull, J. M. (1983). To dream the impossible dream: An agenda for discussion with stepparents. *Family Relations, 32*, 277–230.

Turner, R. H. (1970). Conflict and harmony. *Family Interaction.* New York: John Wiley & Sons. pp. 135–163. See also "Decision Making Process," pp. 97–116; "Determinants of dominance," pp. 117–135.

Vaillant, G. (1977). *Adaptation to life.* Boston: Little, Brown.

Ventura, J. (1987). The stresses of parenthood reexamined. *Family Relations, 36*, 26–29.

Verwoerdt, A. (1967). Comments on communication with the fatally ill. *Omega, 2*, 10–11.

Villard, K., & Whipple, L. (1976). *Beginnings in relational communication.* New York: John Wiley and Sons.

Visher, E., & Visher, J. (1979). *Stepfamilies: A guide to working with stepparents and stepchildren.* New York: Brunner/Mazel.

Visher, J., & Visher, E. (1982). Stepfamilies and stepparenting. In F. Walsh (Ed.), *Normal family processes.* (pp. 331–353). New York: Guildford Press.

Visher, E., & Visher, J. (1988). *Old loyalties, new ties: Therapeutic strategies and stepfamilies.* New York: Brunner/Mazel.

Vuchinich, S. (1987). Starting and stopping spontaneous family conflicts. *Journal of Marriage and the Family, 49*, 591–601.

Wackman, D. (1978, November). *Communication training in marriage and family living.* Paper presented at the Speech Communication Association Convention, Minneapolis.

Waite, L. (1987). Nest-leaving patterns and the transition to marriage for young men and women. *Journal of Marriage and the Family, 49*, 507–516.

Wallerstein, J., & Blakeslee, S. (1989). *Second chances.* New York: Ticknor & Fields.

Wallerstein, J., & Kelly, J. (1980). *Surviving the breakup.* New York: Basic Books.

Walsh, F. (1982). *Normal family processes.* New York: Guilford Press.

Walsh, F. (1985). Social change, disequilibrium, and adaptation in developing countries: A Moroccan example. In J. Schwartzman (Ed.), *Families and other systems* (pp. 244–259). New York: Guilford Press.

Walsh, F. (1989). The family in later life. In B. Carter & M. McGoldrick (Eds.), *The changing family life cycle: A framework for family therapy* (2nd ed., pp. 311–332). New York: Gardner Press.

Walsh, F., & Scheinkman, M. (1989). (Fe)male: The hidden gender dimension in models of family therapy. In M. McGoldrick, C. Anderson & F. Walsh (Eds.), *Women in families* (pp. 16–41). New York: W. W. Norton.

Wampler, K. S., & Sprenkle, D. H. (1980). The Minnesota couple communication program. *Journal of Marriage and the Family, 42,* 577–584.

Waring, E., Tillman, M., Frelick, L., Russell, L., & Weisz, G. (1980). Concepts of intimacy in the general population. *Journal of Nervous and Mental Disease, 168,* 471–474.

Wass, H., & Myers, J. E. (1982). Psychosocial aspects of death among the elderly: A review of the literature. *The Personnel and Guidance Journal, 60,* 131–145.

Waterman, J. (1979). Family patterns of self-disclosure. In G. Chelune and Associates (Eds.), *Self-disclosure* (pp. 225–242). San Francisco: Jossey-Bass.

Watson, J. J., & Remer, R. (1984). The effects of interpersonal confrontation on females. *Personnel and Guidance Journal, 62,* 607–611.

Watson, R. E. (1983). Premarital cohabitation vs. traditional courtship: Their effects on subsequent marital adjustment. *Family Relations, 32,* 139–148.

Wattleton, F. (1986). *How to talk with your child about sexuality.* New York: Doubleday.

Watzlawick, P., Beavin, J., & Jackson, D. D. (1967). *Pragmatics of human communication.* New York: W. W. Norton.

Webster-Stratton, C. (1989). The relationship of marital support, conflict, and divorce to parent perceptions, behaviors, and childhood conduct problems. *Journal of Marriage and the Family, 51,* 417–430.

Weiss, R. L. (1984). Cognitive and strategic intervention in behavioral marital therapy. In K. Hohlweg & N. S. Jacobson (Eds.), *Marital interaction: Analysis and modification* (pp. 337–355). New York: Guilford Press.

Wells, R., & Denzen, A. (1978). The results of family therapy revisited: The nonbehavioral methods. *Family Process, 17,* 251–274.

Werner, C. (1987). Home interiors: A time and place for interpersonal relationships. *Environment and Behavior, 19,* 169–179.

West, J., Zarski, J., & Harvil, R. (1988). The influence of the family triangle on intimacy. *American Mental Health Counselors Association Journal, (10)* 166–174.

Westin, A. (1967). *Privacy and freedom.* New York: Atheneum.

White, B. (1989). Gender differences in marital communication patterns. *Family Process, 28,* 89–106.

White, M., & Tsui, A. (1986). A panel study of family-level structural change. *Journal of Marriage and the Family, 48,* 435–459.

Whitehead, E.E., & Whitehead, J. (1981). *Marrying well: Possibilities in Christian marriage today.* New York: Doubleday.

Wieting, S. G., & McLaren, A. (1975). Power in various family structures. In R. E. Cromwell & D. H. Olson (Eds.), *Power in families* (pp. 95–116). New York: John Wiley & Sons.

Wilcoson, S. (1985). Healthy family functioning: The other side of family pathology. *Journal of Counseling and Development, 63,* 351–354.

Wilkinson, C. (1989). Family first. *Emphasis, 24,* 1–2.

Wilkinson, C. (1990, September). *Family communication: Developing the marital partnership.* Speech presented at the Communicating with Children Conference, Governors State University, University Park, IL.

Wilmot, W. W. (1987). *Dyadic communication* (3rd ed.). New York: Random House.

Wilmot, J., & Wilmot, W. (1978). *Interpersonal conflict.* Dubuque, IA: William C. Brown.

Winter, W. D., Ferreira, A. J., Bowers, N. (1973). Decision-making in married and unrelated couples. *Family Process, 12,* 83–94.

Witteman, H., & Fitzpatrick, M. A. (1986). A social scientific view of Marriage Encounter. *Journal of Clinical and Social Psychology, 4,* 513–522.

Wood, B. S. (1981). *Children and communication: Verbal and nonverbal language development* (2nd ed.). Englewood Cliffs, NJ: Prentice-Hall.

Wood B., & Talmon, M. (1983). Family boundaries in transition: A search for alternatives. *Family Process, 22,* 347–357.

Worobey, J. (1989). Mother-infant interaction: *Proto* communication in the developing dyad. In J. Nussbaum (Ed.), *Life-Span communication: Normative process* (pp. 7–25). Hillsdale, NJ: Lawrence Erlbaum.

Worthington, E., Jr., Buston, G., & Hammonds, T. (1989). A component analysis of marriage enrichment: Information and treatment modality. *Journal of Counseling and Development, 67,* 555–560.

Yelsma, P. (1984). Functional conflict management in effective marital adjustment. *Communication Quarterly, 32,* 56–62.

Yelsma, P. (1986). Marriage vs. cohabitation: Couples communication practices and satisfaction. *Journal of Communication, 36,* 94–107.

Yerby, J., & Buerkel-Rothfuss, N. L. (1982, November). *Communication patterns, contradictions, and family functions.* Paper presented at the Speech Communication Association Convention, Louisville.

Yerby, J., & Buerkel-Rothfuss, N., Bochner, A. P. (1990). *Understanding family communication.* Scottsdale, AZ: Gorsuch Scarisbrick.

Youniss, J., & Smollar, J. (1985). *Adolescent relations with mothers, fathers and friends.* Chicago: University of Chicago Press.

Zacks, E., Green, R., & Marrow, J. (1988). Comparing lesbian and heterosexual couples on the circumplex model: An initial investigation. In *Family Process, 27,* 471–484.

Zeitlin, S., Williamson, G., & Rosenblatt, W. (1987). The coping with stress model: A counseling approach for families with a handicapped child. *Journal of Counseling and Development, 65,* 443–446.

TEXT CREDITS

pp. 10, 11. Froma Walsh, NORMAL FAMILY PROCESSES. New York, Guilford Publications, 1982, pp. 5–6.

pp. 19, 39. From "Circumplex Model of Marital and Family Systems: 1. Cohesion and Adaptability Dimensions, Family Types, and Clinical Application" by David H. Olson, Douglas H. Sprenkle, and Candyce Russell in *Family Process*, Vol. 18, No. 1, March 1979. © 1979 by Jossey-Bass, Inc., Publishers. Reprinted by permission.

pp. 20, 46, 129, 131, 221–222, 287. From *Inside the Family* by David Kantor and William Lehr. Copyright © 1975 by Jossey-Bass, Inc., Publishers. Reprinted by permission.

pp. 24, 50, 51. Excerpts from FAMILY WORLDS by Robert D. Hess and Gerald Handel. Copyright © 1959 by The University of Chicago. Reprinted by permission.

p. 35. From "Systems Thinking and Differentiation of Self" by Robert J. Noone, CENTER FOR FAMILY CONSULTATION REVIEW, 1989. Reprinted by permission of the author.

pp. 36, 37. Harriet G. Lerner, THE DANCE OF INTIMACY. New York: Harper & Row, Publishers, Inc., 1989.

p. 60. Jeanette Kramer, FAMILY INTERFACES: TRANSGENERATIONAL PATTERNS. New York: Brunner/Mazel, 1985.

pp. 81–82. From *Social Penetration* by Irwin Altman and Dalmus Taylor. Copyright © 1973 by Holt, Rinehart and Winston, Inc. Reprinted by permission of the authors.

p. 84. From INTERPERSONAL COMMUNICATION AND HUMAN RELATIONSHIPS by Mark L. Knapp. Copyright © 1984 by Allyn & Bacon. Reprinted by permission.

p. 89. From THEORIES OF HUMAN COMMUNICATION, Third Edition, by Stephen W. Littlejohn. © 1989 by Wadsworth, Inc. This material is adapted from Shirley J. Gilbert, "Empirical and Theoretical Extensions of Self-Disclosure," in EXPLORATIONS IN INTERPERSONAL COMMUNICATION, ed. Gerald R. Miller. Reprinted by permission of Wadsworth, Inc.

p. 102. From THE MARRIAGE DIALOGUE by Lyn Scoresby. Copyright © 1977 McGraw-Hill, Inc. Reprinted by permission.

p. 109. From "Communication with Children: Toward a Healthy Construction of Communication Roles" by Fern Johnson. Paper presented at the Central States Speech Association Conference, April 14, 1978, Chicago, Illinois. Reprinted by permission.

p. 115. "Psychological Dimensions of the Female and Male Roles" by L. B. Feldman from NORMAL FAMILY PROCESSES edited by Froma Walsh. Copyright © 1982 by The Guilford Press, New York. Reprinted by permission.

p. 135. From "Family Power: The Assessment of a Decade of Theory and Research, 1970–1979" by Gerald W. McDonald, JOURNAL OF MARRIAGE AND THE FAMILY, November 1980. Copyright © 1980 by the National Council on Family Relations, 3989 Central Ave. N.E., Suite #550, Minneapolis, MN 55421. Reprinted by permission.

p. 156. From "A Conceptual Approach to Explicit Marital Negotiation" by John Scanzoni and Karen Polonko, JOURNAL OF MARRIAGE AND THE FAMILY, February 1980. Copyright © 1980 by the National Council on Family Relations, 3989 Central Ave. N.E., Suite #550, Minneapolis, MN 55421. Reprinted by permission.

p. 176. "Conflict Styles" from INTERPERSONAL CONFLICT, Second Edition by Joyce Hocker-Wilmot and William W. Wilmot. Copyright © 1978, 1985 by Wm. C. Brown Publishers, Dubuque, Iowa. All rights reserved. Reprinted by permission.

p. 185. From "Marital Conflict and Marital Intimacy" by Larry B. Feldman, *Family Process*, Vol. 18, March 1979, p. 70. © 1979 by Family Process, Inc. Reprinted by permission.

p. 185. From "Sex Roles and Family Dynamics" by L. B. Feldman from NORMAL FAMILY PROCESS edited by Froma Walsh, p. 355. Reprinted by permission of Guilford Publications.

pp. 203, 206, 229. From THE CHANGING FAMILY LIFE CYCLE: A FRAMEWORK FOR FAMILY THERAPY, Second Edition by Betty Carter and Monica McGoldrick. Copyright © 1989 by Allyn and Bacon. Reprinted by permission.

p. 235. "The Double ABCX Model" from SOCIAL STRESS AND THE FAMILY by McCubbin, et al. Copyright © 1983 by The Haworth Press, Inc. Reprinted by permission.

p. 261. From "The Stepfamily Cycle: An Experiential Model of Step Family Development" by Patricia Papernow, FAMILY RELATIONS, 1984, Vol. 33;2. Copyright 1984 by the National Council on Family Relations, 3989 Central Ave., N.E., Suite #550, Minneapolis, MN 55421. Reprinted by permission.

p. 270 Excerpt from BECOMING PARTNERS by Carl R. Rogers. Copyright 1972 by Carl R. Rogers. Used by permission of Dell Books, a division of Bantam, Doubleday, Dell Publishing Group, Inc.

p. 282. From "Living Space in an Urban Ghetto" by Albert E. Scheflen, M.D. in *Family Process*, Vol. 10, © 1971 by Family Process, Inc. Reprinted by permission.

pp. 299–300. From FAMILIES by Jane Howard. Copyright © 1978 by Jane Howard. Reprinted by permission of Simon & Schuster, Inc.

p. 300. From SECOND MARRIAGE by Richard B. Stuart & Barbara Johnson, 1985. Reprinted by permission of W. W. Norton & Company, Inc.

p. 301. From STRENGTHENING YOUR STEPFAMILY by E. Einstein and L. Albert. Copyright © 1986 by American Guidance Service, Inc., Circle Pines, MN 55014. Reprinted by permission.

p. 307. From "Communication Training in Marriage and Family Living" by Daniel B. Wackman, Paper presented at the 64th annual meeting of the Speech Communica- tion Association, Minneapolis, Minnesota, November 1978. Reprinted by permission.

PHOTO CREDITS

Pages **4, 5, 15,** Jean-Claude LeJeune; **35(l),** Myrleen Ferguson/Photo Edit; **35(r),** Richard Stromberg; **52(l),** Jim Bradshaw; **74(l),** Jean-Claude LeJeune; **108,** Jim Bradshaw; **116,** Jean-Claude LeJeune; **183(l),** Jim Bradshaw; **204,** COMSTOCK, INC.: **209, 244(l),** Jean-Claude LeJeune; **244(r),** Thomas E. Medcalf; **283(l),** Bruce Davidson/Magnum Photos.

Author Index

Subject Index

Abandonment, fear of, 103
Abuse, physical, 193
  power and, 144
  in same-sex couples, 267
Acceptance, confirmation and, 87–88
Acceptance stage of crisis, 239
Access dimensions, 129
Access rights, 78
Accommodation, 157–58, 176
Achievement, 120
Active conflict stage, 179
Adaptability (adaptation), 296
  of adolescents, 228
  bonadaptation, 236
  capacity for, 205, 206
  as characteristic of human systems, 42
  communication of affection and, 80
  coping and, 236
  decision-making behavior and, 155
  networks and, 67
  in relationships, 54
  self-disclosure and, 96
  verbal and nonverbal negotiation related to, 210
Adaptability/cohesion axes, 22–23, 205
Adolescents
  autonomy of, 220
  cohesion and adaptability of, 228
  experiences of, 219–22
  family conflict and, 189
  functioning of, 23, 24, 296
  identification with parent's power and, 147
  self-esteem of, 219–20
  sexuality and, 221
  tasks of, 203, 220
Affect
  defined, **129**
  displays of, 77
Affection
  communication of, 80
  displays of, 77–78
  sharing of currencies for, 79
Affective decisions, 154
Affective exchange, in relationship
  development, 82–83

Affective resources, power derived from,
  136–37
Aged, the. *See* Elderly, the
Agenda building, 178
Aggression, intimacy and, 77
Agreement, spontaneous, 170
All-channel network, 70
Ambiguity, 235
Androgyny, 117
Anger, 238
Apologizers, 184
Assertiveness, power and, 139
Assimilation stage of stepfamily development,
  259
Attachment, 210
Authority
  designated, 161–62
  spousal, 143–44
  in stepfamilies, 263
Autonomic power structure, 144
Autonomy, 210
  of teenagers, 220
Average family functioning, 10–11
Avoidance, 176

Bargaining, 238
Behavior(s)
  acceptable, 62
  background and, 113
  family systems and, 36
  negative, 184
  nonverbal, 13, 51
  sequences, 40–41
Beliefs, coping and, 237
Biosocial issues, 29, 30. *See also* Gender; Sexual
  identity
Birth-order effect, 217
Blaming, 238
Blended families, 4, 66–67
Bonadaptation, 236
Bonding, 84
Boundaries, 27–29
  clearing of, 162
  coping and, 236

Dying persons, communication with, 242–43
Dysfunctional families, 296

Economic factors
  economic currencies, 75–76, 80
  impact on family life, 8–9
  power and, 136
  single-parent family and, 254
Ecosystem, family, 42
Education, 157, 303
Efficiency, defined, **53**
Elderly, the. *See also* Older couples
  elder function and, 227
  health of, 226
  housing for, 282
  interpersonal communication among, 226–27
Emotion. *See* Affect
Emotionally divorced couples, 128
Emotional support, as function of family, 119
Empathy
  decision making and, 168
  as function of family, 119
Empty nest stage, 189, 222
Engagement, 208–10
Enmeshed and disengaged families, 20, 191
Environmental context, 274–92. *See also* Home;
      Housekeeping; *and other specific topics*
  factors of, 276–80
    space, 276–78
    time, 278–80
  family relationships affected by, 274–75
  management of, 198
  stress and, 233
  as system element, 34
Equifinality, 43
Ethnicity, 9–10
  communication rules and, 59, 66
  coping and, 233
  roles and, 111, 123
  self-disclosure and, 90
Evaluation, defined, **54**
Expectations, reality of, 113
Experiences, family's community of, 215
Expertise, power and, 137
Exploratory affective exchange, in relationship
      development, 82
Exposure, fear of, 102
Expressiveness, 56
Extended family, 4–5
  power alliances in, 147–48
  stepfamily and, 259
Extended networks, 71

Facial expressions, 77
Fair fighting, 197–98
Family(-ies). *See also specific topics*
  categories of, 3–6
  as communication system, 2
  definitional issues concerning, 2–11
    current status, 7–11
    family systems, 6–7

healthy, 2–3
  identification with, 219
  social context dimensions of, 155–56
  typologies, 129–32
    closed, 130, 131
    open, 130, 131
    random, 130, 131
Family cluster, 306
Family context. *See* Environmental context
Family enrichment programs, 307, 312–13
Family fit
  complementary, 289, 290
  isomorphic, 289, 290
  nonfit category, 289–90
  spatial, 290–91
  temporal, 290–91
Family forms, 252–73. *See also specific forms*
  conflict patterns and, 187–88
  homosexual partners and parents, 265–68
  single-parent families, 253–56
  stepfamily systems, 256–65
Family functioning, perspectives on, 11
Family functions
  affective, 114
  instrumental, 114
  mixed, 114
  primary, 19–24
    adaptability, 21–24
    cohesion, 19–21
  supporting, 24–30
    biosocial issues and, 29–30
    boundaries and, 27–29
    family image and, 24–25
    family themes and, 25–27
Family life cycle. *See* family stages
Family-of-origin, 6
  death and, 244
  influences of, 55–60
    defined, **56**
    ethnicity and, 58–60
    multigenerational transmissions, 56–58
  power processes and, 146
  violent, 193–94
Family stages, 205–29
  the couple, 208–11
  families in later life, 226–28
  families with adolescents, 219–22
  families with young children, 211–19
  launching children and moving on, 222–26
  leaving home, 207
  transitions between, 228–29
Family structure. *See also* Family systems
  defined, **43**
Family systems, 33–48. *See also* Human systems
  assumptions in, 51
  attributes of, 34
  momism and, 125
  perspective, 46–48
  power in, 134–49
    bases of, 136–38
    children and, 146–49

Interpersonal relationships
  child's dealing with, 215
  meaning and, 50
  acceptable levels of, 74–75
  barriers to, 102–4
  commitment of effort and, 104–5
  communication foundation of, 85–102
    confirmation, 85–88
    relationship development and, 80–85
    self-disclosure, 88–96
    sexuality, 96–102
  defined, **73–74**
  development of, 73–80
    relational currencies and, 75–80
  fear of, 102
  low intensity, 103
  marital, 74
  physical, 77
  undeveloped, 103
Intimacy-conflict cycle, 185
Intimate currencies, 75
Intimate space, 276–77
Intimation sequences, 94
Isomorphic fit, 289, 290

Joint physical custody, 271–72
Judication, decision making by, 163
Justice, 171

Kinship maintenance, role function in,
    120–21
Kinship power, 136

Language
  meanings and, 17
  powerless, 139
Last one out, 227
Leadership, child's, 165–66
Leaving home, 207
  delay in, 223
  events in, 222–26
Lesbians. *See* Homosexuals
Life expectancy, 8
Liking, 95
Listening, 76
  in constructive conflict, 196–97
  empathic, 76, 196

Maintenance and management, providing for,
    120–23
Maladaptation, 236
Marital boundary, sexuality and, 98
Marital checkups, 304
Marital enrichment programs, 307–11
  appraisal of, 309–11
Marital satisfaction. *See also* Satisfaction
  cohabiting and, 269
  power and, 145–46
  self-disclosure and, 91
Marital status, self-disclosure and, 90
Marital system, 51

Marriage. *See also specific topics*
  companionship, 128
  dissatisfaction in, 145–46
  first, 7
  initial stage of, 210–11
  institutional, 128
  predictable tasks in, 210
  remarriage, 8
Marriage Encounter program, 308, 310, 312
Mealtime, 287
Meaning(s), 49–71, 129
  acquisition of, 129
  communication patterns influencing, 55–71
    communication networks, 67–71
    communication rules, 60–67
    family-of-origin influences, 55–60
  coordinated, 51–52
  culture and, 17
  development of, 16–18, 31
  in relationships, 49–55
    creation of, 51–52
    in highly developed relationships, 52–55
  shared, 16–17, 18
  worldview and, 52
Meetings, family, 304–5
Membership, stepfamilies and, 263
Men. *See also* Husbands; Fathers
  reaction to conflict by, 187
Merger with loved one, fear of, 102
Message(s)
  confirming, 86
  effectiveness of, 138
  mixed, 139, 171
  one-up, 150, 151
  power and, 139
  reciprocal, 184
  rejecting, 149
Metacommunication, 18
Metaphor, family, 25
Middle ground, 260
Misunderstanding, 78–79
Momism, 125
Money. *See also* Economic factors
  balance of power and, 266–67
  cohabitation and, 270
  as sign of affection, 77
Mormons' Family Home Evening, 305
Morphogenesis (change-promoting processes),
    21
Morphostasis (stability-promoting processes), 21
Mother(s)
  conflicts started by, 184
  momism and, 125
  supermom, 126
Mourning
  divorce and, 247
  handicapped child and, 245
Mutual influence, 61–62
Mutuality, 210
  in sexual experience, 99
Mythology, family, 297